Childhood and
Socialization

Childhood and Socialization

EDITED BY
HANS PETER DREITZEL

Recent Sociology No. 5

Macmillan Publishing Co., Inc.
New York

Collier Macmillan Publishers,
London

Macmillan Publishing Co., Inc.
Collier-Macmillan Canada Ltd.

Library of Congress Catalog Card Number: 72–11677

FIRST MACMILLAN PAPERBACKS EDITION 1973

Printed in the United States of America

"Phenomenology and Socialization: Some Comments on the Assumptions Underlying Socialization Theory" by David M. Rafky is reprinted from *Sociological Analysis*, Vol. 32, no. 1 (Spring 1971) with the permission of the Association for the Sociology of Religion and the Editor of *Sociological Analysis*.

"Violence Against Children" by David G. Gill is reprinted from the *Journal of Marriage and the Family* (November 1971) with the permission of the National Council on Family Relations.

"Kommune 2: Childrearing in the Commune" by Christel Bookhagen, Eike Hemmer, Jan Raspe, and Eberhard Schultz, © 1971 by Verlag Kiepenheuer & Witsch, Köln. Reprinted by permission.

Basil Bernstein, "A brief account of the Theory of Codes" in *Social Relationship and Language*, Block 3 of the Educational Studies Second level course, Language and Learning, The Open University, 1973. Reprinted by permission.

"Assessing Children's School Performance" by Hugh Mehan is adapted from Armer/Grimshaw: *Comparative Social Research* to be published by John Wiley & Sons, Inc. September 1973. Preprinted by permission of the editors and publisher.

"Learning, Teaching, and Television Production for Children: The Experience of *Sesame Street*" by Gerald S. Lesser is reprinted from *Children in Television: Lessons from* Sesame Street, by Gerald S. Lesser. Copyright © 1972 by Gerald S. Lesser. Reprinted by permission of Random House, Inc.

"The Breakdown of Schools: A Problem or a Symptom?" by Ivan Illich is reprinted by permission from the *Journal of Research and Development in Education*, Vol. 5, no. 3 (Spring 1972).

Contents

III

IV

Introduction: Childhood and Socialization *

HANS PETER DREITZEL

THIS COLLECTION OF ESSAYS in socialization theory and research does *not* present a summary of research findings during recent years. Instead, it is my hope to illustrate and illuminate a certain shift in the use of theoretical models and research procedures which has emerged since the middle of the sixties in this field: a new tendency to see socialization as an interaction process which involves the child as an active partner, rather than as a process of unilateral manipulation of the child. While procedures of child rearing have been an important topic of social science research at least since the works of Freud and Piaget, the bulk of research has been confined to the limits of psychological behaviorism. The child was seen as some kind of incomplete organism which develops in different directions in response to different stimuli. This kind of research was for the most part carried out with laboratory experiments, i.e., in artificial situations which tend to cover up the fact that not only has the adult's behavior an impact on children but also that the child's behavior has an impact on adults. In such circumstances, questions like what are the effects of permissive rather than restrictive behavior on children, or, what are the origins of aggressive behavior in socialization, can only insufficiently be answered.

Indeed, the enormous research effort made by anthropology, psychology, psychoanalysis, and sociology to clarify the process of socialization (or, to use the more old-fashioned ter-

* I gratefully acknowledge the help of Susan Hechler with this manuscript.

minology, to detect the influence of different educational strategies) has led to very little useful knowledge. This remains true in spite of the fact that in their childrearing practices parents are more and more influenced by social science concepts as these gradually become part of the popular culture. Thus M. Wolfenstein, in her study of the successive editions of the United States Children's Bureau bulletin "Infant Care" between 1914 and 1951,[1] has demonstrated the changing trends and fashions in the advice given to parents and pediatricians: while the first two editions (1914 and 1921) maintained a very severe attitude toward auto-erotic tendencies in children (thumb sucking, masturbation, etc.), in the 1929 bulletin the emphasis of severity had shifted to toilet training and a rigid schedule for the weaning process. From 1938 to 1951 the tendency is toward more and more permissiveness: under the growing influence of psychoanalysis the sexuality of children is gradually tolerated but not yet positively accepted. Today we know that many psychoanalytic concepts, however useful they may have proved to be for therapeutic purposes, have to be revised when confronted with the results of experimental and comparative research. In fact, the shifts and fashions in what is supposed to be applicable scientific knowledge only serve to demonstrate the enormous complexity and cultural variability of the socialization process. Yet, it seems to me, the cause of the futility and triviality of much socialization research are as much to be found in the behavioristic and metapsychological bases of our scientific approach as in the difficulties of the problem in question. It is the thesis of this book that the phenomenon of socialization can only be understood if seen as a complex interaction process governed by a reciprocity of needs, demands, and perspectives. In other words, rather than treating the adult's behavior as an independent variable, both the behavior of adults and of children must be seen as mutually dependent variables. Children are not simply a *tabula rasa* which mysteriously responds to the input of stimuli by adults, and adults are not simply stable factors of the child's social environment, but are themselves prone to change under the impact of their offspring's challenge.

Superficially seen, it is surprising that, in a time which claims to have established childhood as a sphere in its own right, most socialization research does not conceive of children as psychological, social, and historical beings in their own right. After all, childhood was apparently not a clearly distinguished concept before the advent of the bourgeois family and the modern school. The gradual transference of the child from the private sphere of the nuclear family to the public sphere of the educational institutions is a relatively modern development: as Phillipe Ariès in his excellent study has shown,[2] during the sixteenth century children were indiscriminately and abruptly integrated into the activities of adults after a short period of exclusive attendance by women; no special period of childhood was socially distinguished in which children could grow up within the world of their peers. Public and private spheres only gradually became separated from each other, and, along with this distinction, childhood emerged as a socially acknowledged developmental stage between complete physical dependence on the mother or nurse, and the integration into the adult world of production and reproduction. This development was, however, accompanied by an increasing restrictiveness of childrearing procedures which culminated in the puritanical attitudes of the nineteenth century and which even today have not been completely replaced by more permissive standards. Apparently it was the industrial revolution which has dramatically changed the attitude toward childhood and socialization. Kurt Danzinger in his excellent summary of what we know (and what we don't know) about socialization[3] has described this change:

Whereas before the middle of the eighteenth century the recommended treatment of infants was permissive, an overwhelming emphasis on strictness and control develops during the following period and lasts well into the present century. In the early period babies were to be fed on demand, weaning was to take place at about two years of age and was to be gradual, toilet training was not to be undertaken during the first year of life and the child was not expected to be consistently dry at night until the age of five; no prohibitions against nudity or infantile sexuality are mentioned; the child remained in his mother's bed until weaning and was put to sleep by rocking; he was freely handled and petted by adults and his crying met with a quick and nurturant response. By the early nineteenth century the picture is entirely different. The age of weaning is reduced, feeding schedules are introduced, toilet training is to be begun and completed much earlier; infantile sexuality is to be punished (this becomes general only in the last part of the nineteenth century); rocking, cuddling and an indulgent response to the baby's cry are disapproved of; on the other hand, the child's free motor activity was now encouraged, whereas previously it had been discouraged. A necessarily crude comparison of these data with observations collected in seventy-five different societies across the world strongly suggests that the severity of the nineteenth century was rather unusual in terms of the human norm, whereas the earlier advice was much more in line with the general practice of mankind. (page 140–141)

The question is, of course, how we can account for these changes. It seems that the historical evidence points to a functional relationship between the period of "original accumulation" followed by the industrial revolution and the era of competitive capitalism on the one hand, and a double trend toward the privatization of the childhood experience and the increasing restrictiveness of the childrearing practices on the other. While during the period of extensive exploitation child labor became a market commodity and the working classes were deprived of all opportunities to educate their children, the development of an "inner-directed" social character (David Riesman) became a necessity for the middle classes. Supported by the influence of Wesleyan Methodism in the eighteenth and early nineteenth centuries, the puritanical socialization procedures of the bourgeois family aimed at the development of a character structure which would guarantee a psychological foundation of the protestant ethic needed by the individualized labor market and entrepreneurship. It is interesting to note that with the shift in modern capitalism from extensive to intensive exploitation, i.e., with the growing need for highly skilled workers and the rise of the modern white-collar class, the structure of childhood and socialization again underwent a change: while the tendency to conceive of childhood as a social and psychological stage in its own right grew even stronger with the advent of a modern school system, this century has seen a continuous trend toward more permissiveness in childrearing practices. Apparently the contradiction between the two trends has been a peculiarity of the long period of transition from an agrarian economy with a feudal structure to an industrial economy with a capitalist structure.

Yet this does not mean that present day corporate capitalism provides an enviable social climate for our children. The misery of the nuclear family[4] and the prevailing injustice of the school system are only the symptoms of a widening gap between two contradictory developments in highly industrialized societies: the ever more intensive exploitation of labor, which has long reached the higher echelons of the educated middle classes and the professionally trained, and the decreasing amount of time necessary for the reproduction of our present standard of living. The gap between these two trends is filled with victims, and among these, children may be the most deplorable group. The steady increase in labor productivity, due to the improvement of both the technology of machinery and the average level of industrial skills, creates for each worker and employee problems which he cannot solve on his own on the basis of the compensations he receives for his work. Individually, everybody is helpless when confronted with the numerous psychological disturbances which are caused by the intensified job demands and the technologically polluted environment and which affect, along with his own personality, all his primary group affiliations, especially his family. Thus the typical nuclear family of today provides a pathogenic milieu for the children: the father is absent physically or psychologically to such a degree that the German psychiatrist Alexander Mitscherlich could speak of a "fatherless society";[5] his work is outside of the home and remains abstract and invisible to his children. Instead of being a role model for his children, he can only serve a subsidiary function to the effeminate rule of his economically and erotically frustrated wife. Families often enough react to this situation by those compulsive attempts to save their group cohesion which Professor Richter has described in his essay in this volume (see Article 4) and which only serve to drive the children more and more into the empty "other-directedness" (David Riesman) of their peer culture.

The corporate state, on the other hand, is only interested in the efficient development of utilizable skills and in a socialization which guarantees mass loyalty, i.e., political acquiescence with the prevailing system. Thus it is no surprise that the halfhearted attempts to provide the underprivileged classes with "compensatory education" in Head Start and other programs on the whole have been a failure. The explosion of the educational institutions during the sixties has been a rather ambiguous development. For the corporate system it has served two functions: first, an enormous increase in the supply of skilled labor (i.e., very general skills, like the level of language control or mathematical ability, as well as specific professional skills), which has devalued the price of such labor to the advantage of the corporations; and second, and usually overlooked, a considerable relative decrease in the rate of unemployment: the more and the longer young people are kept in the educational institutions the more they stay out of the labor market. Of course it is an open question to what degree (if at all) this has been the result of a conscious and deliberate policy. In any case some unanticipated consequences have emerged: the students soon became aware that prolonged education of more and more people is a process governed by the law of diminishing returns; no longer can a university education be taken for granted as the automatic gateway toward "professional," i.e. unalienated, work and upper middle class income. Real and anticipated frustrations of this kind were, in my opinion, among the more important objective causes of the student unrest of recent years. At the same time the failure of special "compensatory" programs has frustrated the rising aspirations of ethnic minorities and other underprivileged groups and contributed to their growing radicalization. It may indeed be argued that the recent development of secondary and higher education can be better explained as a contemporary version of the struggle for status and power among different groups than by the functional necessities of the present technological level of production.[6]

This is clearly indicated by at least one other unanticipated consequence of the growth of higher education, namely the overproduction of academically trained students in certain fields. This phenomenon, which probably will grow worse during the next years, is, however, only the tip of the iceberg: more and more former students discover that they cannot really make use of their knowledge and skills in the jobs they are offered. Qualitative as well as quantitative underemployment apparently will become a widely spread characteristic of our economic system in the near future and may well cause a new wave of rebellion. It may well be that our system produces much unnecessary work simply because we have no other system of distribution than the labor market.

This may seem to be somewhat remote from problems of childhood and socialization. However, the described contradictions have a marked impact on the way children are treated in our society. Instead of being the production unit it was in former times, modern family is reduced to the status of a consumption unit. Consequently almost the first thing a child learns in this society is the patterns of consumer behavior which are constantly reinforced by TV and other advertisements, as well as by its parents' struggle against their psychological pauperization. This struggle, however, is doomed to failure as long as the compensations received for their labor determine the emphasis on the quantitative aspect of the market value of individually available commodities rather than on the only collectively attainable change in the quality of their lives. As a result, the children are caught between an increasing psychological stress within their isolated family homes and the growing technological brutalization of street life. The number of children who are yearly killed in the streets need scarcely be emphasized again; those however who are physically or psychologically killed or maimed by violence from their own parents who can no longer control their overwhelming frustration (see Article 5) are in addition the victims of public indifference. In spite of all the public attention given to problems of socialization, modern society creates a generally unfavorable climate for children; the tolerance of childhood as a developmental stage in its own right and the permissive attitudes toward children are probably more the result of resigned helplessness than of positive acceptance of their different needs and perspectives. The nuclear family as a socialization agent is basically a failure because the retreat from a deteriorated public sphere into a Sartrean hell of the emotionally overburdened seclusion of privacy provides for a pathogenic socialization milieu.

The schools as the second major socialization agent are no less in trouble than is the family. As important an institution of modern society as mandatory school attendance has already been challenged by the prophetic voice of Ivan Illich in his widely discussed thesis of "deschooling society" (see Article 11). The fact is that the schools serve more as an agent for the socialization into political acquiescence with an unloved system than as an institution which offers optimal opportunities to acquire useful skills and meaningful knowledge. It should not come as a surprise then, that even children from the middle classes feel frustrated and alienated by the public school system and react with an increasing drop-out rate and by withdrawal into the drug culture—all this in spite of the fact, which sociologists have stated time and again, that the school system is a typical middle class institution in terms of its language patterns and value orientations. The youth from the middle classes, however, react against much of their school-acquired knowledge because of its anticipated uselessness for keeping or raising their class privileges and for finding unalienating work. Lower-class children, on the other hand, understandably feel that the school system functions as a class barrier which deprives them once again of the opportunity to escape their economically and ethnically defined ghettos while claiming the opposite in its ideology. Thus the schools have become an instrument of status conflict rather than an institution of meaningful education.

Of course, children and adolescents do not only bear the marks of the double failure of family and school as socialization agents but also react actively to this situation—which again provokes a (usually authoritarian, sometimes encouraging) response from adults who are in charge of, or care for, children. Unfortunately, the numerous studies on the youth culture have not yet been supplemented by sociological research on the cultural behavior of younger children among their peers. Yet it seems to me that the symbolic interaction processes between children of the age group from five to twelve, and possibly even younger, should be subjected to thorough empirical research, my hypothesis being that already during this age children struggle for the construction and maintenance of a peer culture relatively immune to the pressures of the outside (adult) world. To be sure, there are many who do not survive in this struggle. Journalist Howard James of the *Christian Science Monitor* has written a shocking report on "Children in Trouble,"[7] describing the fate of some 300,000 children who are kept in the deadening brutality of prisons, detention houses, and reform schools in the United States. Yet on the other end of the scale we also find some encouraging attempts to provide children with a healthy learning milieu and a social space in which they can live a creative childhood. More important than Head Start and similar experiments of "compensatory education" (which are all doomed to failure as long as they do not succeed in seriously integrating the language, norms, and values of working class and ethnic cultures) may be the Free School Movement and the Movement for Communal Living, each offering an alternative to the central socialization agents of our society. Both movements, however, are young and not yet fully developed. Moreover, sociologists have as yet rarely turned their attention to such experiments in the counter-culture. With the exception of the socialization practices in the Israeli kibbutzim, which have been the focus of many social scientists,[8] I do not know of any sociological analyses of communal childrearing practices except those reported in the last volume of this series[9] and in the present collection (see Article 7). I also have included in this volume the translation of a report on childrearing practices in a German commune which was written by the members of the communes themselves (see Article 6). It may well be that the most important reason for the establishment of a family commune are the children: overprotective mothers and authoritarian absentee fathers can be more easily controlled and compensated for by a larger number of adults who can serve as additional role models for the children. At the same time a peer group of mixed age and sex outside the boundaries of the school and the dangers of the street helps to emphasize the needs and demands of childhood against the strictures of adult life. However, much more experimentation and much more research into the many patterns and vagaries of communal living are needed before any judgment can be made. Whether the Movement for Communal Living in America and Europe will eventually provide a serious alternative to the socialization patterns of the nuclear family remains to be seen. The same is even more true for the Free School Movement. Many observers agree that the rigidity and insufficient quality of the public school system is in desperate need of change. But which is the right answer—the radical demand of Ivan Illich and his followers in the anarchist tradition for "deschooling" our society, or the many attempts to establish free schools for ghetto or communal family children, or the even more challenging experiments to reintegrate the schools into the public life and the production process[10]—is an open question. Last but not least, the impact of the mass media as a new socialization agent must be considered. While it is very difficult to estimate the real dangers of prolonged television viewing and especially of television violence on children, it is hardly less difficult to find the real causes of the educational effect which a good television program can have, as the research report on the effects of the Sesame Street series in this volume demonstrates (see Article 10).

There can be no doubt that the social sciences are confronted with tremendous new research tasks in the field of socialization and education (for the latter see especially Article 13). It should be emphasized again, however, that all new research efforts will be futile as long as children and adults are not studied in the reciprocity of their mutual symbolic interaction (see Article 12). Phenomenological theory as well as Symbolic Interactionism have both focused on the "social construction"[11] of our "world-taken-for-granted" (Alfred Schütz), a symbolic process in which all members of an interaction system take part—in our case children as well as parents. Therefore a theoretical approach along this line has been emphasized in this volume (see especially the articles in Chapter 1). Little as it may be, what we *have* gained in decades of socialization research supports strongly this view: "the paradigm that equates the parental role with that of the model and the child's role with that of the follower simply does not fit the facts."[12] Beginning with the first smile or the first cry, parents react to their child's behavior and respond with warmth or hostility, encouragement and satisfaction, or discouragement and frustration—depending on their child's character no less than on their own attitudes. Of course, children cannot be understood as active and possibly controlling partners in an interaction process as long as their congenital dispositions are not taken into account. These are, of course, partially hereditary, but there is also mounting evidence that the conditions of pregnancy and delivery as well as maternal anxieties are responsible for such factors as restlessness and social responsiveness. It must be assumed then, that such congenital differences among children provoke different responses on the part of parents, too, and not only vice versa. Other well-known factors in this context are, of course, the relative position of a child among brothers and sisters, the rate of absence of the father, and the existence or non-existence of grandparents in the same household, all contributing to the whole of an interaction framework in which the relative effect of socialization procedures must be understood.

Two problems have been especially well studied in the existing body of socialization research: learning and aggressiveness. The latter can sociologically best be understood as the result of a labelling process: people have accepted many ways of behavior in which aggression plays an important role (sports, for instance), but they feel challenged by someone's behavior that steps outside of the typified patterns of the taken-for-granted normality. The same behavior of a child may be "a nuisance" in one situation and a laudable "effort" in another; some people's nerves can stand a surprising degree of explosiveness in the expressive behavior of children, while for others pedagogically necessary restrictions have shrunk to the boundaries of legitimate self-defense. Learning, as well as aggressiveness, may serve again to support an interactionist approach to, and a critical view of, the nuclear family and the prevailing school system. "There is overwhelming evidence that children learn complex acts through cognitive processes based on observation rather than through being trained by external reinforcements administered by the parents."[13] This does not mean that punishment and reward do not have a certain function, but rather that the acceptance as role models of some people rather than others, in some situations rather than others, plays the most important part in the learning process. Children, however, do not imitate indiscriminately and it is therefore a crucial question: what persons are under which circumstances honoured by being taken as models? This is the underlying problem of an extensive literature devoted to the search for basic dimensions of parental behavior. In spite of much terminological confusion, recently there seems to be a growing consensus among social scientists that there are basically two dimensions which are important here: first, warmth-hostility; and second, restrictiveness-permissiveness. If seen in an interaction paradigm, however, these dimensions are revealed as actually dealing with the reciprocity of need satisfaction, or, in other words, with the mutual claim and satisfaction of demands.[14] The child experiences the satisfaction of its demands as "warmth" and their frustration as "hostility," as it experiences the more or less demanding attitude of parents or other reference persons as a restriction or permission in regard to its own range of activities. Thus the adult-child relationship can be seen as a system of mutual demands. Children as well as parents can display four ideal types of response attitudes:

	demanding (restrictiveness)	undemanding (permissiveness)
satisfying (warmth)	Type I	Type II
unsatisfying (hostility)	Type III	Type IV

These types of behavior may, of course, vary according to such situational factors as mood, stress, available time, health, presence of demands from third parties (especially spouses), etc., as well as in regard to the attitude of the interaction partner himself. Yet the four types may also describe more general attitudes corresponding to certain personality traits and class characteristics. One hypothesis already supported by some research findings is that type I describes the ideal type of lower-class child-rearing patterns, while type II describes middle-class attitudes. Type III, the self-defense reaction, and type IV, indifference, would then point to the direction of deviance in working-class and middle-class socialization patterns, respectively.

It is interesting to note that a number of research findings seem to indicate that type I may be the most favorable attitude for the balanced development of emotional and cognitive abilities, *if* demands are made on the cognitive level and satisfactions are offered on the emotional level. This however does *not* seem to be the typical case of the working-class family, where strong demands are related to a normative rather than cognitive level. Apparently much depends on what kind of demands are made and what kind of satisfactions are given. In the study of the complex interaction process we call socialization, the model of a system of reciprocal demands and satisfactions provides only a preliminary guideline and should be differentiated in regard to the various dimensions of human development. This, however, is not an easy task for research. If, for instance, working-class families seem to be less demanding on the cognitive level than on the level of normative sensibility, it may well be that such an observation is biased by a standpoint alien to the working class and ethnic subcultures. Since the cognitive level is closely related to language abilities, the question arises whether working class and ethnic language patterns can really be understood as a "restricted code" when not measured against the standards of a middle class school system (see Article 9). Professor Basil Bernstein, in his recent report on a decade of his research on the differentiation and application of his concepts of "restricted" and "elaborated code" (see Article 8), has arrived at some rather complex conclusions in regard to this problem. If the goal of the modern school system is supposed to be the development of that ability of abstraction which enables students to learn and deal with technological and scientific paradigms, the lower-class language patterns may be correctly described as a "restricted code." If, on the other hand, education is to emphasize to social abilities of symbolic interaction and role-taking, the "elaborated code" may well prove to be the more restricted language code—provided that the member's own culture and reference groups are taken into account and education does not deteriorate into a struggle for middle- and upper-middle-class statuses.

The latter view seems to inspire the prevalent attitude in the counterculture movements favoring free schools and communal living. In regard to the former view it may be worthwhile, on the other hand, to take seriously Ivan Illich's assumption—however questionable it may be—that certain skills and abilities can be much more easily acquired by means other than the present school system, and subject this hypothesis to a scrutinizing empirical analysis. If we concentrate on the relation of qualities of a person to his ability for symbolic interaction rather than to his intellectual capacity for abstraction, the cognitive level can be associated with normative sensibility, i.e., with the ability to perceive and interpret, to reject and recreate the goals and norms of our society in reciprocity with one's fellow men. In such a paradigm, which would, in the terminology of Professor Habermas, emphasize "communicative" behavior rather than "instrumentalist" behavior,[15] the concepts of ego-identity and role-playing become pertinent. As George Herbert Mead has pointed out, the capacity for the social construction of reality is grounded in that "taking the role of the other," which the child learns in its early role play and games, and through which its self develops its own identity. The establishment of a reciprocity of perspectives in the identification with the other, and thereby the identity formation of the self, should then be regarded as a first step in the socialization process no less fundamental than the development of a need control system, which enables the child (and the adult) to articulate physical and emotional demands and to tolerate frustrations.

Thus optimal conditions for the socialization of children in modern society would mean that the adult-child interaction systems provide for a balanced development of two dimensions: identity formation as the precondition of role-distance and role-identification, and affectivity control as a precondition for the satisfaction of needs and the tolerance of frustrations. The stages of this development can loosely be summarized as follows[16]:

Identity Formation	*Affectivity Control*
1. reciprocity of perspectives; ego-consciousness;	1. structuring of need dispositions; bodily control;
2. internalization of a *norm* of reciprocity;	2. development of the capability to introject and project emotional needs;
3. internalization of general cultural norms ("taking the role of the other"); development of role loyalty and role discipline;	3. self control = internal affectivity control;
4. anticipatory role identifications; impression management;	4. anticipatory emotional gratifications in role play; development of motivations;
5. ego-identity formation;	5. formation of individual needs; equilibrium of the affective drives;
6. development of role-identities;	6. integration of individual needs into role interests, i.e. legitimation of individual needs by their identification with positional interests;
7. equilibrium of the role budget; tension management in regard to role conflicts.	7. equilibrium of frustrations and compensations within the role budget.

Each of these seven developmental stages indicates some necessary achievements of a certain phase in the socialization process. The first stage corresponds to the suckling age, the second and third are identical with the oedipal phase, and the fourth corresponds to the period of latency, or, in Erik Erikson's terminology, the stage of a psychosexual moratorium. The fifth stage then denotes the age of puberty in adolescence, which is gradually followed by adulthood, in which the sixth and the seventh stages must be managed simultaneously.

The advantage of some such system of developmental stages of the socialization process becomes clear only when both—identity formation and affectivity control—are seen as different yet functionally dependent dimensions, as is shown in the chart.

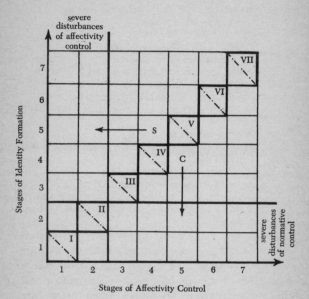

Stages of Affectivity Control

(Arabic numerals 1–7 indicate the stages of task achievement in the socialization process; roman numerals I–VII indicate the socio-genetic position of typical behavioral disturbances; printed lines point to the possibility of incomplete achievements of a development stage and to the direction which behavioral disturbances will take in cases of unbalanced development of the two dimensions during a disruption in the socialization process.)

Obviously the diagonal line of middle fields numbered I–VII indicates an optimal socialization process which is rarely if at all achieved. Normally members of our society are involved in a lifelong struggle at least for the achievements of stages VI and VII. If the socialization process stops at an earlier level however, certain behavioral distrubances will occur which in turn provoke stigmatizations, labelling processes and social control mechanisms on the part of the interaction partners—and thus can initiate the vicious circles of deviant behavior. If the process of socialization has come to an end at a level where affectivity control and identity formation are still balanced the typical behavioral disburbances which occur in the absence of schematically later achievements are:

Stage I:	disturbances in the I-Me relationship (certain forms of imbecility?)
Stage II:	disturbances of the self-formation (certain forms of schizophrenia?)
Stage III:	disturbances in the formation of a "basic personality," or a socio-cultural character (severe neuroses)
Stage IV:	disturbances in behavior management (limited behavioral range caused by relative deprivation)
Stage V:	identity diffusion (lack of equilibrium between role involvement and role distance)
Stage VI:	disturbances in need integration (aggressive reaction to frustrations)
Stage VII:	disturbances in the equilibrium of the role budget (over-identification with some roles, alienation in others)

Of course, if no more than the first or the first two stages can be managed, the person will not be able to play any social roles at all; his behavioral disturbances will be in the order of psychoses. The other disturbances are to a greater or lesser degree manageable and their frequency only serves to demonstrate the miserable failure of our socialization agents. The chart also indicates, however, that behavioral disturbances can be caused by an unbalanced disruption of the socialization process, such that either the identity formation or the affectivity control lags in development behind the other dimension. In the case of primary disturbances, i.e., when the first two stages are not completely managed, this balanced development leads either to severe disturbances of affectivity control (as in the case of sexual offenders, who in other spheres of activity can lead a perfectly normal life) or to severe disturbances of the moral sensibility (as in the case of persons who cannot even adjust to the norms of a deviant subculture). In each case of a "normal" (i.e., balanced) disturbance, the actor can move in either direction: toward less ego identity or toward less affectivity control, depending on his reference groups and the stigmatizing and controlling activities of his original social learning milieu. Thus the examples marked S and C in the chart illustrate the deviant careers of a sexual offender (S) and of an "amoral" criminal (C) respectively. Such deviant careers will begin relatively harmlessly and will only lead to more severe types of behavioral disorders under certain social conditions. Again, the socialization of deviants, too, must be seen as the result of a continuous symbolic interaction with their reference groups no less than as the outcome of objective deprivations.

The interaction paradigm of socialization also points to another problem: namely that nobody can be sure of maintaining the achievements of his socialization, even when he has managed the problems posed by all seven developmental stages, as long as he is not continuously reinforced by his mutual relationships with other people. That human beings are social beings cannot be taken too seriously: sooner or later everybody breaks down under the impact of rejection by his reference persons or in the isolation of "total institutions" (E. Goffman). Depending on the pressure put on him, this may mean a more or less complete breakdown of his ego identity and his affectivity control, or a situational occurrence like those we call misbehavior, intolerable aggressiveness, childishness, and so forth. This calls attention to the fact that we are in constant danger of *regressions* to earlier stages of the developmental system, and that such regressions will usually go in the direction of the weakest points in our socialization. Naturally, everybody has such weak points, which, in an interactionist perspective, represent a sequence of interaction situations which have been failures in terms of a communicative behavior. Thus we all have our ghosts in the closet: parents and teachers, sisters and brothers, spouses and friends, who haunt us with the unfinished communicative situations to which we return in our regressions.

The efforts of the counterculture movements to radically change our major socialization agencies will have to be measured not only against the present miseries of family and school life, but also by their success or failure to realize the interaction paradigm of socialization in order to strengthen communicative abilities and to de-neuroticize our social environment. The efforts of social science research, on the other hand, will have to be measured by their success or failure to spell out the impediments as well as the conditions under which human development can take a course which will enable people to define and redefine, to accept and to criticize the organization of the realities and the interpretation of the relationships of our social systems. For the achievement of these goals a new approach is needed in political life as well as in social science. It is my hope that the following collection of essays will illustrate some attempts in this direction.

NOTES

1. M. Wolfenstein, Trends in Infant Care, American Journal of Orthopsychiatry, vol. 23, 1953, pp. 120–30
2. P. Ariès, Centuries of Childhood, New York 1962
3. Kurt Danzinger, Socialization, Penguin Books, Baltimore 1971
4. See: H. P. Dreitzel, Family, Marriage, and the Struggle of the Sexes; Recent Sociology, No. 4, New York 1972. The present volume no. 5 of Recent Sociology is in many respects a continuation of this previous volume, which, among other analyses relevant to the problem of childhood and socialization, also contains some notes on commercial child-rearing practices.
5. Alexander Mitscherlich, Auf dem Wege zur vaterlosen Gesellschaft, München 1963
6. See: Randall Collins, Functional and Conflict Theories of Educational Stratification, in: American Sociological Review, Vol. 36, 1971, pp. 1002–1019
7. Howard James, Children in Trouble—A National Scandal, New York 1970
8. See as summary: Bruno Bettelheim, The Children of the Dream, New York 1969
9. B. M. Berger et al., Childrearing Practices in the Communal Family, in: H. P. Dreitzel, Family, Marriage, and the Struggle of the Sexes; Recent Sociology, No. 4, New York 1972
10. See the radical demands of so eminent a scholar in the field of sociology of education as J. S. Coleman, Education in the Age of Computers and Mass Communications, in: M. Greenberger (Ed.), Computers, Communications and the Public Interest, Johns Hopkins Press 1971
11. See P. L. Berger/Th. Luckmann, The Social Construction of Reality, New York 1966

12. K. Danzinger, op. cit., p. 58
13. op. cit., p. 34
14. For this and the following see: op. cit. p. 64–65
15. Jürgen Habermas, Toward a Rational Society, New York 1970
16. For the following see: H. P. Dreitzel, Die gesellschaftlichen Leiden und das Leiden an der Gesellschaft, 2nd edition Stuttgart 1972, chapter V,5

I

Alternate Approaches to Socialization Theory

It has been emphasized throughout the Introduction that socialization must be understood as an interaction process which involves the child as an active partner no less than the adult. The three articles of this first chapter all come to the conclusion that symbolic interactionism and phenomenology are the only theoretical perspectives which have consistently held this view. Thus what Robert MacKay calls the "interpretive perspective" as opposed to the prevailing "normative perspective" stands in the phenomenological tradition with some foundations in the symbolic interactionism of George Herbert Mead and his school. Phenomenology has belatedly come to the American academic scene through the work of the late Alfred Schütz, on whose analyses of the structure of the social world the more recent formulations of the ethnomethodological school are based. Robert MacKay, who is Lecturer of Sociology at York University, Toronto, belongs to this school and has collaborated with Aaron Cicourel and others on a research project on problems of language acquisition which will soon be published. Based on the interpretation of his empirical data from this study, he consistently states that the socialization literature tends to confound the topic and the resource of research by a tendency of scientists to identify with the common sense perspective of adults. His article was written for this book.

David M. Rafky, Assistant Professor at Loyola University in New Orleans, summarizes the phenomenological understanding of the socialization process, as developed in the works of Husserl, Mead, Schütz, and Berger/Luckmann. His article

*represents a much needed attempt to integrate these differ-
ent but similar approaches by focusing on the Meadian
interpretation of socialization and an examination of the
differences between child and adult socialization.*

*John O'Neill, Professor of Sociology at York University,
Toronto, concentrates in his essay on the work of the
French phenomenologist Merleau-Ponty, who, in spite of the
great importance of his theories for socialization research,
is still rather unknown in America. This is all the more
deplorable as Merleau-Ponty, in contrast to Husserl, for instance, is a philosopher in the phenomenological tradition
who has extensively dealt with the empirical psychology
and sociology of human development. In order to better
understand the socialization process we have to go beyond
the behavioristic and normative models; the first step in this
direction, however, is to look back at the history of social
thought and to study the neglected theoretical alternatives to
the prevailing approaches.*

1

Conceptions of Children and Models of Socialization*

ROBERT MacKAY

I INTRODUCTION

IN SOCIOLOGICAL WRITINGS characterized as normative,[1] the term socialization glosses[2] the phenomenon of change from the birth of a child to maturity or old age.[3] To observe that changes take place after birth is trivial, but the quasiscientific use of the term socialization masks this triviality. In fact, the study of these changes as socialization is an expression of the sociologists' common sense position in the world—i.e., as adults.[4] The notion of socialization leads to theoretical formulations mirroring the adult view that children are incomplete beings. Investigators have consequently been distracted from the important area of study, which is adult-child interaction and the underlying theoretical problem of intersubjectivity implied in interaction. Writing about the process of socialization, then, has become for me an occasion for exploring the interaction between adults and children.

II TO BE—IS TO BE SOCIALIZED

Children are incomplete—immature, irrational, incompetent, asocial, acultural, depending on whether you are a teacher, sociologist, anthropologist, or psychologist. Adults, on

* I wish to thank Patricia MacKay and Frank Nutch with whom I discussed the ideas in this paper and who at the eleventh hour worked hard to translate the original text into English.

the other hand, are complete—mature, rational, competent, social, and autonomous, unless they are "acting-like-children."[5] Introductory texts[6] in the social sciences suggest that without language and culture, newborn infants are not human, because "language creates minds and selves."[7] An implication is that children who are profoundly retarded or severely brain damaged are never human.

For the sociologist, to be human is to be socialized. To be socialized is to be roles.[8] To be human, therefore, is to be roles. Theorizing is not an indifferent practice, as I have suggested in the Introduction and in footnote 4, it is the formulation of the writer's view of the world (i.e., his self). Considered thus, to conceive of being human as being roles is to conceive an eviscerated view of life. What is more important for the argument presented here, under the auspices of current formulations of socialization, the conception of children as essentially deficient vis-a-vis adults has, in practice, led to no research into children *qua* children. Under the formulation of the world as a process of socialization, children as a phenomenon disappear, and sociologists reveal themselves as parents writing slightly abstract versions of their own or other children.

Socialization is a gloss[9] which precludes the explication of the phenomenon it glosses—i.e., the interaction between adults and children. This glossing is characteristic of normative sociology's reliance on the common sense world as both topic and resource.[10] As Zimmerman and Pollner indicate, "Sociology's acceptance of the lay member's formulation of the formal and substantive features of sociology's topical concerns makes sociology an integral feature of the very order it seeks to describe. It makes sociology into an eminently *folk discipline*, deprived of any prospect or hope of making fundamental structures of folk activity a phenomenon."[11] This confounding is illustrated in the following quotation.

In other words both the *practice and study* of child socialization are "forward looking." It seems *obvious*, furthermore, that of the various later stages which socialization looks forward to, it is the personally relatively enduring and *socially important adult stage* which is the *critical one* to consider. Therefore, a central task of the study of socialization is to enquire into the effects which the experience of the child has on the shaping of the adult. [emphasis added][12]

The terms adults and children are borrowed from the common sense world by sociologists, but if they are viewed as theoretical formulations, then a very serious problem emerges. That is, to suggest theoretically that there are adults and children is to imply that to pass from one stage to the other is to pass from one ontological order to another.[13] The passage from one ontological order to another is also suggested in the formulation of the world as static[14] and as constituted by successive discreet stages—childhood and adulthood, incompleteness and completeness, lack of agreement and shared agreement.[15] If each of these ontological orders implies, on the level of social life, different communicative competencies, then the traditional formulations of socialization make communication between adults and children impossible, since they are assumed not to share common interpretive abilities.

I am suggesting that in the socialization literature the confounding of the common sense world as topic and resource has resulted in the unavailability of interaction between adults and children as a phenomenon of study. The phenomenon of study is adult-child interaction and how it is accomplished.

III THE INTERPRETIVE PERSPECTIVE

For two days I watched some sixty children between the ages of three and six joyfully writing stories of their own, making up poems, exploring the typewriter keyboard and reading paragraphs based on their own conversations. They did this as spontaneously as young children ask questions. I realized then that I had stumbled onto something more important than the mechanical ability to read a few words. Evidently tiny youngsters could reason, invent and acquire knowledge far better than most adults suspected. If they could learn this much through exposure to the talking typewriter for only half an hour a day, the potentialities of preschool children were almost limitless.[16]

I take this quotation to represent what might be sociologists' similar surprise at the ability of children to "reason, invent and acquire knowledge," that is, at their interpretive competencies. In contrast to the study of socialization suggested by normative sociology (discussed in Section II) work in interpretive sociology[17] restores the interaction between adults and children based on interpretive competencies as the phenomenon under study.[18] Without reviewing the literature in this area,[19] the interpretive perspective posits interpretive and surface rules,[20] the reflexive articulation of which enables people to assign meaning to the world. The complexity of the world and its orderliness is seen to rest on persons' (adults and children[21]) interpretive competencies. The focus of investigation is *how* persons display the meaningfulness of the world.

A demonstration of children's interpretive competencies can be found in research conducted in a Grade One classroom.[22] After completing a state-wide reading test designed to measure reading and inference skills, children were asked by researchers how they had decided on answers. The children often linked the stimulus sentence and the answer in ways which the test constructor had not "meant" but which demonstrated their interpretive skills in providing reasonable accounts of the world. For example, the stimulus sentence of one test item was about an animal that had been out in the rain. The "correct answer" was a picture of a room with dotted wallpapered walls and a floor imprinted with a trail of animal tracks. When the child was asked what the picture was about, she replied, "It's snowing." When questioned about the design on the wallpaper—"Do you know what these are?"—she said, "Sprinkles." The child had perceived the picture to be the exterior of a house with snow falling rather than the interior of a house covered with dotted wallpaper. Because of this "misperception" she had chosen an answer which was reasonable under the circumstances—the wrong answer. While the child demonstrated the interpretive skills "measured by the test," no credit was given in this case. This research makes clear that children possess interpretive competencies undiscerned in standard research. The interpretive perspective makes available, then, children as beings who interpret the world as adults do. By revealing the child's competencies, it transforms a theory of deficiency into a theory of competency.

In addition to suggesting that children are competent interpreters in the world, I want to suggest that they are also in possession of their own culture or succession of cultures.[23] Although the evidence for this is only fragmentary, the Opies have presented the most convincing case for the existence of separate cultures.[24] Philippe Ariès also points to the possibility of separate children's cultures and their changing particularity over time.[25]

If the two claims are correct, that children are competent interpreters of the social world and that they possess a separate culture(s), then the study of adult-child interaction (formerly socialization) becomes the study of cultural assimilation, or, more theoretically important, the study of meaningful social interaction.

IV   ADULT-CHILD INTERACTION[26]

I have suggested that adult-child interaction is problematic because of cultural differences. Hall[27] has documented that problems arising out of poor cultural translation can have serious practical outcomes (i.e., misunderstandings, or breaches). Teachers and other adults remain cultural strangers to the world of children, and their interaction with children often results in the generic type of misunderstandings that Hall describes.[28] I have argued on two fronts, first that understanding between two separate cultures requires adequate translation and second that *all* human interaction rests on the participants' interpretive abilities. On a theoretical level, however, there is no difference between these two.[29]

I turn now to an analysis of a specific occasion of interaction between an adult and a child which indicates how understanding based on interpretive abilities is built up through the course of the interaction. The following is a written transcript of the audio portion of a videotaped interview between a Grade One teacher and one child in her class. In the interview, which took place at the end of the lunch hour, the teacher is asking the child about the assignment distributed earlier in the morning. This assignment was to sequence a series of dittoed sentences which were either taken verbatim or paraphrased from a story read earlier in the morning. In the lesson and assignment the teacher had been concerned with introducing the concept of sequencing to the children. The interview was carried out at the request of the researchers to find out how the child would describe his understanding of the lesson and assignment.

INTERVIEW[30]

Teacher 1: Pick out the ones that should come first. Which one would come first in the story? Why did you choose that?

Tom 1: Because that's the first one.

Teacher 2: Why is it the first one?

Tom 2: Whack something fell on Chicken Little's . . . head I guess.

Teacher 3: Umhum. When you read the story in the book w that the very first sentence? Was it exactly like that in the book?

Tom 3: No.

Teacher 4: No but this does tell what happened first. Find the sentence which would tell what happens next.

Teacher 5: Why did you choose that one?

Tom 4: Because I guess that's was what happened (next).

Teacher 6: What, who was the first animal in the story?

Tom 5: Chicken Little.

Teacher 7: And the next?

Tom 6: Henny Penny.

Teacher 8: And who came next?

Tom 7: Goosey Loosey.

Teacher 9: No, not quite, somebody else came after Henny Penny,

Tom 8: ⌐some
     ⌐Cocky Locky.

Teacher 10: Cocky Locky.
            And then?

Tom 9: Henny.

Teacher 11: Goosey Poosey. And then, then what?

Tom 10: Turkey Lurkey.

Teacher 12: In the flannel board story, who came last?

Tom 11: Foxy Loxy.

Teacher 13: Who was not in the book that was in the flannel board story?

Tom 12: Foxy Loxy.

Teacher 14: All right, good, all right see if you can find the sentence then that tells best what happened after Henny Penny went with Chicken Little.

Teacher 15: Why didn't you choose this one it's got Henny Penny and Chicken Little in it?

Tom 13: Ah. Umm. Henny Penny. Cocky Locky and Chicken Little. Cocky Locky and Goosey Poosey he he isn't here yet.

Teacher 16: That's right.

Tom 14: Here Goosey Poosey, here boy.

Teacher 17: That's fine Tom, just tell me quietly please you don't have to act it out right now. There are times for acting but this is not one of them. OK?

Tom 15: They all met Goosey Loosey.

Teacher 18: Alright Why did you choose that "Four animals met Turkey Lurkey" next?

Tom 16: Because he's the last one they met.

Teacher 19: How do you know he's . . . all the other animals like Henny Penny and Cocky Locky are there it doesn't give their names?

Tom 17: Because. . . .

Teacher 20: What does it say?

Tom 18: "The four animals met Turkey Lurkey." There wasn't four animals.

Teacher 21: Weren't there?

Tom 19: One.

Teacher 22: Right.

Tom 20: Two.

Teacher 23: Henny Penny is

Tom 21: One.

Teacher 24: Cocky Locky [is

Tom 22: [two

Teacher 25: Two.

Tom 23: Three . . . Four.

Teacher 26: See there are you are forgetting about Chicken Little? He has met three people but Chicken Little's there too so that makes an extra one. All right what comes next? The animals have seen Turkey Lurkey what would come next?

Teacher 27: Craig would you please take your seat.

Teacher 28: Why did you choose that? Will you read it to me please.

Tom 24: Turkey Lurkey saw a nut under a big tree.

Teacher 29: Why did you choose that [instead of

Tom 25: [because

Teacher 30: that one

Tom 26: Because the sky is not falling. He can't say it because he doesn't know yet.

Teacher 31: Umm. Did Turkey Lurkey know all the time that it was a nut that fell on his head—that fell on ah Chicken Little's tail?

Tom 27: I guess so, I don't know.

Teacher 32: Humm this is interesting. What did it say in the story that Chicken Little ah where the nut fell on Chicken Little?

Tom 28: At the tree.

Teacher 33: Umhum what part of his body did it land on did it say?

Tom 29: Tail.

Teacher 34: Read the first sentence.

Tom 30: Whunk.

Teacher 35: Whack.

Tom 31: Whack something fell on Chicken Little's head.

Teacher 36: Did you notice that when you were putting the sentences together?

Tom 32: Ya, but I always thought.

Teacher 37: In some stories it does fall on his head so it didn't bother you did it that it said head?

Teacher 38: Have you ever heard a story where it fell on Chicken Little's head . . . instead of his tail?

Tom 33: Ya.

Teacher 39: Umhum, so you understood the story and it matter about that word did it because the idea was that on Chicken Little and it was really a nut instead of a of the sky. Thank you very much Tom.

Instruction: Understanding as the Location of the 'Correct' Answer

Given the working assumption that children are *tabu rasa* beings on which to etch programmes, teachers and other adults ignore the fact that understanding rests upon an ongoing reflexive, constructed, convergence of schemas of interpretation.[31] In the transcript it can be seen that the teacher acts as though the world is a static (i.e., not dialectical) place in which she can move the child cognitively from point A to point B while ignoring the child's contributions. In the lesson and review her concern was with moving him from a state of not knowing the concept of sequencing to a state of knowing the concept of sequencing. The teacher thus treats the child as empty of knowledge (i.e., correct answers) and moves him from this state of emptiness to a state of fullness (i.e., knowledge), a process she accomplishes by asking questions and reformulating them until the child gives the 'correct' answer. In some instances the teacher not only asks the questions but also finally *gives* the 'correct' answers (see Segment Teacher 39). Instruction is the occasion for adults to exercise their preference for making sense of the world for the child. The child as more or less passive in the situation is involved only in so far as he is conceived to be an organism capable of memory.[32] The child can/must *remember* the instruction (i.e., in this case the lesson).

Children's Interpretive Competence

I am using interpretive competence in an analytic sense to re   to the ability to use interpretive procedures to assign meaning to the world.[33] If children can be seen to possess the abilities proposed from an analysis of adult-adult interaction, then children have interpretive competence.

: As the Teacher's Assumption

The teacher assumes the child's interpretive competence in doing lessons and reviews. One example of this assumption in the transcript is when the teacher (Segment Teacher 14) asks Tom ". . . see if you can find the sentence that tells best . . ." where "best" implies the careful evaluation of the total situation. This assumption by adults of children's interpretive competence can even be found in situations where children are labelled non-competent. For example in one research study[34] with mentally retarded children (measured I.Q. between 50 and 75) the researcher administered a measure which consisted of a list of 22 personality traits. The children were to rank themselves on a five point scale for each item. The format was:

I am	happy	not	not	some	most	all of
	clean	at	very	of the	of the	the time
	lazy	all	often	time	time	
	etc.					

The researcher assumes that these children have interpretive competence if he assumes that they are able to reflect upon their personalities-as-traits and then rate them on a five point scale. After the measurement is completed, it is assumed that the aggregated measure of self-concept is of persons unable to reason well, they are, *after all*, mentally retarded.

The teacher assumes the child's interpretive competencies at every point. In the transcript this is especially clear in the segments following.

Teacher 39: Umhum, so you understood the story and it didn't make any difference about that word did it because the idea was that it fell on Chicken Little and it was really a nut instead of ah a piece of the sky. Thank you very much Tom.

The above segment was uttered at about 1:05 p.m. The segment below was said by the teacher about 10:45 a.m. the same morning in reference to the story of Chicken Little she was about to tell them.

Teacher: My story might be a little bit different from the way you heard it, the names might be different but the ideas are same.

In both segments she is assuming that what she is saying is obvious. She is asserting that ideas subsume many different words and names and in doing so eliminate what appears to be different. It is important to note that this is a more complex notion to grasp than the one that she makes the topic of the lesson—a concretized form of sequencing. What I am proposing is that she is assuming in an analytic sense the interpretive procedures which define competence. This is evident in the following.

A corollary of this property (reciprocity of perspectives) is that members assume, and assume others assume of them, that their descriptive accounts or utterances will be intelligible and recognizable features of the world known in common and taken for granted.[35]

When the two segments are considered together it can be seen that she is also assuming that the child can *remember* the earlier utterance and find the principle of consistency in the lesson, assuming her use of the word "idea" in the later utterance is a tacit reference back to the earlier utterance as a way of making coherence out of her mistake. (This is discussed further below.)

I offer the following segment as a final example of the child's interpretive competence.

Teacher 32: Humm this is interesting. What did it say in the story that Chicken Little ah where the nut fell on Chicken Little?
Tom 28: At the tree.
Teacher 33: Umhum what part of his body did it land on did it say?

Tom has formulated the correct answer to the question "where was Chicken Little when the nut fell?" i.e. the location of Chicken Little was the scheme of interpretation. While this is a correct interpretation of her question the teacher treats it as 'incorrect' by invoking her own scheme of interpretation "where on Chicken Little did the nut fall?" While interpretive ability is demonstrated, what is also demonstrated is that adults can preempt the interaction with children for their own purposes.

Understanding as Evidenceable

The paradigmatic example of verifying a child's understanding is found in Socrates' encounter with the boy in the *Meno*.

Socrates: Very well. How many times the small one is the whole space?
Boy: Four times.
Socrates: But we wanted a double space, don't you remember?
Boy: Oh, yes I remember.
Socrates: Then here is a line running from corner to corner, cutting each of the spaces in two parts.
Boy: Yes.
Socrates: Are not these four lines equal and don't they contain this space within them?
Boy: Yes, that is right.[36]

The verification of the boy's understanding is in the answer "yes." The *Meno* can be read as a monologue and the "yes" answer by the boy as Socrates' own production. A similar example is found in the transcript, beginning with Segment Teacher 32 and ending at dismissal of Tom. The segment begins with the teacher's recognition that she has made a mistake, "Humm this is interesting." She has incorrectly written the sentence on the assignment sheet to read that the nut fell on Chicken Little's head while in the story it fell on his tail. The rest of the segment is the teacher's attempt to find out if the error made any difference in Tom's understanding of the lesson. What is important, however, is that beginning at Segment Tom 32 it is absolutely clear that Tom no longer has any part in the interaction (i.e., it becomes a monologue), perhaps he no longer even knows what is going on although at the end the teacher seems convinced that Tom understood.

Tom 32:   Ya but I always thought.
Teacher 37:   In some stories it does fall on his head so it didn[...] bother you that it said head?
Teacher 38:   Have you ever heard a story where it falls [...] Chicken Little's head . . . instead of his tail?
Tom 33:   Ya.
Teacher 39:   Umhum, so you understood the story and it d[...] matter about that word did it because the idea was that it [...] on Chicken Little and it was really a nut instead of ah a piec[...] of the sky.
Thank you very much Tom.

A viewing of the videotape[37] reveals that Tom's senten[...] "Ya but I always thought" is not an interruption but a com[...] plete utterance. What is evident from the tape is that To[...] turns his eyes from looking at the teacher down to the de[...] in front of him when he concludes the utterance. He con[...] tinues to look down in this manner until the end of the interview. When he utters "Ya" (Segment Tom 33) it is softly and he does not look up. This is in marked contrast to the rest of the interview where he meets the eyes of the teacher whenever he gives an answer. The teacher, however, continues to find his understanding even though he is no longer a participant. The teacher appropriates the interaction and asserts the child's understanding. In doing this she provides for both speakers and suspends the possibility of the child's use of his interpretive competencies in the interaction, i.e., the child is treated as incompetent. The teacher asserts that Tom has understood ". . . you understood . . ." and points out why ". . . because the idea . . ." not the word was what mattered.

Thus, throughout the interview, the teacher guides the

child to the correct answers and finds in the answers the sense of the lesson which constitutes the evidence of its success, i.e., that the child understood. What is equally important is that the teacher finds both her own competence and the child's understanding in the preconstituted structure of the lesson, i.e., there are no surprises.[38]

The Paradox

The analysis has revealed the paradoxical[39] nature of adult-child interaction. The teacher relies on the child's interpretive competencies to understand the lesson but treats him throughout as incompetent (i.e., she creates or gives the 'correct' answers). The child is treated as deficient and this comes full circle back to the normative sociological view of children, as eminently common sensical. Seeing the child's interpretive competencies implies that the interpretive theory applies to both adult-adult and adult-child interaction. Differences between the two types of interaction are not theoretical but substantive. Substantively, the phenomena of study are one, the way in which adults attribute incompetence to children and create situations for its manifestation, and two, the structure of children's culture. Theoretically the phenomenon of study is the interpretive bases of intersubjectivity.

NOTES

1. Here I follow the formulations of normative found in Thomas P. Wilson, "Normative and Interpretive Paradigms in Sociology" in Jack Douglas *Understanding Everyday Life*, Chicago: Aldine, 1970, pp. 57–79 and in Aaron V. Cicourel, "Basic and Normative Rules" in H. Peter Dreitzel, *Recent Sociology Volume 2*, New York: Macmillan, 1970, pp. 4–45.
2. I use the concept gloss throughout this paper in opposition to the concept explicate. I follow the usage found in Harold Garfinkel, *Studies in Ethnomethodology*, Englewood Cliffs: Prentice-Hall, Inc., 1967, p. 33.
3. Persons concerned with adult socialization see all of life as a process of socialization. For instance see Orville G. Brim, Jr., "Adult Socialization," in J. Clausen (ed.), *Socialization and Society*, Boston: Little, Brown and Company, 1968, pp. 182–226.
4. What I am suggesting here is the same as Alan Blum has ele-

gantly formulated that "Through theorizing the theorist searches for his self, and his achievement in theorizing is a recovery of this self." "Theorizing" in Jack Douglas, *Understanding Everyday Life*, Chicago: Aldine, 1970, p. 304.

5. The problem with children is that they don't think like adults or so it seems in the vast literature on socialization, child rearing and its popular, and usually more empirical, variants in Spock, Ginst, etc. But then not thinking like adults could be applied to other large segments of the world—the people next door, this or that group. There is an extensive literature on how to *train* children, I suppose because they are smaller and less powerful. A similar argument could be applied to the poor, mental patients and prisoners, a similar literature supports this view. Incomplete socialization, deviance, etc. are particular sociological ways of indicating this.

6. See for example Leonard Broom and Philip Selznick, *Sociology 4th Edition*, New York: McGraw-Hill, 1968 and Paul B. Horton and Chester ___unt, *Sociology 2nd Edition*, New York: McGraw-H____ ___68.

7. Leonard Broom and ___p Selznick, *Sociology 4th Edit__* New York: McGraw-H__l, 1968, p. 96.

8. See for example: Orville G. Brim, Jr., "Adult Socialization," in J. Clausen, *Socialization and Society*, Boston: Little, Brow__ and Company, 1968, pp. 182–226; Fred Elkin, *The Chil__ and Society*, New York: Random House, 1960; John A__ Clausen, "Introduction" in J. Clausen, *Socialization and Society*; Alex Inkeles, "Social Structure and the Socialization of Competence," *Harvard Educational Review*, 36, 3, 1966; and Talcott Parsons and Robert F. Bales, *Family, Socialization and Interaction Process*, Glencoe, Illinois: The Free Press, 1955.

9. See Footnote 2.

10. An excellent paper which makes this distinction clear is Don R. Zimmerman and Melvin Pollner, "The Everyday World as a Phenomenon," in J. Douglas, *Understanding Everyday Life*, Chicago: Aldine, 1970, pp. 80–103.

11. *Ibid.*, p. 82.

12. Alex Inkeles, "Society, Social Structure and Child Socialization," in J. Clausen (ed.), *Socialization and Society*, Boston: Little, Brown and Company, 1968, pp. 76–77.

13. This formulation is based upon a footnote to be found in Maurice Merleau-Ponty, "The Child's Relations with Others," translated by William Cobb, to be found in Maurice Merleau-Ponty, *The Primacy of Perception*, Northwestern University Press, 1964.

14. Both theory and measurement in sociology formulate the world as *static*. For example, ideal types and questionaires take a moment in time and freeze it. If the world was not *dynamic* this would be adequate but since change is constant the

models of the world and their concomitant measurement systems are inadequate. Often what passes for theory in sociology is only high level abstractions from which anything can be deduced through the application of common sense knowledge of the world. Measurement systems are misconceived in any event because they do not measure but constitute the phenomenon. Consequently, measurement is by fiat and the world remains to be described.

15. See Footnote 1.

16. Maya Pines, *Revolution in Learning*, New York: Harper and Row, 1966, p. ix.

17. See for example: Aaron Cicourel, "The Acquisition of Social Structure" in J. Douglas, *Understanding Everyday Life*, Chicago: Aldine, 1970, pp. 136–168; Harold Garfinkel, *Studies in Ethnomethodology*, Englewood Cliffs: Prentice-Hall, 1967; John Holt, *The Underachieving School*, New York: Dell Publishing, 1969; William Labor, "The Logic of Nonstandard English" in Pier Paulo Giglioli, *Language and Social Context*, Middlesex England: Penguin Books, 1972, pp. 179–216; A. S. Neill, *Summerhill*, New York: Hart Publishing Co., 1960; and Alfred Schütz, *Collected Papers Volume 1*, The Hague: Martinus Nijhoff, 1962.

18. Perhaps this perspective offers the possibility of freeing political prisoners. See especially Holt, Labor, and Neill.

19. See especially Aaron Cicourel, "The Acquisition of Social Structure" in J. Douglas, *Understanding Everyday Life*, Chicago: Aldine, 1970, pp. 136–168 and "Ethnomethodology" in Thomas A. Sebeok et al., *Current Trends in Linguistics, Volume 12* forthcoming and Harold Garfinkel, *Studies in Ethnomethodology*, Englewood Cliffs: Prentice-Hall, 1967.

20. This formulation is particularly Cicourel's based on his critique of Chomsky.

21. Particularly important to the discusion of children are Cicourel's articles cited in Footnote 18.

22. Robert MacKay "Standardized Tests: Objective/Objectified Measures of Competence," in Aaron Cicourel et al., *Language Acquisition and Use in Testing and Classroom Settings,* forthcoming.

23. For further detailed analysis see Hugh Mehan, *Accomplishing Understanding in Educational Settings*, Unpublished Ph.D. Dissertation, University of California, Santa Barbara, 1971 and David Roth, *Children's Linguistic Performance as a Factor in School Achievement*, Unpublished Ph.D. Dissertation, University of California, Santa Barbara, 1972, also Mehan and Roth this volume, and a related work, William Labor, "The Logic of Nonstandard English," *Georgetown Monographs on Language and Linguistics*, vol. 22, 1969.

24. Opie, Iona and Peter, *The Lore and Language of School Children*, London: Oxford University Press, 1959. The idea of

separate children's culture was suggested by Harvey Sachs in a lecture at the conference on "Language, Society and the Child," Berkeley, 1968. Also see M. Spier, "The Child as Conversationalist: Some Culture Contact Features of Conversationalist Interactions Between Adults and Children," unpublished manuscript.

25. Ariès, Phillipe, *Centuries of Childhood*, New York: Random House, 1965. Also: J. H. Plump, "The Great Change in Children," *Horizon*, vol. 8, no. 1, Winter 1971.

26. The data reported here are part of a larger study that was supported by a Ford Foundation Grant, Aaron V. Cicourel Principal Investigator. Although this research was conceived in part to study children's communicative competencies the videotapes which were taken focus on the teacher's face with the result that often the children have their backs to the camera. In the segment reported on in this paper the teacher's face is clear but when the child looks at the teacher his back is to the camera. This is in part, I would suggest, because of the ubiquity of the adult view of the world and the organization of the classrooms which makes shooting videotapes towards the children almost impossible.

27. Edward T. Hall, *The Silent Language*, Greenwich Conn.: Fawcett Publications, 1959.

28. *Ibid.*, p. 9–13. It should also be noted here that culturally different persons who are serious about understanding each other spend long periods of time working out the translation problems. A good example is an anthropologist doing field work. I can think of no similar attempts on the part of teachers and other adults to understand children.

29. Cultural differences may add an element of practical difficulty created by the problems of doing adequate translation, but this is not a principaled difference. I am following Cicourel's formulation of interpretive abilities as invariant. Under this formulation culture differences are surface rules. See Aaron V. Cicourel, "The Acquisition of Social Structure," in J. Douglas, *Understanding Everyday Life*, Chicago: Aldine, pp. 136–168.

30. During the interview the teacher is seated at her desk looking sideways into the camera, the boy is standing beside her between her and the camera. The sentences to be sequenced are in front of him on her desk.

31. See Alfred Schütz, *Collected Papers I: The Problem of Social Reality*, The Hague: Martinus Nijhoff, 1962 and Harold Garfinkel, *Studies in Ethnomethodology*, Englewood Cliffs: Prentice-Hall, 1967.

32. A persistent feature of the common sense world seems to be a "trust in memory."

33. See Aaron V. Cicourel, "The Acquisition of Social Structure" in J. Douglas, *Understanding Everyday Life*, esp. pp. 147–

157 and Harold Garfinkel, *Studies in Ethnomethodology*, Englewood Cliffs: Prentice-Hall, esp. Ch. 1.

34. C. Lamar Mayer, "Relationships of Self-Concepts and Social Variables in Retarded Children," *American Journal of Mental Deficiency*, 72, 1967, pp. 267–271.

35. Cicourel, *op. cit.*, p. 147.

36. *Great Dialogues of Plato, The Meno*, translated by W.H.D. Rouse, New York: The New American Library, 1956, pp. 48, 49.

37. For a discussion of the methodological consequences of the use of videotape see Aaron V. Cicourel, "Ethnomethodology" in Thomas A. Sebeok et. al., *Current Trends in Linguistics*, Volume 12, forthcoming.

38. This observation has strong implications for the educational system. Learning for the teacher is to find evidence of its accomplishment *now* (i.e. during the lesson and review). When later on (i.e. grade 5) the child demonstrates the ability covered in the grade one lesson it is assumed that the genesis of the ability was in the lesson and not in his ability to learn it *somewhere*. By refering to somewhere I mean to point out that the child has competencies to figure out the world in a variety of different ways and in a variety of settings. The assumption of the importance of the lesson provides the *raison d'être* for formal instruction to be located in organizations called schools. If the focus in schools is on the practical organizational activities *here* and *now* how can these activities produce children committed to the pursuit of knowledge in a larger and more temporally extensive sense. Practically, how is it possible under these circumstances to get children to see that the material "learned" in schools applies beyond its walls?

39. A major assumption of this paper is that phenomena maintain a transparency of being more than one thing at once. Although the phenomenon is unitary the various parts seem sequential when talked or written about. For some phenomenologists (Maurice Merleau-Ponty, The *Phenomenonology of Perception*, New York: Humanities Press, 1962) this is regarded as the perspectival nature of experience and for the Zen monk the unity of experience. One of the most dramatic examples of a phenomenon being two things at once is Carlos Castenada's experiences using "smoke." Reported in Carlos Castaneda, *A Separate Reality*, New York: Simon and Schuster, 1971.

2

Phenomenology and Socialization: Some Comments on the Assumptions Underlying Socialization Theory

DAVID M. RAFKY[1]

INTRODUCTION

THIS ESSAY is addressed to one of the central problems sociology, an area in which there is a concrete nexus b tween theory and empirical research: the process of social ization. This whole area is vague, somewhat muddled, and— according to some sociologists—suffers from an excess of "psychologizing." This essay presents neither new data nor original concepts. Our aims are to bring together some phenomenological strands of thinking on socialization and to make explicit the assumptions underlying much of the current thinking and research in this area. While a great deal of data have been collected on socialization into the profes- sions, especially medicine, nursing and dentistry, *little theoretical integration* has been attempted since the work of George Herbert Mead (1934). The reader may disagree and perhaps cite the Becker *et al.* (1961) study of medical students (*Boys in White*). We believe, however, that sociol- ogists have not attempted to reconcile traditional American socialization literature (mostly in the area of motivation) and the European perspectives of phenomenological reasoning (mostly in the areas of cognition and perception) together with Meadian symbolic interaction.[2] Perhaps this paper will suggest some basis for rapprochement. The following section presents a phenomenological framework for understanding the ends or aims of the socialization process. The concepts of the phenomenological philosophy codified by Edmund Husserl (Farber, 1962) are not new to sociology: witness their influence in the works of Litt (1919), Vierkandt (1896), Gurvitch (1957), Monnerot (1946), and Schütz (1962). Section two focuses on the assumptions underlying the Meadian analysis of socialization, many of which have been made explicit by phenomenologists. The third section examines selected differences between child and adult socialization. Socialization may entail enculturation, the introduction of a cultureless child into the adult culture of his society, or it may describe acculturation, the transition of an adult from one culture into another. Again, the focus is on underlying assumptions.

THE CONTENTS OF THE "WORLD"

A model of socialization ultimately rests on an analysis of the contents of the "world" into which the newborn child[3] is socialized. The infant is born into a world of real objects or artifacts which exist independent of his self and delimit his immediate and protended behavior. For example, a child cannot walk through a tree: he *must* go around it. The nature of this veridical world is not wholly independent of the particular society which inhabits it. If the material substratum is conceived as simply primary or subatomic particles in motion, then there is no ontological reason for one particular object or congeries of particles to be perceived rather than another, for "the relationship between the particles in one object and in another object are just as real and just as important as the relationships found between the particles within any single object itself" (Mead,

1956:5). There are, therefore, an infinite variety of "real" objects which may be carved out of the continuum of the material substratum.

This does not deny that some objects which impose themselves on consciousness are the result of certain particle relations that exist in the very structure of matter; these are ontological necessities. Other objects are carved out of the material substratum by structures and processes in the nervous system.[4] Gestalt psychologists and phenomenologists (e.g., Köhler, 1929) have investigated these physiologically necessary perceptions. Merleau-Ponty (1963: 170-171), the phenomenological psychologist, suggests that the human nervous system contains inborn structures which organize selected stimuli into the objects of ego and other:

For a child, language which is understood, or simply sketched, the appearance of a face or that of a use-object, must from the beginning be the sonorous, motor or visual envelope of a significative intention coming from another. The organization and the sense of understood language can be very minimal at first; it will be the inflection of the voice, the intonation which will be understood rather than the verbal material. But from the beginning the sonorous phenomena—whether I speak or another speaks—will be integrated into the structure: expression-expressed; the face—whether I touch my own or I see that of another—will be integrated into the structure: alter-ego.

Finally, one category of objects obtains its reality or being from social necessity; each culture carves out objects or isolates patterns of particle relations from the panorama of potential objects in accordance with its needs, inclinations, and language structure (Whorf, 1956). The so-called real world of objects which surrounds the infant is, therefore, partly socially defined and structured, and comprises the primary constituent of the world he enters at birth.

The newborn also enters a world of social institutions, the conventionally defined and shared values and norms—symbols—toward which members of his society orient their conduct. Social institutions have a reality identical to that of veridical objects. They exist outside the child in what Emile Durkheim (1938) calls the collective conscience and delimit present and anticipated behavior—they coerce the child in the same manner as a tree.

Social institutions derive their objectivity from the fact that they have real or behavior consequences (Thomas, 1957). For example, the institution of the family consists of rules of descent, inheritance, and conduct which exist or are real only insofar as they are obeyed. They are perceived by the infant as having a prior, external, objective—and thus coercive—existence in relation to himself; that is, social institutions are perceived as veridical objects. Social institutions are the second constituent of the world into which the child is born. In contrast to material objects, institutions are socially defined in their totality.[5]

These two elements, objects and institutions, comprise the world of everyday life. It is this reality into which the child is socialized. The phenomenological analysis of Alfred Schütz (1962) reveals the contents of this world in modern western society. The world of everyday life is characterized by a particular tension of consciousness or level of awareness: this is the wide-awake attitude with which the individual gives his full attention and interest to life. The wide-awake self belongs to a person who is working in the real world, whose actions gear or mesh with those of other egos, who strives to change his environment and become modified by it. Working is subjectively meaningful or intentional because the individual is conscious of a projected state of affairs which he attempts to realize.

The world of everyday life is also characterized by a particular time perspective: the vivid present. The vivid present may be understood as the intersection between one's subjective sense of inner time (*durée*) and cosmic time. *Durée* is the imminent ordering and structuring of one's experiences whereby they "are connected within the past by recollections and retentions and with the future by protentions and anticipations" (Schütz, 1962: 215-216). Cosmic time is the ordering of events in the outer or non-subjective sphere. While participating in the world of everyday life we experience our working actions as a series of events which partake both of outer and inner time: that is, we experience them as a single flux which has an internal or subjective structure which corresponds to an external or cosmic ordering. In this sense, the vivid present may be understood as the standard time of modern western society.

The world of everyday life has a specific *epoché*, the *epoché* of the natural attitude. *Epoché* implies suspension, and as used by Schütz (1962),[6] refers to the individual suspending or giving up any doubt he might have about the existence of the world of everyday life in which he lives. That is, to live in a cultural world and remain sane, one cannot doubt that it is, indeed, real; one cannot seriously entertain the idea that other worlds or modes of reality may be just as real, for this implies that one's own world is unreal. The motive for this is the fundamental anxiety[7] from which all other fears, motives, etc., are derived. Finally, the world of everyday life is characterized by a specific form of sociality. The world is intersubjective: it is made up of other people (selves or subjectivities), and is shared by them. This state of affairs, brought about by communication of symbols and meanings, makes possible social action.

Thus, *our* world of everyday life is characterized by a specific tension of consciousness (wide-awakeness), a prevalent form of spontaneity (work), a particular time perspective (the vivid present), a specific *epoché*, and a unique form of sociality (a common intersubjective world).[8] There is more than one real world: the world of everyday life differs from culture to culture in its contents and cognitive structure (i.e., in the attributes listed above). For example, the level of awareness differs from society to society, just as their forms of spontaneity may not be identical. These life-worlds (*Lebenswelten*) not only change from one society to another, but vary to some extent within a particular society. In western industrialized society, for example, there exists side by side the world of dreams and the world of occupations. Various authors discuss life-worlds: William James (1890) calls them sub-universes; Alfred Schütz (1962) speaks of them as finite provinces of meaning;[9] and Peter Berger and Thomas Luckmann (1966) coin the term "symbolic universe."[10]

Berger and Luckmann (1966) describe the content of symbolic universes or life-worlds as the legitimations (justifications or explanations) of the social institutions that comprise them. In one sense, legitimations integrate the total institutional order of the society so that it "makes sense" to the many people who participate in the various social institutions. On the other hand, legitimations make subjectively meaningful to a single individual the various stages of his own progress through the institutional order of his society. The first level or analysis is pre-theoretical. This level is first in the sense of logical priority, not temporal priority. The brute fact that an institution exists and is named legitimates it. For example, the very fact that a child learns to call an adult "father" legitimates the child's differential conduct towards him. The acquisition of a role is usually coupled with the learning of appropriate labels. "To this first of incipient legitimation belong all the simple traditional affirmations" (Berger and Luckmann, 1966: 87). For example, when a child asks the proverbial question, "Why?" the adult's evasive answer, "Because this is how things are done," constitutes the first order of legitimation.

The second level of legitimation is theoretical in a rudimentary sense. This level is characterized by wise sayings, saws, legends, and folktales. A child may be told not to masturbate because doing so will make him a dullard. The third level of legitimation is theoretical. Thus, in the realm of sexual behavior, a body of psychological theory may be employed as an explanation or justification for punishing a child's masturbatory behavior. On the fourth and final analytical level of legitimation, whole clusters of theories are synthesized and crystalized into a total world view. This world view or ideology legitimates the totality of institutionalized behavior patterns in a given society.

Thus, the life-world the newborn enters contains more than objects and social institutions. It is also characterized by a complex of legitimations which explain and integrate the various action patterns of the group, a "matrix of all socially objectivated and subjectively real meanings; the entire historic society and the entire biography of the individual are seen as events taking place within this universe" (Berger and Luckmann, 1966: 89). In short, the individual has acquired a set or mode for interpreting the world meaningfully; he perceives it in an ordered and subjectively understandable frame of reference. Becker *et al.* (1961) arrive at the same idea by combining the Meadian (1934) explication of socialization with Thomas' (1957) concept of the definition of the situation. Becker *et al.* (1961) thus speak of "perspective," which results from a group's collective adaptation to common problems.

MECHANISMS OF SOCIALIZATION AND THEIR UNDERLYING ASSUMPTIONS

Socialization is the process whereby the objective, i.e., external and coercive world of social objects, norms, values, ~titut~ ..., and legitimations, become subjectively real to the individual. His consciousness is structured in accordance with the world view of his contemporaries and thus the symbolic universe acquires for the individual what William James (1890) calls the "accent of reality." The goal of the socialization process is an individual who identifies with other people or situations. This is a result of the child's introjecting or "absorbing the environment or personality of others into . . . [his] own psyche to the extent of reacting to external events as though they were internal ones" (Warren, 1934: 143). This process is not based on conscious imitation: introjection is an unconscious act (Blum, 1953). The specific mechanisms mediating these processes are examined below and the assumptions that a Meadian analysis of socialization takes for granted are made explicit.

Explanations of socialization ultimately rest on the assumed existence of the unique individual consciousness. The Cartesian statement *cogito ergo sum* cannot be accepted as proof of self-existence; it is merely a *post hoc, ergo propter hoc* statement of faith. The existence of self as a discrete entity is a function of the *ego cogito cogitatum* certitude (Lauer, 1958). According to this scheme, the self exists by virtue of its ability to indicate or "point to" things which transcend it (i.e., which exist as objects in relation to the self). In this way, the self is differentiated from other objects as it takes on a subject-object relationship with them.

The next assumption posits ego's knowledge of the existence of other selves or subjectivities. This constitutes the problem of intersubjectivity which has occupied such scholars as Scheler (1960), Sartre (1943), Husserl (1950), and Schütz (1962); each attempts to explain the origin of the individual's subjective understanding (cognition) of other selves. W. I. Thomas' (Timasheff, 1957) famous dictum, "If men define situations as real, they are real in their consequences," lies at the heart of any consideration of intersubjectivity. According to Thomas (Timasheff, 1957), an actor's "definition of the situation" is only one element in the "total situation" which guides his behavior. Social behavior can only be understood (i.e., is only possible) when is placed within the total situation which includes other subjectivities. Since individual behavior is necessarily situational, and varies widely from one situation to another, the self, if it enters into behavior, must have some situational aspect. Since social behavior is in conception interactive, what others do in response to an action or self presentation will make a difference to the actor; it will influence his behavior. He must, therefore, have some knowledge of other selves.

In a recent autobiographical essay, Talcott Parsons (1970) tackles the issue of intersubjectivity and comes to a position similar to our own; namely, that no satisfactory explanation of this phenomenon has yet been offered. In his discussion of the rational complex and social order, Parsons (1970) asks: How is it possible to gain rational understanding of the non-rational? In an intriguing footnote he traces the origins of his position:

It may be of interest to note that I took a Kantian approach to the problem of order. Very broadly, with respect to the epistemology of empirical knowledge, Hume asked "is valid knowledge of the external world possible?" and came out with, by and large, a negative answer. Kant, on the other hand, posed the question in a more complex way. He first asserted that "we in fact have valid knowledge of the external world" then proceeded to ask "how is it possible?", that is, under what assumptions? Similarly some social theorists have wondered whether social order was possible at all, and often denied its possibility. I, on the other hand, have always assumed that social order in fact *existed*, however imperfectly, and proceeded to ask under what conditions this fact of its existence could be explained (Parsons, 1970: 881).

The existence of other selves may, therefore, have to be accepted as a brute fact—a given with no explanation. It is fruitful, we believe, to first postulate the existence of other selves and then to ask, "How do we acquire knowledge of other subjectivities?" or "How do other selves become real to us?" Thus, we return full circle to Thomas' theorem. Perhaps an adequate approach to the problem of intersubjectivity must await a clarification of the concept of empathy and an elaboration of the Wundtian analysis of body gestures.[11]

The self is assumed to be a process; it flows (Mead, 1956) between subject and object forms—that is, the self is reflexive. The self as subject perceives, feels and acts on or towards other objects. The self bends around and perceives, feels, and literally observes itself as if it were an external object. Because the individual can, in this manner, make himself the object of his own actions, he is able to indicate or "designate things to himself—his wants, his pains, his goals, objects around him, the presence of others, their actions, their expected actions, or whatnot" (Blumer, 1966: 535). The individual acts towards himself as he acts towards others. His own gestures elicit in him the same meanings that they elicit in others. His actions are the result of meanings he bestows (Blumer, 1962) on vocal and other significant gestures which then become symbols.

It is the reflexivity of the self which enables the child to "take on the attitude" (Mead, 1934) or role of significant or important others. He does this in two ways (Mead, 1934). In the first, he simply imitates the behavior of another person in his play activity. For example, children often play mother. Part of their selves (self as subject) imitates the role behavior of mother. The child (self as subject) addresses his self (self as object) with mother's words: "Be a good boy and wash your hands." The child then obeys the command. This mechanism of social control leads to the youngster's development of the child role. In the second case, the child's behavior, which has a particular meaning for his mother, elicits the same meaning in himself. His dirty hands, which typically cause mother to request him to wash, are perceived by the child. He (self as subject) takes on the role of mother and commands himself (self as object) to wash. In either case, the child learns to act in the manner expected by significant others. In taking on the role of the child, the child has also internalized the roles of his significant others; it is this which allows him to interact or relate to these significant others. The internalized roles of significant others are synthesized within the child and make up the role of the generalized other: this enables the child to relate to people in general, to those who are not his significant others, and even to people he has not encountered. The self is, therefore, a conglomeration of roles that the child has introjected. The question, "Who are you?" typically elicits from a child a list of roles or characteristics which represent a synthesis of introjected roles. This is the meaning of the concept of identity. "When an individual becomes involved in the maintenance of a rule [role], he tends also to become committed to a particular image of self" (Goffman, 1956: 474).

Mead (1934) causes some confusion by his use of the phrases "attitude-taking," "role-taking," and "identity" interchangeably. The meanings and interpretations of these concepts *vis-à-vis* the individual and his *Lebenswelt* are clarified in this rather lengthy passage from Berger:

Socialization not only ensures that the individual is "real" to himself in a certain way, but that he will ongoingly respond to his experience of the world with the cognitive and emotive patterns appropriate to this "reality." For example, successful socialization shapes a self that apprehends itself exclusively and in a taken-for-granted way in terms of one or the other of two socially defined sexes, that knows this self-apprehension to be the only "real" one, and rejects as "unreal" any contrary modes of apprehension or emotionality. . . . Every society contains a repertoire of identities that is part of the "objective knowledge" of its members. It is "known" as a matter "of course" that there are men and women, that they have such-and-such psychological traits and that they will have such-and-such psychological reactions in typical circumstances. As the individual is socialized, these identities are "internalized." They are then not only taken for granted as constituents of an objective reality "out there" but as inevitable structures of the individual's own consciousness. The objective reality, as defined by society, is subjectively appropriated. In other words, socialization brings about symmetry between objective and subjective reality, objective and subjective identity. The degree of this symmetry provides the criterion of the successfulness of socialization. The psychological reality of the successfully socialized individual thus *verifies* subjectively what his society has objectively defined as real. He is then no longer required to turn outside himself for "knowledge" concerning the nature proper of men and women. He can obtain that result by simple introspection. He "knows who he is." He feels accordingly. He can conduct himself "spontaneously," because the firmly internalized cognitive and emotive structures make it unnecessary or even impossible for him to reflect upon alternative possibilities of conduct. [pp. 106–107]. . . . Socialization is only possible if, as Mead put it, the individual "takes the attitude" [role, identity] of others, that is, relates to himself as others have first related to him. . . . The combined significance of these root perspectives of social psychology and the sociology of knowledge for the sociological understanding of identity, one may answer in a rather simple statement: *Identify, with its appropriate attachments of psychological reality, is always identity within a specific, socially constructed world.* Or, as seen from the viewpoint of the individual: *One identifies oneself, as one is identified by others, by being located in a common world* (1966: 111).

Several corollaries follow from the above analysis. First, socialization requires other people—significant others—with whom the child interacts. Second, the child's identity is a system, either additive or integrative, of the roles, attitudes, identities or "whatnot" (to use an expression of Blumer, 1966) which significant others display *vis-à-vis* him when relating to him.[12] Third, and most important, socialization is continuous. It is not useful to conceive of socialization as a process that ends at some point in the biography of an individual. Thus, a change in significant others leads to a corresponding change in identity: a child interacts with new significant others and, therefore, makes additions to the sediment of his self-system or identity. For an individual to maintain a stable identity, the presence of significant others must be continuous.[13] A forth corollary is supplied by Goffman (1956), who elaborates the function of context in the development and presentation of self. The self is situational in that other people and objects (social and physical) are necessary for its expression. For example, a person who presents a self defined as important and elevated may do so only to the extent that others act deferentially towards him. Thus, the self as it is presented and interpreted is a product of the interaction of ego, other subjectivities, physical objects (props, make-up, etc.), social institutions, and the symbolic universe (Goffman, 1959).

SOME DIFFERENCES BETWEEN CHILD AND ADULT SOCIALIZATION

The following discussion is not intended to be exhaustive; we do not discuss what to some readers may be crucial differences between child and adult socialization, such as setting, the nature of process, the multiplicity of roles involved, the active contributions of child and adult, etc. We merely point out some selected differences between child and adult socialization which we feel deserve greater attention by researchers and theoreticians. The child, initially a *tabula rasa*, is enculturated: cultureless, he is introduced into the symbolic universe of his parent society. On the other hand, the adult, possessing a world-view, is acculturated: he moves from one symbolic universe into another. A more accurate description of adult socialization is, therefore, re-socialization. The archetype of adult re-socialization is the immigrant who assimilates the world-view of a society very different from the society of his birth. The child is socialized involuntarily whereas the adult may or may not be a willing subject. Adults who enter a new symbolic universe by religious or political conversion, or through psychoanalysis, are willing and often active participants in their re-socialization. Inmates of mental hospitals, political refugees, and prisoners in indoctrination camps typically are involuntary and passive participants.

The infant introjects the external world passively and unconsciously. The world-changing adult is more conscious of the socialization process itself; he imitates (consciously) more and identifies (unconsciously) less than the child. The adult also has more mechanisms than the child to facilitate acquisition of a new world-view. Whereas the infant uses only introjection, the adult introjects,[14] displaces or substitutes, and projects in order to include new people and objects in the structure of his consciousness, i.e., in order to produce a state of internal identification with the external world (Knight, 1940).

Many discussions of identification (e.g., Warren, 1934) stress the importance of an emotional bond between the self and significant others. There is some evidence (Brim, 1966) that an emotional tie between subject and object is more prevalent and decisive during child socialization than in adult re-socialization.[15] Perhaps this is explained by the observation (Dollard, 1939) that the child, in his domestication, is in greater conflict with his trainers than is the adult. The child, lacking a mature reality principle, is driven by primordial lust and rebellion. The adult has already been domesticated (i.e., socialized); therefore, additional socialization is not a new experience—it is the content of the socialization process which is unique. Thus, an emotional link is necessary to overcome the child's initial resistance[16] to a new process, but is not required to overcome the adult's lesser resistance to the familiar process of world-view acquisition.

Physiologists point out another important difference between adult re-socialization and enculturation. The full-term infant is premature. It is not simply that he has not grown to his adult body size; rather, certain physiological processes and structures are not mature at the time of birth. The myelin sheaths have not formed around the pyramidal (nerve fiber) tract by birth, but are completed later; certain endocrine products are lacking in the newborn; and, electroencephalographic recordings are "not mature" (Thompson, 1952). The infant is, while undergoing socialization, developing both morphologically and physiologically. The implications of the interaction of biological and socializing processes have been largely ignored.[17] To speculate that there are biological consequences of social phenomena and social repercussions of biological changes is not to specify the results of this interaction. Needless to say, the adult undergoing re-socialization is fully matured biologically.[18]

The acquisition of language, concomitant with the child's biological development and initial socialization, is completed by adulthood. As the child's ability to symbolize increases, so does his rate of role acquisition. In contrast, the adult's symbolizing capacity is more or less fixed; therefore, the socialization of the adult progresses at a more constant rate than the socialization of the child (Brim, 1966).

Finally, we would like to see additional research on negative and anticipatory socialization, two processes which are quite important in adult re-socialization. A great deal of professional education is not prescriptive, but is proscriptive and focuses on behavior which is defined as inappropriate. Furthermore, many adult socializing institutions screen out recruits who have not already acquired components of the world-view to be pursued in the institution (Becker al. 1961; Becker, 1962; Brim, 1966; Hughes, 196 ogoff, 1957; Stuit, 1949; and Thielens, 1957).

CONCLUSION

Rather than attempting a critique of the massive literature on socialization, we have presented some threads of thinking from phenomenology that bear on socialization. Our aim was to categorize the assumptions implicit in current thinking in the area and to stimulate further questions by theoreticians and researchers. Although many sociologists tend to share our feeling of how things are subjectively, they are uneasy about an analysis of socialization which they believe consciously turns away from what we know empirically about the process through which the behavior of human infants comes to be socialized and turns toward appeals to "the structure of consciousness," "the uniqueness of consciousness," and "introjection" as grounds for the development of an argument. Perhaps they are correct and the position developed in this paper can be equally or better supported by appeals to the knowledge we have about the organization of behavior—better supported because we do not have to totter over the cliff of phenomenological introspection, where every man's introspective report is the ultimate datum.

These doubts can best be resolved by additional synthesis

and research which is theoretically grounded. The task, as we see it, is to identify and codify the assumptions common to traditional American socialization literature, current European phenomenological perspectives, and Meadian symbolic interaction. Once these assumptions are identified, they could be discussed in the concrete terms of, for example, the medical profession. Such an analysis might begin with a demonstration that traditional socialization literature in the area of child and adult socialization (perhaps best represented by Brim and Wheeler, 1966) is inadequate and then point out what phenomenological perspectives can offer by way of improvement. Perhaps a close acquaintance with Alex Inkeles' (1968) formulations of the content of personality may help in such a task.

A first step in such an analysis involves consideration of the following issues:

1. What is the veridical or real world of physicians? This is partly socially defined and structured. It could be argued that physicians perceive objects (fine gradations in muscle tonus, for example) that are invisible to the layman. Psychoanalysts may live in a different veridical world than laymen, in that psychoanalytic theories, inclinations, and language structure enable the physician to carve patterns out of the world that are unknown to others. The veridical world consists of:
   a) ontological necessities.
   b) physiological necessary objects and relations.
   c) patterns and relations determined by needs and inclinations.
2. What is the content of the socially constructed world of physicians? This includes social institutions, conventionally defined and shared values and norms—symbols—toward which members of the medical profession orient their conduct. These permit the physician to interpret the world meaningfully in an ordered and subjectively understandable frame of reference. In short, what are the values, norms, and ideology of physicians which differentiate them from other members of society: norms about patient care, sickness, and so on. Specific elements in the life-world of physicians which may or may not differentiate them from non-physicians are:
   a) level of awareness (in the hospital, office, etc.).
   b) time perspective.
   c) strength of belief in the objective reality of his life-world (cynicism, psychosis in the extreme).
   d) predominant form of sociality.

e) legitimations or world view (in order of increasing complexity).
   i. names and labels
   ii. wise sayings, saws, about medicine and the profession
   iii. theory (germ theory of disease)
   iv. synthetic world-view (ideology of rationality and orderliness in all human endeavors).
3. How does the objective world (all of the above) become subjectively real to the physician? How does his identity become objectified? This process is based on the following assumptions and contingencies:
   a) the self is reflexive and takes both subject and object forms.
   b) other selves (physicians and non-physicians) exist.
   c) the physician "takes on the attitude" of others. That is, he constructs his identity *vis-à-vis* the reactions of others to him, and the reactions of his self as subject to his self as object.
   d) analysis of the procession of other selves (significant others' in the physician's career.
   e) study of the context in which the presentation of self takes place (bedside, hospital, etc.).
   f) to what extent this process is
      i. imitative
      ii. conscious
      iii. characterized by an emotional bond
      iv. anticipatory, and
      v. proscriptive.

We anxiously await a reevaluation of existing theories with a specificity of the kind suggested above.

REFERENCES

Becker, H. S. 1962 "The nature of a profession." Sixty-first yearbook of the national society for the study of education, part II. Chicago: University of Chicago Press, pp. 27–46.

Becker, H. S., B. Geer, E. C. Hughes, and A. L. Strauss 1961 Boys in white: student culture in medical school. Chicago: University of Chicago Press.

Berger, P. 1966 "Identity as a problem in the sociology of knowledge." European Journal of Sociology VII, 105–115.

Berger, P. L., and T. Luckman 1966 The social construction of reality: a treatise in the sociology of knowledge. New York: Doubleday & Co.

Blum, G. S. 1953 Psychoanalytical theories of personality. New York: McGraw-Hill Book Co.

Blumer, H. 1962 "Society as Symbolic Interaction." In A. M. Rose (ed.) Human behavior and social processes: an interactionist approach. Boston: Houghton Mifflin Co., pp. 179–93.

Blumer, H. 1966 "Sociological implications of the thought of

George Herbert Mead." American Journal of Sociology 71: 535–48.

Brim, O. G. 1966 "Socialization through the life cycle." In O. G. Brim and S. Wheeler, Socialization after childhood: two essays. New York: John Wiley & Sons, Inc.

Davis, F., and V. Olesen 1963 "Initiation into a women's profession: identity problems in the status transition of co-ed to student nurse." Sociometry, 26, 89–101.

Dollard, J. 1939 "Culture, society, impulse, and socialization." American Journal of Sociology, 45, 50–64.

Durkheim, E. 1938 The rules of sociological method. Chicago: University of Chicago Press.

Farber, M. 1962 The foundations of phenomenology. New York: Paine-Whitman Publishers.

Garfinkel, H. 1967 Studies in ethnomethodology. Englewood Cliffs, N.J.: Prentice-Hall.

Goffman, E. 1956 "The nature of deference and demeanor." American Anthropologist 58: 473–502.

Goffman, E. 1959 The presentation of self in everyday life. Garden City, N.Y.: Doubleday Anchor Books.

Gurvitch, G. 1957 La vocation actuelle de la sociologie. 2nd edition. Paris: Presses Universitaires de France.

Henle, M. (ed.) 1961 Documents of gestalt psychology. Berkeley and Los Angeles: University of California Press.

Hughes, E. C. 1961 "Education for a profession." Library Quarterly 31: 336–43.

Hughes, E. C. 1958 Men and their work. Glencoe, Ill.: The Free Press.

Husserl, E. 1950 Cartesianische meditationen. S. Strasser (ed.) The Hague: Martinus Nijhoff.

Inkeles, A. 1968 "Society, social structure, and child socialization." In John A. Clausen (ed.) Socialization and society. Boston: Little, Brown and Company, pp. 73–129.

James, W. 1890 Principles of psychology, Vol. II. New York: Holt.

Knight, R. 1940 "Introjection, projection and identification." Psychoanalytic Quarterly 9: 334–41.

Köhler, W. 1929 Gestalt psychology. New York: Horace Liveright.

Lauer, Q. 1958 Phenomenology: its genesis and prospect. New York: Harper & Row.

Litt, T. 1919 Individuum und gemeinshaft. Leipzig: B. G. Teubner.

Mead, G. H. 1956 "Evolution becomes a general idea." In A. Strauss (ed.) George Herbert Mead on social psychology. Chicago: University of Chicago Press, pp. 3–19.

Mead, G. H. 1934 Mind, self and society. Chicago: University of Chicago Press.

Merleau-Ponty, M. 1963 The structure of behavior. Trans. by A. L. Fisher. Boston: The Beacon Press.

Mills, C. W. 1940 "Situated actions and vocabularies of motive." American Sociological Review 5: 904–13.

Monnerot, J. 1946 Les faits sociaux ne sont pas des choses. Paris: Gallimard.

Parsons, T. 1970 "On building social system theory: a personal history." Daedalus 99: 826–881.

Rogoff, N. 1957 "The decision to study medicine." In R. K. Merton, et al. (eds.) The student-physician. Cambridge, Mass.: Harvard University Press: 109–31.

Sartre, J-P. 1943 L'être et le néant. Paris: Gallimard.

Scheler, M. 1960 Die wissensformen und die gesellschaft: probleme einer soziologie des wissens. Bern: Frauke.

Schütz, A. 1962 Collected papers: the problems of social reality, Vol. I. The Hague: Martinus Nijhoff.

Shibutani, T. 1962 "Reference groups and social control." In A. Rose (ed.) Human behavior and social processes: an interactionist approach. Boston: Houghton Mifflin Co.: 128–47.

Stuit, D. B., Gwendolen, S. D., Jordan, T. F., and Schloreb, L. 1949 Predicting success in professional schools. Washington, D.C.: American Council on Education.

Thielens, W. 1957 "Some comparisons of entrants to medical and law school." In R. K. Merton et al. (eds.) The student-physician. Cambridge, Mass.: Harvard University Press, pp. 131–53.

Thomas, W. I. 1957 "The definition of the situation." In L. .A. Coser and B. Rosenberg (eds.) Sociological theory: a book of readings. New York: The Macmillan Co., Houghton Mifflin Co.

Timasheff, N. 1957 Sociological theory: its nature and growth. New York: Random House.

Tiryakian, E. A. 1965 "Existential phenomenology and the sociological tradition." American Sociological Review 30: 674–688.

Tomich, J. 1966 "Home care: a technique for generating professional identity." Journal of Medical Education 41: 202–207.

Vierkandt, A. 1896 Naturvölker und kulturvölker. Leipzig: Duncker & Humbolt.

Warren, H. C. (ed.) 1934 Dictionary of psychology. Boston: Houghton Mifflin Co.

Whorf, B. L. 1956 Language, thought, and reality. New York: John Wiley & Sons, Inc.

NOTES

1. I would like to thank Professor Peter Berger of the Graduate Faculty at the New School for Social Research for introducing me to the current trends in European social thought. Also,

I would like to express appreciation to several anonymous reviewers whose suggestions are incorporated into this final draft.

2. Two noteworthy exceptions are Tiryakian's (1965) essay and Berger and Luckmann's (1966) treatise on the sociology of knowledge, which spell out many of the connections between phenomenological philosophy and sociology. In addition, Mead's (1934) model has been used to guide studies of socialization into the professions; see for example Davis and Olesen's (1963) paper on student nurses and the Becker *et al.* (1961) study of student physicians.

3. The use of the word "child" in this context is questionable. Child implies human-ness: one may legitimately question whether newborn, unsocialized *Homo sapiens* are, indeed, human. It is only after the process of socialization or domestication has taken place, that the infant may be said to be a human or a social animal. Thus, human-ness is an acquired characteristic and feral men are not human in this sense.

4. Kant called this structure the "faculty of understanding." This concept is useful in epistemology, and may be helpful in understanding the origins of purportedly *a priori* cognitions.

5. In the words of Durkheim (1938: 1–2):

When I perform my obligations as brother, husband, or citizen, when I execute my contracts, I perform duties which are defined, externally to myself and my acts, in law and in custom. Even if they conform to my own sentiments and I feel their reality subjectively, such reality is still objective, for I did not create them. . . . Here, then, are ways of acting, thinking, and feeling that present the noteworthy property of existing outside the individual consciousness. These types of conduct or thought are not only external to the individual but are, moreover, endowed with co ~ power, by virtue of which they impose themselves upon him, independent of his individual will.

6. Here Schütz (1962) turns Husserl "on his head." For Husserl (Lauer, 1958), *epoché* is the suspension of any *belief* relating to the existence or nonexistence of the external world, as a necessary procedure in the transcendental phenomenological reduction. Schütz (1962) uses *epoché* to indicate the suspension of *doubt*: that is, the veridicality of the external world is accepted without doubt.

7. Schütz defines the fundamental anxiety as follows: "I know that I shall die and I fear to die" (1962: 228).

8. At this point it may be helpful to make a rather fine—but nevertheless crucial—distinction. *Lebenswelt*, the lived-in-world is also the taken-for-granted world, the world of how-to-do it. These concepts are at different levels of understanding and should not be used interchangeably. See Garfinkel (1967) for a discussion of the how-to-do-it world.

9. Because "it is the meaning of our experiences and not the ontological structure of the objects which constitutes reality" (Schütz, 1962: 230).

10. Berger and Luckman (1966) point out that the concept of symbolic universe is similar to Durkheim's (1938) idea of "religion" and Sartre's (1943) notion of "totalization."

11. Some progress has been made along these lines. See Henle (1961) for an interesting analysis of empathy, and Mills' (1940)—dated, yet still theoretically definitive—discussion of verbal gestures or symbols in the development and expression of motives.

12. To most social psychologists it seems clear that the idea of socialization entails the notion of acting persons who know enough about what they are doing to constitute a society. Perhaps it is not so clear that "the child's identity is a system. . . ." They are correct in the sense that we already know something about processes and products of self-dissociation, and about failures to organize behavior in ways that support inferences to a self (in autistic children, for example) or behavioral disorganization which makes inference to a self difficult or impossible (in so-called "psychotic states," for example).

13. Brim (1966) points out that as an individual becomes older, society's expectations of him change, and as a consequence, the need for adult socialization arises. He fails to recognize, however, that adult socialization is necessary even if new behavior is not required of an individual: socialization and world maintaining mechanisms are necessary to maintain and support *current* behavior. People who "share a common culture are continually supporting one another's perspectives, by each responding to the other in expected ways" (Shibutani, 1962: 143). Interaction with significant others in any context is sufficient to maintain one's identity. For example, physicians who interact with other physicians at the country club do not have to discuss medicine *per se* in order to reinforce each other's professional identity. In fact, interaction with patients is probably sufficient for this purpose (Tomich, 1966). The presence of significant others for the maintenance or change of identity must not be taken only to mean *physical* presence. Mead (1934) has probably been misinterpreted on this point; his discussions of memory and historical biography clearly indicate that the physical presence of significant others is not required. Consider, for example, the religious ascetic or hermit who lives in social isolation. They do communicate, however, if only with God or retentions of significant others.

14. Knight (1940: 335) states that introjection "always involves previous projections onto the object of the subject's own [unacceptable] tendencies."

15. Brim (1966) believes that the emotional tie between significant others and the child is intense, due to the strength and
frequency of physical rewards and punishments administered
by them to the child. This is not to say, however, that there
are no emotional ties evident during adult identification. For
example, during psychoanalysis, positive transference—the
warm feeling which passes between analyst and patient—is a
classic observation. One must determine whether this emotional bond is necessary for the adult to change world-views,
or simply a concomitant of this change.

16. This resistance is described almost poetically by Dollard
(1939: 53):

> It seems clear from the present data that socialization is
> a process full of conflict between the child and its trainers.
> Growing up is not a smooth automatic process of assimilat-
> ing the folkways and mores; on the contrary, society has
> to deal with a rebellious animal full of animal lust and
> anger. The domestication of this animal is without exception
> a process attended conflict and strain.

17. Studies of institutionalized infants (Thompson, 1952) indicate
that their future development is, indeed, affected by early
lack of interaction with parent surrogates. While language
and social responsiveness are most likely to be permanently
retarded, there is some evidence that the child's perceptual
and motor skills may also be affected (although not necessarily permanently). These children exhibit apathy and less
than normal affect. Brim (1966) concludes that primary
socialization is more durable and lasting because it takes place
early in the biological history of the organism.

18. Adult socialization must also take the biological status of the
individual into account. Hughes (1958) discusses the biological requirements of certain roles, such as strength and
vitality. People (Brim, 1966) accommodate to certain biological concomitants of their roles and may thus find themselves
unable or unwilling to adjust to the more "primitive" conditions of new roles.

3

Embodiment and Child Development: A Phenomenological Approach

JOHN O'NEILL

ANY THEORY OF child socialization is implicitly a theory of the construction of social reality, if not of a particular historical social order.[1] In this essay I propose to give an account of the phenomenological approach to the basic presuppositions of child socialization. I shall restrict my account to the writings of Maurice Merleau-Ponty, who, although widely known as a philosopher and political theorist, remains to be known for the lectures on child psychology which he gave for many years at the Sorbonne.[2] For reasons of economy it is not possible to follow the whole of Merleau-Ponty's interpretation and critical evaluation of the literature with which he familiarized himself concerning the physiological, intellectual, moral, and cultural development of the child, not to mention his close reading of psychoanalytical and American anthropological research. Much of the literature is in any case now all too familiar to workers in child psychology, although Merleau-Ponty's close reading and phenomenological critique of Piaget's work[3] might be given special mention because of its continuing interest.

Merleau-Ponty's analysis of the child's relation to others, his family, and the world around him may serve as introduction to the whole of Merleau-Ponty's phenomenology of perception, expression, and the sociohistorical world of human institutions.[4] At all events, the topic and its phenomenological horizons are inseparable and can only be managed in a short space by focusing upon the very fundamental presuppositions of the phenomenon of the child's orientation to the world and others around him through the mediations of the body, language, perception, and reflection. The phenomenological concern with these basic structures of child development involves an implicit concern with the way in which they may be prejudged by the assumptions of unreflexive research.

The starting point in any study of child psychology and socialization must be the child's relation to the adult world, its social relations, linguistic, perceptual, and logical categories. By insisting on this point, Merleau-Ponty dismisses any notion of a psychology of the child, the sick person, man, woman, or the primitive as an enclosed nature. Indeed, ther. is a *complementary feature* of the child-adult relationship, namely, the reverse adult-child relationship. This obliges us in the methodology of child studies to design research procedures which are sensitive to the two-way and even asymmetric relation between the child's orientation to the adult world and the adult world's interests in fostering, enforcing and moralizing upon its own interests and hopes in the child world. We cannot here look down the path toward the "politics of experience" which this first methodological observation opens up.[5] It must suffice to remark that it points to a cultural dilemma that is generic to human relations and thus makes it impossible to conceive of child psychology and psychoanalysis outside of specific cultural frameworks.

Another general conclusion which we may elicit from the interactional nature of the object of child studies refers to a phenomenon that is common to the object of all social studies. The natural scientist for most purposes is concerned only with the observer's experience, however mediated by his instruments, of the object under study. Even if we take into account the problems of interference referred to by the Heisenberg uncertainty principle, the problem here is merely that the scientist must allow for changes in the behaviour of experimental objects due to the interference effects of his own methods of study. But although this problem produces a greater similarity between the natural and social sciences than was imagined earlier, it leaves unchanged an essential difference between them. Namely, where the object of science is a human relationship or set of human relationships, a custom or institution, the "ordering" of the relationship it is not merely a scientific construct. It is first of all a pre-theoretical construct which is the unarticulated "commonsense" knowledge of others as "relatives" who experience dependable needs and wants expressed through the "relevances" of the human body, time, and place.

The burden of Merleau-Ponty's methodological critique of research methods in studies of child perception, language, and morals is that they proceed without the benefit of any reflection upon the way their methods already prejudge the nature of the phenomena they are intended to elicit. In the first place we must rid ourselves of a "dogmatic rationalism" which consists in studying the child's world from above and thereby construing the child's efforts as pre-logical or magical behaviour which must be sloughed off as a condition of entry into the objective, realist world of adults. Such a prejudice overlooks the way in which child and adult behaviour are solidary, with anticipations from the side of the child and regressions on the side of the adult which makes their conduct no more separable than health and sickness. Indeed, the real task of a genuine psychology must be to discover the basis of *communication* between children and adults, between the unconscious and consciousness, between the sick and the sane.[6]

"We must conceive the child neither as an absolute 'other' nor just 'the same' as ourselves, but as polymorphous."[7] This remark may serve as a guiding principle in following Merleau-Ponty's subtle interweaving of the processes of structure and development in the child's relation to others. The notion of *development* is, of course, central to the psychology of the child; it is, however, a complex notion since it implies neither an absolute continuity between childhood and adulthood nor any complete discontinuity without phases or transitions. It is here that we need to avoid the twin reductions of the phenomena of development which Merleau-Ponty labels "mechanist" and "idealist" exemplified respectively by the learning theory approach originated by Pavlov and the cognitive approach of Piaget. Here we are on explicitly philosophical ground because the continuity between childhood and adult life raises the question of how it is in principle that individual and inter-subjective life are possible.

Mechanist, reflex or learning theory accounts of child development involve us in the difficulty that their causal explanations fail to cover the phenomena of adult initiative, creativity and responsibility. Reflex theory reduces conduct to a structure of conditioned reflexes built into increasingly complex patterns whose principle of organization is always conceived as an environmental stimulus to which the responses of adaptation occur without internal elaboration. Reflex theory attempts to explain conduct in terms of physiological process without norms or intentionality. But even at its own level reflex theory is not sure of its foundations.[8] Once one attempts to make the notions of stimulus, receptor and reflex more precise, reflex theory becomes riddled with question-begging hypotheses about mechanisms of inhibition and control, acquired drives and the like. The case of "experimental neurosis" in one of Pavlov's dogs involved in repeated experiments reveals that the consequences of the restriction of a biologically meaningful environment in order to induce conditioned reflexes results in pathological behaviour.[9] By the same token, the acquisition of human habits is not a strictly determined reflex but the acquisition of a capability for inventing solutions to situations which are only *abstractly* similar and never identical with the original "learning situation." What is involved in the formation of human habits is the aquisition of a "categorical attitude"[10] or a power of "symbolic expression,"[11] and it is only in pathological conduct that atomistic and associationist explanations appear plausible.

While rejecting naturalistic reductions of child development, Merleau-Ponty is equally critical of idealist or cognitive accounts of the phenomena of perception, intelligence and sensory-motor behaviour. The basic fault in cognitive approaches to the child's relation to the world and others is that they sacrifice the immediate, *visceral knowledge* of self others and the world which we possess without ever having apprenticed ourselves to the "rules" of perception, language, and movement. This preconceptual knowledge is neither subjective nor objective and requires a conception of *symbolic form* which rests neither upon a realist nor an idealist epistemology but instead seeks what is complementary in them. Because the philosophical presuppositions of psychology are implicitly dualistic, consciousness is usually described as the transparent possession of an object of thought in distinction from perceptual and motor acts which are described as a series of events external to each other. Thought and behaviour are juxtaposed or else set in a speculative hierarchy. Against these alternatives, Merleau-Ponty proposes to classify behaviour according to a continuum whose upper and lower limits are defined by the submergence of the structure of behaviour in content, at the lowest level, i.e., "synenetic forms," and, at the highest level, the emergence of structure as the proper theme of activity, i.e., "symbolic forms."

The conceptualization of behaviour requires the category of Form in order to differentiate the structures of quantity, order and value or signification as the dominant characteristics respectively of matter, life and mind and at the same time to relativize the participation of these structures in a hierarchy of forms of behaviour. Form is itself not an element in the world but a limit toward which biophysical and psychobiological structures tend. In a given environment each organism exhibits a preferred mode of behaviour which is not the simple aim or function of its milieu and its internal organization but is structured by its general attitude to the world. In other words, the analysis of form is not a matter of the composition of real structures but the perception of wholes. Human behaviour, which is essentially symbolic behaviour, unfolds through structures or gestures which are not in objective space and time, like physical objects, nor in a purely internal dimension of consciousness unsituated with respect to historical time and place.

Merleau-Ponty calls the objects of perception "phenomena" in order to characterize their openness to perceptual consciousness to which they are not given *a priori* but as "open, inexhaustible systems which we recognize through a certain style of development." The matrix of all human activity is the *phenomenal body* which is the schema of our world, or the source of a vertical or human space in which we project our feelings, moods and values. Because the human body is a "community of senses" and not a bundle of contingently related impression, it functions as the universal setting or schema for all possible styles or typical structures of the world. These, however, are not given to us with the invariable formula of a *facius totius universi* but through the temporal synthesis of horizons implicit in intentionality. "For us the perceptual synthesis is a temporal synthesis, and subjectivity, at the level of perception, is nothing but temporality, and that is what enables us to leave to the subject of perception his opacity and historicity."[12] The cognitive approaches to child development overlook the *tacit* subjectivity which does not constitute its world *a priori* nor entirely *a posteriori* but develops through a "living cohesion" in which the embodied self experiences itself while belonging to this world and others, clinging to them for its content.

Thus in his analysis of the child's perception of causal relations[13] Merleau-Ponty argues that it is not a matter of a simple ordering of external data but of an "informing" [*Gestaltung*] of the child's experience of external events through an operation that is properly neither a logical nor a predicative activity. Similarly, in the case of the child's imagination,[14] it proves impossible to give any objective sense of the notion of *image* even as photograph, mimicry, or picture, apart from an "affective projection." Imagination is therefore not a purely intellectual operation but is better understood as an operation beneath the cognitive relation of subject and object. The 'imaginary' and the 'real' are two *forms of conduct* which are not antithetical but rest upon a common ambiguity which occasionally allows the imaginary to substitute for the real. The child lives in the hybrid world of the real and the imaginary which the adult keeps apart for most purposes or is otherwise careful of any transgression wherein he catches his own conscience. Again, in the analysis of the child's drawing,[15] it is also improper to treat the child's efforts as abortive attempts to develop "adult," or rather perspectual, drawing, which is itself an historical development in art dominated by the laws of classical geometric perspective. The child's drawing is not a simple imitation of what he sees any more than of what he does not see through lack of detailed 'attention.' The child's drawings are expressive of his relations to the things and people in this world. They develop and change along with his experience with the objects, animals, puppets, and persons around him, including his own experience of his body, its inside and outside.[16] "The child's drawing is *contact* with the visible world and with others. This tactile relation with the world and with man appears long before the looking attitude, the posture of indifferent contemplation between the spectator and the spectacle which is realized in adult drawing."[17]

It is above all in the child's acquisition of language that we observe the complex interrelation of cognition and affectivity which can only be made thematic in later phases of development by presupposing the massive inarticulatable background of the world into which we import our categories, distinctions and relations. Language and intelligence presuppose one another without priority and their development rests rather upon the ability of the child to assimilate his linguistic envir———— —— ?pen system of expression and conduct, comparable .o ... acquisition of all his other habits. Again, for reasons of economy we cannot deal with the broad range of the phenomenology of language.[18] Instead, we must focus attention upon Merleau-Ponty's interpretation of the social contexts of the acquisition of language.[19]

"It is a commonplace that the child's acquisition of language is also correlated with his relation to his mother. Children who have been suddenly and forcibly separated from their mothers always show signs of a linguistic regression. At bottom, it is not only the word 'mama' that is the child's first; it is the entire language which is, so to speak, maternal.

"The acquisition of language might be a phenomenon of the same kind as the relation to the mother. Just as the maternal relation is (as the psychoanalysts say) a relation of *identification*, in which the subject projects on his mother what he himself experiences and assimilates the attitudes of his mother, so one could say that the acquisition of language is itself a phenomenon of identification. To learn to speak is to learn to play a series of *roles*, to assume a series of conducts or linguistic gestures."[20]

This hypothesis on the development of language in relation to the child's familial roles is illustrated in terms of analysis of the expression of child jealousy.[21] Upon the birth of a new baby the younger of two children displays jealousy, behavioural regression (carrying himself as though he were the baby), and language regression. There, phenomena represent an initial response to the threatened structure of the child's temporal and social world of t "latest born" child. The emotional response of jealousy ex presses the child's attachment to a hitherto eternal present. A little later the child begins to identify with his olde brother, adopting the latter's earlier attitudes towards hin self as the "youngest." The chance circumstance of th visit of another child bigger than his older brother relativizes once and for all the 'absolute eldest' and the child's jealousy recedes. At the same time as these 'sociometric' experiences are acquired the child's linguistic experience of temporal structure also expands. "He considered the present to be absolute. Now, on the contrary, one can say that from the moment when he consents to be no longer the latest born, to become in relation to the new baby what his elder brother had until then been in relation to him, he replaces the attitude of 'my place has been taken' with another whose schema might be somewhat like this: 'I *have been* the youngest, but I *am* the youngest no longer, and I *will become* the biggest.' One sees that there is a solidarity between the acquisition of this temporal structure, which gives a meaning to the corresponding linguistic instruments, and the situation of jealousy that is overcome."[22]

The child's resolution of his jealousy permits us to make some general remarks upon the relation of the cognitive and affective elements in the child's conception of the world and others around him which will then permit us to deal finally with the fundamental problem of the possibility of social relations of any kind.[23] In overcoming his jealousy we might, as Piaget would say, speak of the child having solved the egocentric problem by learning to decenter himself and to relativize his notions by thinking in terms of reciprocity. But these are clearly not purely intellectual operations; rather, what is called *intelligence* here really designates the mode of intersubjectivity achieved by the child. The intellectual and linguistic elaboration of our experience of the world always rests upon the 'deep structures' of our affective experience of the interpersonal world against which we elaborate only later our modes of inductive and deductive thinking.

"The perception of other people and the intersubjective world are problematical only for adults. The child lives in a world which he unhesitatingly believes accessible to all around him. He has no awareness of himself or of others as private subjectivities, nor does he suspect that all of us, himself included, are limited to one certain point of view of the world. That is why he subjects neither his thoughts, in which he believes as they present themselves, without attempting to link them to each other, nor our words, to any sort of criticism. He has no knowledge of points of view. For him men are empty heads turned towards one single, self-evident world where everything takes place, even dreams, which are, he thinks, in his room, and even thinking, since it is not distinct from words. Others are for him so many gazes which inspect things, and have an almost material existence, so much so that the child wonders how these gazes avoid being broken as they meet. At about twelve years old, says Piaget, the child achieves the *cogito* and reaches the truths of rationalism. At this stage, it is held, he discovers himself both as a point of view on the world and also as called upon to transcend that point of view, and to construct an objectivity at the level of judgement. Piaget brings the child to a mature outlook as if the thoughts of the adult were self-sufficient and disposed of all contradictions. But, in reality, it must be the case that the child's outlook is in some way vindicated against the adult's and against Piaget, and that the unsophisticated thinking of our earliest years remains as an indispensable acquisition underlying that of maturity, if there is to be for the adult

one single intersubjective world. My awareness of constructing an objective truth would never provide me with anything more than an objective truth for me, and my greatest attempt at impartiality would never enable me to prevail over my subjectivity (as Descartes so well expresses it by the hypothesis of the malignant demon), if I had not, underlying my judgments, the primordial certainty of being in contact with being itself, if, before any voluntary *adoption of a position* I were not already *situated* in an intersubjective world, and if science too were not upheld by this basic δοξα. With the *cogito* begins that struggle between consciousnesses, each of which, as Hegel says, seeks the death of the other. For the struggle ever to begin, and for each consciousness to be capable of suspecting the alien presences which it negates, all must necessarily have some common ground and be mindful of their peaceful co-existence in the world of childhood."[24]

Classical psychology, however, renders the intersubjective world which is the presupposition of all socialization entirely problematic. This arises from the assumption that the psyche is *what is given to only one person*, intrinsically mine and radically inaccessible to others who are similarly possessed of their own experiences. The same assumption is also made with regard to the body, namely, that it is as *individual* as the psyche and knowable by me only through the mass of sensations it gives me. So conceived, the problem of the experience of others presents itself as a system with four terms: (1) myself, my 'psyche'; (2) the image I have of my body by means of the sense of touch or cenesthesia, i.e., the 'introceptive image' of my own body; (3) the body of the other as seen by me, i.e., that 'visual body'; (4) the hypothetical 'psyche' of the other, his feeling of his own existence which I must reconstitute by means of (3) the 'visual body.'[25]

The difficulties intrinsic to the operation of this schema are apparent from what it assumes in the analysis of the child's response to the other's smile.[26] The child responds very early to facial expressions and, of course, verbal expressions of "do's" and "don'ts" without being able either to compare his 'motor smile' with the 'visible smile' of the other or to correlate just what it is that he is doing that meets with approval or disapproval. Rather than engage in point for point comparisons the child can only respond to global situations and attitudes, in other words to his surroundings as motivation or conduct. This means that we must reject the individualist and solipsistic conceptions intrinsic to the dual worlds of the mind and body as conceived in classical psychology and its philosophical tradition.[27] We can no longer conceive of the psyche as a series of enclosed 'states of consciousness' inaccessible to anyone but myself. Consciousness is turned towards the world; it is a mode of conduct toward things and persons[28] which in turn reveal themselves to me through their style and manner of dealing with the world. By the same token we must revise our conception of the body as an agglomeration of senses that are mine and which are only to be guessed at in the case of others. My awareness of body is the activity of a postural or corporeal schema which is the lived experience of a cenestesia or play between my various senses and the senses of others visible in their comportment.

Thus in today's psychology we have one system with two terms (my behaviour and the other's behaviour) which functions as a whole. To the extent that I can elaborate and extend my *corporeal schema*, to the extent that I acquire a better organized experience of my own body, to that very extent will my consciousness of my own body cease being a chaos in which I am submerged and lend itself to a transfer to others. And since at the same time the other who is to be perceived is himself not a 'psyche' closed in on himself but rather a *conduct*, a system of behaviour that aims at the world, he offers himself to my motor intentions and to that 'intentional transgression' (Husserl) by which I animate and pervade him. Husserl said that the perception of others is like a 'phenomenon of coupling' [*accouplement*]. The term is anything but a metaphor. In perceiving the other, my body and his are coupled, resulting in a sort of action which pairs them [*action à deux*]. This conduct which I am able only to see, I live somehow from a distance. I make it mine; I recover [*reprendre*] it or comprehend it. Reciprocally I know that the gestures I make myself can be the objects of another's intention. It is this transfer of intentions to my own, my alienation of the other and his alienation of me, that makes possible the perception of others.[29]

Here we can only point to the complementarity between the role of the corporeal schema and the work of social actors in elaborating the field of impressions and visual data inadvertently and deliberately presented to him as the motives and expectations of social interaction or the typification of personal and institutional conduct, as analyzed by Mead, Goffman, and Schütz.[30] Likewise, without any further comment upon the relation between transcendental phenomenology and mundane intersubjectivity,[31] we must now conclude with an analysis of the formation of the child's corporeal schema in the early stages of socialization.

The problem is to account for how it is that we become aware of the distinction between our own body and the other's body while simultaneously acquiring the ability to transfer our intentions to the facial and linguistic expressions of the other as the *prima facie* basis of their further elaboration and making our own gestures similarly available to the other's intentions and expectations.[32] We may distinguish three principal stages in this process, at each point commenting upon the conceptual revisions which are implicit in their structure and development during the first three years of the child's life.

The first phase is that of *pre-communication* in which the child does not experience himself as a single individual set over against all others. The first *me* is still a latent or vertical possibilitiy within our experience of an anonymous or collective existence. What is sometimes called egocentrism at this stage refers not to an experience of self-other contrast but precisely to the experience of a *me* which dwells as easily in others as in itself and is in fact no more aware of itself than it is of others. For this reason, however, the child's *me* can be extremely demanding and volatile. But the phenomena of the child appearing to be wilfully different from situation to situation, playing several roles with himself and even attributing his experiences to others ('transitivism') mislead us into attributing them to the child's egocentrism. But these phenomena are actually symptomatic of the as yet unacquired structure of his own perspective as an *I* and that of others in which every *you* is also an *I* and neither he nor they an undifferentiated *me* without limits of time and space. The full development of this structure of experience has as its 'correlate' the development of lingustic competence with the system of pronouns which in turn elaborates an interpersonal order through this very perspective.

The second phase which we distinguish intervenes, in the development of the first phase from pre-communication to the acquisition of personal perspective and its implicit competence with orderly social life gained by the child's second year or so. This is the stage of the child's awareness of his *own body (corps propre)* and the *specular image (l'image speculaire)*.[33] At this stage the development of consciousness towards what is called intelligence proceeds by means of an expanded awareness of the child's own body through the acquisition of its specular image which in turn involves a general mode of conduct beyond the episodic event of seeing his body image in a mirror. Moreover, the mastery of this specular image is more difficult for the child to achieve than the distinction between his father, say, and his father's image in the mirror—even though he still allows the image a quasi-reality similar to that we feel in the presence, of portraits, however much we "know better." But in the case of his own specular image the child can make no visual comparison to establish the difference between the experience of his body seen in the mirror and his body of which he can only see the hands, feet or other parts but is otherwise a totality of which he has only a lived experience. Yet the child has now to understand that although he is his own body and not its image in the mirror, his own body is nevertheless visible to others like its mirror image.

Since Merleau-Ponty is not concerned to make an absolute distinction between the three phases of early child development, we may mention the overlap between the second and third phase here, i.e., the "crisis at three years." This phase is marked by the child's refusal of his body and thoughts falling under any perspective or interpretation than his own. He wants his own way and this he works out by stubbornly requiring the resistance of others to his own negativity. Through everything the child refuses, his parents, their words, and their food, there arises the structure of oedipal relations in which again the child's world and his conception of social reality are reducible neither to cognitive nor solely affective factors.

The interpretation of the development of the specular image again involves taking a position on the reduction of cognitive and affective behaviour. Merleau-Ponty rejects the view that the specular image involves a cognitive process in which the relation between reality and image, the body here and its image or shadow over there, is established once and for all. The specular image involves a new form of conduct, a shift from the lived body to the visible body, the object of social attention, projection and mimesis. The body is now a form of conduct, of an identification with others which is never quite stabilized but is the basis of the child's joys and sorrows, his jealousies and tender loyalties which are the experiences of growing up among others—the possibility of a super ego.

Thus one sees that the phenomenon of the specular image is given by psychoanalysts the importance it really has in the life of the child. It is the acquisition not only of a new content but of a new function as well: the narcissistic function. Narcissus was the mythical being who after looking at his image in the mirror of water, was drawn as if by vertigo to rejoin his own image in the mirror of water. At the same time that the image of oneself makes possible the knowledge of oneself, it makes possible a sort of alienation. I am no longer what I felt myself, immediately, to be; I am that image of myself that is offered by the mirror. To use Dr. Lacan's terms, I am "captured, caught up" by my spatial image. Thereupon I leave the reality of my lived *me* in order to refer myself constantly to the ideal, fictitious, or imaginary *me*, of which the specular image is the first outline. In this sense I am torn from myself, and the image in the mirror prepares me for another still more serious alienation, which will be alienation by others. For others have only an exterior image of me, which is analogous to the one seen in the mirror. Consequently others will tear me away from my immediate inwardness much more surely than will the mirror. "The specular image is the 'symbolic matrix,' says Lacan, "where the I springs up in primordial form before objectifying itself in the dialectic of identification with the other."[34]

The acquisition of the specular image introduces the child into the drama of social life, the struggle with the other, ruled by desire and recognition, even to death. It lies outside of the scope of this essay to pursue these themes in terms of the conjuncture between Hegelian phenomenology and

Lacanian psychoanalysis.[35] But this is certainly a direction in which we might pursue the dialectic between personal and public life which we repeat in the spectacle of the *body-politic* and the struggle between the 'organization' of authority and the delinquencies of love's body.[36]

NOTES

1. This is amply illustrated from the comprehensive survey of socialization theory and empirical research edited by John A. Clausen, *Socialization and Society*, Boston, Little, Brown and Company, 1968.

2. These lectures are contained in the form of student notes published with Merleau-Ponty's approval in *Bulletin de Psychologie*, No. 236, tome XVIII 3–6, Novembre 1964. Of these lectures "The Child's Relations with Others" has been translated by William Cobb in Maurice Merleau-Ponty, *The Primacy of Perception*, and other essays, edited by James M. Edie, Evanston, Northwestern University Press 1964, pp. 96–155.

3. *Bulletin de Psychologie*, pp. 112–115; 176–185; 199; 204–210; 216. See Richard M. Zanet, "Piaget and Merleau-Ponty: A Study in Convergence," *Review of Existential Psychology and Psychiatry*, Vol. VI, No. 1 (Winter, 1966), pp. 7–23.

4. John O'Neill, *Perception, Expression and History*: The Social Phenomenology of Maurice Merleau-Ponty, Evanston, Northwestern University Press, 1970. I have drawn on this work at certain points in this essay.

5. R. D. Laing, *The Politics of Experience*, New York, Ballantine Books, 1968.

6. Here I think there is an obvious link between Merleau-Ponty's phenomenological psychology and the work of Lacan in psychoanalysis and Lévi-Strauss in anthropology.

7. *Bulletin de Psychologie*, p. 111.

8. Kurt Goldstein, *Human Nature in the Light of Psychology*, New York, Schocken Books, 1963, Ch. 5; Charles Taylor, *The Explanation of Behavior*, New York, The Humanities Press, 1964, p. 270.

9. Maurice Merleau-Ponty, *The Structure of Behavior*, Translated by Alden L. Fisher, Boston, Beacon Press, 1963, p. 25.

10. Kurt Goldstein and Adhémar Gelb, "Analysis of a Case of Figural Blindness," in *A Source Book of Gestalt Psychology*, edited by W. D. Ellis, London, Routledge and Kegan Paul, 1955, pp. 315–325; Aron Gurwitsch, "Gelb-Goldstein's Concept of 'Concrete' and 'Categorial' Attitude and the Phenomenology of Ideation," in his *Studies in Phenomenology and Psychology*, Evanston, Northwestern University Press, 1966.

11. Henry Head, *Aphasia and Kindred Disorders of Speech*, New York, Macmillan, 1926.

12. Maurice Merleau-Ponty, *Phenomenology of Perception*, translated by Colin Smith, London, Routledge and Kegan Paul, and New York, The Humanities Press, 1965, p. 239.

13. *Bulletin de Psychologie*, pp. 185–187.

14. *Ibid.*, pp. 194–198.

15. *Ibid.*, pp. 130–134; 187–194.

16. Seymour Fisher and Sidney E. Cleveland, *Body Image and Personality*, New York, Dover Publications, Inc., 1968. Despite an extensive bibliography (pp. 415–438) on empirical research into the *body-image* this extremely influential work makes no mention of Merleau-Ponty or Jacques Lacan; cf. Gerald E. Myers, "Self and Body Image," in *Phenomenology in America*, Studies in the Philosophy of Experience, Edited with an introduction by James M. Edie, Chicago, Quadrangle Books, 1967, pp. 147–160; Richard M. Zaner, "Merleau-Ponty's Theory of the Body-Proper as *Etre-au-monde*," *The Journal of Existentialism*, Vol. VI, No. 21 (Fall, 1965), pp. 31–39.

17. *Bulletin de Psychologie*, p. 133.

18. Maurice Merleau-Ponty, *The Prose of the World*, Edited by Claude Lefort and Translated, with an Introduction by John O'Neill, Evanston, Northwestern University Press, 1972.

19. "La Conscience et l'Acquisition du Language," *Bulletin de Psychologie*, pp. 226–259.

20. "The Child's Relations with Others," *op. cit.*, p. 109.

21. *Ibid.*, Merleau-Ponty gives as his reference for the case François Rostand, "Grammaire et Affectivité," *Revue Française de Psychanalyse* Vol. 14 (Avril-Juin, 1950), pp. 299–310.

22. *Ibid.*, p. 110.

23. John O'Neill, "How is Society Possible?" in my *Sociology as a Skin Trade*, Essays Towards a Reflexive Sociology, London, Heinemann Educational Books and New York, Harper and Row, 1972.

24. *Phenomenology of Perception*, p. 355. My stress in the first line.

25. "The Child's Relations with Others," *op. cit.*, p. 115.

26. Frank A. Tillman, "On Perceiving Persons," in *Phenomenology in America*, pp. 161–172.

27. *Phenomenology of Perception*, Part One, Ch. 1 and 2; "Phenomenology and the Sciences of Man," in *The Primary of Perception*, pp. 43–95.

28. Aron Gurwitsch, "A Non-egological Conception of Consciousness," *op. cit.*, pp. 287–300.

29. "The Child's Relation with Others," *op. cit.*, p. 118.

30. For these connections and in particular the affective bases of reciprocity, although he omits any mention of Merleau-Ponty (indeed, this is no fault) see Aaron V. Cicourel, "Basic and

Normative Rules in the Negotiation of Status and Role," in *Recent Sociology No. 2*, Patterns of Communicative Behavior, Edited by Hans Peter Dreitzel, New York, The Macmillan Company, 1970, pp. 4–45; and note 23 above.

31. On this central problem of phenomenological psychology see the chapter "Corporeality and Intersubjectivity" in my *Perception, Expression and History* and the crucial discussion by Alfred Schütz, "The Problem of Transcendental Intersubjectivity in Husserl," in his *Collected Papers III*, Studies in Phenomenological Philosophy, Edited by I. Schutz, with an Introduction by Aron Gurwitsch, The Hague, Martinus Nijhoff, 1966, pp. 51–91; as well as "Scheler's Theory of Intersubjectivity and the General Thesis of the Alter Ego," and "Sartre's Theory of the Alter Ego," in *Collected Papers I*, the Problem of Social Reality, Edited and Introduced by Maurice Natanson, The Hague, Martinus Nijhoff, 1967, pp. 150–179 and 180–203.

32. Erving Goffman, *Interaction Ritual*, Essays on Fact-to-Face Behavior, New York, Doubleday and Company, Inc., 1967.

33. *Bulletin de Psychologie*, pp. 134–136; 300–302. Compare Cooley's notion of the looking-glass self in *Human Nature and the Social Order*, New York, Schocken Books, 1964, pp. 183–185; 196–199 and Mead's conception of the 'I' and 'Me' relation, in *Mind, Self and Society*, Edited and with an Introduction by Charles W. Morris, Chicago, and London, University of Chicago Press, 1967, pp. 173–178; 192–200.

34. "The Child's Relations with Others," *op. cit.*, pp. 136–137, cf. Jacques Lacan, "Le Stade du miroir comme formateur du fonction du je," *Revue Française de Psychanalyse*, Vol. 13, No. 4 (Octobre-Decembre, 1949), pp. 449–455.

35. Lacan remarks that in treating the struggle between Master and Slave in which each seeks to be recognized without in turn recognizing the other as a symbol of the history of the world Hegel "has furnished once and for all the true function of aggression in human ontology, to the point almost of prophesying the iron law of our age." *Ecrits*, Paris Editions du Seuil, 1966, p. 121; Paul Ricoeur, *De l' Interpretation*, Essai sur Freud, Paris, Editions du Seuil, 1965; John O'Neill, "History as Human History in Hegel and Marx," in Jean Hyppolite, *Studies on Marx and Hegel*, Translated with Notes and Bibliography by John O'Neill, New York, Basic Books, 1969; Alexandre Kojova, *Introduction to the Reading of Hegel*, Edited by Allen Bloom, Translated by James H. Nichols, Jr., New York, Basic Books, Inc., 1969.

36. Norman O. Brown, *Love's Body*, New York, Vintage Books, 1966; John O'Neill, "On Body-Politics," in *Recent Sociology No. 4*, Family, Marriage and the Struggle of the Sexes, Edited by Hans Peter Dreitzel, New York, The Macmillan Company, 1972.

II

The Impact of the Family:
Nuclear Versus Communal

The problems of modern family life have been the focus of the last volume of this series, Recent Sociology, No. 4, *and much of the material and perspectives offered in this chapter are a continuation of the arguments in this earlier collection. Whatever the external and internal pressures under which the struggle of the sexes is carried on in marriage and in family life really are, their worst impact is not on adults but on the children. This is clearly the conclusion to be drawn from Professor Richter's study of the "Pathogenic Constellations in Family Dynamics." This essay presents a comprehensive summary of the author's book (in German) on the same topic (1970). Professor Richter is head of the Clinic for Psychosomatic Diseases at the University of Giessen, Germany, and has been a pioneer in family therapy and research for many years. The present article first appeared in* Betrifft Erziehung *(Vol. 5, No. 1, 1972), a journal which addresses a more general public of students, teachers, and parents, and has been translated for this volume. The merit of Professor Richter's views is that they are empirically based on his vast clinical experience.*

David G. Gil's article, "Violence Against Children," demonstrates the worst effects of the pathogenic constellations Richter describes. David G. Gil, who is Professor for Social Welfare at Brandeis University, is among the few who have tried to uncover and analyze data on what amounts to a major scandal of our social system: the degree of brutality with which many children are treated even at home. Professor Gil, whose article is based on a book with the same title (Harvard University Press, 1970), identifies culturally sanctioned use of physical force in child rearing, poverty and discrimination as well as deviance in bio-psycho-social functioning as causal dimensions of physical child abuse, and discusses the scope of the phenomenon in American society. His article first appeared in Journal of Marriage and the Family *(Vol. 33, No. 4, 1971).*

The other two studies of this chapter serve to illustrate the attempts to overcome the pathogenic constellations of nuclear family life by communal child rearing. "Kommune 2" was a highly publicized experiment in communal living in Berlin, Germany, a few years ago. Since most of the members of this family were students of the social sciences, the self-analysis of their experiment is of extraordinary value: there is much to learn from the successes and failures of their serious attempt to overcome the limitations of their own socialization for the sake of a less rigid development of their children. The present version of their report is the translation of a chapter specifically dealing with child-rearing problems, which first appeared in Kursbuch 17 *(1969). "Kommune 2" no longer exists; the failure of this experiment, however, is not due to problems of child rearing but was the result both of the combined impact of their explosive attempt at a radical psychoanalytical group therapy without the opportunity of help by a psychotherapeutic counselor, and of the growing public pressure against communal experiments during the decline of the student movement in Germany. A more detached analysis of communal child-rearing practices in America is presented by Gilbert Zicklin, Assistant Professor of Sociology at the University of Maine, Orono, on the basis of field research. Professor Zicklin, who has published several articles on related topics, has studied three communal families in the eastern part of the United States. Based on his findings, Professor Zicklin concludes that the tendency to stress the autonomy of the child in the communal settlement is the most important difference between the conventional middle-class role of the child and that of the commune-reared child.*

4

Pathogenic Constellations in Family Dynamics[*]

HORST-EBERHARD RICHTER

FOR PSYCHOANALYSIS, the decade and a half between the mid-Twenties and the end of the Thirties was a period of optimism, of faith in education. Numerous analysts believed there was a chance of preventing neurosis by bringing about a radical change in education.[1] In 1926 the *Zeitschrift für Psychoanalytische Pädagogik* was founded. Bernfeld, Reich, Aichhorn, Wolfheim, Hitschmann, Meng, Vera Schmidt, Zullinger, Steff and Berta Bornstein along with Anna Freud numbered among the journal's prominent contributors who on the basis of their psychoanalytic experience suggested ways for revolutionizing childrearing methods. Called for, in particular, was more freedom for infantile sexuality, thorough sex education beginning at an early age, and avoidance of castration threats as well as all abuse of parental authority.

In 1935, its ninth year, the *Zeitschrift für Psychoanalytische Pädagogik* ceased publication. Ten years later, in 1945, it reappeared as the annual *Psychoanalytic Study of the Child* which during the years to come published the most important results of research in the field of child analysis. Meanwhile, this successor publication has dropped not only the name but also to a large extent the cause of psychoanalytic education. How did this come about?

Quite gradually a tendency developed to go farther and farther back into infancy in seeking the causes for psychic disturbances. It was suspected that what the child experiences in early infancy and in the period before he learns

[*] Translation from the German original by Adriana Gottwald.

to talk largely if not exclusively determines whether the later adult will develop a neurosis, psychosis or a sociopathic disturbance. Consequently, leading psychoanalytic researchers concentrated their efforts on tracking down pathogenic traumatic factors in this very earliest phase of childhood.

The best known contributions to this research on the first year of life have been provided by Melanie Klein and her disciples, Mahler, Spitz and, later, Bowlby and associates. Their efforts in this direction have revealed the importance of a constant and reliable object-relationship in early infancy and have disclosed the harmful effects of deprivation, what we now generally call hospitalism.

ANNA FREUD AND PSCHOANALYTIC PESSIMISM

Parallel to this shift in interest to the preverbal phase of infancy, essentially the first year of life, psychoanalysis lost more and more of its earlier enthusiastic confidence in education. Whereas year for year up to 1935 the *Zeitschrift für Psychoanalytische Pädagogik* had reported extensively on activities in the field of psychoanalytic education throughout many countries, after 1945 the *Psychoanalytic Study of the Child* has published little else but clinical or theoretical studies in the field of child analysis.

In a widely discussed paper on psychoanalysis and education, published in 1954, Anna Freud notes that in reference to the chances of preventing neurosis the period of optimistic faith in education was over, having given way to a period of pessimism. According to her, this pessimism had set in "when the origin of neurosis was recognized to be due, not to environmental influences, but to inevitable factors of various kinds." Since an influential section of the Psychoanalytic Society still subscribes to the theses set forth in Anna Freud's paper, I should like to quote her further. She defines the following inevitable pathogenic factors:

(a) qualitative innate factors, such as bisexuality which results in unavoidable deep conflicts between internal strivings;
(b) quantative innate factors, such as the insatiable character

of the infant's instinctive demands, leading to painful and pathogenic frustrations;

(c) the crucial situations in the child's life which give rise to pathogenic fixation points, such as (in reverse order):

the *conflicts of the oedipal phase* with the incestuous fantasies, phallic masturbation, and castration fears;

toilet training, with the accompanying anal and urethral frustrations;

sibling rivalry;

weaning, as the traumatic oral forerunner of later castration ideas, etc.

Anna Freud concludes that she does not believe that "even the most revolutionary changes in infant care can do away with the tendency to ambivalence or with the division of the human personality into an id and ego with conflicting aims." And she ends with the conviction that "the emergence of neurotic conflicts has to be regarded as the price paid for the complexity of the human personality."

Even today, this pessimism retains a hold on many a prominent analyst. This helps to explain why at various psychoanalytic institutes it is a matter of principle to analyze disturbed children individually, i.e. without extending the treatment's scope to include the parents or other factors that have a bearing on the child's upbringing. In 1970 an international conference on child analysis was held in Geneva at which infantile neurosis was once again discussed for the most part as if it was the child's internal problem and no more than that. That parents, traditional child-care centers, school, etc., can have a pathogenic effect, was barely mentioned. This seems logically consistent, given acceptance of Anna Freud's thesis that neuroses develop primarily from within as a result of the human nature's innate disposition toward internal conflicts which are made to emerge by the ubiquitous external stimuli that are appropriate to the respective stage of development.

The Underestimation of Social Influences

There are three, to a certain extent interrelated reasons for the obvious tendency on the part of the psychoanalytic pessimists to underestimate the significance of social influences.

To begin with, we must mention the biologistic element in Freud's original concept, typical of his times. Indicative, for instance, is the assumption that the Oedipus complex is phylogenetically predetermined, a conflict that emerges, as it were, with the natural force of an instinct and is largely unaffected by prevailing cultural influences. As is well known, there are still considerable differences of opinion between ethologists and cultural anthropologists about the extent to which biological or social factors have a bearing on the development of behavior. Nevertheless, comparative studies in cultural anthropology have produced much firm evidence that numerous neurosis-psychological phenomena uncovered by psychoanalysis are determined by social and cultural factors.

Second, there is no mistaking the continuing influence of the programmatical exhortation which Freud repeatedly directed toward his disciples in the years after 1917: according to him, the psychoanalyst should be primarily concerned with uncovering his patients' inner, *psychic* reality, not with their concrete, *material* reality. By material reality, Freud meant all external influences. In his view, the psychoanalyst should not be sidetracked into trying to establish whether his analysand had truly suffered an external traumatic experience or, on the other hand, is only fantasizing that he had. Freud felt that many of these traumas are indeed no more than a product of the patient's imagination; but since even as fantasy they have a pathogenic effect, he felt they had to be analyzed in any event. Many have understood this to mean not only that the psychoanalytic *technique* should take no account of traumatic social factors, but that these should also be considered *theoretically* irrelevant to the pathogenesis of neurosis.

A third reason for the widespread underestimation of social reality lies in what we can presume to call the irrational factor, which may or may not be present in the individual analyst himself. To understand this factor it is useful to recall the classical setting in which the standard psychoanalytical method is applied.

Throughout several years of treatment, the psychoanalyst and the analysand cultivate an extremely close relationship to one another. All emotional conflicts that the patient has suffered within his social matrix are carried over into his so-called transfer relationship with the psychoanalyst. The analyst even encourages this tendency. For it is a fact that, as an instrument, analysis can only be effective when the analysand transfers or projects onto the analyst all the conflict-ridden feelings and conceptions that contribute to his neurosis.

It is by means of this so-called transference neurosis that the analyst is best able to help the analysand understand the background of his conflicts. At some point in any fruitful analytical process all the analysand's emotional problems are funneled through or discharged into this transference neurosis. The analysand's powerful emotional attachment to his analyst has, of course, its dangers for both. The analyst can be tempted to believe in secret that he actually possesses the omnipotence the analysand continually ascribes to him in his transference neurosis. The analyst can be carried away to the extent of relativizing the analysand's concrete social problems, viewing the analysis itself (i.e., himself, without admitting it) as the only decisive external factor so far as his patient is concerned. This corresponds to the delusions of grandeur we find in those overprotective mothers who believe that, for their children, they represent the very world itself.

If the psychoanalyst secretly enters into this kind of rivalry with his analysand's parents, spouse, or other social partners, then he will not only fall prone to employing a restrictive technique; this rivalry problem will also color his theoretical approach. One may therefore suspect that many a solipsistic element in the original psychoanalytical personality theory can be traced back to the practitioner's irrational tendency to deny the power of social reality in order to ward off any threat to his own desire for omnipotence.

In any case, should one not take into account the effect of such inadequately controlled desires for power, it is very difficult to understand how those psychoanalysts who are pessimistic about education can feel capable of exerting an enormous influence on their patients' psychic future through treatment while at the same time categorically denying that the child's personality development depends significantly on the influence of those who raise him. It is as if no one but the psychoanalyst possessed the key for initiating mutative changes in the deep emotional processes of children and adults.

Since the mid-Fifties, however, a counter-movement has been slowly gathering strength against the radical, pessimistic position outlined in the above-mentioned statements by Anna Freud. Still, this counter-movement has yet to have any significant impact on the official image of psychoanalysis as presented at the Psychoanalytic Society's major international conferences.

The Relationship Between Family Dynamics and Psychic Disturbance

Recent studies on the relationship between family dynamics and psychic disturbance have been enlivened by the general interest in group dynamics and group therapy that sprang up in the Fifties.

It became the opinion of a number of analysts interested in social psychology that children's and also adults' inner difficulties could be more fully understood and more effectively treated if more consideration would be given to the dependency of these difficulties on group processes. This assumption led to modifications in the strategy for treating neurotic children and psychotic adolescents, for example. Work was resumed on experiments that had been initiated in the late Twenties and early Thirties. In treating children and adolescents, certain analysts made it a rule to include parents and, as the case may be, siblings, as well. And they resolutely insisted on making unresolved family conflicts the actual object of treatment in every case where these conflicts plainly lie at the root of psychogenic disturbances.

In the process, they soon noticed that the traditional psychoanalytic conceptual model needed to be expanded to accommodate problems of family group dynamics, only then being seen in their full significance. After all, both the classical structure theory and the traditional psychoanalytic theory of neurosis apply explicitly to intrapsychic mechanisms,

functions, and structures and not to the dynamics of interpersonal relations, save in a peripheral sense. Additional
models are therefore needed to provide a theoretical orientation by which the group dynamics of the family can be
understood. For to understand how various members of a
family are entangled with one another, it is of course not
enough to know that the mother has a compulsive structure,
the father a hysterical structure, and the child a sociopathic
structure accompanied, as the case may be, by the corresponding symptom formation. There is little value in tallying
up individual diagnoses in such a piecemeal fashion. It is far
more important to grasp the role situation through the *interplay* of emotional relations. How do the various members
relate to one another? What do they do with one another? A
differentiated theory should make it possible to describe the
relative position of each individual family member in the
general context of interaction, enabling one to come up with
a formula by which to shed light on the group process as a
whole.

It is a widespread and bias-laden overestimation of psychoanalysis to assume that a generally accepted model of this
sort has long since been developed. In reality, work in this
direction is still going on and the debate on pertinent proposals is in full swing. Our own research team, for example,
has been working for some time on a catalogue of so-called
psychosocial defense mechanisms which, along with the classical defense mechanisms, must be precisely defined in order
that one can apply to the family a differentiated, scientific
method of psychoanalytic diagnosis. Psychosocial defense
mechanisms are automatized, subconscious strategies which
members of a family or another small group employ to
deny, deflect or in one or the other specific way abreact
their own tensions with the help of their fellows.

In the family, the psychosocial defense mechanisms of the
individual members as they interact can be subsumed under
the theme of some general strategy according to which the
family as a whole is organized both internally and toward
the outside. For the interplay of individual psychosocial
defense mechanisms is, on the other hand, affected by the
superimposition of group psychosocial defense mechanisms

which the family as a whole employs when necessary to channel off internal tensions toward the outside.

It is unfortunately impossible to give anything even approximating a full orientation as to the various working concepts that psychoanalysts have meanwhile developed in the field of family dynamics. For these concepts vary widely in their formulation and are only to a limited extent comparable. One might imagine that this is the result of inadequate scientific coordination. The trouble, however, is an objective one. The various psychoanalytic teams are doing their research on highly disparate clinical problems. Some are working in psychiatric clinics, almost exclusively studying the families of psychotic patients. Others are primarily concerned with the families of maladjusted and delinquent children. Still others are working on the family dynamics underlying neurotic or psychosomatic disturbances, in child guidance clinics and in centers for treating neurotic children.

Understandably, work in such diverse clinical spheres leads to quite different approaches by which to fruitfully describe and differentiate pathogenic family-dynamic factors. Pathogenic processes in a schizophrenic family can hardly be pinpointed with the help of the same criteria that are applicable to the pathogenic social dynamics operative in families characterized by anxiety neurosis or delinquency.

The study of the dynamics of schizophrenic families or of families in which children acquire a heightened disposition toward schizophrenia has meanwhile developed into what could be called a discipline in its own right. Various research teams in the USA have painstakingly and successfully studied how parents deal with one another and their children and, in the process, make their children prone to a later development of schizophrenic illness. Some of the more important results of these studies on schizophrenic family dynamics have recently been published in Germany in the anthology *Schizophrenie und Familie* (Suhrkamp Verlag) which contains a report on the longitudinal study carried out by Wynne and associates at Bethesda. Their remarkable findings show that the typical symptoms of an acute schizophrenic episode represent no less than an individual replica of the disturbed family organization in which the patient had grown up.

The patient had internalized the disturbed family organization. His fragmentation of experience, identity diffusion, and his impaired ability to perceive things as they are and establish relationships correspond precisely to the conditions obtaining under the family organization as a whole, which Wynne has termed "pseudomutuality." Similar findings have been reported by Lidz and his associates at Yale, who also have demonstrated how the way to schizophrenic illness in the adolescent is quite literally paved by parents who have unconsciously prevented the child from achieving personality integration.

Investigations into the familial factors that induce schizophrenia have produced insights that, taken together, have an importance that goes far beyond their contribution of our understanding of schizophrenia as such. These insights are also relevant to the understanding of many less severe personality integration disorders that never develop as far as schizophrenia, and they provide helpful pointers for preventative counselling and family therapy.

Parallel to such research originally focussed on the genesis of schizophrenia, psychological research on the family and neurosis, in particular, has received new impetus in the past fifteen years. Psychoanalysts and psychotherapists from other schools of thought have taken up the work begun in the Twenties and Thirties and are examining those factors in a family's childrearing practices that contribute to the development of neurosis, psychosomatic illness and sociopathic disturbances. Notable among the specifically psychoanalytic contributions in this field is the work of Erikson, Johnson and Szurek, Ackerman, Grotjahn and Dührssen, to mention only a few more well-known names.

Traumatizing Parents and Their Motivations

These recent studies on family dynamics are generally far more cautiously planned and are considerably sounder, methodologically, than much of the work published earlier in the *Zeitschrift für Psychoanalytische Pädagogik*. It is recognized that the older generation of authors frequently drew hasty conclusions on the basis of short-term, single observations and above all paid too little attention to the deeper family-dynamic processes going on under the purely exterior surface of childrearing practices.

Our psychoanalytical team, originally in Berlin and now in Giessen, is one of several that for some time have been steadily investigating the relationship between family dynamics and the origins of neuroses and sociopathic disturbances. In the following pages we shall try to give the reader an idea of our approach. In a number of respects, our work can probably be considered typical, in mode and objectives, for the more recent trend in psychoanalytical family research.

We began our empirical investigations at the Wedding District Children's Hospital in Berlin, where a combined child psychology counselling and research facility has existed, with interruptions, since the Thirties. Two conclusions served to guide us in our investigations of the primarily working class families of disturbed children and youth:

1. Many psychic disturbances in the children and young people referred to us could be traced back directly to the unfavorable influence of the parents or reference persons involved in the child's upbringing. Such disturbances often improved when we managed to lessen or counter the detrimental effect of the parents or the milieu in which the child was being raised. In identifying the traumatic factors in a family's childrearing practices, we found that it was seldom a lack of information on the part of the reference persons but rather for the most part their emotional attitude that accounted for faulty childrearing practices, whether sustained or incidental.

2. As a result, purely technical parent counselling generally proved ineffective. As a rule, we were successful only when we managed to bring some influence to bear on the parents' subsurface emotional motivations. For we found that all the detrimental constraints, restrictions, punishments, withholding of information, etc., generally turned out to be no more than a product of the total, affective parent-child interaction system. Any promising therapeutic work would have to take into consideration the unconscious as well as conscious dynamics of the parent-child relationship as a whole, which are naturally affected, in turn, by the special dynamics

of the parent's marital relationship. Even at that stage of our work we were struck by the fact that there is a striking discrepancy between many parents' avowed notions about childrearing and their actual behavior toward the child.

In connection with our counselling and therapeutic work during the first ten-year phase of our investigations, we sought to gain a more differentiated picture of the more deep-seated motivations of those parents whose impact on their children is traumatic. At that point we had to take account of a factor which, when ignored, often limits the validity of results of studies on the pathogenic behavior of parents and other persons who have an influence on the child's upbringing: only if from the outset the psychoanalyst avoids stamping the parents as guilty tormentors and exploiters in distinction to their childish victims is he able to work out the motives of parents who exert a detrimental influence on their children. Such prejudiced antipathy all too easily leads to a superficial and uncritical approach, sometimes resulting in precipitous and undifferentiated conclusions that only confirm the analyst's own emotional expectations. This gives rise to such familiar, meaningless generalizations as: the mother and/or father is too repressive, too frustrating, too ambivalent, too protective, etc., whereby all such crude descriptions refer more to the effect than to the actual motivation of parental behavior.

On top of it all, such inordinate antipathies vis-à-vis traumatizing parents or other agents in the child's upbringing place the psychoanalyst in a very difficult therapeutical position. For in his dealings with such persons these feelings easily tempt him to reproduce the same kind of moralizingly dirigistic behavior for which they, themselves, should be condemned. The result, of course, is that the analyst only reinforces the parents' faulty behavior instead of correcting it.

A Catalogue of Parent-Child Relationships That Can Be Detrimental to the Child's Development

In an early series of studies we observed a number of families over a period of as many as seven years, noting how the parent-child dialogue presents itself in psychoanalytic terms. We departed from the traditional sociological concept of role and, proceeding from the psychoanalytical approach, developed a social-psychological role definition. Our questions were: what do parents expect of the child, both consciously and unconsciously? In what way do their own conflicts enter into these expectations?

The structural sum of these expectations we termed *role*. In this sense, the child's role can also be described as a function, established by the parents for the purpose of relieving them of their own inner tensions. In this way one can see how with the help of their children parents seek to satisfy their own unfulfilled wishes, pacify their own unresolved anxieties and ease their own repressed guilt feelings. So it is that a continual dialogue develops between parental role demands and the child's reactions—an interaction that can be unravelled and explained by the means of psychoanalysis. Aside from one particular role variant—the role of the contested ally—all the roles we have described and classified are formulated in bipolar terms. In other words, this concept can help one to determine what sort of a role one or both parents define for the child, and how the child responds to this role demand.

As long as the rules governing role interplay are no rigidly established, all such role relationships constitute an ubiquitous and altogether normal factor in the parents' attitude toward the child. However, the moment the rules assume a dominant position in the parent-child relationship, they acquire an abnormal quality and often have a pathogenic effect.

As a result of our longitudinal studies of families we have worked out a revised catalogue of such potentially traumatic role-play rules, which I shall briefly describe. This catalogue is based on the model of a two-person, parent-child relationship.

1. The child as partner substitute

A parent can unconsciously force the child to play the role of another partner. As a rule, the parent does this in an effort to actualize some early childhood relationship with a person with whom a conflict has not been resolved. The child is now expected, in compensation, to make up for the disappointments left in the wake of that other, unfulfilled or unsuccessful relationship. At the same time, however, this unconscious compulsion to repeat the past forces the child to reproduce those very traumatizing characteristics of the old, unsuccessful relationship that had led to the parent's fixation on the conflict in the first place. Depending on the circumstances, the child's role resembles that of a sibling or either an oedipal or pre-oedipal parent figure. In one frequent variant the child is represented in fantasy as an incestuous sexual partner, the parent having failed to establish a fulfilling relationship with an appropriate sexual object.

2. The child as the idealized image of self

The child can be ascribed the role of becoming an exact replica of the image the parent has of himself. Defining this role is the type of parent who clings, with paranoid intensity, to the notion of his own perfection and grandeur. Since the object is to incorporate the child in this grandiose self-image, the parent must suppress or deny all negative aspects of his own self image as well as of the image he has of the child. Only outside the fantasized parent-child identity may the negativeness be found that is banned from the parent's own narcissistic system. Thus, such a parent is always polarized in a paranoid stance against the outside world. The child is expected to help bring about this polarization. Whenever the child begins to display any of the characteristics associated with the rejected outside world, the parent feels threatened —as if, in doing so, the child was rejecting the parent, himself. If the child wants to avoid the parent's severe disapprobation, he has no choice but to adopt the parent's ideals and behavioral patterns right down to the very last detail.

3. The child as self-ideal

The child is expected to fulfill the ideal the parent had not succeeded in realizing. In contrast to the type described above, the parent does not repress awareness of his own inadequacy but rather suffers on account of it. Yet he is determined to relieve this suffering with the help of the child. The child is pushed relentlessly to attain the goals the parent had failed to reach so that the latter may achieve narcissistic compensation through the mechanism of identification.

4. The child as scapegoat

Here, the child is expected to demonstrate certain tabooed impulses which the parent suppresses but is not capable of fully repressing. The parent is able to avoid becoming aware of his own embarrassing impulse only by finding it constantly present in someone in his own immediate surroundings. This means that he is compelled to continuously project these secretly condemned tendencies onto the child. Once the child demonstrates the condemned impulses, the parent can identify with him in fantasy and thereby secretly attain ersatz-gratification. He can relieve himself of guilt feelings by constantly heaping the child with the punishments he, the parent, secretly believes he himself deserves. This role situation explains the peculiarly ambivalent reaction of many parents toward their children's sexuality.

5. The child as the parent's "weaker self"

This role is new to the catalogue as it was originally drawn up in 1963. Here, the child is expected to take on the role not of the parent's repressed evil self, but rather of a similarly repressed weak self. The parent can only feel powerful and active as long as he finds his own feelings of insignificance, impotence and passiveness mirrored in the child. In other words, the child is expected to express the depression the parent denies in himself. In this role, the child represents the helpless, negative aspect which by means of over-compensation the phallic-narcissistic parent manages to avoid recognizing in himself. The weak, incompetent child allows the parent to see himself by contrast as undisputably magnificent. At the same time, however, the parent is symbiotically able to secretly and vicariously enjoy a measure of his own suppressed passivity and depressiveness. Whereas the casual observer might jump to the conclusion that this impressive figure cannot help but suffer deeply under the burden of having such a pitiable and unsuccessful child, in reality the parent derives considerable satisfaction from this unconscious role play.

6. The child as companion in arms

In this case, the parent is constantly engaged in external conflict and demands of the child that he serve as his ally. All else that the child is and does matters little in comparison to his importance as a companion in arms. In a way, this role appears to be an extreme variant of our second category, the child as self-image. But in this instance, the parent is concerned less wit⁻ screening off what for narcissistic reasons is denied in order to maintain the illusion of omnipotence, than with finding direct support in his need to vent his aggressive impulses. In one frequent and particularly traumatizing situation, the child has the role of a contested ally, caught between his belligerently opposed parents. As important as it is for the child to get to know his adult reference persons as distinct individuals, he cannot fail to have difficulties in his personality development if over a long period of time he experiences himself as the object of an opportunistic rivalry between a set of parents who only use him ruthlessly as a prize or weapon in their own ambivalent struggles with one another.

Over a period of many years, we have observed a number of typical families in order to determine what effects these six role situations have on child development, and have described the particular neuroses and sociopathic personality disturbances that develop easily under the pressure of one or the other specific set of role demands. As psychoanalysts, we were also very much interested in investigating the possibilities of therapeutic treatment to break up or at least modify such pathogenic role situations. Such experimental work ties in with the efforts of other research teams to lay the groundwork for both curative and preventative psychoanalytical family therapy.

The focus of our observations gradually shifted during the course of our investigations. During the first few years we were primarily concerned with pathogenic bi-polar parent-child relationships. As already mentioned, the above role table has a purely bi-personal configuration. The role types resulted from the question: what does the child represent to the mother or to the father?

THE FAMILY AS PATIENT: PSYCHOSOCIAL DEFENSE
MECHANISMS OF THE FAMILY AS A GROUP

The scope of our interest broadened as we progressed in elucidating the dynamics of the parent-child interaction. We then proceeded to ask how the role-defining parent's psychosocial defense system fits in with the dynamic organization of the family as a whole. Can psychoanalytical categories help one to understand the more comprehensive psychosocial defense system of the family as a group, a defense system in which the individual members' own psychosocial defense mechanisms are integrated? For group processes in the family as a whole do indeed have a substantial influence on the individual processes that go on within the family's bi-personal subgroups. The question is only whether the instruments of psychoanalysis are adequate for describing these psychosocial defense structures of the group as a whole, which in turn are superimposed on bi-personal psychosocial processes. Still, this question as to the extent to which psychoanalytic instruments can be applied should not imply that one could or should seek to psychologically analyze sociological determinants in the family. The psychoanalytical model remains a supplementary model to sociology.

Within the context of psychonanalysis it is not only legitimate but also extremely important to extend the discipline's traditionally individual-oriented theoretical model to cover group processes as far as scientifically possible. It is in this sense that we raise the question: does the complex interplay of conscious and unconscious interactive processes within the family group as a whole lend itself to study *in its entirety* and, above all, can it be *conceptualized*? Or in trying to do this would one necessarily wind up with categories so general and superficial that they prove to be unproductive and no longer deserve to be called psychoanalytical?

Family-oriented research on the psychology of neurosis and psychosis has already given rise to a number of general concepts of family which make it possible to answer this question. In this regard, our own team has recently produced a summary of what has been accomplished to date, *Patient Families*, in which we have attempted to define and differentiate various relevant types of family neurosis in their respective overall group-dynamic framework. As usual in the psychoanalytical approach, this model is based on *clinical* definitions. It deals with family structures, the organizational forms of which are defined according to clinical criteria even though a number of the family types studied are by no means what one would consider pathologically conspicuous.

The clinical frame of reference for our psychoanalytical family research is established by pinpointing the particular system of defenses operating in the various families under study. This system of defenses can be described in qualitative terms and, in addition, it can be determined by the extent to which it restricts individual members of the group or its collective ego. Accordingly, we can begin by distinguishing two general types of defense system. The one we call the *symptom-neurotic family*; the other we term the *character-neurotic family*.

The Symptom-Neurotic Family

Characteristic of the symptom-neurotic family are *auto-aggressive splitting processes*. Not simply splitting as it occurs as the rational result of alienation processes, controversy resolution or age-specific decisions to detach oneself from another person. Splitting in the symptom-neurotic family is to be understood not as a solution but only as a means of camouflaging or shifting the focus of a group problem. A brief description of the three most important manifestations of the symptom-neurotic family may help to show how this comes about.

1. The first case concerns the *ostracizing* family. This type

of family seeks to banish everything that is sick, defective and inferior in order to be able to maintain its belief in its own untaintedness. Thus, any handicapped, retarded or troublesome child is sent to an institution or boarding school as soon as possible. This family, anxious to see itself and be seen as a perfect family, can tolerate no misfit or failure in its own ranks. If possible, aged or chronically invalid members are also shunted aside even if they require no undue amount of care. Alone their constant presence poses a threat to the group's fantasy of being perfect and invulnerable. As a rule, the ostracizing family is motivated by the fear of having to be confronted with its own repressed weaknesses, weaknesses that are represented by the member who is eliminated.

2. The second type of symptom-neurotic family appears to behave in an entirely reverse fashion, although it is closely related to the previously mentioned type. Notions of grandeur and omnipotence play a role in this kind of family, as well, but instead of using the technique of ostracism to collectively protect itself from any idea of inferiority or insignificance, this family carries out the split *internally*. One part of the family is permitted to be magnificent, powerful and healthy, while in compensation another part is weak, inferior and ill. The rest of the family needs this sickly, deficient member in analogy to the above-described bi-personal role model of the "weaker self" projection or the scapegoat tactic. It can also happen that, one after the other, several of the children and one of the parents function as the masochistic victim, since such a family knows no other organizational form than a permanent division into a pitiably masochistic part and another part that is hypomanic in its abnegation, both of which unconsciously depend on one another, thus helping to perpetuate this form of family organization.

3. In its third form, all members of the symptom-neurotic family become patients, carrying out a round-robin power struggle with the help of their symptoms and masochistic maneuvers. Each blackmails the other with his ailments and suffering. Only as a patient or would-be patient is a member able to protect himself from the overburdening demands of his rivals within the family. Even the children are integrated

in this perverse competition and generally at an early age, and they learn that by displaying a particular crankiness and particular ailments they are best able to hold their own in a group in which all vital power struggles are carried out with the help of masochistic arguments. It should be mentioned that when after a period of time the belligerent dissociation lessens and the family, for example, begins to solidarize as a sick *group*, then this third symptom-neurotic family variant edges close to becoming a character-neurotic family.

The Character-Neurotic Family

The character-neurotic family displays none of the tendencies toward disintegrative splitting common to the symptom-neurotic family. The emotionally disturbed individual dominates the rest of the family. Its members identify with him and adopt his abnormal way of thinking and behaving, which eases their relationship with him. Despite his disturbance—which may be latent or perhaps even objectively manifest in the medical sense—he no longer needs to organize himself as a patient. On the contrary, by having imposed his sick, distorted and occasionally downright crazy norm system on the other members of the family, he can enjoy the feeling of being the healthiest member of the group. On the other hand, after having gone through this transformation process, the family would regard any member who tries to break free of the newly assimilated norm code as a patient or, at best, an outcast. If the familial character neurosis functions effectively, then the psychopathological transformation in the character of the family as a whole becomes permanently ingrained under the pressure the disturbed central figure brings to bear.

The pronouncedly character-neurotic family is, in any event, homogeneously organized according to a definable neurotic principle. What is specifically neurotic about such a family is that its life is highly restricted thematically by an enormous anxiety defense. Its only reference is to its own particular leitmotif. One can try to outline such leitmotifs in order to arrive at typological distinctions. In what follows I should like to briefly sketch the defense structures of various types of character-neurotic families.

The Hysterical Family

The hysterical family staves off subsurface depression and insecurity as to identity by concealing the depressive void with a constant display of theatrics, a non-stop show the family puts on for others and for itself, as well, because it is not sure "who" it is or whether it is anything at all. This amounts to a frantic flight into activity, into a hectic, unceasing performance of dramatic situations. The inability to develop real relationships is compensated by a wealth of exhibitionistic and voyeuristic pseudo-relationships. Willi, in Zürich, has recently published a subtle description of hysterical marriage structures; his and other studies show that in a hysterical family ensemble not all members need have a hysterical personality structure. Some members are more likely to have a depressive or phobic character. But in the total family interaction they submit to the hysterical principle imposed and enforced, as the leitmotif of the family neurosis, by a strongly dominating, hysterical key figure. This "stage manager" in family hysteria is more likely to be a woman than a man.

The Paranoid Family

The paranoid family lives under the pressure of excessive aggression-rooted tension which it seeks to overcome by establishing an extreme degree of solidarity within the family and by means of the external-enemy projection. To suggest a suitable catchword: what *theater* is to the hysterical family, *fortress* is to the paranoid one. All members of the family fall prey to the compulsion to help create and maintain a polarization against the current external enemy. This over-solidarization, equivalent to a conspiracy, can be explained by the family's enormous fear that the aggressions that have been painstakingly deflected toward the outside could rebound onto the family group the moment one would only begin to openly recognize intragroup divergencies or even conflicts. Just as in the hysterical family the children are compelled at an early age to conform and participate in their parents' as-if theatrics, children in the paranoid family have to pledge loyalty to the paranoid norm system at an age at which they are not at all capable of giving it critical thought. Standing at the center of the paranoid family is a dominant figure who imposes his or her crazily overwrought ideas on the rest of the family. This person's fanaticism is often so terrifying that the rest of the family can see no other means but submission to keep the family from falling apart. These dynamics also explain why many even clinically deluded persons are screened off by their families and not given an opportunity for medical treatment.

The Anxiety-Neurotic Family

In conclusion, a few words about the anxiety-neurotic type of family, the neurotic norms of which largely correspond to the generally accepted ideal of the bourgeois family. Any analysis of this type of family poses particular problems for psychoanalysis, for in decisive points psychoanalytical clinical criteria differ substantially from the criteria of health and illness that are considered valid by society in general and by the rest of the medical profession.

As a rule, the anxiety-neurotic family is dominated by an anxiety-neurotic individual who suffers in a typical fashion under excessive fear of being destroyed. Apart from vegetative complaints, these fears are mainly expressed in a constant death fear and fear of isolation. To calm these enormous fears, the anxiety-neurotic makes an effort to lead a particularly low-risk, scrupulously hygenic life and create exceedingly close, tension-free partner relationships to shield himself from loneliness and isolation. As a result, he puts heavy pressure on the rest of the family to make them become party to his system of defense mechanisms. They, too, are expected to lead a compulsively cautious life, steer clear of danger and conflict, and if at all possible avoid bringing disturbing matters to the attention of the family, even by way of suggestion. Above all, they are expected to live with one another and with him symbiotically, in idyllic harmony, denying everything that could spell conflict. Nothing dare disturb this sanatorium-like peace and tranquility, artificially created by a determined rejection and denial of all anxiety-precipitating stimuli.

If the rest of the family toes the line—among other reasons, to avoid having to suffer guilt feelings vis-à-vis an anxiety-neurotic who is demanding constant consideration—then this person's psychic condition tends to improve. On the other hand, the whole family now lives under a phobic system of avoidance and denial. A restriction on the family's group ego has been imposed and accepted, cementing the familial character neurosis once and for all. The anxiety-neurotic outlook on life is generally passed on from the mother to her children. A systematic inquiry among anxiety-neurotics (heart neurotics) reveals, as our social-statistical studies in Giessen show, that in the parent generation mothers produce the same symptoms eight times more frequently than do the fathers.

These results cannot be explained genetically, i.e., by means of an inheritance model. As a rule, it is apparently quite easy for the parents, particularly the mother, to induce their own type of anxiety-neurotic reaction formation in their children. They neglect to give the children the encouraging ego reinforcement that would reduce the fears and anxieties that normally crop up during certain specific phases in the child's development. Instead, the child is offered—as therapy—the defense mechanisms the family employs to ward off anxiety: 1) retreat in the face of all risks, which, for their part, the parents depict as more alarming than they really are (if you make yourself small and are good and quiet, nothing can happen to you and no one can hurt you); 2) refuge in exceedingly close ties to the mother and to the family group (if you always hang on to us, then we'll make sure nothing happens to you). The child, of course, cannot see that these prescriptions are designed less as a safeguard for him than to help preserve and stabilize the rest of the family's neurotic defenses.

What particularly works in favor of the anxiety-neurotic family in maintaining its system of defenses as an organizational concept and in passing it on from generation to generation is the fact that such a family is able to interpret its compulsively phobic mechanisms as generally accepted social virtues. It can declare its phobic avoidance strategies and tendency to deny all conflict as an expression of its disposition to live and let live. Strong mutual attachments within the family, the product of infantile anxieties, can be passed off as the preservation of genuine, deep-felt love. The adult partners' symbiotic dependence on one another appears, in another light, as pure and noble loyalty. And the mother, having to seek support in her children to appease herself, can appear to herself and the world as the model of altruistic love and care. And if, in constant, hypochondriacal fear of death, one lives a hygenic life from morning to night, exercising to ward off the heart attack, taking vitamins, not smoking, drinking little, and on top of it all using psychopharmacological drugs to protect oneself from unwholesome excitement, then it can be said that one is demonstrating one's moral fiber—this, at a time when at any rate the so-called health ethic is creeping into those regions of the superego from which the Christian ethic, having lost its hold, is disappearing. For the psychoanalyst, in any event, the statistically demonstrated heavy increase in anxiety neuroses and their effects on family dynamics is only fully comprehensible when viewed in relation to those anxiety-neurotic mechanisms that are firmly anchored in our very social norms. This establishes the familial anxiety neurosis as an eminently representative case, a challenge to psychoanalysis to intensify its research in the field of family dynamics.

A Possible Solution: the Extended Family

This typological survey of the various forms that neurotic family deformations take gives rise to the question: what can be done to break the neurotic tradition in the family? And what can psychoanalysis contribute?

It may be that the younger generation is already on the road to finding a way to modify one fateful condition that in the past has proved so highly conducive to the development of most of the family-neurotic mechanisms described above. I am referring to the growing interest in integrating the couple or nuclear family in larger living units or groups. This movement does not give the impression of being a fad. It will probably lead not to the dissolution, but rather to a gradual and fundamental structural transformation of the family as institution.

It appears that, in entering a larger group, many young couples are primarily interested not in devaluating their personal relationship to one another but rather in relieving this relationship of the pressures brought to bear on it by the all too close entanglement and isolation of the traditional symbiotic marriage. If one is interested in lessening mutual dependencies in the couple-relationship and, with this, the danger of each party always striving to abreact his own internal conflicts by placing traumatic role demands on the other, then it is necessary from the very beginning to situate the couple-relationship in a larger community and also bring the children into a large children's group as early as possible. At the moment, such efforts still seem to be in the experimental stage for the most part. An attempt is being made to test:

- How closely people can live together in such collectives, i.e. how much scope do individuals and couples need for themselves?
- What is the optimal size for such groups?
- Having for the most part little experience with such communal living, how can one make group dynamic processes fruitful and productive?
- Above all, how can one avoid the danger of transplanting the neurotic-psychological mechanisms from the traditional nuclear family into the larger community?
- For these larger communities are naturally also vulnerable to both the splitting processes characteristic of the symptom-neurotic family and to the neurotic tendencies toward over-solidarization that we find in character-neurotic families. Unconsciously anchored in every individual are childhood experiences that impel him to seek over and over again to reproduce the dynamics of the old neurosis.

Thus, in such groups, we once again meet up with irrational elimination strategies or here an anxiety-neurotic, there a paranoid denial of internal conflicts, along with a tendency to take refuge in a non-genuine, group-narcissistic collective consciousness which occasionally displays clearly elitarian characteristics. The political involvement that decisively moti-vates many of today's experiments in communal living can occasionally develop into a collective paranoid trend, given the leadership of a particularly neurotic member. There are groups, for example, whose political activities have the exclu-sive or, at least, primary function of serving the group's psychosocial defense against internal aggressive tensions. This aggressive tension can build up into a self-destructive process within the group at any time, given the temporary absence of the repressive external pressure that had been used to achieve solidarization. The best protection against such symptom-neurotic or character-neurotic processes is constant intercommunication and discussion, whereby sufficient atten-tion should be given to self-critical reflection about the group situation and its members' problems.

What the Analyst Can Do

The movement toward these new forms of communal liv-ing quite naturally has a direct bearing on the work of the practicing psychoanalyst, especially in the field of family and child therapy. In addition to the curative and preventa-tive possibilities the therapist has in dealing with the above-mentioned neurotic families, he will also find it important to pay particular attention to these currently relevant experiments in communal living and collective childrearing.

If called upon, the psychoanalyst can and ought to offer his professional advice in these pioneering efforts to realize such new models. This would also give him the opportunity to study the hitherto scarcely known effects these new models have on people, particularly on children. Especially in regard to child development it would seem particularly important to discover what potential these progressive, com-munal-living and childrearing models have for lessening the pathogenic influences on childrearing outlined earlier in this paper.

A valuable start in this direction is the cooperation being established here and there between parent groups who are setting up and running the new type of day-care center (*Kinderläden,* for example) and psychoanalysts. This sort of cooperation can give both parties an opportunity to learn to define the psychoanalyst's role in different terms from those established by the traditional psychoanalytic treatment setting. In such cases, the psychoanalyst should function in a purely attendant capacity, helping these groups of young parents to take, with their children, the course they themselves have ideologically charted, and dealing with neurotic conflicts only to the extent that they obstruct this programmatical course.

Such courageous experiments quite naturally go through crises in which there is always the danger that the group submits to the analyst as to a doctor whose only business is to administer therapy. Or the analyst, himself, may become anxious, lose his detachment and participate as an uncritical ally, giving up the independent position which alone enables him to help the group along in its process of self-critical reflection. Whether as doctor-authority or as undetached, committed ally, the psychoanalyst loses his chances of working with this kind of model. As doctor, he infantilizes the group; as mere comrade-in-arms he is easily liable to want to reduce all of the group's internal tensions one-sidedly by means of external enemy projections, i.e., by reinforcing paranoid structural features within the group. If on the other hand, the psychoanalyst has a proper understanding of his role in this kind of cooperation and if his partners are willing to concede him this role, then I am convinced that psychoanalysis has a new and meaningful contribution to make to child education.

1. Editor's note: ". . . The term education is used in its widest sense, comprising all types of interference with the spontaneous process of development as they exist in the childish organism." Anna Freud, "Psychoanalysis and Education," *Psychoanalytic Study of the Child*, vol. 9, 1954.

5

Violence Against Children[*]

DAVID G. GIL

AMERICAN SOCIETY HAS OFTEN BEEN described as child-centered. This idealized image seems, however, contradicted by various destructive aspects of child life in the United States such as widespread poverty, hunger, malnutrition, neglect and exploitation; stultifying education and inadequate health care; and an ample measure of physical violence inflicted upon children in their homes, in schools, in child care facilities, and in various children's institutions. There can be little doubt that all these phenomena tend to block opportunities for growth and development of many millions of children, and that they prevent the realization of their innate human potentialities.

Physical violence against children has attracted considerable interest during recent decades in this country and overseas among pediatricians, psychiatrists, social workers, lawyers, public authorities, communications media, and the general public. Yet in spite of this widespread interest and concern, which is reflected in numerous studies and demonstration projects, conferences, seminars, articles and books, the underlying dynamics of physical child abuse are still insufficiently understood, and its real incidence and prevalence rates throughout the population and among various population segments are unknown (U.S. Children's Bureau, 1969).

[*] This paper is based on the author's book *Violence Against Children—Physical Child Abuse in the United States*. Cambridge, Massachusetts: Harvard University Press, 1970 (A Commonwealth Fund Book). The series of nationwide studies sumarized here were conducted by the author between 1965 and 1969 with support from the Children's Bureau, U.S. Department of Health, Education, and Welfare. Reports on these studies were published previously in *American Education, Child Welfare, Pediatrics,* and *Social Work Practice.*

The somewhat sensational concern with individual cases of child abuse seems, at times, to have a quality of "scapegoating," for it enables the public to express self-righteous feelings of anger, disgust, resentment, and condemnation toward an individual abusing parent while the entire society is constantly guilty of massive acts of "societal abuse" of millions of children, about which relatively little is said, and even less has been done in recent decades.

One consequence of the extensive interest in child abuse seems to have been the now widely held assumption that its incidence was on the increase. This claim, however, can neither be substantiated nor refuted since no systematic data are available in the form of time series on incidence. One other consequence of the professional and public concern with child abuse was the swift passage throughout the United States of legislation requiring or urging physicians, hospitals and others to report child abuse incidents to appropriate local public authorities. This legislation had been initiated and promoted vigorously by the United States Children's Bureau in order to protect children who had been abused, and to prevent further abuse of these same children and of others in their families. However, since the dynamics of child abuse were not adequately understood at the time reporting legislation was enacted, no proven strategies and policies for prevention and treatment were incorporated into these laws, and their impact on incidence rates is consequently not expected to be significant (U.S. Children's Bureau, 1962; 1966).

The failure of clinical investigators and of various professional groups to unravel the complex underlying dynamics of violence against children in American society seems due mainly to a significant, built-in bias of the social and behavioral sciences, and of the general system of beliefs of our society. This bias is the deeply rooted, yet untested, assumption that behavioral manifestations which are viewed by the majority of society as "deviant" are the result of personal characteristics, failings, problems, maladjustment, or dysfunction. Whatever label is used, the source of all deviance is conceived to be in the individual or his primary group, his family, rather than in characteristics of the society. This general conception of the dynamics of deviance seems to derive from a politically "conservative" premise, according to which American social structure is basically sound except, perhaps, for a few minor, necessary adjustments. Since the design and the findings of social and behavioral research tend to depend on the questions and hypotheses investigated, and since these questions and hypotheses in turn tend to be generated within the framework of the general assumptions of a scientific discipline and its societal context, it is not surprising that most investigations of child abuse in the United States were clinically oriented, and found this phenomenon to be the result of psychological disorders of the perpetrators or, at times, of the abused children themselves, and/or certain pathological aspects of family relationships. This interpretation of the causal context of child abuse is matched logically by intervention strategies aimed mainly at changing the disorders of individuals and the pathology of families, rather than aspects of the social context in which these "disordered" individuals and "pathological" families live.

The series of nationwide studies of physical child abuse discussed here tried to avoid the limitations inherent in the foregoing assumptions concerning the "individual as source" of behavioral deviance. The causal model guiding these investigations was that behavioral phenomena perceived to be deviant tend to result from interaction effects of societal and individual forces rather than from one or the other of these sets of forces acting independently of each other. The corresponding intervention model or social policy perspective of these studies is that intervention at the societal level is likely to be more effective in terms of prevention than intervention at the individual level since intervention aimed at modifying the societal forcefield can be expected to have a more far-reaching impact on the causal context of deviance posited here. This intervention model does, of course, not preclude direct protection and treatment of individuals and family groups involved in incidents of child abuse or in other deviant phenomena.

STUDY DESIGN AND DEFINITION OF SUBJECT

The general causal model of deviance sketched here led to a comprehensive psychosocial-cultural conception of child abuse. To study this phenomenon from such a perspective required an epidemiologically oriented survey design involving systematic review of large numbers of child abuse incidents from all over the country rather than a clinically oriented design involving intensive analysis of small samples in specified settings and localities. Accordingly, the nationwide surveys gathered standardized information on every incident of child abuse reported through legal channels throughout the United States during 1967 and 1968, nearly 13,000 incidents. This broadly-based survey was supplemented by more comprehensive case studies of nearly 1400 incidents reported during 1967 in a representative sample of 39 cities and counties. Further data sources, especially concerning the cultural roots of child abuse, were interviews in October of 1965 with 1520 adults from across the country selected at random so as to be representative of the entire U.S. adult population, and a six months survey during 1965 of daily and periodical newspapers and magazines published throughout the United States.

Studies of child abuse were hampered in the past not only by a certain preconception of the causal context but also by the lack of an unambiguous definition of the phenomenon itself. Definitions were usually derived from observable consequences of violent acts against children rather than from the acts themselves and the underlying behavioral dynamics. However, consequences of abusive acts seem to be an inappropriate basis for developing a conceptually valid definition since such consequences are likely to be affected by chance factors as much as by the intentional behavior of perpetrators, and since their evaluation depends on subjective standards or judgments.

In an effort to minimize ambiguity in defining physical abuse of children, the following conceptual definition was developed. This definition is based only on the behavior of perpetrators, rather than on the variable consequences of such behavior.

Physical abuse of children is intentional, non-accidental use of physical force, or intentional, non-accidental acts of omission, on the part of a parent or other caretaker in interaction with a child in his care, aimed at hurting, injuring, or destroying that child.

The foregoing definition seems sound conceptually, but is not completely satisfactory as an operational definition since it may not always be possible to differentiate between intentional and accidental behavior. Also, the presence of intentional elements in the behavior of perpetrators does not imply complete absence of chance elements. An added difficulty is the fact that behavior which appears to be accidental may be determined in part by "unconsciously intentional" elements. Thus, while the boundary between "pure" accidents and physical abuse can be drawn clearly on a conceptual level, it may, at times, be difficult to differentiate between them without examination of the motivations which underlie manifest behavior in given incidents.

Apart from the difficulty of ascertaining the presence of elements of intentionality, which, by definition, constitute a *sine qua non* of child abuse, the definition reduces ambiguity by including *all* use of physical force and *all* acts of omission aimed at hurting, injuring, or destroying a child, irrespective of the degree of seriousness of the act, the omission, and/or the outcome. Thus, the relativity of personal and community standards and judgments is avoided.

SELECTED FINDINGS FROM THE NATIONWIDE SURVEYS

The Scope of Child Abuse

During 1967 child abuse registries throughout the United States received 9,563 reports. The number of reports rose to 10,931 in 1968. Screening the reports against the conceptual definition of physical child abuse resulted in the elimination of over 37 percent of the 1967 cohort and of over 39 percent of the 1968 cohort, leaving 5,993 children for 1967 and 6,617 for 1968. The post-screening nationwide reporting rate per 100,000 children under age 18 was thus 8.4 in 1967 and 9.3 in 1968.

Analysis of reporting rates state by state suggests that the increase in reporting from 1967 to 1968 reflects primarily changes in legal, administrative, and professional services patterns. The net increase of 624 reports for the country as a whole resulted from an increase of 1,157 reports in 23 states and territories and a decrease of 533 reports in 28 states and territories. No changes in reporting levels were reported from two states. The group of states which reported increases had strengthened their procedures between the two years when compared with the group of states which reported decreases.

There were significant differences in reporting rates per 100,000 children under age 18 among the states ranging from 0.0 to 24.0 in 1967, and from 0.0 to 31.2 in 1968. Reporting rates within the states appeared to be associated with legal, administrative, and professional practices. The more effective these practices were the higher tended to be the reporting rates.

It may be of interest to compare the foregoing reporting levels with a rough estimate of actual incidence of physical abuse of children resulting in some degree of injury. On the basis of a nationwide survey of public knowledge, attitudes and opinions about physical child abuse, the maximum incidence during 1965 was estimated to have been between 2.53 to 4.07 million cases. The actual figure is likely to have been somewhat lower. It should be noted that this figure includes all kinds of injuries from minimal through serious to fatal. The figure would certainly be larger if incidents of abuse which did not result in injury were added.

It is easily seen that official reporting figures bear no relation whatsoever to actual incidence. However, since severity of injury is likely to be one important decision criterion in reporting, reported incidents as a group are likely to constitute the more severe segment of a spectrum of cases ranging from no injury to fatality.

One further comment on reporting patterns concerns reports from metropolitan and nonmetropolitan areas. Reporting rates in SMSAs during 1967 and 1968 were markedly higher than in areas outside SMSAs. While less than 70 percent of the U.S. population live in SMSAs, approximately 80 percent of all reports originated in communities within SMSAs. This concentration of reports in metropolitan areas supports the view that administrative and professional factors are likely to be reflected in reporting patterns.

Characteristics of Legally Reported Abused Children

Slightly more than half the children reported as abused during 1967 and 1968 were boys. Boys outnumbered girls in every age group under age 12, but were outnumbered by girls among teen-aged victims of child abuse. Shifts in the sex distribution during different ages seem to reflect culturally determined attitudes. Girls are viewed as more conforming than boys during childhood and physical force tends to be used less frequently in rearing them. However, during adolescence parental anxieties concerning dating behavior of girls lead to increasing restrictions, conflicts, and use of physical force in asserting parental control. With boys physical force tends to be used more readily prior to adolescence. However, during adolescence, as the physical strength of boys begins to match their parents' strength, the use of physical force in disciplining boys tends to diminish.

The age distribution of the reported children indicates that physical abuse is not limited to early childhood. Over 75 percent of the reported victims were over two years of age, and nearly half of them were over six years. Nearly one-fifth were teen-agers. Age distribution was similar for all ethnic groups.

Non-white children were over-represented in the study cohorts. Nationwide reporting rates per 100,000 white children were 6.7, and per 100,000 non-white children 21.0. This over-representation of non-white children seems due partly to reporting bias but mainly to the higher incidence of poverty and poverty related social and psychological deviance, and to the higher rate of fatherless homes and large families among non-white population segments, all of which were found to be strongly associated with child abuse. Finally, the possibility of real differences in child rearing practices among different ethnic groups cannot be ruled out as a contributing factor to observed differences in reporting rates. Such differences in the use of physical force in child rearing may reflect the violence inflicted upon many generations of non-white minorities in American society.

About 29 percent of the children revealed deviations in social interaction and general functioning during the year preceding the abusive incident, nearly 14 percent suffered from deviations in physical functioning during the same time span, and nearly eight percent revealed deviations in intellectual functioning. Among the school-aged children over 13 percent attended special classes for retarded children or were in grades below their age level. Nearly three percent of the school-aged children had never attended school. Nearly 10 percent of children in the sample cohort had lived with foster families sometime during their lives prior to the incident, and over three percent had lived in child care or correctional institutions. Over five percent had appeared before Juvenile Courts on other than traffic offenses. Taken together, these items suggest a level of deviance in excess of the level of deviance of any group of children selected at random from the population at large.

Over 60 percent of the children had a history of prior abuse. It thus seems that physical abuse of children is more often than not an indication of a prevailing pattern of caretaker-child interaction in a given home rather than of an isolated incident. This impression is supported also by data on involvement in previous abuse by parents, siblings, and other perpetrators.

The Families of Abused Children

Nearly 30 percent of the abused children lived in female-headed households. The child's own father lived in the home in 46 percent of the cases, and a stepfather in nearly 20 percent. Over two percent of the children lived in foster homes, and 0.3 percent lived with adoptive parents. The child's own mother was not living in his home in over 12 percent. Ten percent of the mothers were single, nearly 20 percent were separated, divorced, deserted, or widowed, and over two-thirds were living with a spouse. The homes of non-white children were less frequently intact than those of white children. The data on family structure suggest an association between physical abuse of children and deviance from normative family structure, which seems especially strong for non-white children.

The age distribution of parents of abused children does not support observations according to which parents tend to be extremely young.

The proportion of families with four or more children was nearly twice as high among the families of the reported abused children than among all families with children under 18 in the U.S. population, and the proportion of small families was much larger in the U.S. population. The porportion of larger families among non-white families in the study was significantly higher than among white families.

Educational and occupational levels of parents were markedly lower than of the general population. Non-white parents ranked lower on these items than white ones. Nearly half the fathers of the abused children were not employed throughout the year, and about 12 percent were actually unemployed at the time of the abusive act. Unemployment rates were higher for non-white fathers. Table 1 shows the distribution of income for all sample families, for white, black and Puerto Rican families in the sample, and for all families in the United States.

Compared to all families in the United States, the income of families of abused children was very low and that of families of non-white abused children even lower. At the time of the abusive incident over 37 percent of the families were receiving public assistance. Altogether nearly 60 percent of the families had received public assistance at some time preceding the abusive incident.

Data concerning the personal history of the parents of the reported abused children suggested a level of deviance in areas of psychosocial functioning which exceeds deviance levels in the general population.

Table 1
FAMILY INCOME 1967

Income in $	All families	Percent of Sample Cohort			Percent of all U.S. Families[a]
		White	Negro	Puerto Rican	
under 3,000	22.3	17.7	24.8	34.5	12.5
3,000 to 4,999	26.1	21.9	28.6	41.9	12.8
5,000 to 6,999	16.2	18.5	14.1	9.7	16.1
7,000 to 9,999	12.7	15.9	11.7	5.4	24.3
10,000 to 14,999	2.6	3.1	1.9	1.1	22.4
15,000 and over	0.4	0.9	0.2	0.0	12.0
unknown	19.8	22.2	18.6	7.5	0.0
	N = 1,380	N = 536	N = 630	N = 93	N = 49,834,000

[a] *Consumer Income*, Bureau of the Census, Current Population Reports, Series P-60, No. 59, April 1969.

The Incidents and the Circumstances
Surrounding Them

In nearly 50 percent of the incidents a mother or step-mother was the perpetrator and in about 40 percent a father. However, since about 30 percent of the homes were female-headed, the involvement rate of fathers was actually higher than that of mothers. Two-thirds of incidents in homes with fathers or stepfathers present were commited by fathers or stepfathers, while mothers or stepmothers were the perpetrators in less than half the incidents occurring in homes with mothers or stepmothers present. Over 70 percent of the children were abused by a biological parent, nearly 14 percent by a stepparent, less than one percent by an adoptive parent, two percent by a foster parent, about one percent by a sibling, four percent by other relatives, and nearly seven percent by an unrelated caretaker. Fifty-one percent of the children were abused by a female perpetrator.

Perpetrators tended to have little education and a low socioeconomic status. About 61 percent of them were members of minority groups, 56.8 percent had shown deviations in social and behavioral functioning during the year preceding the abuse incident and about 12.3 percent had been physically ill during that year. Nearly 11 percent showed deviations in intellectual functioning, 7.1 percent had been in mental hospitals some time prior to the incident, 8.4 percent before Juvenile Courts, and 7.9 percent in foster care. Under 14 percent had a criminal record. About 11 percent had been victims of abuse during their childhood, and 52.5 percent had been perpetrators of abuse prior to the current incident.

The types of injuries sustained by the children are shown in Table 2.

The following tabulation of injuries is based on medical verification in 80.2 percent of the cases and the reliability of the diagnoses is therefore quite satisfactory. The injuries were considered to be "not serious" in 53.3 percent. They were rated "serious, no permanent damage expected" in

Table 2

TYPES OF INJURIES SUSTAINED BY CHILDREN
IN REPORTED ABUSE INCIDENTS

Injury	Percent of Children[a]
Bruises, Welts	67.1
Abrasions, Contusions, Lacerations	32.3
Wounds, Cuts, Punctures	7.9
Burns, Scalding	10.1
Bone Fractures (excluding skull)	10.4
Sprains, Dislocations	1.9
Skull Fractures	3.7
Subdural Hemorrhage or Hematoma	4.6
Brain Damage	1.5
Internal Injuries	3.3
Poisoning	0.9
Malnutrition (deliberately inflicted)	4.2
Freezing, Exposure	0.1
Other Injuries	5.4
No Apparent Injuries	3.2
Type Unknown	2.2

[a] The percentages in this table do not add up to 100 since many children sustained more than one injury.

36.5 percent, "serious with permanent damage" in 4.6 percent, and fatal in 3.4 percent. It is noteworthy that 90 percent of the reported incidents were not expected to leave any lasting physical effects on the children, and that over half the incidents were not considered to be serious at all. Even if allowance is made for under-reporting, especially of fatal cases, one must question the view of many concerned professional and lay persons, according to which physical abuse of children constitutes a major cause of death and maiming of children throughout the nation.

Analysis of the relationship between severity of injury and age reveals that injuries of children under age 3 were serious or fatal in 65 percent of the cases while injuries of children over age 3 were serious in 35 percent of the cases only.

Severity of injuries was also found to be related to ethnicity. The injuries of white children were judged not serious in 61.6 percent and serious or fatal in 35.2 percent. The injuries of Negro and Puerto Rican children were judged not serious in 47.3 percent and serious in 52.0 percent.

While severity of injury was thus associated with the age and the ethnic background of the victim, it was found not to be associated with the victim's sex. Severity of injury was about equal for boys and girls.

Several less pronounced associational trends were revealed concerning the severity of injuries sustained by abused children. Severe injuries were more likely to be inflicted by parents and other perpetrators under age 25 than by older ones, by women than by men and especially by single women. Parents who had appeared before Juvenile Courts and who experienced some form of foster care were more likely than other parents to inflict serious injury. Finally, injuries were more likely to be serious or fatal in families whose annual income was under $3,500.

The extent of medical treatment is another crude indicator of the degree of severity of physical abuse sustained by children. The injuries of nearly 60 percent of the children did not seem to require hospitalization, and in nearly 25 percent no medical treatment seemed indicated at all. Of those requiring hospitalization, over 41.7 percent were discharged in less than one week. Hospitalization beyond one week was required by 21.3 percent of the children, and this group seems to represent the segment of severe injury of the child abuse spectrum.

Official Actions Following Abuse

While public and voluntary social welfare agencies were a third choice as an initial source for help following abusive incidents, they carried major responsibility in dealing with and caring for the abused children and their families later on. Social welfare agencies were involved to some extent in 86.9 percent of all cases. Courts were involved in 45.8 percent, the police in 53.1 percent, and District or County Attorneys in 19.1 percent.

Over 36 percent of the abused children were placed away from their families after the abuse incidents. In 15.4 percent of the cases, not only the victims but also siblings living in the same homes were placed away from their families. Placement away from the child's home was more likely to be used when injuries were serious and when children had been abused before. Homemaker service was made available to 2.2 percent of the families, and counseling services were made available to 71.9 percent.

The suspected perpetrators were indicted in 17.3 percent of the incidents. They were convicted in 13.1 percent and jailed in 7.2 percent. Court action was more likely to be taken when children were seriously or fatally injured.

A TYPOLOGY OF CHILD ABUSE

Based on observations throughout the study, the conclusion was reached that physical abuse of children is not a uniform phenomenon with one set of causal factors, but a multidimensional phenomenon. In order to explore the many possible contributing causal contexts which may precipitate incidents of physical abuse of children, lists were prepared of circumstances which may or may not have been present in any given case. The items on the checklist were not designed to be mutually exclusive. Associations between two or more types were therefore expected in many incidents. Responses concerning the circumstances of abuse of 1,380 cases of a sample cohort suggest the following observations concerning types of physical child abuse:

One major type involves incidents developing out of disciplinary action taken by caretakers who respond in uncontrolled anger to real or perceived misconduct of a child. Nearly 63 percent of the cases were checked as "immediate or delayed response to specific act of child," and nearly 73 percent were checked as "inadequately controlled anger of perpetrator."

A second important type seems to involve incidents which derive from a general attitude of resentment and rejection on the part of the perpetrator towards a child. In these cases, not a specific act but the "whole person," or a specific quality of the person such as sex, looks, capacities, circumstances of birth, etc., are the object of rejection. In these cases, too, specific acts of the child may precipitate the acting out of the underlying attitude of rejection. The item "Resentment, rejection of child . . ." was checked in 34.1 percent of the cases. This type was associated with "Repeated abuse of same child by perpetrator," and also "Battered child syndrome" (Kempe, 1962).

A third type is defined by the item "Persistent behavioral atypicality of child, e.g., hyperactivity, high annoyance potential, etc." Cases checked positively on this item may be considered as child-initiated or child-provoked abuse. This item was checked in 24.5 percent of the cases. This type was found to be associated with "Misconduct of child."

A fourth type is physical abuse of a child developing out of a quarrel between his caretakers. The child may come to the aid of one parent, or he may just happen to be in the midst of a fight between the parents. Sometimes the child may even be the object of the fight. The item reflecting this type was checked in 11.3 percent of the cases. It was associated with "Alcoholic intoxication of perpetrator."

A fifth type is physical abuse coinciding with a perpetrator's sexual attack on a child. This item was checked in 0.6 percent of the cases. It was found to be associated with the sixth type, "Sadistic gratification of the perpetrator."

The seventh type may be referred to as sadism sublimated to the level of child rearing ideology. The item was worded on the checklist: "Self-definition of perpetrator as stern, authoritative disciplinarian." It was checked in 31.0 percent of the cases, and was associated with the first type.

Type Number 8 was called "Marked mental and/or emotional deviation of perpetrator." It was checked in 46.1 percent of the cases and was associated with "Mounting stress on perpetrator."

Type Number 9 is the simultaneous occurrence of abuse and neglect. Contrary to observations of many investigators who consider abuse and neglect as mutually exclusive phenomena, this type was checked in 33.7 percent of the cases. It was associated with type Number 2, "Resentment, rejection . . ."

"The battered child syndrome" (Kempe, 1962) constitutes type Number 10. This item was checked in 13.6 percent of the cases.

"Alcoholic intoxication of the perpetrator at the time of the abusive act" constitutes type Number 11. It was checked as present in 12.9 percent of the cases and was associated with "Caretaker quarrel," and "Mother temporarily absent—perpetrator male."

A very important type is Number 12, "Mounting stress on perpetrator due to life circumstances." It was checked as present in 59.0 percent of the cases and was associated with "Mental, emotional deviation of perpetrator."

Type Number 13 is an important "typical constellation" which frequently tends to precipitate physical abuse of a child: The mother or substitute is temporarily absent from the home, working or shopping, or for some other reason, and the child is left in the care of a boyfriend or some other male caretaker. This type was the context for the abuse in 17.2 percent of the cases and seems to deserve special attention in preventive efforts. It was found to be associated with "Physical and sexual abuse coincide," "Sadistic gratification of perpetrator," and "Alcoholic intoxication."

The last type, Number 14, is similar to type Number 13, but quantitatively much less important as a typical context for child abuse. It is the temporary absence of the mother or substitute during which the child is cared for and abused by a female baby-sitter. This item was checked in 2.7 percent of the cases.

The foregoing typology is quite crude. However, it may be of interest to note that this typology seems to have successfully covered most of the circumstances of abuse observed by social workers who completed the checklists. This is reflected in the fact that a residual item—"other circumstances"—was checked only in 2.7 percent of the cases.

Data underlying the foregoing empirically derived typology were subjected to a factor analysis. The final results of this analysis, shown in Table 3, suggest that the typology can be reduced to the following underlying seven factors of legally reported physical child abuse:

1. Psychological Rejection
2. Angry and Uncontrolled Disciplinary Response
3. Male Babysitter Abuse
4. Personality Deviance and Reality Stress
5. Child Originated Abuse
6. Female Babysitter Abuse
7. Caretaker Quarrel

In a certain sense, the seven factors of the spectrum of legally reported physical abuse of children summarize the findings of the nationwide surveys by reducing them into a concentrated paradigm which reflects the underlying structure of the phenomenon. A more comprehensive conceptual summation of these findings, and a set of recommendations derived from them, are presented below.

A CONCEPTUAL MODEL OF PHYSICAL CHILD ABUSE

a. Culturally Sanctioned Use of Physical Force in Child Rearing

One important conclusion of the nationwide surveys was that physical abuse of children as defined here is not a rare and unusual occurrence in our society, and that by itself it should therefore not be considered as sufficient evidence of "deviance" of the perpetrator, the child, or the family. Physical abuse appears to be endemic in American society since our cultural norms of child rearing do not preclude the use of a certain measure of physical force toward children by adults caring for them. Rather, such use tends to be encouraged in subtle, and at times not so subtle, ways by "professional experts" in child rearing, education, and medicine; by the press, radio and television; and by professional and popular publications. Furthermore, children are not infrequently subjected to physical abuse in the public domain in such settings as schools, child care facilities, foster homes, correctional and other children's institutions, and even in juvenile courts.

Strong support for considering child abuse as endemic in American society was provided by the public opinion survey, which revealed that nearly 60 percent of adult Americans

Table 3

FACTOR ANALYSIS OF CIRCUMSTANCES OF CHILD ABUSE ROTATED FACTOR LOADINGS
(ORTHOGONAL VARIMAX, ROTATION BY VARIABLE)

Type of Circumstances	Factors							Communality
	1	2	3	4	5	6	7	
1. Perpetrator response to child's act	—.069	.739°	—.100	—.032	.253	.013	.208	.670
2. Misconduct of child	—.266	.235	.051	—.122	.714°	—.074	.128	.676
3. Inadequately controlled anger	—.050	.805°	—.170	.115	—.009	—.119	—.129	.724
4. Resentment, rejection of child	.620°	.003	—.092	.192	—.083	—.022	—.060	.440
5. Repeated abuse of same child	.729°	.200	.084	.059	.039	—.135	.058	.605
6. Persistent behavioral atypicality	.071	.069	—.007	.053	.797°	—.048	.044	.652
7. Physical abuse and sexual attack coincide	.022	—.235	.673°	—.060	.165	.074	—.143	.565
8. Abuse resulting from caretaker quarrel	—.004	—.068	.057	—.020	—.078	—.048	.880°	.791
9. Battered child syndrome	.675°	—.148	.051	—.110	—.029	—.015	.027	.494
10. Abuse and neglect coincide	.431†	—.328	.068	.340	.026	.050	—.001	.417
11. Mental, emotional deviation of perpetrator	.306	.019	.188	.675°	—.256	.025	—.004	.651
12. Sadistic gratification of perpetrator	—.445†	.017	.546°	.135	—.110	.251	—.080	.595
13. Alcoholic intoxication of perpetrator	—.036	.039	—.493°	.148	—.103	.022	—.499°	.529
14. Perpetrator stern disciplinarian	.212	.522°	.369	.178	.167	.098	.042	.525
15. Mounting stress on perpetrator	—.031	.003	—.121	.813°	.124	—.662	—.040	.697
16. Mother absent; perpetrator male	—.274	.031	—.554°	—.087	—.389	—.365	.267	.746
17. Mother absent; perpetrator female	—.143	—.052	.108	—.051	—.105	.899°	.059	.861
Sums of Squares	2.075	1.762	1.566	1.403	1.547	1.071	1.214	10.638

° high loadings
† moderately high loadings

thought that "almost anybody could at some time injure a child in his care." That survey also indicated that several millions of children may be subjected every year to a wide range of physical abuse, though only several thousands suffer serious physical injury and a few hundred die as a consequence of abusive attacks. Against the background of public sanction of the use of violence against children, and the endemic scope of the prevalence of such cases, it should surprise no one that extreme incidents will occur from time to time in the course of "normal" child rearing practices.

It should be noted that in most incidents of child abuse the caretakers involved are "normal" individuals exercising their prerogative of disciplining a child whose behavior they find in need of correction. While some of these adults may often go farther than they intended because of anger and temporary loss of self-control, and/or because of chance events, their behavior does, nevertheless, not exceed the normative range of disciplining children as defined by the existing culture. Moreover, their acts are usually not in conflict with any law since parents, as well as teachers and other child care personnel, are in many American jurisdictions permitted to use a "reasonable" amount of corporal punishment. For children are not protected by law against bodily attack in the same way as are adults and, consequently, do not enjoy "equal protection under the law" as guaranteed by the XIVth Amendment to the U.S. Constitution.

While, then, culturally sanctioned and patterned use of physical force in child rearing seems to constitute the basic causal dimension of all violence against children in American society, it does not explain many specific aspects of this phenomenon, especially its differential incidence rates among different population segments. Several additional causal dimensions need therefore be considered in interpreting the complex dynamics of physical child abuse.

Difference in Child Rearing Patterns
Among Social Strata and Ethnic Groups

Different social and economic strata of society, and different ethnic and nationality groups tend to differ for various environmental and cultural reasons in their child rearing philosophies and practices, and consequently in the extent to which they approve of corporal punishment of children. These variations in child rearing styles among social and economic strata and ethnic groups constitute a second set of causal dimensions of child abuse, and are reflected in significant variations in incidence rates among these strata and groups. Thus, for instance, incidence rates tend to be negatively correlated with education and income. Also, certain ethnic groups reveal characteristic incidence patterns. Some American Indian tribes will never use physical force in disciplining their children while the incidence rates of child abuse are relatively high among American blacks and Puerto Ricans.

Lest the higher incidence rates among black and Puerto Rican minority groups be misinterpreted, it should be remembered that as a result of centuries of discrimination, non-white ethnic minority status tends to be associated in American society with low educational achievement and low income. The incidence rates of child abuse among these minority groups are likely to reflect this fact, as much as their specific cultural patterns. Furthermore, exposure of these minority groups to various forms of external societal violence to which they could not respond in kind, is likely to have contributed over time to an increase in the level of frustration-generated violence directed against their own members. Relatively high rates of homicide among members of these minority groups seem to support this interpretation.

Higher reporting rates of physical child abuse, and especially of more serious incidents, among the poor and among non-white minority groups may reflect biased reporting procedures. It may be true that the poor and non-whites are more likely to be reported than middle class and white population groups for anything they do or fail to do. At the same time there may also be considerable under-reporting of reportable transgressions not only among middle class and white population groups but also among the poor and the non-white minorities. The net effect of reporting bias and of overall and specific under-reporting with respect to child abuse can, at this time, not be estimated.

It should not be overlooked, however, that life in poverty and in minority group ghettos tends to generate many stressful experiences which are likely to become precipitating factors of child abuse by weakening a caretaker's psychological mechanisms of self-control and contributing, thus, to the uninhibited discharge of his aggressive and destructive impulses toward physically powerless children. The poor and members of ethnic minority groups seem to be subject to many of the conditions and forces which may lead to abusive behavior toward children in other groups of the population and, in addition to this, they seem to be subject to the special environmental stresses and strains associated with socioeconomic deprivation and discrimination. This would suggest that the significantly higher reporting rates for poor and non-white segments of the population reflect a real underlying higher incidence rate among these groups.

It should also be noted that the poor and non-whites tend to have more children per family unit and less living space. They also tend to have fewer alternatives than other population groups for avoiding or dealing with aggressive impulses toward their children. The poor tend to discharge aggressive impulses more directly as they seem less inhibited in expressing feelings through action. These tendencies are apparently learned through lower class and ghetto socialization, which tends to differ in this respect from middle class socialization and mores.

Middle class parents, apparently as a result of exposure to modern psychological theories of child rearing, tend to engage more than lower class parents in verbal interaction with their children, and to use psychological approaches in disciplining them. It may be noted, parenthetically, that verbal and psychological interaction with children may at times be as violent and abusive in its effects, or even more so, than the use of physical force in disciplining them. Life in middle class families tends to generate tensions and pressures characteristic of the dominant individualistic and competitive value orientations of American society, and these pressures may also precipitate violence against children. However, middle class families are spared the more devastating daily tensions and pressures of life in poverty. They also tend to have fewer children, more living space, and more options to relax, at times, without their children. All this would suggest a lower real incidence rate of physical child abuse among middle class families.

Deviance and Pathology in Bio-Psycho-Social Functioning of Individuals and Families

A further set of causal dimensions of violence against children involves a broad range of deviance in biological, psychological, and social functioning of caretakers, children in their care, and of entire family units. This is the causal context which had been identified and stressed by most clinical investigators of child abuse. It is important to note that this dimension of child abuse is by no means independent of the basic cultural dimension discussed above. The choice of symptoms through which intra-psychic conflicts are expressed by members of a society tends to be influenced by the culture of that society. Symptoms of personality deviance involve often exaggerated levels of culturally sanctioned trends. It would thus seem that violent acts against children would less likely be symptoms of personality disorders in a society which did not sanction the use of physical force in rearing its young.

The presence of this third dimension of child abuse was reflected in findings from our surveys, which revealed relatively high rates of deviance in bio-psycho-social circumstances and functioning of children and adults involved in many reported incidents. Often manifestations of such deviance had been observed during the year preceding an incident. Deviance in functioning of individuals was also matched by high rates of deviance in family structure reflected in a high proportion of female-headed households, and of households from which the biological fathers of the abused children were absent.

Environmental Chance Events

A final, but not insignificant causal dimension of child abuse is environmental chance events which may transform "acceptable" disciplinary measures into serious and "unacceptable" outcomes. It is thus obvious that physical abuse of children, like so many other social problems, is a multidimensional phenomenon rather than a uni-dimensional one with a single set of causal factors. This multidimensional conception of child abuse and its dynamics suggests a corresponding multidimensional approach to the prevention or reduction of the incidence rate of this destructive phenomenon.

IMPLICATIONS FOR SOCIAL POLICY

Violence against children constitutes a severe infringement of their rights as members of society. Since distribution of rights in a society is a key aspect of its social policies, modifications of these policies are necessary if the rights of children to physical safety are to be assured (Gil, 1970). For social policies to be effective they must be based on a causal theory concerning the etiology of the condition which is to be corrected or prevented. Accordingly, social policies aimed at protecting the rights of children to bodily safety should be designed around the causal dimensions of child abuse presented in the conceptual model of this phenomenon.

Since cultural sanctions of the use of physical force in child rearing constitute the common core of all physical abuse of children in American society, efforts aimed at gradually changing this aspect of the prevailing child rearing philosophy, and developing clear-cut cultural prohibitions and legal sanctions against such use of physical force, are likely to produce over time the strongest possible reduction of the incidence and prevalence of physical abuse of children.

Suggesting to forego the use of physical force in rearing children does not mean that inherently non-social traits of children need not be modified in the course of socialization. It merely means that non-violent, constructive, educational measures would have to replace physical force. It needs to be recognized that giving up the use of physical force against children may not be easy for adults who were subjected to physical force and violence in their own childhood and who have integrated the existing value system of American society. Moreover, children can sometimes be very irritating and provocative in their behavior and may strain the tolerance of adults to the limit. Yet, in spite of these realities, which must be acknowledged and faced openly, society needs to work toward the gradual reduction, and eventual complete elimination, of the use of physical force against children if it intends to protect their basic right of security from physical attack.

As a first, concrete step toward developing eventually comprehensive legal sanctions against the use of physical force in rearing children, the Congress and legislatures of the states could outlaw corporal punishment in schools, juvenile courts, correctional institutions and other child care facilities. Such legislation would assure children the same constitutional protection against physical attack outside their homes as the law provides for adult members of society. Moreover, such legislation is likely to affect child rearing attitudes and practices in American homes, for it would symbolize society's growing rejection of violence against children.

To avoid misinterpretations it should be noted here that rejecting corporal punishment does not imply favoring unlimited permissiveness in rearing children. To grow up successfully, children require a sense of security which is inherent in nonarbitrary structures and limits. Understanding adults can establish such structures and limits through love, patience, firmness, consistency, and rational authority. Corporal punishment seems devoid of constructive educational value since it cannot provide that sense of security and nonarbitrary authority. Rarely, if ever, is corporal punishment administered for the benefit of an attacked child, for usually it serves the immediate needs of the attacking adult who is seeking relief from his uncontrollable anger and stress.

The multiple links between poverty and racial discrimination and physical abuse of children suggest that one essential route toward reducing the incidence and prevalence of child abuse is the elimination of poverty and of structural social inequalities. This objective could be approached through the establishment of a guaranteed decent annual income for all, at least at the level of the Bureau of Labor Statistics "low" standard of living. No doubt this is only a partial answer to the complex issue of preventing violence toward children, but perhaps a very important part of the total answer, and certainly that part without which other preventive efforts may be utterly futile. Eliminating poverty by equalizing opportunities and rights, and by opening up access for all to all levels of the social status system, also happens to be that part of the answer for which this nation possesses the necessary know-how and resources, provided we were willing to introduce changes in our priorities of resource development, and to redistribute national wealth more equitably.

Deviance and pathology in biological, psychological, and social functioning of individuals and of family units were identified as a third set of forces which contribute to the incidence and prevalence of physical abuse of children. These conditions tend to be strongly associated with poverty and racial discrimination, and, therefore, eliminating poverty and discrimination are likely to reduce, though by no means to eliminate, the incidence and prevalence of these various dysfunctional phenomena. The following measures, aimed at the secondary and tertiary prevention and amelioration of these conditions and their consequences, and at the strengthening of individual and family functioning, should be available in every community as components of a comprehensive program for reducing the incidence of physical abuse of children, and also for helping individuals and families once abuse has occurred:

a. Comprehensive family planning programs including the repeal of all legislation concerning medical abortions: The availability of family planning resources and medical abortions are likely to reduce the number of unwanted and rejected children, who are known to be frequently victims of severe physical abuse and even infanticide. It is important to recall in this context that families with many children, and female-headed households, are over-represented among families involved in physical abuse of children.

b. Family life education and counseling programs for adolescents and adults in preparation for, and after marriage: Such programs should be developed in accordance with the assumption that there is much to learn about married life and parenthood which one does not know merely on the basis of sexual and chronological maturity.

c. A comprehensive, high quality, neighborhood based, national health service, financed through general tax revenue, and geared not only to the treatment of acute and chronic illness, but also the promotion and maintenance of maximum feasible physical and mental health for everyone.

d. A range of high quality, neighborhood based social services geared to the reduction of environmental stresses on family life and especially on mothers who carry major responsibility for the child rearing function. Any measure which would reduce these stresses would also indirectly reduce the incidence rate of child abuse. Homemaker and housekeeping services, mothers' helpers and baby-sitting services, family and group day-care facilities for pre-school and school age children are all examples of such services. It should be recognized, however, that unless a decent income is assured to all families, these social services are unlikely to achieve their objectives.

e. Every community needs also a system of social services and child care facilities geared to assisting families and children who cannot live together because of severe relationship and/or reality problems. Physically abused children belong frequently to this category.

The measures proposed herewith are aimed at different causal dimensions of violence against children. The first set would attack the culturally determined core of the phenomenon; the second set would attack and eliminate major conditions to which child abuse is linked in many ways; the third set approaches the causes of child abuse indirectly. It would be futile to argue the relative merits of these approaches as all three are important. The basic question seems to be, not which measure to select for combating child abuse, but whether American society is indeed committed to assuring equal rights to all its children, and to eradicate child abuse in any form, abuse perpetrated by individual caretakers, as well as abuse perpetrated collectively by society. Our affluent society certainly seems to possess the resources and the skills to eradicate the massive forms of abuse committed by society collectively as well as the physical violence perpetrated by individuals and societal institutions against children in their care.

REFERENCES

Gil, David G. 1970 "A systematic approach to social policy analysis." The Social Service Review 44 (December).
Kempe, D. Henry et al. 1962 "The battered child syndrome" Journal American Medical Association 181 (17).
U.S. Children's Bureau 1962 The Abused Child: Principles and Suggested Language on Reporting the Physically Abused Child. Washington, D.C.: U.S. Government Printing Office.
1966 The Child Abuse Reporting Laws—A Tabular View. Washington, D.C.: U.S. Government Printing Office.
1969 Bibliography on the Battered Child. Washington, D.C.: Clearinghouse for Research in Child Life, U.S. Government Printing Office.

6

Kommune 2: Childrearing in the Commune[*]

CHRISTEL BOOKHAGEN, EIKE HEMMER,
JAN RASPE, EBERHARD SCHULTZ

THE MOST STRIKING CHARACTERISTIC of the "sex wave" currently sweeping Germany's mass media is the attention being devoted to a pseudo-serious discussion of the extended family and communal life. No longer is it enough to raise aloft the image of the intact family in answer to the misery of living life at the mercy of the pie-in-the-sky promises made in the name of total consumption. The ideologists of this family ideal still cry out at the filth, sexual perversion, child neglect and disregard for private property they see in the communes. Yet at the same time they are seeking ways to explain rejection of one man, one woman life: the love-hate syndrome, brutality, the suppression of woman and child are no longer seen as individual tragedy but rather in terms of the apparently historical fate of the nuclear family in our society.

In the early capitalist era (according to the studies on *Autorität und Familie*, published in 1936 by the Frankfurt Institute for Social Research) the family carried out a specific set of rational functions for both the individual and society. As the smallest independent production unit, it served to transmit socially essential knowledge and the cultural techniques necessary for later job training. This gave the justification for the father's rational authority. In addition, the family functioned as the basis for joint reproduction, for consumption, and for the sexual satisfaction of the adults. In a squandering capitalism, all these objective functions of the family are reduced to consumption. In this

[*] Translation from the German original by Adriana Gottwald.

kind of capitalism the nuclear family is the most profitable unit for the consumption of "essential luxury articles" (such as television sets and washing machines) which can be produced with planned obsolescence in mind in a socially unnecessary volume. The family continues to remain the most important socialization center for the capitalist system, for with its authoritarian and pleasure-denying education it produces the desired conformist, passive, bourgeois character.

The family as psychic refuge against social competition and the pressures to achieve is steadily disintegrating. The tenacity with which the family continues to survive under late capitalism is not due simply to its economic function. Under prevailing conditions, women and children are still not able to do without the economic and social guarantee of a "secure existence" as provided by the family, although this security is brought at the price of a decisive measure of suppression. With the loss of the positive psychic function the family once had for the individual, aggressiveness has increased in the more advanced capitalistic societies, permeating even the most intimate human relations. Vietnam crops up again and again in the growing tendency toward sadistic and masochistic forms of sexual gratification, in partner-swapping and in the commercialization of stimulants to increase potency. Highly developed forms of ersatz gratification are supplemented by the open propagation of coitus for its own sake; all erotic contact is reduced to the physiological functions which are thought to bring about the orgiastic *Endsieg*.

The objective of the first Berlin communes, which were established in 1967 in conjunction with the radical student movement, was to overcome and do away with the bourgeois family's traditional forms of domination. People everywhere were fascinated—some positively, some negatively—by the attempt to overcome individual isolation by creating a nexus between the private sphere and revolutionary politics. Even in the anti-authoritarian camp, the new way of life met with rejection as well as enthusiasm. Left wing theoreticians saw it as a collective designed exclusively for work and militant action—or, at best, as a suitable vehicle for making the transition from puberty to a new type of family—and, in this sense, gave their approval. Thus Reimut Reiche, writing in *Sexualität und Klassenkampf* in 1968, issued the following programmatical warning:

There is one classical family function that this type of commune can only assume with difficulty, if at all: childrearing. As Brückner says, "One cannot play around with the socialization process"— a statement that should be taken very seriously. In none of the highly developed industrial nations do we find one single example of a functioning model for infant socialization, other than the family, that could possibly produce significantly better results than what, on average, comes out of the more successful incidences (or accidents) of family socialization at the hands of normal or loving parents, given generally favorable secondary conditions (a secure income; good living conditions; role distribution between the parents; time the mother can devote to the child). (p. 160)

Reiche's matter-of-fact enumeration of the conditions needed for successful socialization tends to obscure the matter in point: the theoretical and practical critique of the bourgeois, constraining family. The "happy family" is being smuggled back in as the normal one through the back door of affirmative childrearing. Reiche fails to point out that "normal" families are incapable of loving and the existing family structure can only be maintained in the presence of extreme constraints on all its members. In the material sphere, this pressure is brought to bear through the irrational economic dependency of wife and child. The erotic and sexual desires that are constantly aroused by the promises held out by consumption cannot be satisfied in an institutional framework that is based on mutual dependency.

Material and psychic dependency prevents the total disintegration of the family as institution from producing a corresponding increase in the number of divorces. Instead, the majority of married people make life hell for one another. It is the children, above all, who are affected by the pressure. The average nuclear family produces clinging, unstable individuals who have a fixation on infantile needs and irrational authority-figures. This fact remains despite the parents' good intentions or their childrearing practices. Only a radical break with the traditional triangular family structure can clear the way for forms of collective living in which the individual is able to develop new needs and imagination with the goal of creating a new human being in a revolutionized society.

The solution to the problem of the neglected, rebellious child in particular, and childrearing in general, depends on whether and how it will prove possible to prevent the incestuous and guilt-ridden hate-bind between parents and children from playing a role in the development of the psychic structure. It follows that this cannot succeed if the children are not introduced to collective childrearing *before* they are able to develop emotionally destructive ties to the parents—in other words, even *before* the age of four. This means destruction *not* of the natural ties of affection between parents and children, only of the neurotic ones. There will certainly be no solution to this problem if the contradiction between collective and family is not overcome in a broader social context. (Wilhelm Reich, *Die sexuelle Revolution*, Frankfurt, 1966, p. 316)

Reich's statement touches one of the central issues of what was then called the *Sexpol* movement. This is why childrearing is a matter of central concern for the communes, which are carrying forth the ideas developed in the Thirties in the context of the socialist movement. In the following pages we shall describe our experience in one of these communes, placing the focus on childrearing. This contribution has been taken in part from a book on *Kommune 2*, in which the political significance of this new form of living was analyzed in greater detail.

In view of the public discussion we feel it is necessary to make brief mention here of the distinction between the extended family and the commune. The extended family, limited in its objectives to promoting a freer mode of interaction among its members without taking their work situation into account, can certainly provide existential relief for those involved. However, just as is the case which the movement toward sexual liberation, collective forms of living are liable to become integrated into the present system as long as the individual members of such collectives go on, individually, in their jobs, fulfilling their social function. This can seem to do away with the contradiction inherent in the family as an instrument of constraint, but it does not attack the actual source of repression. It is an illusion to assume that individual and social relations can be totally revolutionized by simply multiplying the number of new, collective forms of living. What matters is to politicize the contradictions that emerge as the nuclear family dissolves and so create a revolutionary consciousness capable of doing away with the fundamental contradiction that exists between social production and private appropriation under the capitalist mode of production.

Communes can claim to have a revolutionizing effect only if they take part in political organizing to further the struggle in the institutions, factories and workshops. A beginning toward establishing such collectives in the production sphere is being made in West Berlin in the communes set up by younger workers and apprentices. Only in a very limited sense is our experience applicable to these communes. It still has to be considered a privilege to be free, as students, from having to perform alienated work. We hope to be able to justify the luxury of our greater freedom by working toward the goal of abolishing privilege for once and for all.

THE CREATION OF KOMMUNE 2

We understood the commune as a political collective when we set out to establish it early in 1967. Through it, we wanted to draw the organizational consequences from our SDS activity during the previous months. The commune was initiated by a group of about 30 comrades, all of whom had played a leading part in the first provocatory actions carried out in West Berlin. The group was composed primarily of students, members of the SDS. In view of the struggle for emancipation in the colonial world, they were no longer merely satisfied with developing a theoretical critique of the status quo, but rather wanted to proceed to the practical matter of revolution. All the time we had been dreaming of a liberated society, romantically identifying ourselves with the guerrillas in Latin America, our everyday life continued to be dominated by the almost unbroken norms and constraints of capitalist society. This could be clearly seen in the status of women in SDS, who gave the men's discussions a decorative touch and otherwise were relegated to the private sphere. During our first night-time poster-pasting sorties and confrontations with the police over something other than possible traffic or registration violations, we were inhibited by anxieties that were constantly reinforced by the bourgeois life we were leading. As isolated individuals we were again and again forced to conform by our fear of the landlady, the professor, bureaucratic officials and by the overwhelming power of capitalism in everyday matters. We knew that genocide in Vietnam was part of this everyday life. But when we tried to challenge this life—say, on some isolated point such as traffic regulations—we ran up against an inner resistance, a functional mechanism that had been built into us, day for day. The idea of moving together into a collective grew out of our theoretically motivated radical determination to revolutionize all prevailing conditions, as well as out of our need to create our own milieu in order to make us psychologically more fit for rebellion.

In February 1967, seven adults and two children moved into the SDS Center in Berlin. They wanted to work together politically. Little time passed, however, before individual problems began to dominate the scene. There was no overlooking the fact that while the men sat around talking politics, the women were doing the cooking. Or, living as we were all day together, a troubled relationship could no longer be concealed behind carefully erected private walls. Although we had initially believed that in the process of political cooperation individual difficulties would become amenable to group treatment, we quickly discovered that before we could settle down to productive political work we would first have to deal with individual problems that for years had been ignored (inability to maintain a loving relationship, incompatible marriages). In our preoccupation with ourselves we became annoyed by the political demands our SDS comrades would make upon us. In August of the same year we moved out of the SDS Center.

In our new apartment we were four men (three of them

students), three women and two children, at that time three and four years old. The girl's mother and the boy's father lived with us in the commune.

ORGANIZATION OF EVERYDAY LIFE

Without any set program, certain customary patterns had developed in our everyday life. All income—for the most part from scholarships and from re-issuing out-of-print books —went into a common kitty. All expenses were paid from this kitty. Commune members took turns, two a day, doing the shopping, cooking and washing up. We also intended to raise the children collectively and work together on political projects.

After two years of living together, we can summarize our positive experiences in jointly organizing our everyday life:

1. Consumption can be more rationally organized in a collective. Together, we required less money than we did earlier to satisfy the same needs on an individual basis.

2. By providing the money and organizing expenditures on a collective basis, each person was relieved of the pressure of having to work individually, for himself or his family, and of having to devote a considerable amount of energy to managing his budget.

3. If it did not happen to be one's duty day—which, with seven people, came up twice a week—then one was completely relieved of all household cares. There was no need to bother about shopping and cooking, looking after the children or cleaning up. For those, at least, who had previously had to care for their children on their own, this meant that they had more time for themselves and their own interests.

4. Since men and women had the same household and child-care duties, we were able to do away with some of the socially determined division of labor according to sex. According to society's role definition, men and women are ascribed specific spheres of activity and modes of behavior. This means that all perceptive, expressive and productive capabilities that are not defined by sexual role are curtailed or suppressed. In organizing our everyday life together, we learned that there is no biological distinction between man and woman in the desire and ability to cook, dance, chose clothes or express the need for affection. Thus, each individual found a greater opportunity to express his individual potential.

CONFLICTS AND ATTEMPTS TO RESOLVE THEM

The second important improvement in connection with communal living lay in our attempt to deal with conflicts systematically. At the beginning, we gathered practically every evening to talk about daily irritations, the interplay of aggressions or individual grumpiness. We felt the need to share problems that, up to then, each of us had had to contend with individually. Bourgeois standards force the individual to suppress his spontaneous emotions to a very large extent. Wilhelm Reich has described this suppression as "character armor-plating" (cf. *Charakteranalyse*, 1st ed., 1933). In a society in which each person is in competition with the other, no one can afford to display his inner weakness (anxiety, sadness, the need for tenderness and love) except in the rare intimacy of a love affair. The pressure of having to come up on top in a competitive situation—to perform and excel, as we experienced this in SDS political discussions—makes people continually steel themselves against their own desires and vent the most malicious kind of aggression toward other people's needs.

In the commune we gradually learned to recognize our own suppressed needs in those of the others. When, for example, one of us related what kind of anxieties he felt during his first semesters at the university (nervous perspiration, speech inhibition in class) and then would hear how another member of the group described having the same difficulty, then he became more secure in having recognized himself in the other's description. It became easier for him to discuss his own problems. This new chance to talk openly about our anxieties and experience one another as weak gave us all an immediate sense of relief, one we often felt at the end of these group discussions. However, we soon ran up against a barrier. We discovered that we could only express our emotions in abstract terms, not spontaneously. Certain conflict situations emerged again and again; in other words, we had not succeeded in penetrating through to their real causes.

One typical conflict erupted each time a new couple-relationship developed within the group. Trivial incidents would escalate into highly aggressive conflicts which would then affect the whole group. Such aggressive behavior as slamming doors and yelling at each other failed to function as a release for either of the persons involved, but rather made the women depressive. Nor was it possible to resolve sexual conflicts simply by labelling them and discussing them with the others. We were forced to delve into the childhood roots of such difficulties, and we tried to develop methods of group analysis. The main characteristics of this method were: 1, one member of the group would analyze another member in the presence of the group, which functioned as a control factor; 2, the "analyst" would actively respond to the "analysand's" wishes to the extent this was necessary in order to give him an opportunity for alternative experiences to his own infantile anxieties; 3, despite our theoretical misgivings about it, we had to do without a trained analyst. Through analysis we succeeded in releasing emotions and repressed urges. This had the immediate effect of producing a greater degree of spontaneity and lovingness in all members of the group. After three months we had to discontinue the analysis, however, for the dynamics created by all our released desires, fantasies and infantile demands threatened to obliterate every reference point in reality. Since we were all simultaneously involved in this process, we lacked a person who would have been able to relativize all the impulses being released.

A collective such as ours, in which no one was forced to work regularly, stands in danger of gradually losing all reference to social reality. This loss of reality and preoccupation with a utopian fantasy world can be observed in many subcultural groups in West Germany and West Berlin, particularly those in which hallucogenic drugs and opiates are used. We were frequently tempted—particularly during the group analysis phase—to succumb to the desire for total regression into an infantile dream world. We envisioned a state of affairs in which every form of external organization would be done away with, where every person could sleep as long as he wanted and eat whenever he felt like it, and no one would have to clean up, wash dishes or go shopping unless he happened to want to. We wanted to set up a common bedroom, listen to music, dance, and simply play together as our children do. On the basis of the observations we can now make of other groups, we are inclined to doubt whether this form of collective regression has any therapeutic effect if, in the long run, the collective fails to develop any other common activity. The lack of a factor representing the reference to external reality (such as parents do in childhood) seems as a rule to lead to a progressive disintegration of the psychic structure rather than help develop personalities that are more autonomous and resistent to social manipulation.

We were able to indulge in our regressive desires only to a limited extent, and never as a group or for any longer period of time, because our original political understanding and the existence of the children continued to represent an objective reality.

THE ARRIVAL OF THE CHILDREN

When the children joined us (up to September 1967 they had lived in *Kommune 1*), they both bore the marks of traumatic experiences: for Nessim, a four year old boy, it had been his parents' separation and mother's leaving; for Grischa, a three year old girl, it had been the temporary separation from her unmarried mother. Nessim's father and Grischa's mother were now living with us in the commune.

Not all of us had been in favor of bringing the children into the group. K. and Jan felt that children would upset our group relationship and disturb their own concentration on their studies. Eike was afraid he would have to bear sole responsibility for rearing Nessim. At that time, Nessim was extremely closely tied to his father. On walks together he would cling to his father's hand. Through the loss of his mother he had developed a strongly passive, feminine posture vis-à-vis his father, evidenced by his tendency to avoid all competition with Eike. He would try, for example, to climb a tree. If Eike climbed up, Nessim would give up immediately, whining, "I can't do it." Eike felt over-burdened and strongly inhibited by this exclusive claim on him. He therefore demanded that the group rear Nessim collectively. Marion, Grischa's mother, made the same claim on the group. The rest of us looked forward to the new experience, and although we were all very much in agreement with the plan to look after and rear the children as a collective endeavor, there was one reservation: they should not monopolize our lives. Thus we made arrangements for them to attend a public nursery school. Although the nursery school was already full, the commune children were accepted immediately. The child welfare authorities seemed highly relieved that we were voluntarily prepared to place the children under state control, thus sparing the administration the trouble of having to venture into some wild-eyed anarchists' den to look after the "well-being of the children." Only in terms of biological instinct can the proto-fascist bourgeoisie grasp the fact that left-wing radicals are capable of loving their children.

In a column that appeared in the *Tagesspiegel* on October 7, 1967, the author struggled to establish an analogy to the wolf and its cubs:

Don't the members of these so-called communes make too little use of soap and morals? It's a two-edged question in the sense that morals, understood as a convention—and on closer examination, what else would they be, more a detergent than a token of cleanliness. And second, what prevents a person who provokes others by dress and behavior from showering more often than a social conformist? However reluctant one is to accordingly dump the communards out with the bathwater of individually and socially motivated hygenic prejudices, one still has the suspicion that their brood may have to do without nest-warmth altogether. Each of the communes has a nestling whose welfare had to be officially attested when application was made for the children—three and four years old—to attend all-day nursery school. Prior to this, the customary interview had taken place with the parents and according to official reports, their concern met up to middle-class standards very well indeed. As far as the children are concerned, the district commissioner for juvenile affairs could not conceal a certain amount of surprise when he reported that they are altogether well nourished, strikingly well groomed, seem to be well behaved, and had no difficulty fitting in with the group of middle-class tots. This could prompt one to say: why not? Even the wolf looks after its cubs. Well enough—but what wolf is accustomed to behave as differently from other wolves, as these communards do?

Right down to the fully garbled sentences, this article reveals the burgher's helplessness in the face of his antagonist's humanity.

PHASE 1: INTELLECTUALIZED CHILDREARING

In order to prevent the children from once again clinging to their parents exclusively, we organized child-care on the same basis as we had our other everyday duties. We took turns getting up with the children to help them dress, fix their breakfast and take them to nursery school. Another would pick them up, play with them until dinner and bring them to bed in the room they shared.

At the beginning, the goal of our collective approach to childrearing was to loosen and then abolish the children's fixation on their respective parents. The children were to be given an opportunity to enter into more intensive relations with several adults so that they could carry their wishes and anxieties to persons other than their parents. Our aim was to raise the children to be independent.

In retrospect we can see that the men's behavior toward the children was marked by a rigid schematism. They frequently pushed through their way of doing things against the children's expressed wishes. If at bedtime a child demanded to see a particular adult, the answer was often, "It's not his turn today!" If a child cried, it was usually his own parent who comforted him. This sometimes brought criticism from Eberhard, who felt that in such cases the person on duty that day ought to look after the child. The children were expected to wash and dress themselves, and often the adult whose "turn" it was would wait half an hour before responding to the children's wish to be dressed rather than dress themselves. At that time, we were proceeding from a schematic evaluation of the children's level of development. We thought that, at three and four, they ought to be old enough to dress themselves and overlooked the fact that the children's emotional development had been held up by traumatic experiences. Their refusal to independently employ certain abilities commensurate with their physical maturity stemmed from their wish to regress into the state in which, as babies, their mothers had lovingly cared for them.

Anna Freud has described the mechanism of intellectualization in children and adolescents as a means by which they come to terms with overwhelming inner drives:

In general, asceticism, the outright denial of his urges, fails to give the juvenile what he expects it should. Since the danger remains immediate for the time being, he has to seek out many means for overcoming it. One such means seems to lie in thinking out the conflict of urges—in intellectualizing it. In this case, instead of escaping from the drive, as in asceticism, one confronts it directly. But confronting it remains an intellectual act. What the youth achieves in his abstract intellectual conversations and accomplishments has nothing to do with seeking to solve the problems posed by reality. Instead, his intellectual effort amounts to an intense alertness to inner drives and to a translation of what he feels into abstract thought. (Anna Freud, *Das Ich und die Abwehrmechanismen*, Kindler, Munich, p. 126)

Without going into Anna Freud's rather problematical notion of defense, we would like to note that the fear of inner drives is always preceded by some real, external threat that through prohibitions, punishment and withdrawal of affection has impaired or blocked satisfaction of the child's urges. We know that a substantial portion of these sanctions against infantile drives is imposed by the parents unconsciously, more likely in the form of a repressive emotional atmosphere than through verbal dictates or proscriptions. If the mere registration of an inner urge is distressing to the ego, then it can be assumed that any expression of the urge is or was at one time associated with an external threat.

In keeping with their middle-class background and education at high school and college, the four men displayed this rationalizing approach to human emotions to a very marked degree. They had difficulty in interpreting the children's actions intuitively and they had to make a constant effort to press these actions into intellectual categories in order to understand them and be able to react to them. When the children intentionally swept their food off the table or urinated on the floor, the men would ask angrily, "Why did you do that?" or "What's that supposed to mean?"

It took us some time to realize that this apparently wanton destruction of food had the nature of a signal; that, by doing this, the children wanted us to see something—that we adults, for instance, had always talked among ourselves at meals, ignoring the children. Since they were unable to protest verbally against this lack of attention, they did it by means of a provocative act that we adults could not help but notice. It took us a very long time to learn to respond to infantile modes of communication. That we could, first became apparent in play situations where the children would go on and on imitating our words or delight in twisting them around.

Here is an example from the reports we kept, among other reasons, to record our children's development:

Both children want to operate the elevator at the same time. (For the children, to operate the elevator by themselves means to satisfy their desire to be independent and identify with the adults, and so for a time this was an emotionally highly sensitive matter.) At first, the adults often sought to settle the conflict between the children by rational argument: Grischa can push the button today, and tomorrow it's Nessim's turn. That usually produced a violent protest on the part of the one who had to be put off until the next day. The postponement of wish-fulfillment until what, for the child, is a far-off point in time seemed anything but pleasurable. The apparently rational justice, meted out at the adult level, was not acceptable to the children. They found a better way to solve the conflict on their own. Nessim, for example, would say: now it's my turn, and then it's yours. This developed into a word game which ran something like this: I can push it now—you later; your turn now—mine later; me me—you, too; not you—me me, etc. When the adults joined in, this turned out to be great fun for all. The conflict dissolved in the pleasure of playing, and the postponement of the wish to operate the elevator no longer seemed exclusively unpleasurable and could thus be accepted by the child.

It was far easier for the women than for the men to respond spontaneously to infantile forms of expression. Although on balance the rationalistic approach dominated and the children's needs were consequently often frustrated, one can say that this first phase of communal life had the positive result that the parents were relieved of exclusive responsibility for their respective children. This gave the parent an opportunity to develop a degree of detachment toward his own behavior vis-à-vis the child and critically examine his own entrenched irrational reactions with the help of the group's more objective observations.

Expanded Latitude for Free Expression

Day's report: It's duty day for Eberhard and Jan. Eberhard gets up at eight o'clock. The children have been up for two hours and are romping around the apartment, naked. They have fetched bananas from the pantry and have eaten them, along with the raisins. Sugar is scattered all over the kitchen. Things look pretty chaotic. Eberhard tries to suppress his irritation. He asks the children, "Shall we all clean up?" The children run out of the kitchen. Eberhard takes a rag and wipes off the table. He calls out to the children to get dressed. When he comes into the children's room five minutes later, Grischa has one sock on. Nessim is playing under the blanket. Grischa doesn't want to go to nursery school. Eberhard: "Why don't you want to go to nursery school?" Grischa: "Just don't." Eberhard tries to convince her: "Look, Grischa, there's still time to go for a walk and buy some gum, and this afternoon I'll come and get you, and the three of us can go and pick up the VW bus from the garage." Grischa: "Is the bus ready?" Eberhard explains what was the matter with the bus. Grischa sits down on the bed and gets dressed with Eberhard's assistance. She doesn't want the dress he hands her. She wants the one with the red polka dots. Eberhard tries to explain that that dress is dirty and needs to be washed. Grischa insists on the polka dot dress. Eberhard puts it on her. Nessim makes no attempt to get dressed. Eberhard hands him his pants and a shirt and says, "Here, put these on." Nessim: "Can't. You help me." Eberhard: "Come on, you can get dressed by yourself." Nessim refuses. Finally, Eberhard has to dress him since time is running out. He takes them to nursery school and picks them up at five o'clock.

Jan has cooked dinner. The children eat at the same table with the seven adults. Grischa wants to help herself to the noodles. She takes a huge portion and wants to pile on even more. Jan: "Start eating and when you're finished you can have more." Nessim doesn't want anything to eat. Nobody pressures him. After watching the others for a few minutes, he helps himself. He finishes half, gets up and goes over to his father, saying: "I want to come up on your lap."

All stay at the table for twenty minutes, talking, while the children shove chairs together to make a train. Then Jan says to them, "Come, let's go into your room." But the children don't want to go to bed yet. Jan suggests that they first take a bath and then play for a while in their room. Grischa dashes off to the bedroom, followed in due course by Nessim. Nessim and

Grischa stay in the tub for a long time, playing with boats, fooling around and splashing water all over the floor. After they are dried off, brought to bed, and their hair is dried with the drier, they romp on the beds, hide under the blanket, toss the blanket over Jan's head, and then protest when he places a dark green cloth over the lamp for the night. The children want Jan to stay and tell them a story. Nessim wants to hear about airplanes. Jan complies and is frequently interrupted by Nessim, who changes the story according to his own wishes and notions. Grischa has meanwhile fallen asleep. Nessim stays awake for a while and wants Eike to come in.

It should be added that when Eike and Marion are home, they make it a rule to go in to see the children at night and play with them for a while.

When the children demanded attention, we took pains to avoid continually reacting with sanctions and aggressive behavior even when their way of expressing themselves clashed with our previous notions of cleanliness and order. In doing this, it often happened at the beginning that we gave in to the temptation to use manipulation in order to break down the children's defense against some particular demand. (Cf. the report on Eberhard's attempt to get Grischa to drop her clearly expressed opposition to going to nursery school by diverting her attention with talk about the VW bus.) One often encounters this subtle form of repression among liberal parents who are reluctant to issue open sanctions or use physical force. This prevents the child from recognizing the conflict that objectively exists between his own wishes and his parents' demands. His aggressive energy cannot be vented against the source of the repression and must find other outlets. With this kind of upbringing, the child will either tend to strike out indiscriminately or will masochistically turn his aggression against himself, as we see in the whining and nagging of some children.

Our group discussions quickly put us on the track of tendencies to play down the children's needs by manipulation. When there seemed to be no other choice, we preferred to issue straightforward prohibitions (and tried to justify them) rather than use tricks to prevent the children from doing certain things such as using the record player or playing in the study.

In important spheres the children enjoyed a great deal more freedom to do as they pleased than there would be in the bourgeois family. We tried as much as possible not to interfere with their play or force ourselves upon them with store-bought toys and story-telling. The toy-filled children's room is the corollary to the sanction against playing with objects from the adult world. In the commune apartment, the children had considerable liberty to use furnishings and utensils—mattresses, chairs, tables, kitchen utensils—in their games. We feel it is important for the process of mastering reality through play that particularly those adult-world objects that are threatening be stripped of their set function and receive a new one in play (for instance, when chairs are assembled into a train). As our reports show, the children were not forced to eat or empty their plates. We preferred to let them wear soiled clothes if they really wanted to, and we did not let ourselves be bothered by the nursery school teacher's disapproval. We felt that a child's attachment to a particular piece of clothing was more important than the exaggerated social pressure to be clean. Until well in the fall, the children bathed every evening. In this way we did not have to urge them to wash, instead achieving the same goal by letting it be the by-product, as it were, of an activity that the children found highly pleasurable—playing in the tub. Only in the morning before they went to nursery school did we wash their faces and we all joined in in washing hands.

Ah-Ah, Po-Po, Pee-Pee: Reactivating the Anal Phase

In our society, toilet training is central to the development of authority-oriented, ego deficient individuals. In psychoanalysis, the psychic structure that displays particularly strong signs of repressive training during the anal phase, is known as the anal character.

The anal character is distinguished by the fact that the ego-capabilities that ought to expand in the process of coming to terms with anal pleasure (namely the various orderly functions that develop on the basis of a systematic control of bowel activity) are asserted in a particularly rigid, ruthless and uncompromising fashion. Fastidious, conscientious and socially intimidated parents feel their child's unsocialized and instinctual nature in no way more strongly than in his anal delight, in his obstinacy in clinging to the products of these body zones as to dearly loved objects. The means by which this delight is driven out of the child are the same means by which his ego-capabilities are deformed. This we see in the anal character's punctuality, conscientiousness, in his warped approach to sexual objects, and in the rigidity that governs all his actions. (R. Reiche, *Sexualität und Klassenkampf*, p. 35)

The example of Nessim shows that in the commune it was possible to correct part of what had gone wrong during earlier developmental phases. Nessim had learned to control his bowel movements at age one and a half. At that time he was spending six weeks with his grandmother, separated from his parents. When Nessim came into the commune, he expressed revulsion in the face of filth, and kept himself quite clean when eating and playing. If he saw dog turd on the street, he would sometimes say "Ugh!" and would get upset if he happened to step in it. He showed little interest in making mud pies or playing with clay or paints. If he painted, he only drew contours and seldom filled in a space. For a period of several weeks he was anxious on walks to avoid stepping on the cracks in the pavement. (We see this avoidance compulsion in adult neuroses. It is always connected with the fantasy that by adhering to the compulsive rule, an unpleasant event could be avoided or a desired one occur. Many children's games revolve around attempts to deal with this compulsion—the result of toilet training—not to step on or over certain lines. In playing "Heaven and Hell," for example, the object is to hop across certain marked fields without stepping on the dividing lines. The winner goes to heaven, the loser lands in hell. In play children seek to assimilate the notions of order their parents demand they observe.)

Nessim was very responsive to rational arguments and readily suppressed his own wishes when the adults took pains to explain intellectually the necessity of doing so.

Excerpt from a report by Jan:

Petra and I were eating; standing on the table was a portion of curds left over for our dessert. Nessim stood at the table and asked us very earnestly whether we were eating, whether we were planning to also eat the curds, and then something to the effect that we shouldn't eat any because he wanted some. We asked him whether he had any and he answered, shame-faced, that he had. Petra and I went on eating. Nessim sat all the while at the table, playing. Finally we came to the fatal dessert. I had intended to give him some and offered him a spoonful. I had to ask him a couple of times before he even looked up. Then, with a sadly serious expression on his face, he said in an even tone—terribly reasonably—"No, I've already had some." I asked him, "Don't you want some more? You can have part of mine." This he accepted and came happily over to me, and of course he couldn't get enough.

As time went on, some of the urges repressed in the anal phase became reactivated and were expressed, for instance, in an obvious interest in excrement. Nessim and Grischa often delighted in repeating over and over such word games as "ah-ah, po-po, pee-pee." During one vacation, Nessim would stop at every dunghill, delightedly say "muck!" and then ask what animal it came from. We would respond, come to a stop every time and explain patiently that this is from a horse, that from a donkey. We tried to reinforce Nessim's newly awakened interest in excrement without showing any aversion. Because of his previous developmental difficulties in this respect, we felt it was important not only to let Nessim have his way, but also to clearly affirm his anal interest. After two years in the commune, the positive effect could be seen in his much less compulsive attitude toward cleanliness. Excrement no longer particularly interests him, nor does he show any aversion. When he paints, he is much freer, covering large spaces with strong colors. He no longer displays compulsive symptoms such as the previously described avoidance of lines. He has become freer and less inhibited in his whole behavior. Only after we had learned to release our own repressed urges were we able to come around to this emotionally, not just intellectually affirmative attitude toward anality (Eike, for example, ceased to be nauseated when he cleaned the sink).

PHASE 2: LOOSENING THE HOLD OF FIXATIONS

For months after the children came into the commune, both continued to feel the shock of having been separated from their mothers. Grischa developed an enormous appetite. She was forever stuffing anything she could into her mouth and vehemently demanded a pacifier, which she would keep in her mouth even out on the street. There was something clearly aggressive about the way she gobbled her food. This regression into an emphasis on oral behavior revealed her desire to return to the state of affairs that had existed before her temporary separation from her mother. At first, Grischa was unable to openly express her aggressive feelings toward her mother, feelings that stemmed from her fury over her mother's temporary disappearance. These impulses surfaced in her urge to aggressively devour her food. If one failed to grant her wishes, she would throw herself onto the floor, roll up in a ball and refuse to respond to anyone at all. Is someone touched her, she would lash out with her legs and scream, "Leave me alone!"

During the first few months, Nessim rejected all gestures of affection from women. If they caressed him or wanted to cuddle him, he would push them away, demanding that they leave him alone. He never mentioned his mother. If he wanted something, he would usually ask for it in a whining tone. During this time, both children tended to wake up, screaming, in the middle of the night. It was impossible to get them to say what was upsetting them. If one asked, they just went on crying spasmodically.

We had no success at first with our plan to gradually loosen the children's fixation on their respective parents. Whenever the two of them fought, sought affection or were frightened, they generally tended to turn to their respective parent. As time went on, however, it turned out that the opportunity to let out their feelings, as it were, on a trial basis vis-à-vis other adults gradually enabled the children to vent aggression against their own parents. Nessim, in particular, avoided all outward signs of aggression toward his father for a long time.

Excerpt from a report by Jan:

Nessim, Jan and Eike are sitting in the main room. Jan and Nessim are rough-housing. Jan tries to grab Nessim, Nessim runs away and then edges closer again and tries to hit Jan. Nessim is deeply involved in this playful tussling, laughs delightedly, and doesn't need to be considerate of Jan. He strikes out as hard as he can, displaying no fear. Suddenly we're interrupted by the telephone and Jan goes to answer it. In the meantime, Eike tries to go on playing with Nessim. But Nessim acts as if transformed: he abruptly stops playing, obviously can't rough-house with Eike, starts to whine and says, "No, no. When he's off the telephone I'll go on fighting with Jan."

Today, Nessim energetically hits Eike or calls him names if he happens to be angry at him. The child's ability to vent aggression against his own parent developed parallel to his ability to turn to other members of the commune for the affection he needs. The children's libidinous fixation on their parents lost its exclusiveness to the extent that the relationship of the adults among one another took on a more libidinous character. During the time the analysis was going on, the group developed its greatest degree of internal cohesion and stability. Group integration ceased to be merely a program, and we developed strong libidinous ties to one another. During this phase, the children turned more and more often to other adults for the satisfaction of their needs, accepting them to some extent as ersatz-parents. Nessim's defensive rejection of women began to break down; he gradually came around to accept their affection and began to demand it. Grischa developed a strong and affectionate attachment to Eberhard. Whereas up to this point Nessim had clearly dominated in play, never letting Grischa do more than assist, she now began to create her own games. The tantrums and nightly screaming ceased. The more the adults broke through their emotional barriers through analysis, the more spontaneous and less intellectualized their behavior became toward the children. Although at the beginning the children had stood more or less on the fringe of our communal life, now we began giving them more and more attention. In the children we discovered the same repressed urges we ourselves had become aware of in the analysis, and this helped us to develop a much greater understanding of their non-verbal forms of self-expression. The greater degree of sensitivity that we had acquired through analysis and our intensive observation of the children helped us to learn to better understand our own concealed desires and needs.

Excerpt from a report by Eike, April 23, 1968:

It's evening, and both children are lying in bed. I caress Nessim, fondling his penis, as well. Grischa: "I want a penis." I try to explain to her that after all she has a vagina that one can caress, too. Grischa rejects this: "I want a penis for pissing like him." I recalled a conversation with the psychoanalyst, Hans Killian, in which we talked hypothetically about the possibility that men no longer need to regard their penis as their sole property. I say: "Well, Grischa, you *can* have Nasser's (Nessim's) penis. You can fondle it!" Grischa responds immediately and wants to stroke Nessim's penis. At first, Nessim refuses, clearly afraid that Grischa will launch an aggressive attack on his penis. I tell them that the penis has to be stroked very gently. Nessim is now willing, but insists on fondling Grischa's vagina, as well. Grischa backs off the way Nessim had done. I tell them that one must stroke the vagina very gently, too. Now both are in agreement, but they argue about who is to have the first turn. It's all right with Nessim that Grischa stroke his penis first. Argument about how many times she may. She wants to "lots and lots," and counts how many times on her fingers. Nasser says only once. I mediate. Grischa strokes Nasser's penis very gently with one finger and then, just as gently, Nasser plays with Grischa's vagina. Then the two try to copulate.

Eike's ability to imagine himself in the children's situation and overcome their fear of being touched in the genital region is surely connected with his own renewed experience of castration anxiety during analysis and with his improved capacity to deal with it. Children become aware of sexual differences quite early. Learning to deal with this on the emotional and intellectual levels is one of the most important steps in the development of the child's personality. As our reports show, we tried to behave in such a way as to help the children understand sexual differences not as an anxiety-producing threat, but rather as an opportunity for entering into an affectionate relationship with another person.

Affirmation, not Tolerance of Infantile Sexuality

To us, a positive attitude toward infantile sexuality means not only explaining sexual functions to the children openly but also that one must be emotionally prepared to appreciate the pleasurable sensations children experience in connection with their own genital spheres.

However minor the difference between mere tolerance and affirmation of infantile and pubertal sexuality may seem on the surface, it is decisive for the formation of the youngster's psychic structure. The tolerant attitude prevailing in small circles of people concerned with childrearing can be seen as nothing less than total sexual negation. The child senses tolerance as non-punishment for something that is basically forbidden; moreover, mere tolerance or a "permissive attitude" toward sexual play fails to offset the overpowering pressures exerted by the social climate. An explicit and unmistakable affirmation of infantile sexuality on the part of those responsible for the child's unbringing can, on the other hand, provide the basis for the formation of ego-structure components that affirm sexuality even if they are not able to counteract the social influences. This view is to be understood as criticism of the behavior of those psychoanalysts who do not dare to take the important step from tolerance to affirmation. It is nothing less than shirking responsibility to maintain that this is a matter that ought to be left up to the children. Just as one should never force something on the child that the infantile organism does not want, it is indispensible that support be given those tendencies in the child or patient that are leaning toward sexual economy. Society's sexual barrier stands between tolerance of sexuality and its affirmation. To say yes to sexuality means to overcome the social barrier." (Wilhelm Reich, *Der Einbruch der Sexualmoral*, 2nd ed., Copenhagen, 1935)

The following report by Christel demonstrates how important infantile sexuality is for the understanding of social roles and social abilities:

February 25, 1968. It's evening. The children are in bed chatting with Christel and Petra. Topic: babies (something that has often interested Nessim).

Nessim: How little are babies? (Measuring with his hands, bringing them closer and closer together.)

Christel: They're about this big when they are born. (Shows him with her hands.)

Nessim: What does that mean, to be born?

Christel: Babies are tiny to begin with (showing him) and then they grow in the woman's belly—you've surely seen a young woman on the street with a big, big belly. She had a baby in her belly, and when it's big, then it comes out. (Shows how big.)

Nessim: How?

Christel: Through the vagina.

Nessim: And how does it get into the vagina?—I wasn't in a vagina.

Christel: No, babies grow in the woman's belly.

Nessim: I once had a baby.

Petra: No you didn't, but *you* were once a baby.

Christel: Only women can have babies. You know that Grischa has a vagina, and you have a penis. When a boy and a girl care about each other very much, then the boy puts his penis into the girl's vagina. When the two of you are bigger, you can do that, too. Then a whole lot of semen comes out into the vagina, and that's how babies come about. But it takes a long time before the baby is big enough to come out.

Nessim: Grischa has a vagnia. (Turning to Petra) You, too?

Petra: Of course.

Nessim: I've got a penis, and I can drive a car, too.

Petra: Can a person drive a car only if he's got a penis?

Nessim: Only boys can drive cars.

Petra: But I can drive, and I'm a girl.

Nessim: But Christel can't!

Petra: Yes, but she can learn like you—there are driving schools.

Nessim: And Grischa could learn, too?

Petra: Of course. (Explaining to him how one learns, that there are instructors, etc.)

All this time Grischa was very disinterested, listening, but obviously not as concerned as Nessim.

Christel: Grischa, did you hear what I was just saying?

Grischa: Yes, but now I want to tell about something, alright? But first you've got to be quiet. (Says something altogether out of context.)

Christel: So, lie down again now. Shall I go on?

Nessim: Yes—about learning and driving.

Christel: Shall I go on talking about babies? Have you understood everything?

Nessim: No, only about learning and driving . . .

Nessim shows us here clearly how objects become infused with sexual energy. The autonomy and feelings of strength and superiority connected with driving are associated by Nessim with possession of the male genital organ. Here we see how the woman's alleged social inferiority and her lack of autonomy and dynamic energy are psychologically motivated by the low value the child places on the female genital sphere. This low evaluation is an expression of woman's thousand-year history of oppression by man. It is constantly reproduced in the child's upbringing, whereby the boy is expected to perform certain typically male activities, while according to traditional childrearing practices the girl is expected to assume a primarily passive, homemaker role. The exaggerated value placed on the male genitals leads, on the one hand, to a psychic devaluation of the woman; on the other hand, it intensifies the boy's fear of castration—of being robbed of the highly valued organ. Of being, in other words, like women. In general, sex differences are explained to children in the following terms: "Boys have a penis, and girls don't have one." This reduces sexual differences to a matter of having or lacking a particular organ.

In contrast to this approach, we made an effort to convince the children that male and female genitalia are functionally equal in value for the attainment of pleasure. We also tried to avoid characterizing the children's various games in terms of what many consider typical male or female behavior. This was made easier by our gradual abolition of sex-specific distinctions in our everyday activities. In this way we feel we can counteract the tendency to fetishize consumer goods as surrogate sex-objects. The car, for example, becomes a love-object because its possession unconsciously provides its owner with a strong and impressive penis. When fear of sexual distinctions is reduced, more genuine satisfaction in sexual relations is possible. The car, like other consumer goods, can then be seen more objectively in terms of its utility, and its value can be judged critically. This can be demonstrated by the example of driving: whereas the children always used to insist on driving the car in traffic (whenever possible we let them steer), they have now gradually come around to realizing their wish-fantasies in *play* situations, having come to accept that driving requires an adult's strength and skill.

Given an affirmative attitude toward infantile sexuality, sooner or later the children's sexual interest will focus on adult genitalia. Even in any "free" childrearing atmosphere, this is generally the point where the adults' own inhibitions set a limit on the children's sexual curiosity.

Report by Eberhard, April 4, 1968

After getting undressed, Grischa comes to me and says, "I want to sleep with you." Because I'm tired and frustrated, I lie down next to her on the bed, fully dressed, wanting to get her to fall asleep as fast as possible. Grischa keeps me awake by leafing through the newspaper and asking me "why" questions. She doesn't let me close my eyes. When I ask why I should keep my eyes open, she doesn't answer with words. She's only very restless, rubs her legs together, shoves the blanket between them, and keeps on tugging at her sweater and stockings. It's impossible for me to respond to her sexual interest, and after twenty minutes she takes her pillow and goes back into her room, frustrated. When I follow her, she first sends me away and then says I should tell her a story and lie down next to her. Nasser is already almost asleep, and so she whispers various questions to me that I don't understand. I can't manage to make her sleepy. When I ask her whether she wants to sleep in her room or mine, she happily comes into mine. I lie down next to her on the bed in underpants and undershirt.

Grischa says she doesn't need a blanket to go to sleep. Furthermore, I shouldn't close my eyes. Then she wants to stroke me—my hands and face. I'm only allowed to caress her after she has carressed me, and then only for a short while. I have to pull up my shirt while she strokes my belly. I'm lying on my back. Grischa caresses my belly, and imagines that my protruding ribs are breasts. I explain that these are only ribs and that I have a flat chest with nothing but nipples. She fondles them and shows me hers. We talk about girls' breasts when they are older. Then she wants to caress my "bottom". I have to turn over. She pulls down my shorts and strokes my buttocks. When I turn over again to stroke hers, as she desires, her interest immediately focusses on my penis. She fondles it and wants to "shut" it (meaning pull the foreskin over the glans) until I'm all worked up and have an erection. She beams and fondles it for a couple of minutes, making comments like, "Touch and touch! Looky penis! Big! Make it shut! Make it little!" She's kneeling next to me, laughing and moving nothing but her hands. A couple of times I shyly try to make her conscious of her vagina, saying that I'd like to caress it, too, which doesn't divert her in the least. Then, however, she has her "reaction". She grabs my peter with her whole left hand, wants to pull down her tights, and says, "Come one, stick it in." I had expected something of the kind (Marion had talked about bathtub games where Nasser had held his peter up close to Grischa's stomach and had pushed her back in such a way that one could play "stick penis in vagina," which didn't work for lack of an erection) but then she became so self-conscious that I quickly said, well, it's too big, anyway. Grischa drops the idea immediately and very reluctantly lets me rub her vagina. Then she goes and fetches a mirror and looks again and again at vagina and peter. After renewed fondling and attempts to "shut" my penis, she again expresses the wish to "stick it in," this time more energetically than before. I say, "Give it a try!" She holds my peter up to her vagina and then gives up in resignation: "Too big!"

Children's sexual curiosity, if not inhibited by intimidation and prohibitions, goes as far as pretend-intercourse in imitation of adult sexual behavior. As this report shows, the children discovered on their own that it was impossible to satisfy their desires in terms of genital sexual activity with adults. For the children to experience this directly it was essential that the adults not only issue no prohibitions, but also managed to overcome their own inhibitions. Personal experiences, made conscious, function as an incentive for the children to satisfy their genital sexuality in a more realistic fashion, with contemporaries instead of with adults. The precondition for such a better process of coming to terms with reality is growing up in a children's collective.

Custodial Child-Care

Public nursery school not only fails to meet this requirement; it also hampers children's development. At first, our children were happy in nursery school. After a few weeks, however, they began to show more and more aversion. They refused to get dressed in the morning, were dead set on staying home, and had to be persuaded to go almost every day. Grischa would often simply sit down on the sidewalk, say, "I don't wanna go to nursery school," and would scream if one of us picked her up. When we came for the children in the afternoon, they were usually very aggressive toward one another. They would quarrel, for example, about which one was to take the adult's right hand, would insist on stopping to buy gum or candy or demand to be picked up and carried. They would look for opportunities to hit each other. Once we were home, it generally took an hour before they were able to play with concentration. We sometimes could think of no better way to give them an outlet for the aggression that had accumulated in nursery school than to give them hammers and encourage them to smash bottles. Once home, they usually wanted to take off all their clothes right away. Never did they continue an activity begun in nursery school. When we would ask what they had been doing there, they either gave a token answer or none at all.

When bringing them or picking them up, we were able to see that the nursery school was no more than a combination pen and drill establishment. The children were crowded into tiny rooms. Play was essentially limited to what could be done at a table. A dreary inner yard, supplied with a simple jungle gym to climb on and a couple of sandboxes, served as a playground. There being no special place for naps, cots were set up each early afternoon and put away after the rest period. There was one teacher for at least twelve (and sometimes over twenty) children. Even with the best intentions, she could hardly take the children's needs and wishes into consideration under these conditions—and this in the middle-class Charlottenburg district; we are aware that conditions are worse in other public nursery schools. In the eyes of the children, nursery school teachers represent an essentially disciplining, prohibiting and commandeering authority. They, for the most part, decided what games were to be played. Longer stretches of play were impossible; games were forever being interrupted by the rigid daily routine. Under nursery school conditions, all intrinsically pleasurable activities were transformed into something humiliating, unpleasurable and compulsory. The children ate under the pressure of having to eat up everything. The last one to finish was ridiculed for being a "slow poke." This reduced meals to a kind of achievement test. It was impossible for the children to rest when they felt like it; instead, a rest period was enforced for all even when the children were not tired. The objective reason was probably that these two hours gave the overworked nursery school teachers a chance to recuperate. The children were commanded to close their eyes and no contact was permitted during the rest period. The children's interest in their sexuality and body functions was consistently squelched. When we came to pick out youngsters, we could often observe how children who wanted to watch others go to the toilet were chased off. Their needs could only be articulated in terms of their dependency on restrictive adults. They had no way of learning to synchronize and reconcile their own needs with those of the other children.

A children's collective ought to make it easier for children to practice truly social behavior. There, they discover that to enforce one's own will may well mean restricting another child in expressing *his* individual needs. It is necessary for the development of close relationships among children that they experience this conflict. No such possibilities were offered in the public nursery school.

PHASE 3: THE SOCIALIST STORE-FRONT CHILD-CARE CENTER

The contradiction between the relatively large degree of freedom they enjoyed in the commune and the strict discipline and suppression experienced in nursery school became more and more unbearable for the children. The more spontaneous our relationship to the children became and the more they were consequently able to satisfy their needs in the commune, the greater this contradiction became. This confronted us with the necessity of creating a children's collective that would correspond to our own ideas. At the beginning of February, 1968, we reissued Vera Schmidt's report on the Moscow Home for Children in order to stimulate discussion on the problems of childrearing. In the preface to this brochure—the first product of our thinking on the subject—we set forth our ideas about the children's collective. What we had in mind was a children's home, where the children would live in. This idea fitted in with the work then being done by the Action Council on Women's Liberation which at about that time was founding the first two store-front day-nurseries (*Kinderläden*) in the Berlin districts of Neukölln and Schöneberg. Empty stores were rented, remodeled and furnished for approximately eight children, supervised daily by two parents on a rotating basis. In the following months additional *Kinderläden* were opened in other districts of the city.

For the time being there was absolutely no chance of

realizing our rather elaborate plan for setting up a children's home to be run on a psychoanalytic basis. On the other hand, we did not want to continue sending our children to public nursery school, so in April we began to work out plans for setting up an additional *Kinderladen*. Until we could find suitable quarters we decided to organize daily excursions with the children to the Havel River. Most of the children were only willing to go along if one or both of their parents attended. At the beginning, therefore, the parents accompanied the group in order to help the children get used to the new experience. Their fear of going off with other adults and children was connected with the new experience of being together with many unfamiliar children and adults and not, for the most part, the result of a neurotic separation anxiety. After a few weeks most of them had lost this fear; only the smaller children (two to three years old) and a few of the older ones continued to insist on having their parents come along. Our children had no difficulties in this respect.

From the very outset we had held the view at our weekly parent discussion meetings that we needed to find a "neutral" person to accompany the children on these excursions and later look after them in the *Kinderladen*. In this point we differed from the prevailing attitude in other *Kinderläden*, where the parents took turns, day for day, looking after the children. Our view was confirmed by the experience we gained on our daily excursions. Those children, in particular, whose parents took turns accompanying the group all tended to have special difficulties: they were particularly aggressive, were always checking to see if their mother or father was about, were to a certain extent unable to tolerate seeing other children carry their needs to "their" parents, and had trouble on that particular day playing with other children; generally, they wanted to put on a show for their own parents.

This situation was also new for the parents. Above all, they had trouble behaving normally toward their own children and would assume a forced neutrality, trying to treat their youngsters exactly the way they treated the others. This, of course, intensified their own child's anxiety. About a month after we began taking the children on these group excursions we managed to find a trained teacher who has remained with the group ever since on a regular basis. She had quit her job in a public nursery school because the practical conditions under which she had to work had forced her to regiment the children constantly. In cooperation with the parents she tried to run the *Kinderläden* in such a way that the children would become freer and develop a greater degree of individual or group initiative. The West Berlin Central Council of Socialist *Kinderläden* regularly publishes the practical and theoretical results of the *Kinderläden* experiment in a series of brochures, one of which contains an extensive description of our particular endeavor.

For the children, the teacher was essentially a person who laid down few limitations and sanctions, and instead encouraged them to participate in pleasurable activities. Before long, the children developed a strong affection for her and thoroughly enjoyed going to the center. Their libidinous relationship to her helped them to loosen anxiety-producing ties to their parents to some extent. Only then did it become possible for the children to develop more stable relationships within their own group; thus, a collective came into being which had its own sense of identity.

Commune and Kinderladen

Once the children had become more closely acquainted, Nessim and Grischa often expressed the desire to spend the night with other children. Whenever possible, we encouraged this interest. The other children were delighted whenever Nessim and Grischa or one of the two wanted to spend the night. Soon after the children began going to the *Kinderladen* daily, the other children also began to want to go home with one another. But they never wanted to spend the night there. In the beginning it was primarily the fear of being separated from the parents that accounted for their ambivalence, displayed in the conflict between the need to continue playing with other children after *Kinderladen* and the refusal to stay on and spend the night. This anxiety clearly shifted after half a year of regular experience in the *Kinderladen*. Nessim and Grischa and S. enjoyed spending the night with other children and did so frequently. When they arrived at the *Kinderladen* in the morning the others often begged them to go home with them at night. Sometimes all three or one of the three would be promised some favor in return for going home with one of these other children. This shows clearly that the other children have a strong need to be with their fellows in the evening, as well. Still, they themselves are not interested in spending the night elsewhere—save, perhaps, that their parents come along. These children need the assurance that their parents really approve of their sleeping out. In the case of parents whose children are unwilling to sleep at another child's home, one can assume that they unconsciously reject having their children spend the night elsewhere.

As we can see, the children are definitely interested in expanding the collective experience beyond the confines of the *Kinderladen*. There are similar tendencies among the parents. For some time there has been a discussion on whether those adults not living communally should not also form communes of their own. Without exception, there has been strong friction from the outset between couples living in nuclear families. In the course of our work together in the *Kinderladen* it has become pretty well clear to all concerned that these marriages are not viable. Participation in the parent collective called long established response patterns toward the children in question. At one of our first discussion meetings the mother of a four year old boy still managed to state, "He's not at all interested in his penis. Sometimes he'll take hold of it and say it hurts him. But then he immediately lets his attention be diverted." Or another couple: "We always sleep together naked in the presence of the children. That doesn't interest them in the least." What with our group discussions and the open sexual interest demonstrated by other children in the *Kinderladen*, it was not long before these parents were no longer able to repress their own children's manifest interest in sexuality.

Children as Conflict Deflectors

In the adults' psychic system in almost all marriages, the child functions as a screen on which the parents project their own conflicts, anxieties and longings.

This, then, is how transferences also turn up in the emotional relations between parents and child. Parents with chronic neurotic conflicts often unconsciously tend to revivify some old traumatic constellation with the help of their child. They direct feelings toward the child that are actually not meant for him at all, but rather for another, perhaps long vanished partner. The child, absolutely blameless, has no choice but to serve as that background figure's representative. This role is thrust upon him. Such parent-child transferences are facilitated by the actual existence, in the child, of certain special traits that correspond or are at least very similar to traits found in the partner-figures through which the mother or father seeks to create a bridge to the child." (Horst-Eberhard Richter, *Eltern, Kind und Neurose*, Rowohlt, 1969, p. 76)

Such unconscious transferences also turn up regularly in parents who are not obviously neurotic. Through taking part in our parent collective and observing other children, the parents became conscious of some of these unconscious projections. This forced them to work out more of their conflicts between themselves rather than abreact them on their children. For the children, the *Kinderladen* represents long-term security and the parents no longer need bear sole responsibility for their upbringing—conditions under which constantly suppressed marital conflicts could break out into the open. Ever since a sense of collective responsibility began to develop within the *Kinderladen*, the question, "What will become of our children if our marriage breaks up?" has ceased to arouse all the anxiety, both concretely and psychologically motivated, that had been associated with it. For the women, in particular, this meant a release from the compulsory requirement of providing constant childcare. The immediate, short-range goal which the Action Council on Women's Liberation had set in founding the *Kinderladen* is beginning to be realized: relief from these pressures gives the woman an opportunity to recognize her own interests and pursue them even in the face of male opposition.

PHASE 4: WIDENING THE COLLECTIVE

Kommune 2 is now setting out to expand the children's collective. Three adults and two girls, both the same age, have joined us from the *Kinderladen*. (Two adults from the original commune are now living in other collectives.) Experience with the *Kinderladen* and with our own group of children has prompted us to substantially revise our original, rather utopian notions about the children's collective. In the beginning, we imagined that the children would be able to establish their own self-regulating collective, a group that for the most part would develop its own play-interests and resolve its own group conflicts. We felt that the adults should interfere as little as possible and imagined that this would enable the children's group to develop a certain autonomy and inner strength vis-à-vis the adults.

In regard to behavior toward the outside world, a measure of group resistance against the repressive behavior of adults can indeed be noted.

Kinderladen *report, November 1968*

T., the teacher, is in the park with the children and they cut across a lawn. A park attendant comes up. "That's not permitted. I'm going to call the police. After all, you are responsible and have to see to it that the children don't go off onto the grass." T. says, "How can it hurt the grass if the kids walk or play on it?" Several of the children call out, "That's a stupid man—you stupid man!" They ask the attendant, "Why can't we play on the grass?" The attendant yells at the children, "I'm calling the police. Get off the grass this very minute!" The children continue to walk around on the grass and say, "But we're playing here now." The park attendant gets on his bike in a fury and rides away.

But to what extent can the children's collective also function to reduce psychic pressure and promote the child's understanding of reality in conflicts with the decisive reference persons, the parents? In our experience, it is always with the parents that the crucial conflicts come to a head. (We are referring, reservedly, to our only empirically verifiable experience to date—an experience with children who had already lived in a nuclear family for some time before coming into a commune or children's collective.) We therefore have to pose the question: what external conditions can the commune and children's collective provide in the interest of promoting an ego-strengthening resolution of such conflicts? One basic condition is that the parents have an emotionally affirmative attitude toward the children's collective and do not unconsciously seek to bind the children to themselves (see the above example of spending the night in other homes). A positive attitude on the part of the parents depends, on the other hand, on the degree to which they themselves are integrated in the commune or *Kinderladen* collective. Successful integration depends, in abstract terms, on two prerequisites: a) a large measure of mutual interest and b) the development of methods for promoting a greater degree of sensitivity toward the feelings and emotions of other group members.

The difficulty in *Kommune 2* was that at no point did all members share a common productive interest (for instance, in political work). Furthermore, our attempt to find methods for releasing emotions and expanding awareness focussed mainly on group analysis—which, as previously stated, was broken off. We are only just beginning to develop other techniques (group role-play and use of consciousness-expanding drugs). For this reason we have experienced a rather considerable fluctuation. Grischa's mother moved out in February, leaving Grischa with us, so that she could live for a while in another group, without children. With such limitations it is impossible to present conclusive, empirical evidence for the positive influence the commune and children's collective have had on the two children, who by now have lived almost two years in the commune. But there are indications that the children's collective does help them substantially in resolving crucial conflicts.

In the *Kinderladen*, Grischa is able to verbalize and act out her current problem—that her mother is no longer living in the commune. Since her mother left, she has occasional temper tantrums. The children then ask T., the teacher, "What's the matter with Grischa?" T. will then explain that Grischa is sad because her mother is no longer living in the commune. This usually prompts a number of children to go over to Grischa and try to comfort her. Then they try to get her to play with them again.

Report, April 17 and 18

The teacher is spending the evening in the commune. Grischa wants to tell T. a story about a "funny lady." She says, "The lady has a white nose and a red mouth. And eyes like Grischa. But the color is very pale blue. And crazy-colored hair. It's a witch. Her shoes are gold and silver. And her skirt has lots of colors. And she's got a blouse on. There's a baby on it. Isn't that funny —a blouse with a baby on it?" Next day in the *Kinderladen* Grischa plays television. She says, "I know a funny, funny witch." She repeats the description from the previous evening, ending with the comment, "That's mommy."

After that she plays family (as she has often done recently) with I. They cook together. Then Grischa goes on and on about her baby. I. had lain down on the mattress, put his thumb into his mouth, and let himself be tucked in and cuddled. Grischa goes over to the other children and demands that they come and see her baby. When I.'s mother comes to pick him up, Grischa says, "I have to dress my baby. We're going home." Eberhard comes to pick up Grischa. She says, "Look, that's my baby. I've got to sleep with my baby." Eberhard reassures her by saying that she may go home and spend the night with I., but later asks once again, "Are you sure you don't want to come home?" Grischa: "No, but I'll come back tomorrow. You can pick me up."

As we can see, even in the case of a traumatic conflict such as when a child's mother disappears from the scene, children are able to come to terms with their own problems more realistically in their own collective setting. Grischa identifies with a mother figure. At the same time, she is able to vent her anger at her flesh-and-blood mother by calling her a witch. This makes it unnecessary for her to repress the conflict. This does not mean that the conflict has been resolved, as we see in Grischa's reaction when her mother visits the *Kinderladen*. She throws herself onto the floor, is aggressive toward her mother or other persons, refuses to come home, or screams, "I want to go to my grandma!"

Nessim, who had not dared to display any aggression toward his father, is now able to express his negative feelings toward Eike openly. He strikes him, wants to shoot him or expresses the wish that Eike die, telling him, "You've only got a day to live." The children's group and the commune have quite definitely exerted a favorable influence on him in releasing the aggressive side of his ambivalent attitude toward his father.

Report, April 1969

It's noon and Eike is cooking the midday meal in the *Kinderladen*. Nessim is pressing him to go away alone with him. Eike says, "But I can't. I've got to cook for all the children." In the afternoon a car comes to pick them up with the rest of the commune children. Nessim wants his father to take him home alone, by public bus. Eike says, "Sure, we can do that, but I'd rather go with the others because it's raining and if we take the city bus, then we'll have to walk through the rain." Nessim is pretty angry. He goes over to I. and makes arrangements to spend the night at his place. Outside, Eike asks Nessim whether he'd rather not go back to the commune after all (having realized that it was only because of his negative reaction that Nessim wanted to sleep elsewhere). Whereupon I. says to Eike, "Look, Nessim doesn't belong to you. He can do what he pleases." The two children go off together with I.'s father.

This example shows that the children's collective gives children an opportunity to work off their aggressive impulses toward their parents. It is too soon to judge what function the children's collective and commune have in the process of altering the structure of typical conflicts such as the Oedipus complex. But one can at least suggest, as a working hypothesis about children's collectives and communes in relation to their function in socialization, that they allow children to bring out the negative side of their ambivalence toward their parents instead of having to repress it, as is typical in the nuclear family. Repressed aggressive energy either becomes directed toward one's self or it lends itself to manipulative deflection against some social scapegoat. If the child is able to untangle his ambivalent drives as he has experienced them in relationship to his primary reference persons, then he is able to direct his aggressions against the actual source of the repression he feels. He develops a strong ego. "If this hate remains conscious, then it can become a powerful, individual, revolutionary force; it can then become the motive force in breaking free from the family association and can be easily made to serve the rational objectives of the struggle against those conditions that give rise to this hate in the first place." (Wilhelm Reich, *Die sexuelle Revolution*, p. 112 f.)

7

Communal Child-rearing: A Report on Three Cases *

GILBERT ZICKLIN

PRESENT-DAY COMMUNES, it must be noted at the outset, include groups and settlements with remarkably divergent beliefs, practices and organizations. At the same time, all of these new creations seem to emerge from the same spirit of disenchantment with contemporary life choices, thus giving the appearance of a coherent if not cohesive movement. Yet as diverse as they are, it is safe to assume that they resemble one another *sub specie sociologicum*. For, all are faced with fundamental social structural issues which must be resolved in order for the group to survive. The resolution of these problems may be approached by the group from either an ideological or "practical" perspective or it may be achieved as a consequence of individual decisions without group discussion or debate. One of these issues, which is the focus of attention of this paper, concerns the way in which children are to be socialized, an issue resolved in the larger society (for good or for ill), through the workings of the class system, nuclear families and the schools.

The question of who will raise the children, or to put it another way, to whom do the children belong, poses a fundamental problem for a group with distinct collective goals, quite apart from the vexing issue of what a "child" is, and therefore what it means to "raise" one.[1] The question brings to the fore the issue of group solidarity and the extent to which the group has priority over its individual component

* This paper is based on research made possible by NIMH Grant No. 1–RO1–MH 16570–01A1–SP to Scientific Analysis Corporation, San Francisco, California.

members. The group must eventually choose, through delib-
eration or otherwise, whether the children shall belong in
principle to the group and be reared and educated by the
group through its delegated agents, or whether they shall
belong to their parents. The determination to raise the children in one or the other manner can be seen as both a
consequence of prior conditions affecting group solidarity,
namely, the pervasiveness of ideological commitment and
group identity, the degree of economic integration, the existence of long-term goals, etc., as well as a constitutive factor,
in itself affecting solidarity. If the socialization of children
is the basic responsibility of individual parental units, then
independent units of solidarity arise which can compete
with the group for the members' loyalty, unless it is clear
that these parents are merely used by the group to help
rear its children. In the latter case, however, they would
function less as "parents" than as agents of the group.[2]

The establishment of separate child-rearing families introduces a competing focus of solidarity and commitment which
at least in theory can serve to diminish the authority and
importance of the group.[3] In the past, communal groups
"solved" the problem of separate child-rearing families by
either choosing celibacy, so that no children are born within
the group, or group marriage with institutionalized child-
rearing in children homes. In this way all the adults presumably felt a relatedness to one another as brothers and
sisters or husbands and wives. Not that there haven't been
intentional communities structured around individual home
units; they have ranged in kind from Robert Owens' New
Harmony through the Israeli Moshav and in a vague sense
to the typical Levittown suburb. But these have been clearly
defined in advance as cooperative communities of a limited
sort. Where the inspiration and guiding motif is "all things
in common" and what is wanted is the creation of intense
bonds of solidarity, the existence of separate family units,
each rearing its own children will either be temporary or can
be considered a stumbling-block to the self-realization of the
community.

This talk of limited cooperation as against all things in
common indicates a degree of self-awareness, if not out-

right planning, which observers of the present-day communal movement, myself included, note by its relative absence. That is, the question of what kind of group shall we form, with what lines of solidarity and with what sort of provision for bringing up children is not laid out before the membership either before or after the founding. Certainly nothing like the elaborate planning of an Owens or a Fourier has preceded the attempts at communal living we are talking about here.[4] Communes have sprung up by and large without planners or plans, without the formation of leagues, or prior meetings of the membership.[5] In many cases, though certainly not all, the founding of the commune was achieved by a small fraction of the eventual membership. In these cases, to a nucleus of original members might be added compatible hitchhikers, curious passers-by, interested visitors, guests from a different commune, etc.[6]

It is no wonder that a movement which exhibited so little planning in its formation should also manifest little concrete reflection about questions concerning the direction of the group and the nature of its social bond. The questions that did absorb the reflective energies of these young people prior to their joining communal settlements were in the main related to the dialectics of self-liberation and not to the formation of new economic and social ties which preoccupied 19th century Utopians.[7] The early founding and joining of communes in cities and, then, increasingly, in rural areas, which began around 1967 represented an attempt to create an environment wherein the pattern of the emerging counter-culture and its dynamics of self-liberation could be worked out.

This absence of planning and the rather spontaneous origin of communes may provide one explanation of what I have perceived to be a relative absence of communal institutions geared toward collective child-rearing. Such an explanation would emphasize the individualistic nature of what seem to be collectivist-minded groups, stressing the idea that the goals of self-liberation are unproductive of communal institutions and intensive solidarity ties. Such a view lends conviction to the belief that these communes are merely way-stations for searching, alienated youth, and are not meant to endure as settled communities. However this may be, one can find other explanations for the relative absence of institutionalized communal child-rearing. First, given the age distribution of those recruited to the communal movement, there are relatively fewer children in the communal population to begin with, and these children are most often in the infant or toddler stage. Since the adult population of communes tends to be around 10-20 members, the typical commune might have from two to five children, most likely of infant or toddler age. In such cases, though it is possible to develop communal child-care arrangements, they would be rudimentary indeed. Given the further tendency for women to play traditional female roles,[8] one may conclude that there is little incentive to establish communal child-rearing patterns at this stage. Another explanation which does not rule out the serious collective nature of the commune, nor indicate a lack of long-term commitment to the settlement, concerns the stages through which such groups may go. As Bettelheim notes of the Kibbutz, child-rearing functions do not have immediate priority when the survival of the group depends on achieving a viable economic order, including the building of residences and other domestic facilities.[9] This view suggests that until the group feels established and safely past the physical dangers of extinction it cannot afford the time and energy needed to create a radically different mode of child-rearing. Accordingly, if and when a group does reach the stage of physical security and a sense of having weathered the initial strains of building a viable community, then one may expect to find attention paid to new ways of institutionalizing the socialization of its children. During the intervening time, however, one may assume that the way children are raised in the commune will diverge markedly from the norms of the rejected larger society, especially its middle class, from which, by most accounts, the communal membership is predominantly drawn. It is the purpose of the remainder of this paper to discuss the ways in which communal child-rearing does in fact differ from the basic middle-class pattern.

The three communes I shall discuss had a total of 23 children during the time of my research, five of whom were visitors on either a summer or longer term basis.[10] In one of these communes, the yoga-oriented group calling themselves Satna,[11] there were three infants, four pre-schoolers, four school-age children, and one high school boy.[12] Four children lived in the second group, called Arroyo's, and three more children were just summer visitors. One of the children was under six, with the rest between ages seven and twelve. This group had six permanent adults with a series of adult visitors staying from several days to several weeks. At the third commune, called Haney, the children numbered four, two of whom were long-term visitors. In addition to these visitors, age 12 and 14, were a brother and sister, aged seven and four, respectively. This group included nine adults.

Some further demographic notes are in order. The adults in the first group numbered 21 at the beginning of my stay.[13] They comprised fifteen households, eight of which had children in them. Of these eight, three contained both biological parents, two contained the biological mother and a stable mate,[14] three included only the mother and her children. At Arroyo's, one of the six adults was the mother of three children, while the other children had biological parents elsewhere. The father of the youngest of the three siblings lived with the group at first, left, and then returned after a three month absence. He and the mother no longer lived together as a couple. Of the four children at Haney, two were visitors whose parents lived elsewhere, while the other two came with their divorced mother, who at first, had sexual relations with several men. By the time it was decided to live at Haney through the hard, snow-bound winter she had begun living with one man. This relationship lasted at least as long as the duration of my research.

I mention these elementary statistics not in anticipation of sustaining future hypotheses about communal child-rearing, for our numbers, deriving as they do from a fragmentary sample of a population whose parameters have not been well charted, are doubly inadequate for that purpose. Rather, I want to convey something of the demographic character of the three groups to the reader so that he may have some familiarity, if not with the feel of the place, at least with its bare social structure.

Of the communes I am dealing with, two may be said to have their roots in the broadly-labeled counter-culture movement. In the case of Haney, land was made available by a well-off young man who saw himself as part of the counter-culture. The available land attracted some of his acquaintances who, in turn, "recruited" others.[15] The members adhered to no particular political ideology or religious doctrine and showed no desire to publicize the communal way of life.

The six core members of Arroyo's, five of them women and one man, had known each other prior to settling in their rural-based commune. One of the women bought the land with a small inheritance used as a down payment. This group, too, had neither a central creed nor any missionary zeal. As with the group at Haney's, they seemed uninterested in promoting their way of life either through publicity or by helping to establish similar communal settlements.

The third communal settlement, Satna, was begun by an American swami. It attracted both those who had little, if any, knowledge of yoga, constituting the majority, and those more familiar with the teachings and the discipline. Among those initially ignorant of the yoga tradition, almost all had participated in one or another manifestation of the counter-culture. After an early clash over what would be permitted in the settlement, part of the counter-culture faction withdrew, strengthening the swami's position. Thus, though elements of the counter-culture can be found at Satna, its basic orientation, including its future direction, is that of a spiritual community.[16] New members must now show familiarity with Satna's spiritual creed, and be willing to conform to its devotional practices. The founder, to the displeasure of some, hoped to establish a virtually self-reliant village community with a membership of between one and two hundred. The objectors didn't want so large a membership, though they acknowledged the desirability of making their way of life available to others.

To proceed with a discussion of child-rearing, after these brief descriptions, we may begin by asking who socializes the child, whose primary responsibility is it, in the absence of institutionalized collective child-rearing, to tend the infants and teach the children the rules by which they ought to live. To speak of the infants first, which is to talk only of Satna, their care was the task of the individual mother, though she would often meet her co-infant-watchers at the central house where they kept a collective eye on their children. However, I have not recorded an instance when any one of the three mothers of infants picked up another mother's child, either to cuddle, comfort or feed. The ties between mother and infant were intimate and exclusive, though a father would occasionally spell his mate during the day and get up at night to feed or comfort the baby.

Each mother had her own way of attending to her infant and in one case a male communard was reproached for having said "no" to a baby whose mother attempted to avoid using negatives with him. Each infant slept "at home" with his parents, even if "home" were a tipi or a converted shack, and had his own toys and clothes. With respect to infant socialization, the community had little, if any, direct effect.

The pre-schoolers, on the other hand, were of an age to be taught rules and inducted into the diverse elements of the group's culture. At Satna, the four little children played together much of the day on their own. However, one often heard complaints about the children's wildness and tendency to steal food from others. The group originally decided to build a nursery school for the little children, but the material proved unusable, and neither time nor money was found to complete the structure. At a later time, concerned mothers did seek to take collective action at a general meeting, stressing the need for a school with adult direction. Prior to this, one member had volunteered to spend time with the children and introduce them to a love of nature and the yoga tradition, but his effort lasted only a short time. Occasionally, members would attempt to restore peace to the group of squabbling kids and as often would chastize them for their disorderliness by pointing out that this was, after all, a peaceful community. By and large, the non-parental adult members spent little time with the pre-schoolers and did not seek to cultivate a relationship with any of these children. The general lack of interaction between non-parental adults and pre-schoolers can be attributed in part to the busy schedule of the adults and in part to the dissatisfaction with the way these children behaved.[17]

This was not the case with the pre-schoolers at Haney and Arroyo's. In these two smaller groups, relations between each of the pre-schoolers and certain adults could be characterized as warm and intimate. Here we encounter a feature of group life that is peculiar, perhaps, to the counter-culture and can best be seen in a small commune of this sort. I am referring to the way in which a child is perceived as a distinct being capable of forming a relationship with an adult other than his or her own parents, rather than a simple off-shoot or mere adjunct of the parents. At Arroyo's, the five year old Heather went to one of several adults to be read to, to get food, to find clothes and to be put to sleep. Though her mother did not appear to be neglecting her needs and responded to her more than did other adults, nevertheless, the child easily approached the other women when her mother was busy or not interested in interacting with her. Similarly, when seven year old Arty became visibly upset by a remark from one of the older girls and could not get a satisfactory answer from her, I observed one of the adult women approach and ask him how he felt about not getting the response he wanted. She offered the boy a chance to talk things out. The boy seemed willing to do this, and showed no surprise that anyone besides his mother would seriously concern herself with his own doings.

At Haney, this way of responding to a child was considered incumbent upon an adult. Rachel, one of the Haney adults, pointed out another adult member's interactional difficulties with Lara, the four year old. "He tried to do the right things for her, what her mother would want done." She explained that this adult, Michael, could not see Lara as a person in her own right, as the rest of the group presumably did, but only as an extension of her mother. He viewed her as an object which had to be treated a certain way, which was the way her mother would want her to be treated. While Michael was downgraded for acting like a surrogate parent, Rachel, on the other hand, treated Lara as a little friend, and indeed, maintained a lively relationship with her. In fact, Lara's mother's mate felt that Rachel was closer to Lara than to her own mother and urged Jane, Lara's mother, to win Lara away from Rachel. Jane didn't share her mate's sense of wrongfulness and was rather glad that Lara had such a good friend in Rachel.[18]

While the parent(s) retain primary responsibility for the health and well-being of their children, the commune, with its extended family atmosphere, does provide certain socialization services. As we have seen with the pre-school children in the two smaller settlements, the presence of other adults permits the children to form on-going relationships with them which may range from the significant to the casual. This is true of school-age children as well, and is sensed as an important benefit by divorced mothers. At Satna, such a mother of three children gave as one of her reasons for moving to the commune the opportunity it offered her seven year old boy to relate to older males. This particular boy could often be seen talking to the men while they worked around the farm, asking about the work they were doing and offering to help. Another divorced mother was grateful to the commune for the opportunity it gave her oldest son, aged 14, to work together with the men.

Men were at a premium at Arroyo's where the core group of six consisted of five women. The divorced mother of three of the children voiced the hope that more men would show up, not only for the sexual fulfillment of the adult women, but also for the boys' sake. She felt they needed some males to identify with in this otherwise female-dominated environment.

At Haney, too, the presence of other males was seen to be of help to Rod, Jane's seven year old son. When Jane's mate attacked Rod for unmasculine behavior, the other males rose to the boy's support.

In general, then, neither the form nor the content of socialization, about which we have not said much, attempts to communalize the children. Unlike the Kibbutz system of education described by Spiro and Bettelheim, these children are not reared collectively, nor are they taught that the collective is more fundamental or important than their parents.[19] Nor, for that matter, are the parents required to vow an oath of overriding loyalty to the community, as among the Bruderhof. The community does participate in the socialization of the children, doing so unprogrammatically, merely in the way that it resembles an extended family. The community does not raise the children nor is it the originator or master of what they are taught. This is the parent's domain. But it does provide the children with close and sometimes intimate contact with other adults, united in a common effort with their parents, and available as friends and as role models.

But to what extent, if any, do these children identify with this communal group formed by their parents and neighboring adults, and do they sense their difference from other children in this respect? Put another way, how strongly do the children identify themselves with a collective larger than the one formed by their parents and siblings? To be fair, this question is somewhat premature. Of those children at an age to be aware of such things, most have come from non-communal settings and have had relatively little exposure to the commune's way of life. There are indications, however, that children raised in counter-culture settings before moving to a commune are aware of ways in which they and the group of which they are a part do differ from others. For instance, Lara knew that other children her age didn't curse the way she did or do "freaky" things like invite a guest at the farm to fuck her in the barn. On trips to town, Lara would observe the way parents treated their children and comment about how straight they were. On one of these trips to town, she saw a sheriff's car and excitedly burst out, "Pigs, Rachel, pigs! We could get busted." Rachel reassured her that "the pigs" had no reason to bust her, but Lara seemed uneasy when police were around.

While the adults at Haney did not give themselves any special identifying label, and consequently the children did not call themselves freaks or hippies, the adults at Arroyo's did. This was especially true of Lou, the mother of three of the children, who was a fan of Tim Leary and considered herself an "early-on hippy." Her son, seven year old Arty, used to ask about people mentioned in conversation whether "they are hippies like us?" When he found out that I spent some time at Satna, he wanted to know if they, too, were hippies.

The Satna member could not easily be typed with the social imagery of a term like freak or hippie. They did not consider themselves Hindus or self-realized Yogis, though they aspired to the status of the latter. Some were seasoned drop-outs who had been in heavy drug scenes in San Francisco, a couple were off-beat middle-age adults, and two or three were young middle-class housewives who had gotten "turned on." What they all had in common was a desire to be "on the path" toward enlightenment, but this did not seem to constitute a usable self-description for the children. Unlike the Haney and Arroyo adults, who saw themselves as freaks and hippies, Satna adults were neither straight nor freaky, as such "worldly" distinctions counted for little at Satna.[20] The tradition in which they saw themselves participating, that of Yogic self-realization, long antedated the counter-culture movement. There are numerous adherents of this spiritual tradition besides the people at Satna, many of whom occupy middle-class positions. Nevertheless, as noted above, quite a few of the young adults at Satna had been involved in the counter-culture and a real tension existed between those prior values and their present spiritual life.[21] With respect to the important matter of schools, Satna parents selected the "straight" option of having them attend the local one-room public school. Haney and Arroyo children, on the other hand, did not attend school, though they might have gone to a free school had there been one available.

Satna aims at becoming a self-sufficient village community of about 100 families, including its own schools. If and when this hope is realized, one would expect a distinct identity to develop of the sort that might characterize the Amish or Bruderhof communities. The Satna children, then, will be faced with a more difficult choice than the Haney or Arroyo children; it will be impossible for them to be *in* Satna and *in* the world at the same time.

I have mentioned the children's freedom to relate to non-parental adults, especially in the smaller communes, but I want now to consider directly the subject of autonomy. What is at stake here, I believe, is a growing tendency in the counter-culture to attribute to a quite young child, even an infant, a self capable of unfolding in directions of its own. I am not simply talking about the Rousseauian conception of man as a being born free and everywhere fettered by the limitations built into human institutions, though certainly this conception flourishes in the communal movement. What I am referring to, rather, is the institution of parenthood itself, as it embodies emotions, images, and beliefs concerning the way parents relate to a child.

Traditionally, the parent-child relationship has involved the following elements:

1. Parents are the masters of the child's environment.
2. They are the authority on what is good or bad for the child.
3. They have the right to discipline and punish a child.
4. They are responsible for conveying the cultural norms to the children and for preparing them for adulthood.
5. They are to be praised when the children turn out successfully.
6. They must share the responsibility if the child turns out badly.

At one time, parents had sole disposition of the child and were entitled to select a mate for him or her, hire out the child's labor, sell the child, etc. With the rise of the centralized state, in the modern era, a slow erosion of parental rights has occurred, the justification of which has been three-fold. First, the state has become a guarantor of the child's rights vis à vis his or her parents, ensuring, for example, that the child be protected against damaging punishment. In this sense, the state stands as ultimate protector of the child. Secondly, the state has recently begun to assume the responsibility of assuring favorable conditions for the child's future growth and productivity. Here, the justification is not only in terms of the child's welfare, but the society's as well, for a "damaged" child as it grows to be an adult can be a costly burden to the society.[22] Various groups in the society are demanding that in the case where parents are incapable, financially or morally, of doing so, the state play an increasingly large role not only in protecting the child, but in fostering its intellectual and emotional development. A third aspect of the state's enlarged role with respect to the child derives from the political critique of class structure and the advantages and disadvantages it entails to children born in a certain class. Here, the attempt is made to enlist the state under the banner of equalitarianism in order to promote equal opportunity for lower-class children in their competition with children of higher classes. The force of these developments has been to enlarge the domain of the state's role with regard to child-rearing and to limit the authority of the parent. Nevertheless, in areas of social life untouched by state control and in the more privileged classes generally, parental control and domination in child-rearing remains relatively undiminished.

Implicit in parents' treatment of children in communes, examples of which I will offer momentarily, is the reduction of the degree of domination common in the larger society. Equally important, perhaps, is the tendency to transform the status of the child from that of a possession of the parents to something resembling a trust, whereby the child is given to its parents for a period of time, but has its course of being elsewhere.[23] For some communards, parenthood in the larger society is seen as a form of ownership of the child and an entitlement to both the rights of domination and the opportunity for prideful display that ownership of a valuable commodity affords. A child, in this view, is a reflection of its parents, which behooves the parents to produce the most prestigious version of a child their culture recognizes. In the straight world, these communards maintain, the child is another aspect of nature which must be subdued and capitalized. For the communards, on the contrary, it is the naturalness of the child which must be respected. He or she must be given the dignity to live in the ways natural to it, with guidance to be sure and advice that might be useful, but in a direction of his or her own choosing. Parents cannot form the child; they must allow the child's own form to emerge.

In Satna, these ideas are tied closely to the Hindu belief in reincarnation, that people have a long-lived soul and must play out a further portion of that soul's destiny in its present incarnation. For example, mothers at times referred to their infants as "the baby Krishna," referring to its status as an incarnation of the Hindu Lord of Creation. Two of the three mothers of infants were known to believe that their infants in this life were destined to go quite far on the path toward eventual enlightenment.[24] One mother, a visiting friend of several Satna members, in speaking about the tribulations of raising her son, whose astrological chart indictated an extremely active sexual nature, related tales of the many incidents that led her to feel guilty about the way she was raising Todd. After prolonged self-scrutiny, including psychological counseling, she reported having the insight that it was not her fault, but rather Todd's *karma*, his inheritance from past lives, that was working itself out and that she could only respond by giving him the freedom to be himself: "There is a reason why the kid gets the mother he gets. It's all part of the divine plan. The kid has to work out things on his own and gets the mother who will help him do it."

This awareness of inherited *karma* and spiritual destiny was not so much present in the parents of older children at Satna.[25] Yet with these parents, too, one finds a desire to give rein to the child, to let him or her lead an independent life, and to consider the child capable of adult-like experience. For example, one of the communards saw an itinerant handyman of about 60 who helped build some of the houses at Satna and was known to everyone there, in sex play with a three year old girl. This particular communard revealed what he had seen to the child's mother, and to others. While the reaction of the members varied, some showing sympathy for the old man, others not knowing how to feel, one or two desiring to punish him, the mother believed nothing bad had been done. She felt that her child did not appear to be harmed by the experience. A similar incident took place at

Haney. There it involved a "mind-blown" but gentle long-hair about 25, named Sid, who didn't do any work and spent a lot of time picking mushrooms and wandering about out of touch with what was happening at the farm. He and Lara were discovered naked in bed making love. The girl's mother felt it was nobody else's business, and had to restrain Rudy from doing violence to Sid. Though again several communards were quite ambivalent, at least two felt that Sid wouldn't do anything to hurt Lara because his love for her was genuine and innocent. They also believed that Lara, who had already been sexually involved with boys, didn't think it was weird to be in bed with Sid. Her mother shared this view.

Another illustration of this complex of attitudes toward children concerns a seven year old boy at Satna named Carlton. Satna wasn't far from a river which, in summer, served as a campsite for groups of local youngsters. Many of them spent the summer "down at the river" with frequent trips to town or home for provisions. Carlton met a 16 year old girl at Satna who was going to the river and arranged to go with her, but she wanted to know if it was all right with his mother. Carlton told his mother of his plan and she assented. In recounting her decision, Anna said she knew it was somewhat risky to let a 7 year old go down there in the company of a 16 year old girl who might not pay enough attention to him or the hazardous things he might do, but she felt how much it meant to him to go and this outweighed her caution. According to Anna: "I want to give my children as much freedom to be themselves as possible."

A further illustration of these attitudes concerns a situation which developed while I was chatting with Anna in her tiny trailer-home. Marianne, a six year old, had come to visit and was playing by herself in a corner of the trailer while we talked. Anna described her experience in a conventional marriage as a wife of an engineer, her discovery of acid, the extra-marital sexual relationships that developed and her ultimate divorce. She went on telling about her oldest son's needs and difficulties and the incident involving the handy-man and his sexual encounter with three year old Trish. At no time did Anna censor her conversation because of

Marianne's presence, nor did she hesitate to talk about such matters in front of her (though I did). Intermittently, Marianne showed Anna her crayon drawings and scissor cutouts which Anna praised, stroking her head.

At Haney, and at Arroyo's, too, the unwillingness to overrule a child, to exercise seemingly arbitrary authority, or to exclude a child from harsh or complex adult affairs because of the tenderness of a child's age made up part of the attitude toward children. At Haney, both of Jane's children, Lara and Rod, could arrange with visiting adults to accompany them home without first securing permission from their mother. Jane felt that it was the children's right to go as long as the visitors wanted to look after them. Moreover, the children could be present at all meetings, even during those in which their mother came in for criticism. It was thought that Rod and Lara kept things in good perspective, not feeling they had to protect their mother, and understanding that condemnation coming from individual A was between that individual and their mother, and didn't affect them.

The adults at Haney sometimes got angry at the children and would holler at them, but they did not hit or "punish" them. (At Satna, however, I did see two sets of couples threatening to punish their whining, noisy children by excluding them from dinner, though these threats were not carried out.) During the summer in which the commune began forming, Lara used to take other little kids' clothing off and Rachel once called her "a mean little fuck" for doing it. Lara could get angry at other kids and adults—swear, spit, kick, yell at them. She had no special "respect" for older people. Yet, it was felt that she could recognize when a person's anger against her was justified. Many of the communards at Haney believed they had no more authority over Lara than over another adult, so that it was up to Lara to change her offending ways or not. She would not be forced to change through physical punishments or withdrawal of her rights.

At Arroyo's, the children's freedom of action was made manifest in several ways, though not without some ambivalence on the part of the adults. The children aged 10-13 could smoke dope or "drop" a hallucinogenic at their will, and had equal access with adults to the communal drug supply. (The younger ones had to have a reason for wanting to "drop" and an adult not on drugs had to be present.) Some concern developed on Lou's part when her 10-year-old began using the psiloscibin with increasing frequency. Since one was supposed to use the hallucinogenic in a serious manner as a part of self-discovery, Lou was able to question Donny about his intentions in using the drug without denying him his right to do so. Perhaps because he sensed he had been cautioned, Donny's use did, in fact, diminish.

The adults at Arroyo believed in an ethic of unburdened, pleasurable and frequent sexuality, which was applied to the children as well. It was a source of satisfaction that 11 year old Donny was reputed to be "making it" with his 12 year old girlfriend, and that the three other girls, around 12 or 13 years old, were interested in fucking two teenage boys who lived at a neighboring home down the road.[26] Moreover, no effort was made to shield the children from adult remarks about "the good fuck" they had last night or the frustration of not having a man.

Though the adults indicated no ambivalence about the right of children to engage in sex, in other areas the results of the child's freedom of action proved problematic. I have already mentioned the way in which Donny's mother, Lou, balked at the boy's increasing use of hallucinogenics. In another matter, Lou worried that her two youngest children were not showing much interest nor making much progress in reading and basic arithmetic.[27] She had read *Summerhill* and subscribed to what she believed to be the author's non-directive approach. Her children did not attend the local public school, but she herself had offered to help them with reading and math. From my observations, it was mainly Lou who initiated these study sessions. Lou had graduated from college; her second husband had been a research psychologist at a reputable University in the West. She and two of the other women read a great deal and had numerous high-quality books on subjects ranging from ancient Egyptian mythology to the gestalt therapy works of Fritz Perls, in addition to some delightful children's books. Lou expressed some concern over the children's lack of progress in learning the things normally taught children at that age, but felt there was little she could do if they did not want to learn. She believed they were happy children, yet she herself would have preferred them to show more enthusiasm for schooling.

I have tried in these variegated examples to illustrate the ways in which parents try, not without some ambivalence, to foster the autonomy of their children. I have suggested that the ways chosen by these parents to handle certain problematic situations and even the very situations that arise differ considerably from those of middle-class households. Whether it be in the way a parent at Satna conceives of him or herself as, at best, a helpful guide in the self-realization process of a soul now temporarily inhabiting his or her child, or in the child's openness to experience in sexual matters as well as drugs, or in the manner in which children determine their own bed-time, choose their own clothes, eat or not eat, or in the ability to arrange trips and visits for themselves, leaving parents for days and weeks at a time, or in being present during discussions normally open to adults only, I venture to say that these children no longer live in the same world of childhood as their age-mates in conventional society.[28] What we have called the stress on autonomy is equally a collapsing of the walls between childhood and adulthood, the elimination of many of the normative practices and distinctions which link the child with an inferior status vis à vis an adult. It seems to me that the commitment to equality is most noticeable in just this area of communal social life.

The granting of adult-like prerogatives to children can be seen as part of the evolution of the concept of equality now embodied in the counter-culture in which all forms of domination are suspect. In this new view, no part of creation has the rightful authority to dominate another, whether it be whites over blacks or reds, men over women, parents over children, or man over nature.[29] Adherence to such a worldview, particularly with respect to children, can and does raise difficult problems. If the adult has no rightful authority over a child how can he or she obtain the child's consent in meeting adult expectations and desires? What if the child cannot be persuaded to do what the parents request? This is not simply an academic question, for in these communities, situations arise of just such a nature. At a Satna dinner in Charles and Dinah's new *hogun*, the five adults present became increasingly annoyed at the disruptive antics of the two children. In each case the non-biological father requested that the children calm down and, with continued "misbehavior," suggested a punishment if consent was not forthcoming. The children kept up the disturbance, repeatedly saying No! to the parents' requests for quiet, while the adults alternately besought and threatened until dinner was ready and peace finally restored. On numerous other occasions, Celia, the leader of the group of pre-schoolers, resisted suggestions made by adults on the proper demeanor for Satna children. It is true that these children had been raised for most of their lives in a different setting with more traditional forms of obtaining compliance. Perhaps children raised from birth by parents who believe in persuasion and the right of children to be free from adult domination will know when they are acting selfishly and accommodate themselves to perceived legitimate requests, as Rachel claims Lara did.[30]

The problem of obtaining the child's consent to adult wishes is more complicated in a situation where the child is seen as rightfully exercising his or her individuality. Such was the case when Lou's youngest children showed, from her point of view, insufficient interest in learning how to read and use numbers. Lou wanted them to feel free enough to refuse her promptings if they so wished and yet she clearly desired that they learn the things she wanted them to know. In such situations, one may be compensated for the lost power to impose one's will upon the child by the feeling that such self-imposed restraint indirectly strengthens the child's sense of autonomy.

There are few areas of adult life in the communal settlements from which the children are excluded. Even the sexual life of the adults is a subject of interest and speculation among them. Within the one-room home-site, the child might observe his parents making love and want to participate directly. This was reported by two mothers at Satna. One girl asked her mother if she could make love to her the way Charles does.[31] At Arroyo's the children sometimes slept in the loft of a cabin where two adult women had separate sleeping quarters. The older children were well aware of the nocturnal love-making that took place when men were there and would on occasion jokingly refer to overheard sighs and groans.

In certain key activities, however, the children either did not participate or maintained an ambivalent position. At Arroyo's, a central concern of the group was the matter of openness in interpersonal relationships. There was a great deal of talk about feelings in the fashion associated with sensitivity groups and encountering. The children, though not directly excluded from these therapeutic sessions, were not asked or encouraged to participate in them. On two occasions, Lou "encountered" her children about an uncomfortableness she had in their way of relating, but she was the only adult to do so; the children did not "encounter" any adult or each other.[32]

No one did much productive work at Arroyo's, so that the children were neither included nor excluded from this important activity. They were given some specific chores, like the feeding of pets and the gathering of fire wood, which they seemed to accept willingly. In general, the absence of a work ethic helped to make long stretches of leisure time available, which, in turn, served to enhance the status of children by ruling out invidious discrimination against them with respect to work accomplishments. Moreover, it allowed them to make their mark in an endeavor for which they were well-suited, namely, the effortless spending of leisure time.

At Satna, work was considered necessary in building up and maintaining the community as well as a service to one's fellows. Members plowed, raked, cultivated and watered gardens, constructed homesites for each other, built a dam, worked in the several cottage industries turning out foot lockers, incense, candy bars, and costume jewelry, were employed at enterprises outside the settlement, tended the compost heap, built a temple, fed and milked the goats and did general maintenance work. The children did not work, however, with the exception of the one teenager and his two friends.[33] As a consequence, children were excluded from an important status-generating activity and also had little interaction with the adults, including parents, during the long working day. Moreover, the discipline and seriousness that went into adult work contrasted sharply with the aimless, and at times, raucous playing that characterized the children's world.

At Satna, spiritual things were considered of utmost importance. Knee-babies often sat with their meditating mothers, who felt the experience was beneficial to the children. One mother of a three year old included her daughter in the rituals she performed at her homesite, instructing the child in the meaning of the events as well. On Sunday, when all those who could get transportation went to chanting and meditation services at the retreat, the children were taken along. Often they would appear bored and shuttle in and out of the service area. This led to a move to initiate a special children's service on Sunday, though at mid-week services on the farm the children were still welcome. By and large, the religious activities interested and attracted adults far more than they did the children.

At Haney, work was seasonal, almost all of it done during the time between the spring thaw and the first snows. The two visiting boys and seven year old Rod would occasionally help the men around the farm. But according to one source, the boys were asked if they wanted to lend a hand, not so much because their effort was needed, but because the adults thought it would give them a chance to feel grown up. Nevertheless, one of the visitors, 14 year old Sam, had lived at the farm previously and knew a great deal about the surrounding woods. It was generally acknowledged that his woodsman's skills made an important contribution to the settlement. I had no way of ascertaining whether the status accruing to Sam because of his knowledge of the woods simultaneously raised the status of his peers, as well, in the eyes of the adults.

The direction of the settlements, insofar as it took place in general meetings and in smaller committees, involved only the adults. Children might attend a meeting, or they might be asked by an adult to voice an apparent grievance, but basic decisions about finances, work schedules, recruitment of new members, and relations with the outside world, were in the hands of the adults.

I mention these adult activities in order to give a more complete picture of the status of children in the commune. While I have spoken of the ways in which the traditional prerogatives of adults have been eroded, I also want to make clear that in some respects the distinction between adult and child status remains intact. It is the *tendency* to stress the autonomy of the child in the communal settlement that I maintain to be the important difference between the conventional middle-class role of the child and that of the commune-reared child. The communard parents feel little pull from the conventional society to instill in their children a sense of discipline and obedience to conventional social norms. They do not operate on the premise that the child must learn to behave in ways that will be useful to him or her in the pursuit of status and career in "straight" society and the freedom that the child needs to be him or herself counts more than the inculcation of conventionally good manners. Nor is the child seen to be helpless and innocent and in need of protection from the adult world. Many communal parents believe the child to be possessed of adequate intellectual and emotional resources to cope with the knowledge and freedom of action reserved to adults in the larger society. In the Satna community, moreover, one finds the belief that the child possesses a soul with an independent karmic destiny, adding further to the status of the child as an independent being. In this way, the responsibility for traditional parenting, for controlling the child and securing his adaptation to the larger culture, and for instilling useful attitudes and habits in the competition for status and rewards, is lessened. As a consequence one may predict that the parents' identification with the child and their concern with the child's present behavior insofar as it relates to his or her achievement of future status in the world, have both been reduced. It is in this overall context that the reader is asked to understand the reported tendency toward equalization of adult-child status and the growth in intimacy made possible by the change in the relationship.

One difference alluded to above between conventional child-rearing and that practiced in the communal settlement deserves further mention. Whereas a middle-class family tends to think of its sons and daughters as potential occupants of relatively high-status positions, the communal parent does not.[34] For the latter, the future status and condition of the child seems unknowable and is not a referent for present action. Given their own experience of a radical break with more traditional modes of living and their not-quite-settled, often rather precarious existence in the commune, one can comprehend how the future might seem largely unpredictable. While informally interviewing parents at Satna, we asked what hopes they had for their children. We received either a homily on the uselessness of expectations or statements the essence of which are contained in the cliché "what will be, will be." They felt it made as much sense to predict that their children would be on a spiritual path like themselves, in a community like Satna, as back in the world with a materialistic outlook. They could not say how their children would turn out; the very question struck them as inopportune. They had no distinct plans for either their own or their children's future. Their time perspective was days, weeks, and months, rather than years. When one does not know where one will be living in a year, what one will be doing and with whom, and whether one's fundamental ideas about man and the world will remain the same, it might, indeed, appear fruitless activity to seriously plan for, or even contemplate the distant future.

We are long past the time when the raising of children and the child's place in the family and society was taken for granted, a cultural given which all possessed as an inheritance from the previous generation. Today as a result of decades of thought and observation, we probably have more information available about the growth of children than at any other time previously.[35] What is more, we have professionally trained experts and therapists to spread new insights and investigate new areas in the domain of childrearing. The intensive exploration of the world of the child has not been without its effect. It is safe to assume that it has been a factor in the shifting balance of authority within the family that is more and more characteristic of the middle-class.[36] To quote from *Crestwood Heights*, a study of the culture of upper-middle class suburbia:

The ideal Crestwood family, is, therefore, greatly different from the ideal family of previous decades. If we might use an analogy, the Crestwood family now seems a little like a country which, having operated under an authoritarian form of government, has suddenly switched to a democratic form, without too much preparation for the change. The parents, who are still held legally responsible for the rearing of the children, are, at the same time, shorn of the moral sanction they once had for the exercise of absolute power over the subordinate children, an authority then thought to follow "naturally" from age and the dominant economic position of the parents, (particularly the father), and further buttressed supernaturally by traditional religious norms. The father, it is true, still holds the economic power, but he is now culturally enjoined from exercising it in "despotic" ways. A central problem of the family now appears to be the allocation of power among its members so that each may participate, not in the earning of the family income, but in the emotional and social life of the family unit . . . Just what (now) constitutes "over-severe" discipline or "over-permissiveness" cannot be stated in unequivocal theoretical terms, nor, frequently, agreed upon in practice. No longer are there any precise canons of behavior for children towards their parents or for parents towards their children.[37]

The declining adherence to authoritarian norms on the part of communard parents, far from being strictly a counter-culture phenomenon, then, represents a general shift of values affecting the entire society. What participation in the culture has done, perhaps, is to remove the rationale for the continuing influence which parents in respectability-bound, career-and-suburb families seek to exert on the attitudes and aspirations of their children. Whereas middle-class parents want and expect their children to eventually assume the type of social role generally held by adults in that class, communard parents, having rejected the larger society which makes such roles available, need no longer feel responsible for inculcating in their children the key values of that society. But lacking a clear and established alternative network of adult social roles into which their children can move, these parents are attempting instead to rear independent, relatively autonomous children in the hope, perhaps, that as adults they will have the inner resources to find or make their own way.

Communal parents, in confronting the problem of raising children without possessing more than a vague notion of what they are destined to become, are responding to an extreme version of a general condition shared to some degree by all contemporary parents. The shifting strands of modern life, whether it be in work, leisure, sexual mores, education or family life, have substantially unravelled the web of tradition with which the future is bound to the past. Communard parents face this discontinuity squarely, for they have chosen to reject the future awaiting them in middle-class society and in most cases have not yet found an adequate substitute. Middle-class parents, however, continue to plan for the future on the assumption that it will be an extension of the present, and they try, with their remaining influence, to insure that their children will lead lives recognizably, if not wholly, like their own. Whether participation "in the emotional and social life of the family unit" under the leadership of the parents, but now with diminished authority, can effectively socialize the child to want to continue this way of life remains to be seen.

As for the communal movement itself, it is still very much in its beginning phase, and the character of its children still largely undetermined. To a great degree, what will happen to the children depends on the fate of the counter-culture generally. While, at present, certain aspects of the counter-culture are being passed on to the children, there is still little clarity about what kind of roles these young people will be expected to play as they mature.

Until the counter-culture becomes much more consolidated, indeed, if it ever does, and a form of sub-society developed with its own network of communications, institutional life and collective consciousness, including the emergence of an appropriate form of education for the children, communard parents will lack the supporting social context which could strengthen their commitment to presently held child-rearing values. As has been noted elsewhere,[38] many of those who identify with the counter-culture are still in the process of searching for an over-arching cultural tradition, be it American Indian, frontier American, Hindu, Zen, early Christian or anarchist, with which to link and consolidate their disaffection from mainstream American life. Whether out of these manifold traditions an identifiable subsociety with its own social system will emerge is perhaps the critical question concerning the counter-culture as a movement.[39] Failing this, we can expect to see the sustained growth of a few communal settlements, a process of formation and disintegration with respect to many more and a continuation of the vagabondage and marginal living characteristic of much of the counter-culture's adherents today.[40]

NOTES

1. The "world of childhood" is essentially shaped by adults within limits established by adult expectations of children's capabilities. We must assume that these expectations do not coincide with the potential range of childhood experiences, since they vary from class to class and from age to age, as if they were a question of manners. To maintain otherwise, one would have to say that the natural ability of the child depended upon the era or social class to which he belonged. Sociologists are increasingly able to recognize and document the ways in which adults do their work of creating the world for the child, including his place in it.

2. The Bruderhof community described by Zablocki (1970) maintains the nuclear family form, but members considering marriage must vow primary allegiance to the community, which may even involve betraying the trust of the marriage partner. In this sense, they function more as agents of the group than as parents conventionally defined.

3. For a discussion of "commitment mechanisms" in 19th century communal settlements which derives a member's sense of commitment to the group essentially from the internal structural arrangements that prevail in a settlement, see Rosabeth Kanter (1968). Kanter's argument assumes only that the continued survival of a settlement depends upon the devices employed to secure the members continued commitment to the enterprise. Actually, a settlement can survive even if the commitment of all but a core membership lapses, as long as there exists a supply of available recruits to take the place of the defectors. More importantly, longevity

ought not be considered the sole criterion of a successful venture. As Cuber and Harroff, (1965), have shown, a married couple for a number of reasons may be committed to a marriage which both may consider an unhappy one. Long-lived as it may be, such an arrangement could scarcely be called a successful example of marital relationships. Similarly, members who remain committed to a communal settlement may do so for reasons having little to do with their own fulfillment, but rather with the pressures and constraints of their position. Use of the term "success" to describe such a settlement would be misleading, a problem that Kanter never faces.

4. I except the few groups that have based their settlement on B. F. Skinner's *Walden II*, or Robert Rimmer's *Proposition Thirty One.*

5. I know of only two attempts at forming inter-communal lines of communication, both of which were in northern California and consisted of the distribution of rudimentary communal newspapers. I have seen nothing in this country as sophisticated as the *Journal of the Commune Movement*, published in Great Britain.

6. In a similar vein and surely with even less discrimination, Robert Owens took out newspaper advertisements extolling the potential virtues of New Harmony as a means of recruiting new members. See Bestor (1971) for a discussion of the early 19th century communitarian movement.

7. Only recently, after five or so years of commune formation, have young dropouts begun to organize around larger socio-economic issues such as the need for land reform, the development of land trusts and land banks, the establishment of federated rural cooperatives with marketing operations for farm produce and handicrafts, etc. A movement based on these issues open possibilities for an alliance between counter-culture youth and the more disgruntled elements of rural America.

8. The presence of "male chauvinism" in the communal movement is a live issue in counter-culture circles. From my observations, no commune has adopted an "affirmative action" policy with respect to women. But at the same time that women tend to assume the traditional roles of mother and housekeeper, they also take an active part in the overall direction of the settlements. The frontier ambiance of many communes makes the sexual division of labor seem "natural," while the communal structure seems to encourage universal participation in decision-making.

9. See Bettelheim, (1968), pp. 31–35.

10. My observations on the communal movement began with some preliminary field work in 1968–69. In 1970–71, I spent some three months in the field at Satna and Arroyo's. My observa-

tions on Haney derive from two brief visits and extensive interviewing of two members. The names of the settlements used in this report are fictitious in order to preserve the groups' anonymity.

11. By the end of my field work at Satna, there were several more children present. Satna, perhaps because of its spiritual rather than counter-culture orientation and its more viable economy, attracted older adults, as well, and therefore had an unusually high number of children. Two families headed by adults over 30 accounted for six children, as many as the seventeen adults under 25.

12. The number of children present has about doubled as of this writing.

13. This number has also doubled as of this writing.

14. By a stable-mate, I mean that the relationship lasted at least as long as I knew the couple, or about a period of one year.

15. One of the members learned about Haney at a country store a few miles from the settlement. He and his two companions were passing through, when they met someone from the settlement who suggested they come by for a visit.

16. By keeping the composite nature of Satna's membership in mind, the reader will find it easier to understand why at times Satna resembles the other two settlements and can be joined with them in making a point, while in different instances it must be treated as a separate case, in contradistinction to the others.

17. As will be mentioned later, these children, as well as the older ones, had only lived from six months to a year in a communal setting.

18. Jane's mate, an ex-New Yorker named Rudy, came from a strong working class background. Jane had lived in an enclave of the counter-culture for about two years prior to coming to Haney but Rudy was not the typical hippy. When, on one occasion, he saw Jane's son engaged in sewing, he called the boy "a fucking pussy." Though Rudy's apparently obsessive concern with masculinity could get out of hand, as seen in this instance, when better modulated it fit more comfortably into the frontier-farm atmosphere which prevailed at Haney.

19. See M. Spiro (1965) and B. Bettelheim (1968).

20. When a group of Satna members were shot at while swimming at a nearby waterhole, they were disturbed not only by the attack but by the thought that they had been taken for "dirty hippies." An incident reported by the equivalent of the treasurer of Satna also bears retelling. When buying supplies in the nearest town, she always had lunch at the same place. The woman working the counter knew that Jenny was affiliated with Satna and treated her cordially. Once the counter-woman even rose to Jenny's defense when

some lumbermen began insinuating that she was a loose-living "hippy chick." To Jenny's satisfaction, the woman explained that the Satna people were different from the others, and deserved to be treated respectfully. This incident led Jenny to suggest that the townspeople were beginning to distinguish between "our hippies" and the "dirty kind."

21. One example of this tension concerned the issue of whether those who worked in the garden could do so in the nude. The swami who founded Satna believed that working in the nude might be considered bizarre by "straight" visitors to the settlement who might otherwise be attracted to a spiritual community, and that therefore it behooved those who could be seen by visitors to wear appropriate apparel. Several members who worked in the garden disputed the swami's contention, basing their claim on both the naturalness of the human body and the encumbrance of clothing while working in the garden. One woman especially, spoke of her need to accept her body and to feel free to be naked in front of others. This belief in the natural beauty of the human body and in the goodness of being naked without shame pervades the counter-culture, though it did not convince the swami to alter his position.

22. Of late, psychiatrists like R.D. Laing and his colleague, David Cooper, have contended that much more damage is done to children in families than has hitherto been realized. See, R. D. Laing and A. Esterson (1964), and D. Cooper (1967).

23. This view is expressed poetically in Kahlil Gibran's meditation on childhood: "Your children are not your children, they are the sons and daughters of life's longing for itself. They come through you but not from you. And though they are with you yet they belong not to you. You may give them your love but not your thoughts . . . You may strive to be like them, but seek not to make them like you. . . ." K. Gibran (1923).

24. At the same time, one of the babies had bow legs and his parents were in a quandary about whether to take him to a straight doctor. They wanted to "heal" him through the power of the spirit, but hedged their bet by eventually going to a medical doctor. Since the doctor indicated that the baby's legs would probably straighten out as he grew older, the parents felt somewhat vindicated. People at Satna seemed to make the implicit assumption that physical ailments reflected moral or spiritual failure.

25. It seems easier to see a spiritual dimension in the behavior of infants than in the activities of older children. Moreover, the birth of the infant children corresponded more closely with the time the parents became involved in spiritual life. One mother of a six year old at Satna, who was expecting to become pregnant again soon, commented about how this time

she was "going to do it right." She intended to follow the advice offered in a spiritual guide to child-rearing, called *Child Equals One* published by the Aurobindo Community in India. The guide informs the prospective mother among other things, to talk openly with the growing embryo in her womb, and to explain her activities and introduce fellow members to the future neonate.

26. Though members wished the girls luck, they were also afraid that the boys' straight parents would get upset by two freaky girls "coming on" to their sons.

27. The decision to keep the children out of public school was said by Lou to have been taken by her and the children collectively. She maintained that if the kids wanted to go, they would. Yet, if they had elected to go, the effort of getting them to and from the school bus stop would have been considerable, involving a five-mile drive on a winding dirt road that floods out with the onset of the fall rains.

28. Not all communal parents treat their children this way. At Satna, Mark, the young man living with 3 year old Celia's mother, was quite upset when he stumbled upon Celia and 9 year old Stevie together in sex play. He felt that somebody ought to have set Stevie straight, and that if his mother didn't, he would. Similarly, Stevie's mother, Lee, a woman in her forties, considered her other son's temporary absence as his having "run away." She showed a kindly indulgence toward the boy's departure, but presumably the boy himself felt he would not be able to leave the community if he had to consult with his mother. Both Mark and Lee were among the least involved in the counter-culture before coming to Satna. Both came there chiefly to further an already initiated contact with Eastern spirituality.

29. For individuals with such a *weltanschauung*, the callous treatment of animals has been a thorn in the side. Members of the Jain sect in India use extreme caution when walking, lest they inadvertently kill an insect on the path. Strict vegetarians argue that man has no right to use animals for his exclusive benefit by raising them for slaughter or taking their milk or eggs. At Satna, a guest raised questions about the propriety of separating kid goats from their mothers in order to have a supply of milk for the commune. The guest provoked a vigorous discussion; the possibility of curtailing the practice was considered. Disputes between meat-eaters and vegetarians have been responsible for breaking up communal settlements into antagonistic camps, which, on occasion, has led to the creation of new communes for the dissenters. Some meat-eating communes slaughtering their own animals have purportedly adopted a rite in which they ask the animal's understanding and consent in the taking of its life. One Yogic wit, an American who at one time had been in the New York

literary scene, and described himself currently as "in the used Karma business," while visiting the Satna community once said jokingly to a mosquito he had just dispatched: "May you proceed to a higher incarnation." One might see the joke as a gesture aimed at dispelling the collective unease caused by killing even so minor a fellow creature.

30. Sylvia, a visitor to Satna, explained that when she wanted something that her children wouldn't relinquish, she used to tell them that "it was now this Krishna's turn." Another example of the use of religious doctrine in gaining leverage over the child is illustrated by the following incident. A small child was made to cry by a playmate. After running to his mother and receiving comfort, he returned with a message to his tormentor, saying: "Look, you're only building up bad *karma* for yourself."

31. In this case, the mother clearly informed the girl that only people of the opposite sex make love. A few days later, she tested her daughter to see if the lesson had sunk in. She asked the girl if she still wanted to make love and received the reassuring reply that they couldn't since neither of them was a man.

32. In point of fact the children got along more harmoniously and seemed more joyful and creative than the adults, who were continuously bickering and reviewing their feelings and dreams. Even the adults appeared to recognize that the children were a happier group.

33. In many respects, 14 year old Kelly was considered an adult and a full member of the community. He even moved out of his mother's mobile home into a homesite of his own. Yet, having been entrusted with the overseership of the community's tractor, he found others consistently by-passing his authority. His mother claimed that this hurt his feelings and was the principal reason for his eventually leaving the settlement.

34. See, for example, Aberle and Naegele, (1952) on the future orientation of middle-class fathers.

35. See Bernard Wishy (1968) for a discussion of the child nurture movement in early 19th century America. Wishy agrees that a history of *expertise* on the child can only begin with the advent of the 20th century. See Wishy (1968), p. viii.

36. The rise of child-psychology as an important technique in the production of well-balanced adults contrasts sharply with the older moralistic treatment of child-rearing: "The child's nurture is one important key to a more controlled and rational future and, presumably, parents with the right kind of ideas will assure him the best possible nurture. Together . . . parental wishes and prejudices as well as enlightened ideas have made every child a test of the worthiness of our passports as modern human beings." Wishy (1968), p. viii.

37. Seely, Sim, Loosley (1956), p. 167.
38. Zablocki, (1971), Mungo (1971), Diamond (1971), Houriet (1971), Roszak (1969).
39. See Paul Goodman's (1967) nightmarish idyll for a vision of such a sub-society.
40. Satna has recently experienced a growth in membership, and has begun its own high school, grade school, and nursery school. It appears as if the group has successfully weathered the critical founding stage, though tensions still exist between the more counter-culture oriented and the more spiritually devoted members. Defections have occurred but the addition of new members has more than offset the number of those who have left. More is involved in the relative success of Satna than the existence of a spiritual commitment. Nevertheless, the example of Satna seems to indicate again the important role that religious ideology plays in the establishment of group solidarity in communal settlements.

REFERENCES

Aberle, David F., and Kaspar D. Naegele. "Middle-class Fathers' Occupational Role and Attitudes Toward Children." *American Journal of Orthopsychiatry*, 22 (1952), 366 378.
Bestor, Arthur. *Backwoods Utopias: The Sectarian Origins and the Owenite Phase of Communitarian Socialism in America, 1663–1829.* 2nd edition, Philadelphia: University of Pennsylvania Press, (1971). Originally published in 1950.
Bettelheim, Bruno. *Children of the Dream.* New York: Macmillan, (1969).
Cooper, David. *The Death of the Family.* New York: Vintage, (1971).
Cuber, John F., and Peggy B. Harroff. *The Significant Americans: A Study of Sexual Behavior Among the Affluent.* New York: Appleton-Century, (1965).
———. "The More Total View: Relationships Among Men and Women of the Upper Middle-Class." *Marriage and Family Living,* Vol. XXV, No. 2, (May, 1963), 140–145.
Diamond, Stephen. *What the Trees Said: Life on a New Age Farm.* New York: Delacorte Press, (1971).
Gibran, Kahlil. *The Prophet.* New York: Alfred A. Knopf, (1972). Originally published in 1923.
Goodman, Paul. "1984." *Ramparts,* Vol. 6, No. 2, (Sept., 1967).
Houriet, Robert. *Getting Back Together.* New York: Coward, McCann and Geoghegan, (1971).
Kanter, Rosabeth Moss. "Commitment and Social Organization: A Study of Commitment Mechanisms in Utopian Communities." *American Sociological Review,* Vol. 33, No. 4, (1968).
Laing, R.D. and A. Esterson. *Sanity, Madness and the Family.*

Baltimore: Penguin Books, (1970). Originally published in 1964.

Mungo, Raymond. *Total Loss Farm: A Year in the Life*. New York: E. P. Dutton and Co., (1971).

Rimmer, Robert. *Proposition Thirty One*. New York: Bantam Books, (1968).

Roszak, Theodore. *The Making of a Counter-Culture*. Garden City, New York: Doubleday, (1969).

Seeley, J.R., R.A. Sim and E.W. Loosley. *Crestwood Heights: A Study of the Culture of Suburban Life*. New York: John Wiley and Sons, (1963). Originally published in 1956.

Skinner, B.F. *Walden II*. New York: Macmillan, (1969). Originally published in 1948.

Wishy, Bernard. *The Child and The Republic*. Philadelphia: University of Pennsylvania Press, (1968).

Zablocki, Benjamin. *The Joyful Community*. Baltimore: Penguin Books, (1971).

III

The Impact of the School: Traditional and Beyond

Next to the family the schools are the most important socialization agent of modern society. No wonder then that the school system has been the focus of public debate and scientific research almost since its founding. Whole libraries have been written about the schools and the flood of literature has increased rather than decreased. Thus the purpose of this chapter can only be a limited one. The first two articles are to illustrate the recent status of an ongoing debate in sociological and psychological literature on the class character of our schools. This debate has focused on the problem of language acquisition and the so-called theory of codes. Professor Basil Bernstein, from the University of London, Institute of Education, is probably the most prominent promoter of socio-linguistic research; in his numerous theoretical and empirical studies he has developed the concept of a "restricted" and an "elaborated" language code which determines to a large extent success and failure of children in the school and which shows a correspondence to their family and class origin. In his present paper, which was first published within the framework of an Open University course book, he presents an excellent summary of a decade of his research. In this most recent statement of his he has reformulated and modified some of his earlier concepts while at the same time attacking some of his critics and adversaries.—Hugh Mehan's paper on "Assessing Children's School Performance," which was written for publication in this volume, continues the discussion of language codes in a different framework. Professor Mehan, *who is director of the Teacher Education Program at the University of California, San Diego, collaborated with Professor Aaron Cicourel and others on a research project concerned with language development and school performance. With his ethnomethodological approach he is able to demonstrate empirically that children from lower classes and from ethnic minorities are discriminated against by the unreflected use of psychological tests in school. This once again casts light on the fact that the school system is a middle class institution which furthers adjustment to unquestioned values and norms rather than intellectual capabilities and skills—With the failure of "compensatory education" for underpriviliged children in special school programs it came as a natural question whether the tremendous impact which the mass media have today on the socialization process could not be steered into a more fruitful direction. Thus the famous "Sesame Street" program was started and proved to be a remarkable step toward an educational use of national television. How difficult it is to control such an experiment and to assess its relative success is thoroughly described by Gerald S. Lesser, the chairman of the National Board of Advisers to the Children's Television Workshop, which produces "Sesame Street." Dr. Lesser's article, which is adapted from his new book on "Children and Television: Lessons from Sesame Street" (Random House, New York 1972), reflects on the experience of researchers and television producers working together to develop television for children on the basis of knowledge (and hunches) about how children learn. This article was first printed in Harvard Educational Review (Vol. 42, No. 2, May 1972). The fact that children apparently can learn to read in a playful way at a much earlier age than that established as appropriate in the schools opens up the question of whether the schools can be replaced by other means of education, especially in regard to the learning of specific skills. The strongest voice in a recent chorus of critics of the school system has become that of Ivan Illich with his famous thesis of "Deschooling Society." Dr. Illich has established his reputation as a radical Catholic ex-priest through his work at the Centre CIDOC in Cuernavaca, Mexico, which serves as a language school for Spanish as well as an international meeting ground for Western intellectuals and Latin American radicals. In his present essay on "The Breakdown of Schools," which is reprinted from "Journal of Research and Development" (Vol. 5, No. 3, 1972) he criticizes the schools (and the media) for offering what he calls "pre-cooked knowledge," which serves as a barrier against the immediate experience of reality, and suggests a number of radical alternatives.*

8

A Brief Account
of the Theory of Codes

BASIL BERNSTEIN

A MAJOR AIM of the research has been to try and understand the basic social controls on the form and contents of symbolic orders transmitted initially in the family and in the process of education. Thus, there have been two major strands in the work I have been trying to do over the past decade: the research into socio-linguistic codes, and the research into education as an agency of social control. The underlying conceptual connection between these two strands was made explicit in the first draft of the classification and frame paper, written in 1969 ("On the curriculum"). I shall give a brief account of this development.

The first paper, in the series of four on the school, was written in 1964 and was published in 1966 ("Sources of consensus and disaffection in education"). This grew out of a paragraph in a paper entitled "Some sociological determinants of perception" (1958). The major idea was to create a simple conceptual framework capable of showing the interrelationships between the family, peer group, school and work. In this analysis, the school was the basic variable and an attempt was made to show, theoretically, how the response of the pupil to the school was influenced by the form of the transmission of what I termed the instrumental and expressive orders of the school.

I distinguished between the organisational structure which controlled the curricula, pedagogy and assessment (the instrumental order) and the organisational structure which attempted to control the definitions of acceptable conduct, character and manner (the expressive order). I suggested a classification of types of relationships a pupil might develop (which had its basis in different forms of consensus and disaffection), according to the pupil's experience of the school's instrumental and expressive order. These pupil relationships can be summarised, with *great* over-simplification, as follows:

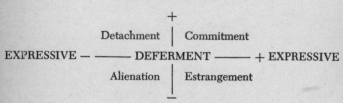

INSTRUMENTAL

+

| Detachment | Commitment |

EXPRESSIVE — ——— DEFERMENT ——— + EXPRESSIVE

| Alienation | Estrangement |

—

INSTRUMENTAL

LEGEND: + high involvement/acceptance
— low involvement/rejection

I argued that "What the school does, its rituals, ceremonies, authority relationships, its incentives, rewards and punishments, its very image of conduct, character and manner can modify or change the pupil's role as this has been initially shaped by the family. Thus the number of pupils initially involved in a particular role can be modified or changed by the school."

In the "Ritual in Education" paper, (1966a), the analysis was taken a stage further. Here I distinguished between two different organisational structures for the transmission of the instrumental order and the expressive order. Each of these orders could be transmitted in such a way that each could give rise to social relationships which were highly stratified (strong and hierarchical definitions of roles, groups, subjects) or to social relationships which were differentiated (weaker and less hierarchical definitions of roles, groups and subjects). In this paper, I explored changes in the forms of social control as expressive and instrumental orders moved away from stratified towards more differentiated social relationships. I suggested that non-examination children were more likely to experience the differentiated type. "For the non-examination children, the school functions not so much as a delicate instrument of the division of labour, but much more as an instrument of social control regulating the behavior of such pupils, their emotional sensitivities, their modes of social relationship to what is considered acceptable to a section of society to which the pupils often feel they do not belong. At a higher level of abstraction, the shift from stratified to differentiated was derived from Durkheim's two forms of solidarity, mechanical and organic."

In the "Open schools—open society?" paper (1967), the distinction between "stratified" and "differentiated" was dropped, and it was replaced by the distinction between "open" and "closed." The diagram sets out the basic analysis of the paper, and also provides a scale for the degree of openness or closure. It is possible to see how changes in the distribution of power and the principles of social control affect the what, how, where, when, with whom, of school learning. *Thus the realisation of elaborated codes varies with the form of their institutionalisation.*

At this point, the link with the socio-linguistic work begins to emerge. From one point of view, the concepts of restricted and elaborated codes took their starting point from Durkheim's two forms of solidarity. From another point of view, the socio-linguistic thesis attempted to demonstrate how the class structure affected the social distribution of privileged meanings and the interpretative procedures which generated them. It is also the case that as the organisational structure and "knowledge" properties of the school change, so do the nature of the processes and the procedures of communication.

In the "Open schools—open society?" paper (1967), I made use of Professor Douglas's exciting book *Purity and Danger* (1966). I analysed the curriculum in terms of it representing a structure which celebrated *purity* of categories (strongly bounded subjects) or in terms of a structure celebrating the *mixing* of categories (weakly bounded subjects). I linked the shift from one curriculum to another to changes in the form of authority and in the patterns of control. There was a conceptual error in this paper, for I had applied the concepts of mechanical and organic solidarity without making a sufficiently detailed analysis of the two types of "knowledge" structures. The problem was more complex than I had anticipated. I developed the *New Society* paper in February 1969, but the draft was never published, although it existed in manuscript form (University of London Institute of Education Library 1969a). In this manuscript, I suggested "Now we can begin to see that if we are to discuss curriculum we have also to consider pedagogy and evaluation . . . The selective organisation, transmission and evaluation of knowledge is intimately bound up with patterns of authority and control." I distinguished between two forms of the transmission of educational knowledge, "collection" and "integrated," and I speculated on their effect upon the formation of identities, concepts of property, the relationships between teachers and pupils, and upon the distribution of power and the principles of social control.

I was now in a stronger position to bring together the two strands. It has always been very clear to me that the class structure affected access to elaborated codes through its influence upon initial socialisation into the family *and* through its fundamental shaping of both the organisational structure and contents of education. I was also very sure that there were a variety of ways in which an elaborated code could be transmitted. (See later discussion of positional and personal family types which preceded "stratified" and "differentiated" schools.)

It is entirely incorrect to suggest that I placed no emphasis upon the school as a creator of educational problems for pupils. Indeed, it should be clear from this brief summary that I have been preoccupied with the analysis of the form and contents of education.

In the most recent paper in the series on the school ("On the classification and framing of educational knowledge," 1970a), the lower order concepts of stratified/differentiated, open/closed finally disappeared as they could be derived from the concepts classification and frame. In this paper, I regarded curriculum, pedagogy and evaluation as message systems and I attempted an analysis of their underlying principles in terms of the relative strength of their classification and framing.

Formal Controls
ORDERS
INSTRUMENTAL

Mixing of Categories	*Purity of Categories*
Teaching groups: Heterogeneous—size and composition varied	**Teaching groups:** Homogeneous—size and composition fixed.
Pedagogy: Problem setting or creating / Emphasises *ways of knowing*	**Pedagogy:** Solution giving / Emphasises *contents* or states of *knowledge*
Teachers: Teaching roles co-operative/inter-dependent / Duties *achieved* / Fluid points of reference and relation	**Teachers:** Teaching roles insulated from each other / Duties *assigned* / Fixed points of reference and relation
Curriculum: Subject boundaries blurred (inter-related) / Progression: deep to surface structure of knowledge / Common curriculum	**Curriculum:** Subject boundaries sharp (less inter-relation or integration) / Progression: surface to deep structure of knowledge / Curriculum graded for different ability groups
Pupils: Varied social groups reducing *group* similarity and difference—increased area of choice / Aspirations of the *many* raised / Fluid points of reference and relation	**Pupils:** Fixed and stable social groups emphasising group similarity and difference—reduced area of choice. / Aspirations of the *few* developed / Fixed points of reference and relation

TYPE—OPEN	TYPE—CLOSED
1) Ritual order celebrates participation/co-operation	1) Ritual order celebrates hierarchy/dominance
2) Boundary relationships with outside blurred	2) Boundary relationships with outside sharply drawn
3) Internal organisation: wide range of integrative sub-groups with active membership and success roles across ability ranges / If prefect system—wide area of independence from staff, but limited exercise of power / Range of opportunities for pupils to influence staff decisions, e.g. opportunities for self-government	3) Internal organisation: narrower range of integrative sub-groups with active membership and success roles confined to high ability range / If prefect system—under staff control and influence, but extensive exercise of power / Limited opportunities for pupils to influence staff decisions, e.g. limited opportunities for self-government.
4) Teacher-pupil authority relationships: Reward and punishment less public and ritualised / Teacher-pupil relationships of control—inter-personal	4) Teacher-pupil authority relationships: Reward and punishment public and ritualised / Teacher-pupil relationships of control—positional
Mixing of Categories	*Purity of Categories*

EXPRESSIVE

CLASSIFICATION AND FRAME

Classification, here, does not refer to *what* is classified, but to the *relationships* between contents. Classification refers to the nature of the differentiation between contents. Where classification is strong, contents are well insulated from each other by strong boundaries. Where classification is weak, there is reduced insulation between contents for the boundaries between contents are weak or blurred. *Classification thus refers to the degree of boundary maintenance between contents*. Classification focusses our attention upon boundary strength as the critical distinguishing feature of the division of labour of educational knowledge. It gives us the basic structure of the message system, curriculum. The concept *frame* is used to determine the structure of the message system, pedagogy. Frame refers to the form of the *context* in which knowledge is transmitted and received. Frame refers to the specific pedagogical relationship of teacher and taught. In the same way as classification does not refer to contents, so frame does not refer to the contents of the pedagogy. Frame refers to the strength of the boundary between what may be transmitted and what may not be transmitted, in the pedagogical relationship. Where framing is strong, there is a sharp boundary, where framing is weak, a blurred boundary, between what may and may not be transmitted. Frame refers us to the range of options available to teacher and taught in the *control* of what is transmitted and received in the context of the pedagogical relationship. Strong framing entails reduced options; weak framing entails a range of options. *Thus frame refers to the degree of control teacher and pupil possess over the selection, organisation, and pacing of the knowledge transmitted and received in the pedagogical relationship*.

There is another aspect of the boundary relationship between what may be taught and what may not be taught, and consequently, another aspect to framing. We can consider the relationship between the non-school everyday community knowledge of the teacher or taught, *and* the educational knowledge transmitted in the pedagogical relationship. We can raise the question of the strength of the boundary, the degree of insulation, between the everyday community knowledge of teacher and taught and educational knowledge. Thus, we can consider variations in the strength of frames as these refer to the strength of the boundary between educational knowledge and everyday community knowledge of teacher and taught.

From the perspective of this analysis, the basic structure of the message system, curriculum, is given by variations in the strength of classification, and the basic structure of the message system, pedagogy, is given by variations in the strength of frames. The structure of the message system, evaluation, is a function of the strength of classification and frames.

It was now possible to make explicit the concept of educational knowledge code. The code is fully given at the most general level by the relationship between classification and frame.

In terms of the early work, *but with much over-simplification*, stratified or closed schools would now be schools employing strong classification and strong frames, which realised types of collection codes; whereas differentiated or open schools would employ weak classification and weak frames, which would realise types of integrated codes. Because these new concepts operated at a much higher level of abstraction than the earlier ones, their analytic power was very much greater.

In the classification and frame paper, the linkage with the work on socio-linguistic codes has been forged, to my mind, in a fundamental way. This can be seen if we raise the following question. If the social assumptions which give rise to restricted codes are those of intimacy, what are the social assumptions which shape the realisations of elaborated codes? Basically, all social assumptions must manifest themselves in the form taken by social relationships in the context of interaction, and in the structure of communication. I suggested that the realisations of elaborated codes vary according to the strength of classification and the strength of frames which regulate their transmission in schools or formal educational relationships. As the classification and frames of formal education change their strength, so does the system of meanings and the interpretative procedures, which are realised by code elaboration. The social assumptions which shape elaborated codes express themselves in classification and frames of various strengths. Thus collection codes which are transmitted through strong classifications and strong frames will give rise to elaborated codes very different from those created by integrated codes transmitted through weakened classifications and weakened frames. It follows from this that elaborated codes are not necessarily middle-class communication procedures; they are not necessarily instruments for the alienation of the working-class; neither does it follow that they function as repeaters of a particular class structure. Whether such codes perform the above functions depends more and more in industrialised societies upon the classification and frames which control their transmission in formal education.

In this way, the work on socio-linguistic codes is vitally and inextricably inter-related with the work on so-called "knowledge" codes made available through public education. I am not here concerned with the empirical truth of the thesis, only with the question of tracing the conceptual inter-relationship of its two strands. In one sentence, whilst the division of labour inevitably exerts an influence upon the contents of education, the class structure and its legitimising ideology regulates the classification and framing of such contents. It is a travesty to relate the concepts of elaborated or restricted codes to superficial stylistics of middle-class and working-class forms of conversational behaviour, as implied by Labov (1970).

It is more than likely that the thesis, like any other in the field of social science, will be shown to be inadequate, empirically false, in some respects partial, even misleading, but at least one has a right to expect recognition that one has attempted to treat a problem at the level it deserves. The exploration of the concepts developed to understand the form and contents of education inevitably influenced, and were influenced by, the concepts developed to understand forms of language use and *both* become further developed by empirical research.

I now want to turn to the development of the concept of socio-linguistic codes, to the exploration of their generating and maintaining social relationships, and to their relationship to the wider social structure. I have given some accounts of this process in the Introduction to the book *Class Codes and Control* Vol. I (1961).

I have difficulty in understanding, and I have very little sympathy with, complaints that the socio-linguistic thesis of 1958 is in some respects different from the thesis in 1972. Such a critique is based upon a complete misunderstanding of the nature of research. The single most important fact of research is where it *leads*, not where it starts. In one sense, of course, where it starts—i.e. the initial formulation of the basic problem—already pre-determines the extent of the exploration. To have an idea is not difficult, but the attempt to clarify it, to rescue it from a local intuition, to make it explicit, yet always to be aware of the ambiguity upon which its growth depends, is quite another matter.

The basic thesis has been that forms of communication may be distinguished in terms of what is rendered implicit and what is rendered explicit. Thus the fundamental characteristic of a public language given in 1958 was that a public language is a language of implicit meaning. This idea of implicitness and explicitness underwent a series of transformations:—

(1) Universalistic/particularistic (1962b)
(2) Context independent/context dependent (1969)

Now what was it that was rendered implicit or explicit? Clearly, any communication depends upon shared assumptions and rests upon inherent ambiguities, but the nature of the assumptions and the nature of the ambiguities may vary. Implicit/explicit represented for me the extent to which the *principles* underlying the social structuring of relevant meaning were made public and elaborated through the use of language *in the process of socialisation*. The problem then became one of constructing defining criteria of *such forms* of implicitness and explicitness realised and transmitted in the use of language. It appeared to me (as to many others) that as the emphasis changed from implicitness to explicitness (*as previously defined*) then such a change in emphasis would act selectively on the grammatical and lexical choices. At no time did I ever consider that I was concerned with differences between social groups at the level of competency; that is, differences between social groups which had their origin in their basic tacit understanding of the linguistic rule system. I was fundamentally concerned with *performance*, that is; I was interested in the sociological controls on the use to which this common understanding was put. In the same way, I never believed that there was any difference between social groups in their *tacit* understanding of logical rules; of the rules of inference. The difference which concerned me was the usage to which this common tacit understanding was put. It was also made very clear in print that I was not essentially concerned with dialect or so-called sub-standard speech (1958, 1959, 1960).

The identification of implicit usage with dialect or "substandard" speech probably arose out of the first characteristic given of public and formal language use, in which "Short grammatical, simple, often unfinished sentences, a poor syntactic structure stressing the active mood" was contrasted with "Accurate grammatical order and syntax regulates what is said." None of the other characteristics in the list pointed towards "standard" or "substandard" speech. Neither have I ever considered that these characteristics were in any sense the crucial determiners of the form of language use. Indeed, even in the early papers it is clear that the primary paradigm of a public language is a context of intimacy. However, given the class structuring of speech, it was likely that formal language use would be associated with so-called standard speech. Such speech, in *itself*, could not serve to indicate either public or formal language usage. In other words, I have never been concerned with what Labov and others call the superficial stylistics of middle-class speech. *Indeed, if I had been concerned with the relative presence or absence of such niceties of conversation, why did not Lawton or myself in the early research count such deviations from standard speech?* It would not have been difficult! I certainly would not wish to defend the indices created in those two lists, but I would resolutely oppose the view that the distinction between the two forms of communication rested upon, or necessarily pointed to the difference between, "standard" or "substandard" speech. Indeed, even the relationship between codes and social class was seen as contingent (1962).

The second formulation (1962) in terms of restricted and elaborated codes represented an attempt to formulate the regulative principles which I considered to underly implicit and explicit forms of communication. These terms pointed to the way the class structure acted upon the social distribution of privileged meanings and upon the interpretative procedures which generated them. The class structure distributes power unequally; it distributes access to, control over, facility to exploit property; whether this property is physical or symbolic. It does this through its penetration into educational arrangements and processes and through its penetration into primary socialisation within the family, in such a way that a vicious self-perpetuating circle is often set up between home, school and work. Any analysis of how class structures repeat themselves in the process of socialisation must necessarily show the class realisations in the family *and* school *and* work.

During this period of the re-formulation of public and formal language use into restricted and elaborated codes, I moved away from a descriptive correlational association between speech forms and certain demographic attributes of families such as level of education and economic functions, to the formulation of two different types of families with differently focussed communication structures. ("Family role systems, communication and socialisation" (1962b)). Different role options were made available in these hypothetical types of families and I connected causally the nature of these role options with the nature of the linguistic options; for the role options initially created and defined the social structuring of relevant meanings and established the interpretative procedures underlying their generation and reception. There were two aspects to the communication structure within the types of families:

(1) The communications could focus upon either positional or personal attributes of family member (see con-

nection between "stratified" and "differentiated" schools, "collection"/"integrated" codes).

(2) The realisation of these attributes could be regulated by either restricted or elaborated codes.

We can express this formulation diagrammatically:

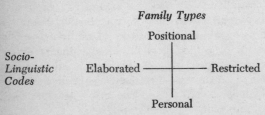

Family Types

Positional

Socio-Linguistic Codes   Elaborated ——————— Restricted

Personal

Thus, by about 1962, the crude correlation between forms of language use and social class had been made more sensitive, so that the basic unit had become a family type with a particular communication structure and focus. It was further possible to distinguish *both* within the middle-class and the working-class according to the type of family and to relate the incidence and change of the types to the more macro-institutional features of the society. The same model allowed for the distinction between object-focussed codes (positional) and person-focused codes (personal).

Whilst the sociological aspect of the analysis had now been more carefully specified, there were still major difficulties with the linguistic aspect. The code definitions in 1962 emphasised the relatively extensive range of alternatives in the case of an elaborated code and the relatively reduced range of alternatives in the case of a restricted code. These definitions brought the role options, at the sociological level, into a hypothesised causal relationship with the linguistic options. There were a number of conceptual problems in this formulation. To begin with, the concept of role option, or discretion, as it was then called, operated at a different logical level from the concept of code. Role options or discretion refer to sociologically controlled choices in specific interactional contexts, whereas the concept code referred to a regulative principle which shaped a general orientation. What was the relationship between these two concepts; essentially what was the relationship between code and context? If we turn now to the code definitions, it can be seen that I considered that the possibility of combination and re-combination of syntactic alternatives was greater in the case of an elaborated code, therefore I considered that the possibility of predicting such alternatives was less than in the case of a restricted code. I associated complexity with a greater variety of choice. This was partly because at the time I knew very little linguistics, and, more importantly, because of the influence of information theory at the Department of Phonetics, University College London, where I held a junior position of honorary research assistant.

The two parts of the thesis were now at odds with each other. The sociological aspect had its roots in roles and so it directed attention to interactional contexts or situations; whereas the linguistic aspect defined codes independently of context or situation. This was the conceptual position at the start of the major enquiries of the Sociological Research Unit, under my direction, in 1964. A descriptive account of these enquiries was given in the Introduction I wrote to the first SRU monograph (Brandis and Henderson (1970)).

Despite the inconsistency between the sociological and linguistic aspects of the thesis, the major research activity was directed towards examining code realisations in different contexts. In the first interview, for example, the mothers who took part in the research were asked how they *might* answer questions their child *might* put to them. Two and a half years later many of the same questions, together with a range of others, were put to the children of these mothers. This was the beginning of the exploration of the instructional context (Robinson and Rackstraw (1972)). In the same interview the mothers were asked what they *might* say *if* their child committed a series of misdemeanours. Two and a half years later the same questions (but with some modification) were put to the children. This was the beginning of the analysis of the *regulative* context (Cook (1970, 1972), Turner (1972a & b). We also obtained from the children at age five years and seven years, examples of speech elicited from convicted, imaginative and instructional contexts.

It was clear to me that we had to choose a linguistic

theory to guide the analysis of the speech. The major linguistic theory at that time (1964) which was attaining supremacy, was transformation grammar. I deliberately decided for the following reasons not to use Chomsky's theory.

(1) The theory divorced linguistics from semantics. I could not see how such a theory could be appropriate to a study where the major area of enquiry was precisely the problem of the relationship between the social structuring of relevant meanings and the form of their linguistic expression.

(2) Chomsky's theory rested upon certain psychological, even neurological assumptions which underpinned the concept of *competence*. The theory I was exploring rested upon clearly *social* assumptions about the nature of *performance*. I foresaw major difficulties in any attempt to bring together two theories which differed so markedly in their basic assumptions and focus.

(3) Chomsky's theory did not permit any linguistic descriptions above the level of the sentence. I considered that one of our major tasks was to carry out such a description which would entail an examination of the integrating devices between sentences. A major problem of the non-linguistic analyses carried out by Dr. Lawton and myself arose out of the attempt to characterise the overall patterning of speech on the basis of counts of isolated frequencies of selected speech elements. Whilst intuitively I believed that differences in such relative frequencies (sometimes even quite small differences) created a distinctly different overall patterning, there was no means (in the sense that I was not aware of the means) of making this intuition explicit and formal. It was also clear to me that the logical levels of the sociological and linguistic analysis must match. A necessary condition for this was the construction of a linguistic description above the level of the sentence from which could be *derived* a justification for any individual counts of speech elements. Such a linguistic description in turn would need to be directed by a primitive (in the sense of elementary or simple) specification of the semantic structure of codes. Interestingly enough, when such a specification was accomplished it was, and indeed, had to be, a context-free formu-

lation (Context dependent/independent: high/low specificity).

(4) In 1964, Chomsky had not developed a phonological analysis. I considered (though in fact we never carried out such an analysis) that such an enquiry might at some point become necessary.

A year before the major research enquiry, we had used an early form of Professor Halliday's Scale and Category Grammar in an analysis of the written texts obtained from children aged eleven years. Geoffrey Turner, senior linguist of the SRU, carried out this application. As a result, we adopted Halliday's linguistic theory, for it satisfied all the requirements created by the sociological aspects of the thesis. The long association with Professor Halliday which followed provided for both of us a constant source of mutual stimulation and influence. Dr. Hasan's development of Halliday's analysis of cohesion marked an especially critical step in the analyses of the speech. Perhaps the key to this analysis, and so to the relationship between the "socio" and the linguistic features arose out of the exploration of the regulative context.

I had earlier (1962b) developed a set of concepts which distinguished three basic modes of control; imperative, positional and personal. (Quite independently, Dr. Hanson (1965) published a paper setting out a similar approach). My own approach was never officially published until 1970, although the concepts were used in a paper given at an International Meeting in 1964. The concepts of imperative, positional and personal modes of control were operationalised and applied to the social control data we had collected from the mothers and children. Dr. Cook and myself (in discussion with other members of the SRU, notably Dr. Peter Robinson) created a coding grid for the analysis of the data. Briefly, we distinguished a number of sub-systems which could be applied to a range of parent-child regulative contexts. Each sub-system opened the way to a range of choices, all of which were derived from the thesis. We could then examine which of the sub-systems a mother or child entered *and* nature of the choice within any sub-system. Further, each choice could be given a precise linguistic description. In other words, we had constructed a semantic network, derived from the thesis, which made possible an analysis of its contextual linguistic realisation.

Thus:

Theory→model of social control (regulative context)→ semantic specification of alternatives→linguistic realisation of the alternatives.

It was this formulation which allowed us to take over Professor Halliday's network theory, and theory of language functions. We could also show the *different* linguistic realisations of different contexts *and* decide whether each context had evoked either a restricted or an elaborated variant. We now could examine both the emphasis and the range of choices (alternatives) an individual took up in the network. In this way, it was possible to return to the definition of codes in terms of the range of alternatives; *yet these alternatives would always be context specific.*

I certainly do not want to give the impression that the problem of the operationalising of codes was solved, but at least a way had been found of approaching a possible solution. Geoffrey Turner, who was a graduate student of Halliday, played a vital role in the construction of networks used for the analysis of the regulative context. The way was now clear for the final definition of codes, which first appeared in "A critique of compensatory education," published in the book edited by Rubinstein and Stoneman, *Education for Democracy* (1970). That paper had been given earlier as a public lecture at Columbia University (1969b).

I will now summarise the development of the final definition.

1) Public and Formal Language Use — list of apparently unrelated characteristics with no explicit conceptual backing.

2) Elaborated and Restricted Codes (object or person focussed) — context-free definition in terms of the predictability of syntactic alternatives. No explicit linkage with semantics.

3) Elaborated and Restricted Codes (object or person focussed)   context-independent definition in terms of semantics.

Semantic Structure

universalistic

Specificity: High ——————————— Low

particularistic

but context-dependent linguistic analysis, on the basis of derivations from the above model appropriate to the contexts, crucial to the thesis.

I will now turn to the research on the family. The second interview with the mothers took place two and a half years after the first. It took the form of a set of closed questionnaires. I have commented on the methodological problems in such an approach in the Introduction to *Class Codes and Control*, Volume II, 1972 (see also Cook, J., chapter in the same volume). The basic research aim was to test out the ideas of the positional and personal types of families as these might be realised in *both* the middle and working classes. To have a model is one thing, to explore it empirically takes a little time and normally it gives rise to more questions than answers. I considered that if we were to study communication in families in a way *relevant to the thesis*, we would need to see such communication as being shaped by the following variables:

(1) strong-weak linkage with family of origin
(2) strong-weak linkage with neighbourhood and local community
(3) strong-weak role definitions of family members
(4) strong-weak insulation between the meanings active in the family and the meanings active in agencies external to the family, to which members of the family were connected, e.g. work/family, school/family, T.U./family.

Clearly, the above variables would have to be examined against the economic, demographic and local characteristics of the family. The above formulation was very much influenced by *Family and Social Network* written by Elizabeth Bott (1957). One of the advantages of this approach was that we could distinguish between families within a particular social class category in terms of the strength or weakness of the various linkages and then examine the mothers' *reported* orientation to communication and control (see Bernstein and Henderson (1969c); Henderson (1970)). In principle, it would also be possible to examine the relationships between the language use of the mothers and their children, and changes in the strength of the various linkages. In general, the stronger the linkages, the more likely that the family would resemble a positional type. At this point, one can begin to see that strong linkages (positional families) are families which create rather strong boundaries, whereas person-centred families tend to create weak or blurred boundaries. In this way, it should be possible to consider families rather like schools in terms of their *classifications* and *frames*.

There is a danger to such an analysis, because it appears to separate the communication structure from the power relationships of society, but this can be avoided if the same analysis can show the relationships between class structures and communication structures; which is where we began.

I have tried very briefly to give some idea of the relationships between the work on "knowledge" codes and sociolinguistic codes, the development of the concept of code and some indication of the approach to communication within the family. In other papers I have tried to analyse, perhaps very inadequately, how macro institutional features of the society affect the nature of primary and secondary socialising agencies.*

Finally, I should like to comment on a particular interpretation of the thesis offered by Labov ("The logic of nonstandard English," reprinted in the Course Unit). I am not here concerned to examine Labov's analysis of the speech of Charles, M., and Larry, or the dialogue between Larry and John Lewis, for I have never asserted that differences

---

* It is possible for a code to be restricted in the verbal channel, but elaborated in others, e.g. music, painting.

between codes have any basis in speaker's tacit understanding of the linguistic rule system, that non-standard forms of speech have, in themselves, any necessary conceptual consequences, or that reasoning is only possible in an elaborated code, nor have I ever suggested that differences between codes have anything to do with superficial niceties of speech. It has become very fashionable in the USA now to find the villain who was responsible for leading research astray. It is a matter of interest that over 50% of the references (39) which I used in the first two papers (1958, 1959) came from American sources. Perhaps Americans have some difficulty in acknowledging the potential or actual influence on Americans by Americans. Indeed, it took me a little time to free myself of the standard USA work on socialisation.

Labov, like Ginsburg (1972), confines his analysis to early work, presumably up to 1961, yet the work I have supposed to influence was not published until 1966–68 (Bereiter, G. and Englemann, S. *Teaching Disadvantaged Children in the Pre-School*, Prentice-Hall, 1966; Deutsch, M., et al. (eds.) *The Disadvantaged Child*, New York, Basic Books, 1967; Deutsch, M., Katz, I., Jensen, A.R. *Social Class, Race and Psychological Development*, Holt, Rinehart and Winston Inc., 1960). Between 1961 and 1966, I had written a number of papers which it seems much of the USA ignored, so busy were they confining their attention in an uncritical way to papers written up to 1961. The reader might care to contrast Ginsburg's or Labov's account with that of Lillian Weber, who compares the overall impact of the thesis in England and the USA in her book *The English Infant School and Informal Education*, Center for Urban Education Book, Prentice-Hall, 1971.

Whilst there is much I agree with in Labov's paper (published in 1970), I find the following puzzling, to say the least. "The most extreme view which proceeds from this orientation and one that is widely accepted is that lower-class Negro children have no language at all. This notion is first drawn from Basil Bernstein's writings that "much of lower class language consists of a kind of incidental 'emotional' accompaniment to action here and now" (Jensen,

1968, p. 118). Bernstein's views are filtered through a strong bias against all forms of working-class behaviour so that middle-class language is seen as superior in every respect, "more abstract and necessarily somewhat more flexible, detailed and subtle" (p. 118) (Labov). In order to ensure that the ambiguity of the writing should not stand in the way of truth, when Labov had this paper reprinted, he *removed* Jensen's name from the quotations, so that the reader could identify these statements as coming from me (*Atlantic Monthly*, June 1972).

Compare with "A public language contains its own aesthetic, a simplicity and directness of expression, emotionally virile, pithy and powerful and a metaphoric range of considerable force and appropriateness. Some examples taken from the schools of this country have a beauty which many writers might well envy."* "This is not to say that speakers of this language interact in a completely uniform manner, for the potential of a public language allows a vast range of possibilities." (Bernstein, 1959)

"I must emphasise the point that in restricted code relationships, people are not non-verbal. There is no such thing as a non-verbal child; if a child is limited to a restricted code, it means not that this child is non-verbal, but simply that the kinds of roles he has learned have created in him a particular way in which he verbally transforms his world. *It is a whole lot of nonsense to speak of a non-verbal child, although he may be inarticulate in certain social contexts.*" (Bernstein, 1966b, Public Lecture, New York, published 1967)

"Isn't it (the elaborated code) also turgid, redundant, bombastic and empty? Is it not simply an elaborated style rather than a *superior* code or system?" (my italics) (Labov 1970)

"The preparation and delivery of relatively explicit meaning is the major function of this code. The meanings are not necessarily abstract, but abstraction inheres in the possibilities. Moreover, it cannot be assumed that because a person moves towards an elaborated code, the meanings he is signalling are of any great significance. A lot of nonsense can be signalled in this code. Regardless of the actual content, this code promotes the transmission of certain kinds of meanings rather than others." (Bernstein, 1966, op. cit.)

"Again, let me underline that neither of these codes is good or bad in itself." (Bernstein 1966, op. cit.)

* All children, irrespective of code, explore the creative potential of language. Indeed, where the initially received code is restricted, such exploration may be less trammelled than in the case of an elaborated code, for in its transmission, children may well be constrained by too early socialisation into explicit criteria.

"Clearly one code is not better than another, each possesses its own aesthetic, its own possibilities." (Bernstein, 1964)

"Again, let me be quite clear. This description (of the codes) implies no value judgment as to whether the exchange of individualised verbal signals or communalised signals is better. The value of one over the other depends upon the context." (Bernstein, 1966, op. cit.)

I am well aware that the issues raised by Labov and others cannot be settled by exchange of quotations; for it is always possible for a sentence, paragraph or a paper to be abstracted from the spirit of the total work.

The verbal deficit thesis has one of its roots in an American theory of learning (stimulus-response) which, when applied to language, becomes a particular type of theory of verbal mediation. In turn, the theory tends to give rise to an approach to change by means of "behaviour modification" (various forms of conditioning responses by rigorous control over the stimuli). The verbal deficit thesis also draws upon American child development studies which place an overwhelming emphasis upon the significance of the early years of the child's life. Both of these two groups of theories, for different reasons, are likely to view problems of educability as arising out of inter-actions which are considered to be deficient, inadequate or even pathological. These theories offer little purchase upon the wider institutional and cultural contexts which define the form, content and evaluation of what is to be learned, how it is to be learned, and the organisational context. It is also the case that, certainly up to the middle-sixties, much of the research into the problem of "who is able to learn what" was carried out by psychologists whose intellectual training and whose own socialisation led them to define the problem in a limited way.

It was only with the radicalising of American academics through Vietnam, the rise of black power, through the exposure of the failure of the American urban school, that fundamental questions were raised about the political implications of forms of education during the late sixties.[*]

I believe that the following extract was among one of the first public critiques of the deficit thesis:

[*] "Like many Americans, I belatedly discovered the "crisis" in urban education in the late 1960s." (Ginsburg (1972), Preface, p. ix.)

Mario Fantini: I am wondering if you can offer us some clarification on how we can actually use your model in terms of the problems that we face: for example, the problem of deprivation.

Basil Bernstein: I think what underlies this particular problem (in my thesis) is a notion of the formation of social experience somewhat different from the notions of social experience that inhere in some intervention approaches. Let me make this very concrete. It follows from my view that the notion of deficit is inadequate and perhaps misleading. Deficit is not a theory, it is simply a statement of certain lacks or deficiencies. This notion of treating children as exhibiting various kinds of deficits turns the social scientist into a plumber whose task is to plug, or rather fill, the deficits. It may lead to a partial relation with the child. You see a child as a cognitive or perceptual deficit, and so lose track of the vital nature of the communal experience of the child, and the many cultural and psychological processes at work in him, when he is to be "enriched."

It is of critical importance to draw into our work researchers in sociology and anthropology, in order that the various socializing agencies can be seen in relation to each other, and that the dynamics which flow from the political and economic nature of the society can inform our thinking and our actions. We must have more work of a sociological nature on both the school and the college of education as sociocultural systems. (Bernstein, 1966, op. cit.)

In a fundamental sense, a restricted code is the basic code. It is the code of intimacy which shapes and changes the very nature of subjective experience, initially in the family and in our close personal relationships. The intensifications and condensations of such communication carry us beyond speech and new forms of awareness often become possible. An elaborated code is the basic code by means of which our experience of persons and things is objectified and a different exploration of consciousness is possible. The social controls on the distribution, institutionalisation and realisation of elaborated codes may, under certain conditions, create alienation; this is not necessarily in the order of things.

APPENDIX ON THE TEST SITUATION

When we obtained the speech from the children we constructed a number of different situations which the children were invited to talk about. Although the researcher spent one day in the classroom with the children, the interview situation was an unusual situation for a child for at least the following reasons:

(1) The child is removed from both his normal school *and* non-school setting.

(2) The child enters a situation (the experimental setting) which is unlike any other setting he has met.

(3) He is presented with tasks which are unfamiliar and he is asked to create meanings often far removed from those he offers and receives in his day-by-day experience or even perhaps in his infant class.

(4) He inter-acts with a relatively strange adult, who provides only minimal guidance in a setting where he is given minimal clues as to what is or is not an appropriate response.

The question immediately arises as to what inferences can be made from the child's behaviour in this context to other contexts. Further, why should any measures of the mother's behaviour or social setting (e.g. social class position of the family) bear any relation to the child's behaviour? We could say that the experimental setting abstracts the child from his normal settings, abstracts the child from his normal tasks, abstracts the child from his normal social relationships with other adults, and finally abstracts the child from the meanings he normally creates and receives. The setting, tasks, social relationships and meanings are independent of the child's normal settings, tasks, relationships and meanings. In this sense, the experimental setting is a *context-independent* setting for the child. Now some children in this setting produce speech or responses which differ markedly from the speech or meanings of other children. Why do the children differ in their interpretation of the context? It certainly has nothing to do with differences in the children's tacit understanding of grammar and little to do with differences in the children's vocabulary. I suggest that what we are witnessing are differences in the *ground rules* the children are using to generate their meanings and so their speech.* One group of children are applying rules for the creation of

* Ground rules lie behind manifest behaviour almost in ways similar to the way grammatical rules lie behind speech. Elaborated and restricted codes from this perspective have their basis in different ground rules.

context-independent speech, whereas another group of children are doing this to a lesser extent. In the language of the thesis, one group of children are realising elaborated speech variants, whereas the other group are realising more restricted speech variants. The children are following different ground rules. Thus the experimental setting is itself, in its *totality*, that is, in terms of the setting, social relationships, tasks and meanings, acts *selectively* upon the ground rules the children are using. One group of children, through their initial socialisation, are applying one set of ground rules, and another group of children are applying a different set. What is being measured at a fundamental level is the process of socialisation which underlies the children's selection of ground rules. Let me give an example. When the children were seven years of age, they were asked (after two earlier attempts) to explain how the game "Hide and Seek" was played, to a child who did not know the game. Miss Lesley Lineker's (who is a Research Assistant in the S.R.U.), analysis of the speech indicates that there is a tendency for L.W.C. children to explain the game very much in terms of their family/neighbourhood setting, whereas there is a tendency for the M.C. children to refer much less to a local setting; their explanations are relatively context *independent*, whereas the L.W.C. children's explanations are rather more context *dependent*. Now it may well be the case that the L.W.C. children's form of explanation, as a teaching device, is more efficient than that of the M.C. children, but from the point of view of the thesis, the orientation to *different* forms of explanation is the crucial interest.

Thus, the inference from the experimental setting to other settings is based less upon differences in the spoken grammar and lexes, but more upon what *ground* rule the children will select in what context. Similarly, when we find a relationship between the speech and meanings of the mother and those of the children, it is, I suggest, because what has been taken over by the children is less the particulars of a grammar and lexes (although these are of some importance), but more a ground rule for developing meanings and speech. The child is not explicitly taught these ground rules by his parents. These ground rules are implicit in the meanings, speech and social relationships realised in the process and contexts of socialisation.

It is also a matter of some interest that the means we often (but not always) use for testing children in schools involve:

(1) The removal of the child from his normal non-school environment.

(2) An unusual setting where the child is isolated from other children.

(3) Inter-action with an adult who provides minimal guidance and support, and where he is often given, at the time, minimum clues as to what is or is not an appropriate response.

(4) Tasks which are very different from the ones he is concerned with outside of the school.

Thus, there is a broad analogy between the experimental setting and the test situation in the school. They are both relatively context independent, although it is true that the child is given opportunities to learn the requirements of the school test situation. Basically, I am suggesting that there are certain social assumptions underlying the experimental setting and test situations, and that the M.C. child, at least from the age of five years, has an understanding of the ground rules of these assumptions and so he is differently oriented to context-independent settings. If we see the problem from this point of view, we can go on to ask how it is that some L.W.C. children do select the ground rules for context-independent meanings, and how it is that some M.C. children do not. Why, for example, in a similar experimental setting, do M.C. children at five years of age score much higher on verbal tests than W.C. children, but on non-verbal tests this advantage is very much reduced. This opens up, of course, how it is that context-independent meanings are both assessed and acquired in a particular way; a way which is more favourable to M.C. children than to W.C. children. The basic argument applies equally to the mothers' response to the interview situation.

REFERENCES

Bereiter, G. and Engleman, S. 1966 *Teaching Disadvantaged Children in the Pre-School*, Prentice-Hall.

Bernstein, B. 1958 "Some sociological determinants of perception," *British Journal of Sociology*, IX.

1959 "A public language: some sociological implications of a linguistic form" *British Journal of Sociology*, X.

1960 "Language and social class" *British Journal of Sociology*, XII.

1962a "Lingustic codes, hesitation phenomena and intelligence" *Language and Speech*, 5.

1962b "Family role systems, socialisation and communication," Unpublished Manuscript, S.R.U., University of London Institute of Education.

1964 "Social class speech systems and psychotherapy," *British Journal of Sociology*, XV.

1964 "Elaborated and restricted codes; their social origins and some consequences," *American Anthropologist:* special issue, *Ethnography of Communication*.

Bernstein, R., with Elvin, H.L. & Peters, R.S. 1966a "Ritual in education" *Philosophical Transactions of the Royal Society of London, Series B.,* Biological Sciences, No. 772 C.I. 251; also reprinted in Open University Reader *School and Society* (1972)

1966b "The role of speech in the development and transmission of culture," Public Lecture to Bank Street Fiftieth Anniversary Symposium, published in *Perspectives on Learning* (eds.) Klopf, G.L. and Hohman, W.A., Mental Health Material Center Inc. 1967.

1967 "Open schools, open society?" *New Society*, Sept. 14th.

1969a "On the curriculum" University of London Institute of Education Library.

1969b "A critique of contemporary education," Public Lecture to Teachers College, Columbia University, published in *Education for Democracy* (eds.) Rubenstein, D. and Stoneman, C., Penguin Books, 1970.

(with Henderson, D.) (1969c) "Social class differences in the relevance of language to socialisation," *Sociology, 3.*

1970a "On the classification and framing of educational knowledge." Closing Address, B.S.A. Annual Conference on the Sociology of Education, reprinted in *Class Codes and Control*, Vol. I. (see below).

1970b "A socio-linguistic approach to socialisation, with some reference to educability." *Human Context, II.*

1971 *Class Codes and Control, Vol. I.,* Routledge and Kegan Paul.

1972 *Class Codes and Control, Vol. II*, Routledge and Kegan Paul (forthcoming).

Bott, E. 1957 *Family and Social Network*, Tavistock Press.

Brandis, W. and Henderson, D. 1970 *Social Class, Language and Communication*, Routledge and Kegan Paul.

Cook, J. 1970 *An Enquiry into Patterns of Communication and*

Control between Mothers and their Children in Different Social Classes. University of London Library (Ph.D.).

1972 *Socialisation and Social Control,* Routledge and Kegan Paul.

1972 Chapter X, *Class Codes and Control, Vol. II,* (ed.) Bernstein, B., Routledge and Kegan Paul.

Douglas, M. 1966 *Purity and Danger,* Routledge and Kegan Paul.

Deutsch, M. et al. (eds.) 1967 *The Disadvantaged Child,* New York, Basic Books.

1968 *Social Class, Race and Psychological Development,* Holt, Rinehart and Winston Inc.

Ginsberg, H. 1972 *The Myth of the Deprived Child.* Prentice-Hall.

Hansen, D. 1965 "Personal and positional influences in informal groups" *Social Forces, 44.*

Henderson, D. 1970 "Contextual specificity, discretion and cognitive socialisation," *Sociology, 3.*

Labov, W. 1970 "The logic of non-standard English" *Language and Poverty* (ed.) Williams, F. Markham Press, reprinted in *Open University Course Unit.*

1972 "Black intelligence and academic ignorance" *Atlantic Monthly,* June.

Robinson, W.P. and Rackstraw, S.J. 1972 *A Question of Answers, Vol. I* and *II,* Routledge and Kegan Paul.

see also Robinson W.P., Chapter VIII, *Class Codes and Control, Volume II.* (ed.) Bernstein, B. Routledge and Kegan Paul.

Turner, G. 1972a Chapter VII *Class Codes and Control Vol. II,* op. cit. (forthcoming b) "A socio-linguistic analysis of the regulative context."

Weber, L. 1971 *The English Infant School and Informal Education,* Center for Urban Educational Book, Prentice-Hall.

9

Assessing Children's
School Performance[*]

HUGH MEHAN

SOCIALIZATION AND EDUCATION

THE CONVENTIONAL AMERICAN SCHOOL is a major socializing agency in the United States. Compulsory education laws place the child in school most of his waking hours nine months of the year from the age of six until 16 or 18. The school has assumed responsibility for instructional activities which were previously accomplished informally or at home, including the transmission of cultural values, and the acquisition of the skills and abilities considered necessary for competent societal membership.

The conventional American school is a classic example of a bureaucratically organized institution. Its governance is hierarchically arranged, and responsibility is allocated among highly trained specialists. A superintendent is in charge of a school system composed of a number of schools, each of which is directed by a principal. The principal is in charge of an administrative and a teaching staff. The administrative staff is responsible for budgetary, custodial, and business matters, while the teaching staff is concerned with instructing the pupils. Work and responsibility is

[*] This chapter reports about one phase of a larger research project concerned with language development and school performance (See Cicourel, et al., in preparation) supported by a Ford Foundation Grant (Aaron V. Cicourel, Principal Investigator). I am grateful to the research team of Aaron Cicourel, Kenneth Jennings, Sybillyn Jennings, Kenneth Leiter, Robert MacKay, and David Roth, and to Marshall Shumsky for their cooperative assistance in formulating and carrying out my phase of the project, and for their critical evaluation of the results. Carolyn Mullins provided unusually expert editorial assistance on an earlier report. Portions of this chapter are scheduled to appear in: J. Michael Armer and Allen D. Grimshaw (eds.), *Methodological Problems in Comparative Sociological Research*. The editors' permission to use that material here is gratefully acknowledged.

further divided within the teaching staff. Some teachers specialize in teaching at the primary grade level, others at the secondary level. Some teachers are subject matter specialists, teaching math, science, history, etc., exclusively.

Performance Assessment in Elementary Schools

Specialization and compartmentalization also characterize the way subject matter is presented to pupils and the way in which the pupil's academic performance is evaluated. Lessons are generally taught in compartments of equal physical size during periods of equal temporal length. A concern for objective evaluation has led to the use of standardized educational tests to assess the child's performance. The child's performance on reading, IQ, and language development tests, among others, inform decisions which school officials make to promote or retain children, and to place them in certain "tracks" or "skill groups" within classes. Children's test results are also used by school superintendents and state education officials to gauge the quality of teachers' performances and to evaluate and compare schools and school districts.

Although the teacher in the classroom has daily, personal contact with the children in her[1] class, sees them in a wide variety of teaching-learning situations, at various motivational and performance levels, she does not have well documented reports of her children's achievement and progress. Consider the classroom situation. There are often more than thirty children constantly making demands on the teacher. She has to keep track of each child's rate of progress, remember current interests and peculiar problems. Often she has to involve many different children in diverse activities simultaneously. While she is explaining a math problem to one child, another may be seeking help with his art work. The teacher must be able to encourage both without discouraging either. If the teacher decides to work closely with a small group of children, she must also monitor from a distance the rest of the children who may be playing, working alone, or with a teaching aid.

Because often more than 30 children make constant

demands on the teacher's attention, and because educational activities blend into each other without "time out" or breaks in between, the teacher is not able to write out a detailed progress report for each child's performance in such subjects as arithmetic, spelling, and science each day or after each lesson. Instead she has vague, loosely assembled impressions about each child in her class which are subject to constant change as the child's performance varies from lesson to lesson and day to day. The teacher takes time once or twice a semester to write reports about each child which are placed in his cumulative record, perhaps sent home to the child's parents, or are discussed with them if they visit the school for "parent-teacher" conferences. In preparing the report, the teacher is faced with the problem of transforming the swarm of impressions she has had about each child into a coherent and orderly form. The teacher produces descriptions like "Johnny seems to have trouble with fine motor control"; "Suzie has mastered initial consonants, short vowels, initial digraphs, initial blends, and is ready for elementary readers"; "Max is unable to make left-right discriminations which hinders him when he reads" which, in their abbreviated, summary form, are far removed, high level glosses of the moment to moment, day to day changes in attention, interest, and performance which led to those formulations.

Parents complain that such descriptions are uninformative and meaningless, and do not explain the "successes" or "troubles" their child is having in school. Teachers who read such descriptions about the children they inherit each year complain that they are unreliable and do not instruct them on how to construct the child's program of learning.

Because teachers often do not have documents to support their claims about the child's performance, and because the documents they do have are considered vague and unreliable, teachers and other school officials turn to standardized intelligence and achievement tests to measure the child's ability and to assess his academic progress. Standardized tests have all the features found lacking in teachers' subjective reports. They can be uniformly, simply, and neatly applied; all children are examined on the "same" material.

Each child receives a score which can be compared to "national norms" and scores of other children.

Although the use of standardized tests seems to have solved the problem of subjective and non-uniform teacher evaluation, the child's performance on standardized tests and his performance in class and out of school are seldom formally compared. Test performance is taken as an unquestioned, non-problematic reflection of the child's underlying ability. When informal comparisons of children's classroom performance and test results are made (teachers constantly make remarks like "I thought Johnny was smarter than that IQ test showed" and "I didn't think Max was as good as that test showed, but I guess he must be smart after all"), the authority of the test to measure the child's "real" ability is not challenged. The evaluation of the child's ability obtained by test measurement is accepted by teachers and other school officials, while teachers' evaluations which contradict test results are dismissed by principals (and soon by the reporting teachers) as biased, subjective, and inaccurate.[2]

CONTRASTIVE PERFORMANCE ASSESSMENT

As part of a larger sociolinguistics study,[3] I investigated the school performance of elementary school children in contrasting educational environments by videotaping and analyzing adult-child interaction in the classroom, in testing encounters, and the home (Mehan, 1971).

One of the Southern California schools studied used a series of psycholinguistic tests to evaluate the child's language skills. Children's results on these tests contributed to decisions made to place children in one of the three first grade classrooms (see Leiter, in Cicourel, et al., in preparation). The children who scored lowest on the diagnostic tests were all placed in one classroom. Their poor test performance, coupled with their low SES (and often Chicano origin) seemed to make these children prime examples of the "culturally deprived child"[4] placed in a special classroom designed to accelerate their academic progress.

One of these children's sources of trouble on the school's diagnostic tests was an inability to respond correctly to questions asking for discrimination's about sentences with prepositional phrases which express locational reference. Because the children had had difficulty with prepositions and other grammatical forms, the teacher presented them with "language development" lessons to teach them the requisite grammatical forms. My informal comparison of the children's responses on the Fall diagnostic test with their work in early language development lessons showed that some children gave correct responses in one situation but not the other. The children's differential performances on tests and lessons prompted me to examine those situations to see whether the socially organized features of the interrogation procedure itself contributed to the children's performance and the school official's evaluations of it.

Examining the Assumptions of the Formal Test

The educational test is constructed with the following assumptions about (1) the nature of cognitive abilities, (2) the meaning of test items, (3) the basis of the respondent's performance, and (4) the testing situation.

(1) The educational test, though not always an IQ test, incorporates the assumptions about the nature of mental abilities which originated in intelligence testing theory. Spearman (1923) proposed that each individual possesses a general intelligence factor (g). Intelligence is viewed as a fixed mental capacity "of the individual to act purposefully, to think rationally, to deal effectively with his environment" (Wechsler, 1944:3). The implication is that intelligence is an underlying mental ability. Underlying mental abilities are composed of previously learned experiences, accumulated knowledge, and skills. Simply stated, if learning opportunities and all other factors are equal, those persons who learn the most and perform the best probably have greater innate mental capacity than those who learn and perform most poorly" (Mercer, 1971:322-23). Tests measure these experiences learned in the past.

(2) The tester assumes that the meaning of instructions,

questions, and answers is obvious to the test taker and is shared among the test constructor, test taker, and test administrator. The test items serve as unambiguous stimuli which tap the respondent's underlying attitudes about or knowledge of certain factors.

Each test item is considered to be clear and unambiguous because the test constructor assumes that persons taking the test have had experience with the test items, whether they be words, pictures, or objects, and that the test experience will be the same as the prior experiences he has had with these items. Because of this assumed similarity of experience, test takers will interpret the items in the same way the test constructor did when he compiled the items. Because each test item will be interpreted only in the way intended by the test constructor, the test taker's reasons or purposes for making certain choices, or for giving certain explanations are assumed to match the purposes of the tester.

Each question asked has a correct answer which consists of a connecting link between stimulus instruction and test item. The respondent who answers questions properly is assumed to have searched for and found the intended connection between questions and materials. While correct answers to questions are seen as products of correct search procedures, incorrect answers are seen as the products of faulty reasoning, or the lack of underlying ability, knowledge or understanding.

(3) The educational tester makes the same assumptions about the measurement of behavior that the experimental psychologist makes: "A psychological experiment, then, can be symbolized by S-O-R, which means that E (understood) applies a certain stimulus (or situation) to O's receptors and observes O's response" (Woodworth and Schlosberg, 1954:2). The test taker, like the experimental subject, responds to the stimulus, and his response is a direct and sole result of the "stimulus acting at that moment and the factors present in the organism at that moment" (Woodworth and Schlosberg, 1954:3).

(4) The respondent's behavior is considered to be the sole result of his underlying abilities and stimulus applica-

tion because other factors and variables which might be influential are able to be standardized and controlled.

Standardization implies uniformity of procedure in administering and scoring the test. . . . Such standardization extends to the exact materials employed, time limits, oral instructions to subjects, preliminary demonstrations, ways of handling queries from subjects, and every other detail of the testing situation (Anastasi, 1968:23).

The tester (or experimenter) is supposed to present the stimulus while holding other factors in the situation constant. The test is supposed to be standardized in its presentation of stimuli so that all respondents face the same conditions which make comparisons of performances and replications possible.

The assumptions made by the formal test include: (1) the abilities being tested are the products of past experience, (2) cultural meanings are shared in common by tester and respondent, (3) the respondent's performance is an exclusive function of underlying abilities and stimulus presentation, (4) stimuli are presented to respondents in standardized ways, extraneous variables in the testing situation are controlled, and (5) the tester passively records the respondent's performance.

The structure of the testing encounter was examined in two ways. First, six of the first grade children who took the Spring test were videotaped. After the test was over, I informally interrogated the children about their perceptions and understandings of the testing materials. Second, versions of the formal test which systematically altered its features were presented to the first grade children.

The language development tests employed by the school are picture identification tasks in which children are asked to identify the grammatical forms represented by a series of pictures by pointing to the one that correctly characterizes it. Instead of using only one kind of stimulus, I used three alternative versions of the picture identification task. I had children demonstrate their knowledge of orientational prepositions by manipulating their hands, manipulating small objects, and by drawing pictures in response to the instructions I gave. I contrasted the formal testing characteristic of a strange and unfamiliar environment by presenting the "orientations tasks" to children in the less formal surroundings of the classroom, and (to a few) in the familiar settings of their homes. To examine the "common culture" assumption, the general research design required that one test be presented in Spanish to those children familiar with that language, and that all children's definitions and conceptions of testing materials be analyzed. Six classroom and six home testing encounters were videotaped.[5]

Results of Children's Performances

The results of the children's performances on the two sessions of school administered tests and the "orientations tasks" appear in Table 1. A table of scores like this one, or a more general comment like: "Adam has command of prepositions," or "Sarah does not comprehend the negative or the orientational preposition" is characteristically provided to teachers after a testing session and is entered into the child's school record. I will now examine this table of scores to see that it reports about the child's abilities and the manner in which results are reported. Such a table of scores or a general descriptive statement (1) obscures the child's understanding of the materials and task, (2) does not capture the child's reasoning abilities and (3) does not show the negotiated, contextually bound measurement decisions which the tester makes while scoring the child's behavior as "correct" or "incorrect."

The Child's Conception of the Task

One question on the school language test (the Basic Concept Inventory, Englemann, 1967, henceforth BCI) asks the respondent to decide which child in a group is the tallest. Because the heads of the children are obscured, the child taking the test is supposed to reply that he can't make that judgment. However, many children examined selected one of the children in the picture as the tallest. When I interviewed the children after they took the Spring test, and I asked them why they chose that boy, they replied that

Table 1
RESULTS OF LANGUAGE TESTING IN THREE FIRST GRADES

Part A: Individual Results

Child	School Tests		Variations	
	Fall	Spring	Class	Home
1 (Jean)	73	69	93	100
2 (Clarc)	10	50	86	86
3 (Lesli)	46	76	44	65*
4 (Lora)	10	25	33	60*
5	50	61	86	
6	52	54	77	
7	75	85	75	
8	65	70	80	
9	60	75	75	
10	40	50	50	
11	15	25	37	
12	60	75	55	
13	35	70	75	
14	55	85	87	
15	35	65	67	
16	63	77	80	
17	50	54	60	85*
18	85	95	93	
19	56	86	55	75*
20	10	35	33	
21	85	95	95	
22	35	50	45	
23	75	85	85	
	1140	1512	1566	

* Tested in Spanish at home.

Part B: Results by Classroom

Classroom	School Tests		Classroom Variations
	Fall	Spring	
#1	49.5	65.7	68.0
#2	73.0	87.0	
#3	77.0	82.0	

he was the tallest boy because "his feet are bigger." Investigating the thread of reasoning used by the children, then, showed that they understood the *intent* of the question—to discriminate and compare—but they were not using the same criteria as the tester. Because they were not using the criteria *intended* (but never explicated), answers which indicated that one child was taller than another were marked wrong. However, in this case, a wrong answer does not index a lack of ability, but rather the use of an alternative scheme of interpretation.

Another question on the BCI asks the child to decide which of two boxes a ball is in after the tester has told him which box the ball is *not* in. The child is expected to point to the box which the tester hasn't touched. The question following that on the BCI asks the child to decide which of *three* boxes a ball is in after the tester has told the child which box does not contain the ball. The child is expected to say the problem can't be solved. Many children failed to answer this question correctly; they chose one, or sometimes both, of the remaining two boxes. In a follow-up interview, when I asked the children why they chose one of the other boxes (instead of saying the problem could not be solved) they replied: "You said it's not in that one." I think children find it untenable to doubt an adult's word. An adult has told the child that a state of affairs actually exists: "There is a ball in one of these three boxes." He has been told that the ball isn't in one, so, he reasons: "It must be in one of the other two because the adult said so." That is, these children's answers may have been wrong, but not necessarily because they didn't have the proper reasoning ability; rather, they lacked the sophistication necessary to doubt an adult's word.

A question from another language development test instructs the child to choose the "animal that can fly" from a bird, an elephant, and a dog. The correct answer (obviously) is the bird. Many first grade children, though, chose the elephant along with the bird as a response to that question. When I later asked them why they chose that answer they replied: "That's Dumbo." Dumbo (of course) is Walt Disney's flying elephant, well known to children who watch television and read children's books as an animal that flies.

On another BCI question the child is asked to "find the ones that talk" when presented pictures of a man, a boy, a dog, and a table. Children frequently include the dog along with the man and the boy as an answer to this question. For those children who have learned to say their pets "speak" or "talk" that is not an unlikely choice. Deciding that the child doesn't know how to use the verb "talk" correctly would, in this case, be erroneous, for that decision would have resulted from an unexamined assumption that both adult and child attribute the same characteristics to objects or are attending to them in the same way.

For a question from another language development test, children are presented a picture of a medieval fortress—complete with moat, drawbridge, and parapets—and three initial consonants: D, C, and G. The child is supposed to circle the correct initial consonant. C for "castle" is correct, but many children choose D. After the test, when I asked those children what the name of the building was, they responded "Disneyland." These children used the same line of reasoning intended by the tester, but they arrived at the wrong substantive answer. The score sheet showing a wrong answer does not document a child's lack of reasoning ability; it only documents that the child indicated an answer different from the one the tester expected.

These descriptions demonstrate that the child can exist simultaneously in a number of different "realities" or words (Schutz, 1962:207–59), i.e., the "factual" world of everyday life and the world of fantasy. The child who says that animals can fly and talk is (from the adult point of view) mixing and blending the characteristics of fantasy and everyday worlds. The test, however, assumes the child is attending to stimulus items only from the viewpoint of the everyday world where dogs do not talk and elephants do not fly. The test assumes further that the child keeps the world of play, fantasy, and television out of the testing situation. Yet, as these anecdotes demonstrate, the child of age 4-6 does not always keep his realities sequentially arranged. Because the child may be operating simultaneously in multiple realities, valid interrogations must examine why a child answers questions as he does and must determine what children "see" in educational materials; they must not use test results exclusively.

In sum, a document of the children's correct and incorrect responses, such as Table 1, does not show the variation in the children's answers across materials, test, and languages of interrogation. Conventional testing techniques cannot determine if a child's wrong answers are due to his lack of ability or are due to his equally valid alternative interpretations. Differences in tester and child meaning of educational materials does not lend support for the "common culture" assumption of the educational test.

The Test Assembly Process

A table of correct answers (e.g., Table 1) is a static display which does not capture the contextually bound, fluid and dynamic activities which constitute its production.[6] When I reexamined the videotape of the testing sessions which produced Table 1, I found that these results were not as unequivocal as they appeared in tabular form.

Testers deviated from the requirements of a mechanical, uniform presentation of instructions and stimuli to respondents. The school test required a series of pictures to be presented to respondents, each with the instruction "look at the picture." The following variations on that introductory comment are just some of those recorded during the school administered testing session which I videotaped. (Similar deviations occurred in the informal tests that I presented and may be observed in any interrogation) cf., Friedman, 1968, who documents the same phenomenon in social-psychological experiments.)

FT[7]	1:7	Look at that picture and show a find . . .
	4:17	Y'see all the things in that picture
	8:1	Let's look at that one
	11:1	Now you look at those pictures
	3:3	I want you to look at that picture and tell me what you see by looking at the picture
	1:8	Look at this picture now
	5:9	See all those pictures?
	5:10	What those?
	5:11	Okay, now I want you to find the right ones

Under the criteria of the formal test, test takers are supposed to respond only to stimulus materials presented to them, but these respondents are not receiving the same stimulus instructions. Some are being told to look and find the correct pictures; others are being told just to look. No child, however, is told what constitutes a correct answer. The child is expected to operate without this information.

When I reexamined the testing videotapes, I found that when children were asked a question, they presented many displays. If I looked at one of the other displays the children presented, rather than those originally scored, a substantially different evaluation of each child's performance would have been obtained. In cases where a child had been marked wrong, an instance of the correct display was apparent in his actions, and vice versa. If that display, rather than the one noted by the tester had been recorded, the child's overall score would have changed.

When answering questions, the child is supposed to touch that picture or part of it that best answers the question asked. Often the children either did not touch any part of the objects represented in the picture, or covered more of the picture than was required by the question. Because the child's response was ambiguous, the tester had to determine the boundaries of the answering gesture to the stimulus picture. Depending on which picture the space between the pictures was assigned to, the tester either marked the child right or marked him wrong.

When the children touched two or more pictures in succession, the tester had to decide which of the movements was intended by the child as his answer. On a number of occasions, the children began to answer before the complete question was asked. Regardless of whether or not the correct picture was touched, the tester did not count the action as an answer. It seemed that the responses had to be given *after* questions had been completely asked in order to be considered answers-to-questions.

Some children touched the page of pictures with both of their hands simultaneously, and also laid their palms flat on the page while answering a question. In these cases, one hand touched an "incorrect" part of the page while the other hand touched the "correct" part. To count the child's answer as correct in these cases, the tester had to assign the status of "hand indicating an answer" to one hand and not the other.

The following example is representative of the way in which the tester assigned the status of "answer" during the orientations tasks. In the hand manipulation phase of the orientations task, after I finished my instruction: "Put your hand below the table," Clarc placed his hand in the air:

(1) hand raised

I repeated the substance of the instruction: "Below the table," and Clarc modified his initial response. He lowered his hand slowly until it was parallel with and off the side of the table top:

(2) hand off to the side

He paused there, and I said nothing. His hand continued in the arc he had been circumscribing until it was as far down below the table as it would go:

(3) hand underneath, but not touching the underside of the table.

At that point, realizing that I had, in fact, influenced his behavior and thereby modified his answer, I attempted to neutralize this influence by saying, "Put it anywhere you want." Clarc left his hand in the last position (3), and I scored that "final" placement "correct." But note, there are at least three separate displays given in response to the question asked. The production of multiple responses was obviously influenced by the challenges I made of the child's responses. With each challenge, the child modified his behavior until his arm could literally go no further under the table. Had I recorded either of his first two displays as his "answer" rather than challenging those displays, the child would have been considered wrong for this question.

The protocol conditions of the formal testing procedures are violated in other ways. In the school tests, the child is supposed to touch the correct picture as soon as the question is read. Often more than one picture is to be touched in response to a question. Ideally, the child is supposed to touch all pictures as soon as the question is read. Often the child only touches one. When this occurs, a tester employs various practices to elicit further answers from the child. A tester may prompt the child with verbal cues like "that one," or "is that the only one?" These cues tell the child to continue searching for more answers in the series. A similar cue is provided non-verbally when the tester pauses after a response and does not immediately go on to the next question. The pause serves as a cue to the child to keep looking for a correct answer. When the tester provides a commendatory comment like "good," "fine," or goes immediately on to the next question, the child is prohibited from providing any more responses or changing answers he has already given.

Not only do testers contribute to respondents' productions, but respondents interrupt and thereby contribute to their interrogation. During a test, the tester is supposed to ask questions and the respondent is supposed to answer them. But if a respondent asks the tester a question instead of just answering the tester's question, the adult is forced to respond to the demand made of him by the respondent, i.e., the adult/tester has to respond to the demand made of him by the child/respondent *before* the child answers the original test question.[8] The tester can ignore the child's request and repeat the original question, he can pause and say nothing, or he can provide a "neutral" comment like "do whatever you think is best." Regardless of the tester's reaction to the child's request, though, the child gains further information that influences his interpretation of the original request made of him.

The following interchange exemplifies the manner in which the child gains supplemental information from a tester's responses to his questions. A child was asked to draw a circle above the line. She placed her pencil on the paper at a point slightly above the diagonal line she had drawn and asked: "Above?" "Right here?"

I interpreted the child's action as a request for information about the suitability of an answer which she was considering giving. She had not yet committed herself to producing a particular answer, but was asking for confirmation of a possible answer in advance of its production.

That request for information required me to respond in some way. Regardless of my action, the child would learn something about the suitability of the answer she was proposing. I chose to repeat the question as a way out of the dilemma posed by her question. The child then reviewed the entire paper. Her pencil wandered all around the area of the line—both above and below it. She finally settled on this point:

While performing this act, she asked: "Right here?" Perhaps exasperated, perhaps convinced that she now "knew" the answer, perhaps unable to restrain myself, I said "Okay." The child drew a circle at the second point and got the question right.

Summary

This examination of testing interactions shows test assumptions are not met in practice. Stimulus items are not presented in standardized ways. Test materials do not always have the same meaning for tester and child. The child's performance is not just the result of his ability and the stimulus presented but is also influenced by contextually provided information. The respondent's answers are not the product of the tester's passive record keeping; they emerge from the tester's interpretive assessment of the child's actions.

The tester is not just examining and recording the child's response. He is actively engaged in assigning the status of "answer" to certain portions of the child's behavioral presentation. The tester is according differential status to similar behavioral displays produced by the child as answers-to-questions because the tester is not seeing the child's display in isolation from other aspects of the testing situation. The fingers used to point and the hand laid on the page are included in a perceptual field and are seen against a constantly changing background of features which includes the questions asked, the child's restlessness, his performances on previous questions, teachers' reports about him, and the tester's expectations for the child's performance on any particular question. Therefore, the "same" behavioral display, seen against different backgrounds, is interpreted differently; it obtains a different reading. In short, test taking and test scoring are interpretive interactional processes which should be approached and studied as such.

EDUCATIONAL IMPLICATIONS

Performance in Different Interrogation Contexts

I have suggested that examining only educational test results makes it impossible to determine the child's understanding of test materials, and prohibits comparison of his test performance with his daily experiences. When I assessed first grade children's abilities in different situations and with different materials, their performances varied. Comparing the results of the children's performances on two sessions of school administered tests with my informal variations (Table 1) shows that the children scored better on the informal tests than on the formal tests.

These results are consistent with other studies which examine the child's performance in different contexts of interrogation. Labov (1969) and Lewis (1970) have shown how Black children produce more vivid, complex, and spontaneous utterances in peer centered, unstructured situations than they do in the power relationship of adult over child. Abrahams (1970), Mitchell-Kernan (1969), and Ward (1971) give numerous examples of the Black child's oral expressiveness outside the classroom. Phillips (1970) documents the reluctance of Indian children from the Warmsprings Reservation to participate in classroom verbal interaction when it is competitive, adult organized, and controlled, in contrast to the eagerness of these same children to speak out when activity is unstructured, unsupervised, and group centered. These results suggest that the structure of the interrogation encounter influences the assessment of the child's abilities. Cultural deprivation proponents say the minority child's school failure is the function of the child's lack of language and culture. These studies demonstrate that the minority child possesses language and culture, but his are often different than that demanded in the white middle class oriented classroom. Therefore, it seems that the minority child's poor school performance may be due to the inability of current educational interrogation methods to assess the child's abilities and may not be the result of the minority child's lack of ability, language, or culture.

Language and Meaning in Educational Testing

The scores of the children tested who speak both Spanish and English show they scored higher when questions were asked of them at home in Spanish than when questions were asked of them in English at school. If this difference in performance were shown to be systematic across all bilingual children, it could lead to the conclusion that these children understand instructions better when they are presented in their native language, which, in turn can lead to the recommendation to instruct and test bilingual children in their native language.

Due to the difficulties inherent in developing "culture free" and "culture specific" tests,[9] educational tests have commonly been modified by translation in response to the problems raised by the need to test children from different cultures (Mercer, 1971). Darcy (1963) summarized the bilingualism testing literature. The consistent findings reported were (1) bilingual subjects received significantly lower scores than comparable monolinguals, (2) bilinguals received lower scores when tested in their native language than when they were tested in English, (3) bilinguals scored lower on verbal tests than they did on non-verbal tests. The second result was explained by the fact that the children were instructed in English, while their native language training stopped, for all intents and purposes, when the children entered primary school; thus, the translated versions of the formal test probably differed significantly from the native language familiar to the children.

Translating assessment materials will not solve the school problems of the lower class or bilingual child because the content of the entire interrogation encounter, not just the words of the test, is culture bound. Questions, materials, and referents reflect the content of the culture in which the test was developed. Simply translating the content of a test designed for persons socialized in one culture into the language of another does not eliminate culture differences.

Furthermore, the respondent's performance and the observer's evaluation of that performance is an interpreted and negotiated process. Although my analysis of interrogation encounters is not finely enough calibrated to decide which particular situational features available to a child contribute to his answer on a given occasion, I have shown that much more than just the presentation of stimulus items serves as the source of the child's answer. Although the tester assumes variations in stimulus presentation and his intervening activity do not contribute to the child's understanding of testing materials and are unimportant features in his evaluation of the respondent's performance, I have shown the child is not attending to stimulus items in isolation and the tester is not passively recording "answers." The questions and materials appear against a background composed of the negotiated aspects of the question-answer sequence, verbal and non-verbal cues. Because the respondent has to interpret the entire interrogation setting, the translation of materials, or the substitution of one mode of interrogation for another, does not solve the respondent's test taking problems, for he must interpret the materials against a situationally provided background. Simple translation and the exclusive reliance on any single kind of instrument to evaluate competence is limited, for such practices fail to recognize that each communicative encounter is self-organizing (Zimmerman and Pollner, 1970:94–100), and each question-answer sequence imposes its own perceptual demands and interpretive requirements on respondents and evaluators.

In short, each encounter between interrogator and respondent has its own social organization and unique features which produce different (not necessarily better) evaluations of a respondent. Therefore, instead of searching for a single best test or a best single learning environment, the recommendation being made here is to study the interpretive process in any educational environment, and to examine a child's performance in different situations so that the encounter best suited to the child's experience can be utilized.

NOTES

1. The feminine pronoun is used to reflect the high proportion of women teachers in public schools.

2. A number of writers, e.g., Dennison (1969), Friere (1970), Holt (1964), Kozol (1968), Illich (1970), have criticized the prevailing structure and organization of conventional schools. The research of which this report is a part is focusing on the procedures used to evaluate the child's performance and is attempting to point out the practical problems facing the teacher in the classroom regardless of organizational structure.

3. The overall contrastive study of language acquisition, language use, and school performance utilized data gathered in 1969–1970 from two elementary schools in Southern California. Cicourel is studying the demands that multiple sources of information make on teachers' and children's information processing. Jennings and Jennings are studying the interactional aspects of the psycholinguistic assessment of the child's acquisition of syntactic structures. Leiter is analyzing the decision-making processes school officials use to place children in elementary school classrooms. MacKay is contrasting teachers' and children's conceptions of classroom and testing materials. Roth is examining the conception of the child's abilities which intelligence tests provide educators (see Cicourel, et al., in preparation). In related studies, Boese (1971) described the deaf child's acquisition and use of natural sign language, and Shumsky (1972) describes the structure of interpretations of an encounter group session.

4. Lower class American Indian, Black, Chicano, Puerto Rican, and other "minority" children perform poorly in school by comparison with their middle class school mates. This poor performance has been said to be the result of a cultural or hereditary deficiency by some educators and researchers (see Jensen, 1969; Hernstein, 1971; Bereiter and Englemann, 1966; Hunt, 1964; Deutsch, 1964). The *hereditary* deprivation argument, defended primarily by Jensen and Hernstein, is explained and critically examined by Roth in this volume. The *culturally* deprived child is said to be the product of an impoverished environment. It is argued that overcrowded facilities, infrequent social contact, inconsistent discipline, absence of cultural artifacts provide limited opportunities for the lower class child to be verbally expressive, develop cooperative, perceptual, and attitudinal skills. As a result, the child is said to possess an impoverished language and has few of the skills and experiences required by the middle class oriented school.

The two forms of the cultural deprivation explanation of the lower class child's school failure have been attacked by linguists, sociologists, and anthropologists (see, for example, Labov, 1969; Gumperz, 1972; and a collection of essays in Williams, 1970), who argue that the lower class child does not come from a *deprived* environment or speak a *degraded* language, but rather possesses a *different* culture and speaks a language which has some different grammatical rules and rules for social usage. These cultural and linguistic differences produce anomalies for the lower class child in the classroom as he is expected to perform in ways he has not been taught.

Care must be taken in saying the Black, Chicano, or other minority child possesses a different culture. Although many proponents of the "difference" thesis recognize the existence of alternate cultures, it is possible that the child's behavior which is called culturally different may be treated in the same way that behavior which is called culturally deficient: as behavioral attributes to be eradicated. A third proposal, called "bi-cultural" by Valentine (1971) and others recognizes and seeks to preserve the ethnic child's unique cultural identity while allowing him to develop skills which allow him to operate in the white middle class culture if he so chooses.

Although the "deficit" rather than the "difference" or "bi-cultural" thesis has been the dominant view among educators during the last two decades, the "deprived" child's "impoverished" cultural or linguistic system has not been shown to inhibit actual classroom interaction. Instead the academic and behavioral difficulties of the "deprived" child have been documented by the use of data gathered from formal tests conducted outside the classroom. This report, then, is in part an examination of the "deficiency" thesis which advertises its findings without a critical examination of the methods used to assess the child's abilities.

5. This is obviously not the first critical examination of educational tests. Educators, psychologists, and sociologists have long been concerned with the accuracy and fairness of educational tests. Previous criticisms of testing, however, have dealt only with the *product* and *results* of testing, i.e., the test scores of different groups of children have been compared. When differences in test scores (read: ability) have been found, attempts have been made to make tests "culture free" (e.g., Goodenough draw-a-man, David-Eel's games, the Raven Progressive Matrices), or to develop culture-sensitive tests (e.g., by translating tests into the respondent's native language, (e.g., the Peabody Picture Vocabulary Test, the Stanford-Binet, and the WISC). (Mercer, 1971 presents a concise summary of his literature.) The examination of tests reported here differs from previous ones in that testing is treated as an interactional accomplishment. The meaning of the testing situation, the source of the respondent's answer, and the tester's scoring are examined from within ongoing testing situations.

6. The way in which production procedures and practices are said to constitute socially organized settings is explained by Garfinkel (1967), Garfinkel and Sacks (1970), Cicourel (1968b, 1969, 1970, and forthcoming), and Zimmerman and Pollner (1970).

7. Numbers refer to the full transcript of the school administered testing session; transcripts which are part of this study may be examined upon request.

8. Sacks (1967–1970) and Schegloff (1968, 1971) have proposed that when one question follows another in conversation, the question asked second is answered before the one asked first. Schegloff (1971) calls this an "embedded question" sequence:

Turn	Speaker	Response
1	Tester	question
2	Child	question
3	Tester	answer
4	Child	answer

9. From its appearance in 1926, Goodenough's "draw-a-man" test was considered a possible culture-free test of intelligence because it was non-verbal, presumably not subject-matter related, and the referent drawn was universal. Recent testing has shown, however, that Goodenough's scores correlate highly with the presence, familiarity, and encouragement of representative art in a society, a factor which seems to be

a function of a society's degree of modernization (Dennis, 1966). These kinds of findings have led Goodenough to say: The present writers would like to express the opinion that that search for a culture free test, whether of intelligence, artistic ability, personal-social characteristics, or any other measurable trait is illusory, and that the naive assumption that mere freedom from verbal requirements renders a test equally suitable for all groups is no longer tenable (Goodenough and Harris, 1950:339).

REFERENCES

Abrahams, Roger 1970   Deep Down in the Jungle. Chicago: Aldine.
Anastasi, Anne 1968   Psychological Testing. New York: Macmillan.
Bereiter, Carl and Siegfried Englemann 1966   Teaching Disadvantaged Children in the Preschool. Englewood Cliffs, New Jersey: Prentice-Hall.
Boese, Robert 1971   Natural Sign Language and the Acquisition of Social Structure. Unpublished Ph.D. dissertation, University of California, Santa Barbara.
Cicourel, Aaron V. 1964   Method and Measurement in Sociology. New York: The Free Press.
1968a   The Social Organization of Juvenile Justice. New York: Wiley.
1868b   "Verso una Sociologia Evoltiva del Linguaggio e del Significato." Rassegna Italiana di Sociologia 9:211–58. Reprinted 1970 as: "The Acquisition of Social Structure: Towards a Developmental Sociology of Language and Meaning." In: Jack Douglas (ed.), Understanding Everyday Life. Chicago: Aldine.
1969   "Generative Semantics and the Structure of Social Interaction." In: International Days of Sociolinguistics. Rome: Luigi Sturzo Institute.
1970   "Basic and Normative Rules in the Negotiation of Status and Role." In: Hans P. Dreitzel (ed.), Recent Sociology 2: Patterns of Communicative Behavior. New York: Macmillan.
Forthcoming   "Ethnomethodology." To appear in: Thomas A. Sebeok (ed.), Current Trends in Linguistics, Vol. XII. The Hague: Mouton.
Cicourel, Aaron V., Kenneth Jennings, Sybillyn Jennings, Kenneth Leiter, Robert MacKay, Hugh Mehan, and David Roth
In preparation   Language Acquisition and Use in Testing and Classroom Settings. New York: Seminar Press.
Darcy, Natalie T. 1963   "Bilingualism and the Measurement of Intelligence." Journal of Genetic Psychology 103:259–82.
Denison, George 1969   Lives of Children. New York: Random House.

Dennis, Wayne T. 1966 "Goodenough Scores, Art Experience, and Modernization." Journal of Social Psychology 68:211–28.

Deutsch, Martin 1964 Teaching the Disadvantaged Child. Englewood Cliffs, N.J.: Prentice-Hall.

Englemann, Siegfried 1967 The Basic Concept Inventory. Chicago: Follet.

Friedman, Neil 1968 The Social Nature of Psychological Research. New York: Basic Books.

Friere, Paolo 1970 Pedagogy of the Oppressed. New York: Herder and Herder.

Garfinkel, Harold 1967 Studies in Ethnomethodology. Englewood Cliffs, New Jersey: Prentice-Hall.

Garfinkel, Harold and Harvey Sacks 1970 "The Formal Properties of Practical Actions." In: John C. McKinney and Edward A. Tiryakian (eds.), Theoretical Sociology. New York: Appleton-Century-Crofts.

Goodenough, Florence and D. L. Harris 1950 "Studies in the Psychology of Children's Drawings." Psychological Bulletin, 369–433.

Gumperz, John J. 1972 Language in Social Groups. Palo Alto: Stanford University Press.

Holt, John 1964 How Children Fail. New York: Putnam.

Hunt, J. McVeich 1964 Intelligence and Experience.

Illich, Ivan 1970 Deschooling Society. New York: Harper and Row.

Jensen, Arther 1969 "How Much Can We Boost IQ and Scholastic Achievement?" Harvard Educational Review, 39:1–123.

Kozol, Jonathan 1969 Death at an Early Age. Boston: Houghton Mifflin.

Labov, William 1969 "The Logic of Non-Standard English." In: George Alatis (ed.), Linguistics and Language Study, Monograph Series #22. Washington, D.C.: Georgetown University Press.

Lewis, Louisa 1970 "Culture and Social Interaction in the Classroom." Working Paper #38, Language-Behavior Research Lab, University of California, Berkeley.

Mehan, Hugh 1971 Accomplishing Understanding in Educational Settings. Unpublished Ph.D. dissertation, University of California, Santa Barbara.

Melmed, Paul 1971 Black English Phonology, Monograph #1, Language-Behavior Research Lab, University of California, Berkeley.

Mercer, Jane R. 1971 "Institutionalized Anglocentricism." In: Peter Orleans and William R. Ellis, Jr. (eds.), Race, Change, and Urban Society. New York: Russell Sage Publishers.

Mitchell-Kernan, Claudia 1969 Language Behavior in a Black Urban Community. Unpublished Ph.D. Dissertation, University of California, Berkeley. Working Paper #23, Language-Behavior Research Laboratory, University of California, Berkeley,

Also Monograph #2, Language-Behavior Research Lab, 1971.

Phillips, Susan U. 1970 "Acquisition of Rules for Appropriate Speech Usage." In: George Alatis (ed.), Linguistics and Language Study, Monograph Series #23, Washington, D.C.: Georgetown University Press.

Sacks, Harvey 1967–70 Unpublished Lecture Notes, UCLA, UC Irvine.

Schegloff, Emmanuel A. 1968 "Sequencing in Conversational Openings." American Anthropologist 70 (6): 1075–95.

Schütz, Alfred 1962 Collected Papers I: The Problem of Social Reality. The Hague: Martinus Nijhoff.

Shores, David L. (ed.) 1972 Contemporary English. Philadelphia: Lippincott.

Shumsky, Marshall 1972 Encounter Groups: A Forensic Science, Ph.D. Dissertation, University of California, Santa Barbara.

Spearman, Carl 1923 The Nature of Intelligence and the Purposes of Cognition. London: Macmillan.

Valentine, Charles A. 1971 "Deficit, Difference, and Bi-Cultural Models of Afro-American Behavior." Harvard Educational Review, 41:137–158.

Ward, Martha Coonfield 1971 Them Children. New York: Holt, Rinehart, Winston.

Wechsler, David 1944 The Measurement of Adult Intelligence. Baltimore: Williams and Wilkens.

Williams, Frederick (ed.) 1970 Language and Poverty. Boston: Markham.

Wilson, Thomas P. 1970 "Conceptions of Interaction and Forms of Sociological Explanation." American Sociological Review 35 (4): 697–709.

Woodworth, Robert S., and Harold Schlosberg 1954 Experimental Psychology. New York: Holt.

Zimmerman, Don H. and Melvin Pollner 1970 "The Everyday World as a Phenomenon." In Jack Douglas (ed.), Understanding Everyday Life. Chicago: Aldine.

10
Learning, Teaching, and Television Production for Children: The Experience of *Sesame Street* *

GERALD S. LESSER

SESAME STREET is an experiment joining the technical capabilities of television with some premises about children's learning. The experimentation extends not only to the television product itself but to the production process as well, which has allowed academics, teachers, creative artists, and television producers to reflect upon and reshape their own assumptions in dialogue with each other. This essay discusses one aspect of our experiences: the translation of educational goals and ideas about learning and teaching into actual television programming.

° Adapted from the forthcoming book, *Children and Television: Lessons from Sesame Street*, by Gerald S. Lesser. Copyright © by Random House, Inc. Reprinted by permission of the publisher.

This paper discusses some informal ideas about learning and teaching and certain suggested strategies of television production for children. The ideas about learning and teaching have been available for some time, but the observations of children responding to various forms of television production are new. They are the property of my colleagues at the Children's Television Workshop: Edward L. Palmer, Samuel Y. Gibbon, Barbara Reeves, David Connell, Patricia Hayes, Joan Ganz Cooney, Jon Stone, James Henson, Jeff Moss, Joe Raposo, Vivian Horner, Norton Wright, Joan Lufrano, Sharon Lerner, Barbara Fowles, Joyce Weil, and others.

In addition, Maurice Sendak, the children's author and illustrator, has contributed to the Children's Television Workshop's projects since their inception. During our early planning sessions, Maurice periodically slipped into states of reverie, producing the illustrations used throughout this paper. I am most grateful for his permission to use them here.

DEFINING EDUCATIONAL GOALS FOR TELEVISION PRODUCTION

Sesame Street has sought to provide a supplementary educational experience to help prepare children for school by stimulating their appetite for learning. Its specific goals include instruction in (1) symbolic representation—letters, numbers, and geometric forms; (2) cognitive process—perceptual discrimination, relationships, classification, and ordering; (3) reasoning and problem-solving; and (4) "the child and his world"—concepts regarding the self, social units, social interaction, and the man-made and natural environment.

How a child develops a view of him or herself as competent and effective remains a profound mystery. Surely the process does not proceed in a neat succession of discrete steps, but there must be important effects upon a child's self-concept when he acquires certain elementary symbolic skills (letters, numbers, the names of geometric forms), exhibits them in the presence of someone who cares about him, and receives attention and admiration. The child then knows that he is capable of learning something worth knowing, and thus acquires a sense of competence that motivates further learning.

Our emphasis on cognitive skills was based upon a series of important premises which also guided our work as we translated goals into television programming. Because television reaches a mass, national audience, we had to aim to teach only certain universal goals that we hoped all children would achieve. We assumed that all children would learn to read and to write, for example, but we did not expect each child to play the violin or to become an architect or a poet, these being particular goals defined by the individual child's aptitudes, interests, and experiences.

We assumed that television is a special and limited kind of educational medium, that it is unable to provide sequenced instruction, that it needs to be entertaining as well as educational, and that television does not control the behavior of either parents or children in the viewing audience as a classroom teacher might. All of this led us to the premise that television can serve only as one additional alternative to supplement other forms of early experience, that its curriculum cannot cover the full range of preschool objectives. Television must never be designed to replace or compete with other educational experiences. It can only aspire to complement whatever else the child has available.

Our decision to establish preparation for school as a goal of *Sesame Street* did not presuppose an uncritical attitude toward the schools. Nonetheless, preparation for schooling seemed a plausible goal. We were aware that the parents of inner-city children, toward whom our efforts were primarily directed, want their children to be competent in reading, writing, and arithmetic, even though many of them perceive that schools do not function to their children's benefit. Perhaps it is not always best to give people what they say they want—but knowing what they want is not a bad place to start if you intend to help.

In our attention to inner-city children, we rejected the "deficit" model of what these children need. Our contrasting premise was simply to give children what they could use in order to cope with and improve their own environments.

Arriving at these relatively general goals and writing a curriculum statement defining our specific education objectives was a long, collaborative process. The Children's Television Workshop brought together both academics and non-academics, creators of ideas and materials as well as critics, professionals with confidence in the schools and persons who believed schools too corrupt to reform, professionals who approached their work intuitively and those who depended upon explicit, analytic problem-solving approaches, professionals whose disciplines contained a specialized vocabulary and those without any special professional language. At the seminars in which the premises and goals of *Sesame Street* were hammered out, these differences produced diverse suggestions for educational goals, but also to repeated conflicts.

Early in our discussions we did not allow ourselves to be constrained by what the production staff thought feasible in the production of a show. But as we came to setting priorities this became a primary concern. The creative producers and writers reminded us that our task was the concrete and practical one of constructing a set of educational goals that could be understood clearly and converted into actual television programming. They were especially insistent when other seminar participants used esoteric jargon. On these occasions, the staff resembled a Greek chorus, intoning repeatedly, "What do you mean by that? What do you mean by that?"

We had made a fundamental decision to do our best to meld production and research activities into a single force directed towards continuous program improvement. Still, there was skepticism. As production and research began to search for ways to collaborate, writers and producers expressed some doubt that it could be done; perhaps there were some very good reasons why it had never been done before. David Connell, Vice President of the Children's Television Workshop and its executive producer, described his early skepticism:

My background was in commercial television where we felt we had developed a pretty good set of instincts about what kind of show would appeal to children of any given age. I frankly was skeptical about the idea of researching every moment of a television show, and certainly of being told how to design it. There was the risk of intellectualizing the material to death and ending up with a program most notable for its monumental boredom. It would be like trying to analyze the elements of a joke, only to find that when we had isolated all the pieces, there was nothing learned and nothing to laugh about. But if *Sesame Street* was an experiment—and it very definitely continues to be one—this notion of broadcaster/researcher cooperation was the most bold experiment within it. I kept thinking of the biologists who crossbred a crocodile with an abalone in hopes of getting an abadile. Only something went wrong and they ended up with a crocoblone. Nothing quite like this had ever been attempted before. (Connell and Palmer, 1970, p. 3)

As the project progressed, both the researchers and producers learned a great deal about how to be useful to each other. The researchers not only learned to make useful observations about what worked or did not work with children but also how to convey this information to the producers. The producers learned how to absorb and use this information and how to ask reasonable questions of the research staff.

Early on, the researchers took the producers' question "What do you mean?" very seriously. What did we mean by "symbolic representation" and "cognitive process?" Statements of goals were clarified in terms of behavioral objectives for the child. What would the child actually be able to do, what behavior would an observer see, if the child had mastered a particular skill? For example, one of the limited number of social goals we selected was the ability to take another person's point of view—to understand that another person may see and feel things differently from the way you do, and then to be able to imagine yourself in that person's place. Although some estimates in the psychological literature suggest that taking another person's physical or social perspective is an advanced skill that, roughly speaking, cannot be acquired before age seven, we decided to experiment with it for several reasons: it seemed especially suitable to treatment through a visual medium; its importance for school preparation could be defended; and it appeared to be a general skill that could help a child to acquire other specific skills and information. The behavioral objectives for this goal were described as follows:

Social interactions: Differences in perspective. The child recognizes that a single event may be seen and interpreted differently by different individuals. Ex.: given a picture showing one boy in a bathing suit and another boy in a snowsuit, the child can express the feelings of both boys in the event of snow.

To further clarify the meaning of this goal for the producers and writers, some general teaching strategies also were proposed:

(1) Start with the child's point of view and then present the opposing point of view in juxtaposition with his; (2) have the child pretend he is someone whose point of view is obviously different from his own; (3) start with a two-person situation where one person is totally oblivious to another's point of view and develop a need for communication; (4) keep the situation constant and have several characters enter, in turn, and react differently in the same situation. (Reeves, 1970, p. 4)

Even with the behavioral objectives and illustrative teaching strategies, the goal statements still did not specify at which levels the producers should begin. The producers and writers obviously needed some indication of the initial level of competence of their potential audience and how high these children might be expected to reach. Occasional normative data are scattered throughout the educational and psychological literature, but estimates of initial competence in most of our goal areas were not available, particularly for urban disadvantaged children, and therefore they had to be collected by the Children's Television Workshop research staff (Reeves, 1970). These data gave the producers rough estimates of the levels of skills they should aim to present.

The research staff made another resource available to the producers and writers, the Writer's Manual. This Manual suggests an array of situations familiar to young children in which each goal could be played out, along with specific teaching strategies that might be used in those situations. Without expecting that all or even many of the ideas in the Manual eventually would be used by the producers, the researchers prepared it to serve as another bridge between statement of goals and script development.

Thus, script writing was tied to goals and priorities, the translations of these goals into behavioral terms, the data on competence levels in different goal areas, and the suggestions for familiar situations and teaching strategies contained in the Writer's Manual.

The instincts of the creative staff and the early observations of children by the researchers suggested some guiding principles for television production. These principles were continually modified as the program developed and can be understood retrospectively as the scaffolding on which *Sesame Street* was erected. The following sections discuss our assumptions and observations, some deeply felt, others hesitantly advanced—some carefully researched, others spontaneously developed. All of them concern how to teach through television, and how children can use television to learn.

SOME ASSUMPTIONS ABOUT CHILDREN'S LEARNING

Some children can view television for hours with their eyes rarely leaving the set. We were so struck by this viewing style . . . that we coined the term 'zombie viewer' to refer to the child that sat seemingly hypnotized, in front of the set. Other children constantly keep a check on all outside activities in the room while they view. We found these styles to be no guarantee of how much the child was absorbing from the program. (Reeves, 1970, p. 11)

Styles of television viewing differ so much among children that no single program should be expected to teach all children with equal impact. We probably never will understand precisely what goes on in the minds of young children when they watch television, but variations in overt viewing styles began to appear early in the researchers' observations. These different overt styles, however, do not seem to relate closely to how much a child will learn; each style can be effective or ineffective, depending on how the child uses it.

One viewing pattern, in which children seem able to watch television while simultaneously keeping track of other interesting events around them, has been described as "dual attention" in other psychological research (e.g. Maccoby, 1967, 1969; Maccoby and Konrad, 1967; White, Watts et al., 1972) and seems to characterize competent young children. What may appear to be distractibility in the child may in fact be a constant alertness and monitoring of many events. Of course, in other children what appears to be distractibility is just that. Similarly, "zombie viewing" may reflect either intense concentration or stupor.

In addition to "zombie" and "dual attention" patterns, another common viewing style displays overt, active physical and verbal participation in the televised action. Certain children sing or talk along with (or even talk at) the televised characters, reply to questions directed toward the children on the program or toward the viewing audience, yelp or tremble in mock fright at monsters or cliff-hanging sequences, offer delighted or disdainful comments on what they see, and generally respond with a high level of both physical and verbal activity. Although active participation is encouraged through numerous programming devices, we do not yet know how it facilitates or inhibits learning. It does ensure the child's orientation to the set, interrupts a period of physical passivity, and reflects active rehearsal by the child. On the other hand, participation can become so compelling or engrossing in itself that some children seem carried away by their own activity, losing contact with the material that initiated their participation in the first place. How this viewing style relates to the effectiveness of learning also remains to be established.

Some people work hard at odious tasks because they have acquired an exotic taste for doing so. But most children probably learn best what they want to learn. Thus the fact that television is a nonpunitive medium becomes important. Children have nothing to fear when tuning in, no threat of humiliation, no possibility of disappointing others' expectations for them. If they do find television threatening or simply uninteresting, they can tune it out, literally and mentally. This principle of personal initiative in television viewing, allowing children to control the direction of their own attention, seems crucial to children's learning, but it is in sharp contrast to our hardy belief that children never do what is good for them unless they are forced to. Since we always have seen entertainment (acceptable when it is momentary relaxation earned by diligent work, but not really good for you) as competing with education (which *is* good for you, but is earnest and hard), we have little experience in combining them to reinforce each other. In discussing production techniques, we shall return to the idea that entertainment and education need not be "either-or" alternatives.

Modeling

We presently do not understand the exact mechanisms by which "observational learning" or "modeling" occurs. We do know that simply watching others—without any direct reinforcement for learning—can teach a child a wide variety of both socially desirable behaviors (e.g., Bandura, Grusec, and Menlove, 1967; Bandura and Menlove, 1968;

Bryan and London, 1970; Bryan and Schwartz, 1971; Bryan and Walbek, 1970; Rosenhan and White, 1967) and socially undesirable behaviors (e.g., Bandura, 1969; Berkowitz, 1962; Bryan and Schwartz, 1971; Surgeon General's Scientific Advisory Committee on Television and Social Behavior, 1972).

Our early observations of children watching television contained innumerable instances of specific modeling. It became obvious that children frequently imitate the physical motions of televised characters. When *Sesame Street* cast members count on their fingers or use their fingers or other parts of the body to shape letters or forms, many children copy them. In particular, one device used on *Sesame Street* has evoked a remarkable amount of physical imitation: all the viewer sees on the screen is a hand trying in various ways to make a noise. As the hand tries snapping its fingers and making other movements, children often imitate these actions. When the hand delightedly discovers that, with the cooperation of the other hand, it can make a clapping sound, the hands of young viewers tend to share in this gratifying experience. Giggling, washing, scratching, hopping, rubbing, and various comical actions also evoke considerable imitation. If a character on television does something absurd, such as stepping in a bucket, children will get up and pretend to walk around with buckets on their feet, too.

Modeling, of course, extends far beyond simple physical imitation. Modeling of effective verbal communication has been a guiding principle behind many writing and production methods. Whenever possible in the production of the show, attempts are made to demonstrate models of constructive communication among the live characters, both adults and children. For example, televised children are shown asking questions as a way of acquiring information, talking together until they solve a problem, or simply enjoying the feel and the sound of words. Since modeling effects are strengthened through children's identification with the character they are watching, we decided to introduce varieties of speech forms on the program, including some spoken dialect and a considerable amount of informal "street" language. Several forms of Spanish speech and culture also are presented. In order to enhance their identification and to contribute to their self-concepts, viewers are implicitly assured that their speech patterns are recognized and accepted. Children are also encouraged to accept speech forms different from their own.

Observational learning does not demand direct teaching to be effective. Simply displaying activities that convey an implicit or underlying attitude also can produce effective modeling. In this way, altruism, kindness, courage, and tolerance can be communicated indirectly through the actions of the televised characters, without explicit labeling. The discovery of writing and production methods that will convey these attitudes effectively to young children has only just begun, but the principle of modeling provides another powerful base for writing and production efforts. It is conveyed succinctly by the young Black child who exclaimed while watching Sesame Street, "Look! He's Black like me and he knows the right answers!"

Narrow-focusing

In communicating a message to a young child, the less "noise" masking the message, the better (Reeves, 1970). In many learning situations, preschool children will have difficulty discriminating what is essential or relevant from what is incidental or irrelevant to the specified goal, and this certainly is true when they respond to film or television. Young children are readily distracted from the central content of a program and often respond to peripheral details. As children get older, they become more capable of attending selectively to those features that have the greatest potential utility (Collins, 1970; Stevenson, 1971). In a confused situation, older children can more easily pick out what matters and ignore what does not, an extremely important skill identified as "distinctive feature learning" (e.g. Pick and Pick, 1970). Since we know that young children have difficulty making such discriminations and attending selectively, special care must be given to make salient what the child is expected to learn. For young children, television's special capacity (Deutschmann, Barrow, and McMillan, 1961) to isolate and highlight the central concept must be exploited, and this becomes an important principle behind many writing and production techniques.

Television can be designed to screen out irrelevancies, reducing the extraneous material, either visual or auditory, that confuses the child and causes him to lose interest. For example, "The Triangle and the Square" presents two animated geometric forms against a solid background. To a musical accompaniment, they each demonstrate what they can do and how they differ from each other. The episode is deliberately bare of irrelevant or peripheral detail.

Total stripping of irrelevance from the material to be learned must be handled judiciously, because several risks are involved. At times, children seem to learn most from what are considered irrelevancies by adults. One man's irrelevancy may be another's primary source of learning, and this especially may be true when an adult decides what will be trivial to a child. Second, total stripping may render the material so bare and unembellished as to be simply uninteresting. When a televised episode is repeated, children will seek new aspects and meanings and sufficient embellishment is necessary to supply these new meanings. Third, if an entertaining way cannot be found to teach the central content without adding a nonessential but amusing feature to hold the child's attention, the risk of adding this peripheral element may be worth taking. Then the writing and production problem is to tie this non-essential feature to the central content, or, at worst, to keep the peripheral content from totally distracting the child from the content to be learned. Whatever the risks, however, television can provide for the young child a narrow, precise focus on central content, carefully eliminating irrelevancies and distractions. This provides another useful principle for children's television production.

Learning from Format as well as Content

Every communication medium has its conventions. Starting with the simple understanding that books written in

English are read left to right, with lines read in descending order, many more subtle conventions affect the ways in which books are written and read. Television's conventions seem to have evolved without deliberate design, but operate strongly to expedite a viewer's understanding. Certain conventions have become so conventional that their triteness no longer expedites but instead intrudes upon the viewer's attention; swelling music, dramatic pauses, fade-outs and zoom-ins, and freeze-frames now elicit groans from adolescents who have grown up on television and regard these conventions as unimaginative and archaic.

But format cues can provide important prompting devices to facilitate learning. For example, in *Sesame Street's* first year, speech balloons were introduced in ten-second segments to teach letter names; soon viewers learned that the appearance of the balloon itself was a signal to the learning of letters. During *Sesame Street's* second year, we decided to expand the reasoning and problem-solving curriculum to teach children that their minds can perform several essential functions for them, including pretesting alternative solutions to problems imaginally before acting, planning a sequence of steps to solve a problem, guessing intelligently from progressively-revealed clues, etc. We adopted another convention to signify the mind at work, in which the televised thoughts appeared above the character's head, signalling the viewer that the character was thinking and working through a problem in his mind before acting.

The educational uses of other common television conventions remain to be exploited. Can zoom-in techniques teach a child who has difficulty in discriminating salient cues to attend more selectively? Can the format in which a speech balloon appears above a character's head to display his thoughts be used to teach children the value of mental mediation in solving problems? Can slow-motion techniques help an impulsive child to develop a more reflective mental pace? Split-screens can visually juxtapose two or more events that actually are distant from each other; can the technique teach the child to juxtapose objects or events in his or her own mind? We are familiar with the use of television-format conventions to supply a setting for learning (e.g. the consistent use of a song or a particular visual display) but we have not experimented yet with their possible effects on a child's mental operations. Will the visual representations of television foster corresponding mental representations in the child? It seems overly simplified to expect such direct effects upon a child's thinking, but, given the importance assigned to the development of mental representations (or Piaget's "schemata"), it probably is worth finding out how the visual and mental representations connect.

In contrast to these positive cases, format clues, including music, can be distracting and interfere with learning. For example, a child may concentrate on the music or on the quality of a voice and miss what the speaker is saying. In evaluating the appeal of stories read on television, Lauren Bacall's voice "sounded funny" to many children and they concentrated on this voice quality instead of the story itself. These children may have been engaging in significant incidental learning about variations in vocal patterns, but their attention had been diverted from the intended focus.

Visual and auditory formats can provide valuable vehicles to facilitate the learning of content. The "either-or" form of argument should be avoided. We do not ask if a child learns more effectively from format or content; instead, we seek to discover how format and content can be melded into the most effective combination.

Cross-modal Reinforcement

Another of the perennial "either-or" arguments in which researchers have entangled themselves is "Which works better, words or pictures?" They have not solved this one either (Lumsdaine, 1963; Yamamoto, 1969). The search continues, however, based on theories that human information-processing is characterized by low capacity and a single-channel transmission system (e.g. Broadbent, 1958; Travers, 1964, 1970), suggesting that there is no advantage to supplying redundant information through more than one sensory modality and thus flooding the learner with more information than he can handle. According to these views of information-processing, messages fed simultaneously through two modalities will tend to interfere with each other. Although there are rare occasions when television will present either pictures or sounds, one without the other, its special capacity is in their coordinated combination. For instance, in a segment designed to teach letter discrimination, Big Bird, an eight-foot-tall feathered puppet who tends to be confused easily, is shown painstakingly drawing an E and an F side-by-side on a blackboard. Viewing children attend to Big Bird's efforts until the letters are completed (they are alert to Big Bird's tendency to make mistakes, which they enjoy correcting); then their interest fades. Soon, however, while Big Bird watches in befuddlement, the bottom line of the E migrates mysteriously to the neighboring F, making an E of the F and an F of the original E. As the bottom line of the E begins its magical move, a slide-whistle sound accompanies its jerky progress.

In this example, the principle of synchronizing sight and sound to provide cross-modal reinforcement instead of interference is clear. Carrying the principle into actual writing and production required that we learn how one modality can be used to support another, instead of cancelling out or interfering with the other. Since most existing research asks how the different modalities compare when considered singly, much remains to be learned.

SOME ASSUMPTIONS ABOUT TEACHING

We always have regarded entertainment and education as competing for a child's attention. We view entertainment as frivolous; too much entertainment produces flabbiness and decadence. Education is seen as serious and earnest, but awfully good for you if you have the strength of character to persist in tedious, hard work; not only does education teach but it builds character by forcing children to work at what is not, and should not be, much fun. Entertainment can only contaminate education, robbing children of the opportunity to learn how to do things that they really do not want to do. And doing things that you do not want to do is what life is really about, isn't it? How will a child learn, after all, to accept the confinement of a job and other responsibilities if we do not start early to teach him to accept tedium? In this view, making education exciting or entertaining is a disservice to the higher purpose of producing disciplined character. To use entertainment in the service of education is tantamount to coddling.

Since we have been maintaining this lunatic view for some time, it is not surprising that we do not understand how to combine entertainment and education to the mutual benefit of each. We have begun to recognize that they need not be incompatible but have not pursued or found ways to make them compatible. We perhaps acknowledge that entertainment need not be empty of educational value and that education need not be unentertaining. What we now need to discover is how to make entertainment instrumental to learning and how to frame a child's learning experiences so that they contain the excitement and joy that he or she has experienced only while not being "educated."

Television Tutelage

Teachers always have known that new learning is expedited by starting from a base of objects and experiences that are familiar to the child and then building and extending into new and unfamiliar material. Several examples of using the familiar as a bridge to the unfamiliar are provided by our televised episodes on letter recognition, in which similarities are illustrated visually between the letter forms and the shapes of familiar real objects. At the start of one animated film, two boys are invited by an unseen narrator to watch a story about the letter "J." As a large, upper case "J" descends between them, one of the boys remarks that the "J" looks like a fishhook. The voice of the narrator intones, "It's not a fishhook, it's a J." This is followed by a rhythmic sequence in which the letter is used as part of a short story filled with "J" sounds and with words beginning with "J." At the end of the story, the second boy says, "So that's the letter J." The first boy replies, "It still look like a fishhook to me." Similar analogies are developed between other letters and familiar shapes. "Y," for example, has on different occasions been compared visually with a fork in a road and a branching trunk of a tree.

Another example of a bridge from the familiar to the unfamiliar is the search for letter forms embedded in the child's real environment. In one *Sesame Street* segment, a puppet finds the letter "E" repeated in the structure of a door, and in another, "T" is discovered embedded in the railing around the basement windows of an apartment house. When such embedded letters are found, a cutout letter is latched to the embedded letter to confirm the presence of the embedded form for the child who may not have seen it. This search for embedded letters not only teaches letter recognition but also provides practice in another essential cognitive skill, distinguishing between figure and ground by isolating relevant characteristics. In all these instances, the child's familiarity with his or her real environment is used as a base upon which new and unfamiliar concepts are introduced.

Only a small part of what children learn is taught to them directly. The importance of informal learning opportunities in undirected play is beyond dispute. On television, direct teaching might be expressed by both telling and showing the children what you intend to teach them, then teaching them by telling and showing it to them, and finally by telling them and showing them again what you have taught them. Many television commercials use this direct approach: here is the product, here is what it does better than any other product, buy it (please).

In contrast, most of television's messages are covert and indirect; the message is illustrated in action but not taught directly. On commercial television's family-situation comedies, father is bumbling and helpless, but lovable—doubly so if he happens to be a professor. We are not told this in words but we watch him constantly bumble. On game shows, women are greedy, grasping, and hysterical with gratitude when receiving a refrigerator or dishwasher for nothing. On soap operas, only bad people have sexual impulses; good peoples' sex is apologetic and engaged in solely for purposes of reproduction. Good children are respectful and reverent, dogs are heroic and loyal, fish are clever (dolphins) or vicious (sharks). The stereotypes abound, but are communicated indirectly through action.

Indirect teaching on television indeed can be extremely effective. Recall the long list of behaviors that children can learn by modeling the behavior of others without any direct reinforcement, deliberate teaching, or overt practice, ranging from self-sacrifice to aggression and back to altruism. *Sesame Street* uses direct methods to teach basic intellectual skills, but adopts indirect teaching methods to display certain social attitudes, such as people treating each other with kindness and courtesy, respect for racial differences, taking another person's point of view, modes of conflict resolution, and accepting rules of justice and fair play. Indeed, almost all the aspects of social development that *Sesame Street* experiments with are approached in this way. We decided to employ the full range of direct and indirect teaching methods on television, trying to discover how to fit the approach to what we were trying to teach.

Showing the World

One of television's great powers is its capacity to transport, to show the world to children—to display people, events, and ideas that they have never encountered before and are unlikely ever to have the opportunity to confront in person. Granting this capacity to transport, difficult choices still remain: What parts of the world, and what events and experiences? If a child lives in a city ghetto, what do we gain in using television to depict its harsh realities? What does the child gain if, instead, we show the brighter and gentler, indeed, the sweeter side of how things are and what they could be? In our early planning of *Sesame Street*, we tried to keep the full range of options open on these questions, but as we went along our drift toward the sweeter side of life emerged. We knew that if we persisted in this drift, we would be criticized for sugar-coating and distorting the unpleasant realities, and for abdicating the responsibility to show conditions that children must learn to change rather than tolerate passively. Our judgment, however, was that *Sesame Street* should not add more stridency and bitterness to the harshness already present in the child's environment. The drift continued toward showing the warmth and kindness that might exist. With all its raucousness and slapstick humor, *Sesame Street* became a sweet show and its staff maintains that there is nothing wrong in that.

The issue of showing the world as it is or as it might be centers on how to depict the difficulties of urban living. *Sesame Street* has taken children visually to an automobile assembly plant, a fishing ship, the back of a bakery, an African play area for children, a farm, a junkyard, several zoos, down a mail chute, and to several other places that they could not visit on their own. One such trip is a bus ride around town, showing what the driver does and how the passengers handle things. Now, we all know that a bus driver often is not society's best example of someone who is kind and courteous. But on *Sesame Street's* bus trip, the driver responds to his passengers' hellos and thank yous, tells a child who can not locate his money, "That's all right, you can pay me tomorrow," and, when seeing a young woman running after his bus just as it has left the curb, actually stops to let her on. Why present to gullible little children such an outrageous misrepresentation of the realities of a city transportation system?

Here are two extreme options: (1) display how people can and even sometimes do act with decency toward each other, or (2) display common uncivil and inconsiderate behaviors so that children will recognize these occasions and be prepared to cope with them more effectively. Although we did decide to include on *Sesame Street* some incidents of conflict among people in order to display possible forms of conflict resolution (the curriculum contains a major section on "conflict resolution"), our basic position was to show the child what the world is like when people treat each other with decency and consideration. Our act of faith—supported by some evidence on the modeling of kindness and altruism —was that young children will learn such attitudes if we take the trouble to show them some examples, even if we stretch familiar reality a bit in order to do so. The harsh realities of a child's world surely are out there. We lose credibility to the child if we ignore them entirely and no effort to teach can afford this. But, even at the risk of sugar-coating these realities, perhaps we can suggest a vision of better things.

While modeling positive behaviors seems worthwhile, preaching on television does not. We have qualms about directly lecturing children on how they should conduct themselves. Many of us still believe we know what is right for others, especially for children, but we are not quite so sure any more and we have begun to wonder about the justice of preventing children from struggling through to reach their own conclusions about virtue and morality. Even without these general reservations about preaching, we know that preaching on television, in particular, simply does not work. Maybe preaching demands a captive audience and television's audience exercises free choice. Maybe the difference between preaching and what people have come to expect from television is too great. In designing *Sesame Street*, we never did consider preaching to children but we did give considerable thought to the various forms that preaching on television has taken, in order to avoid slipping into them. Others before us had done so. Our assumption about teaching by television was that children abhor preaching and that our first inadvertent excursion into it would be the last time that many children would watch the program.

For some reason, when adults on television speak to children, their voices often assume a strange "talking to children" quality. Although we have no evidence of how children perceive the "voice talking down," its unctuousness seems inescapable and as belittling as any other continuous, undeserved punishment.

Equally unctuous is the common practice on children's television of trivializing or reducing a topic in the misguided effort to present it at the child's level of understanding. It is often quite necessary to simplify material for children, extracting the essence of the message and presenting it without distracting irrelevancies. But simplifying and trivializing are not synonymous, and children probably know the difference when they see it.

PRODUCTION TECHNIQUES

Many of these ideas about learning and teaching are incorporated in the writing methods and production techniques used on *Sesame Street*. Several principles converge in pointing to the importance of catching, directing, and holding the child's attention and of providing extensive and varied opportunities for active mental rehearsal.

Catching Children's Attention

Given the child's natural motivation to explore, finding ways to elicit his attention should be less difficult than finding ways to direct and sustain it. This should be especially true with television viewing, since most children apparently have a natural attraction to the medium. But when a child turns on the television set, he usually has many programs from which to choose, some worthy of his attention and some unworthy. What does it take to get the child to watch an "educational" program instead of something else?

Children are accustomed to watching television that is expensively produced, with high quality in visual appearance and form if not in content. The primary exceptions are the inexpensive, locally-produced children's shows (Bozo the Clown, Romper Room, and many others) and the "instructional television" programs that are created locally for in-school use. Neither example of inexpensive production seems to elicit much attention from children; the programs simply do not resemble the expensive look of the television that is most familiar to them. Indeed, instructional television produced for school use (showing teachers lecturing in front of blackboards, and science instructors demonstrating experiments from behind laboratory tables) is not regarded by some children as "television" at all.

Recall that commercial advertisements use animation, appealing music, and other sound effects, all designed to get the viewer's attention quickly and to hold it tightly for the commercial's short duration. The situation comedies that the child knows so well use skillful professional actors, attractive and realistic settings, and a variety of camera techniques to hold attention. Science fiction shows are full of visual gimmicks, often slickly contrived and convincing in appearance. The young viewer's attention will not be diverted to an educational program by the program's good intentions. The show must compete for his attention with others that spend large amounts of money on professional, high quality production.

Music and sound effects seem to play an especially important role in eliciting children's attention. Music in films and television often is referred to as "background," and perhaps for adults its primary function is to provide accompaniment to action and dialogue. But for children it plays more essential roles.

Music's most obvious function on television is to regain a child's lost attention by signaling the entrance of a familiar, appealing character or episode. In viewing television, young children tend to drift in and out of visual attention. As this happens, the "dual attention" abilities of most young children allow them to listen without quite listening, even when they are not actively watching. Auditory cues, usually in the form of music or sound effects, then signal them that an uninteresting sequence has ended and that a new character or episode, recognized by a consistent musical signature, has begun.

Equally obvious is music's function as an aid to memory in learning material in sequence. Almost any child can more easily sing the alphabet than recite it, and the learning of other sequenced materials, such as counting or recalling the order of the days of the week and months of the year, seems easier for young children when put in rhythmic and music form.

Music and sound effects also provide a direct means of teaching basic skills. For example, the *Sesame Street* curriculum suggests teaching "auditory discrimination" skills, one sub-category being "sound identification: the child can associate sounds with familiar objects or animals, e.g., car horn, wood saw, moo of a cow, etc." Here sound effects can provide one direct teaching device, as in the following episode. One puppet character, dressed in hat and overcoat, comes to the door of another puppet's house asking if he may use the telephone to call an auto repair shop for help. The puppet making the request looks and acts perfectly normal and explains that when he stopped his car to wait for a train to go by, his car stalled and he was unable to get it started again. As he talks, however, he displays one unusual characteristic—whenever he arrives in his narrative at a key phrase (e.g. car driving, train going by, car stalling) he delivers this part of his message in the sound effect representing what he is describing. His story involves a baby crying, a cow mooing, and other distinctive sounds, all of this delivered with accompanying sound effects as the other puppet listens in increasing amazement. When the other puppet then tries to repeat the message to see if he has heard it correctly, he finds to his own surprise that he also speaks in the same sound effects.

The use of sound effects in direct teaching can also be more subtle. An example is provided by one of our efforts to communicate a basic reasoning and problem-solving skill. Instead of prompting children to act upon the first problem solution that occurs to them, we wanted to show them that they could try out different possible solutions, pretesting them in their minds before choosing one to act upon. In one episode, a puppet (Ernie) approaches another (Bert) to ask his advice on where to place a large vase. Ernie has to decide among several different-sized shelves, only the largest shelf being sufficient to accommodate it. Bert, distracted from reading his newspaper, tells Ernie to "figure it out for yourself." Ernie then imagines what would happen if he were to place the vase on the small shelf. We see no action; all we see is Ernie's face as he thinks about possible consequences. But as we watch Ernie thinking we hear the vase falling (a slide-whistle sound effect), breaking (crashing sound effect), and Ernie's ejection from the house (Bert's angry voice, door slamming). Having pretested this option imaginally and rejected it, Ernie then imagines the likely consequences of placing the vase on the shelf of correct size; sound effects again play out the placing of the vase, exaggerated congratulatory voices, a trumpet signaling success, and finally a magnificent fanfare. Having imagined the consequences of this option, Ernie proceeds to act it out, successfully, in reality.

One reason for music's great impact on young children is its capacity to evoke physical participation. Variations in musical style evoke different forms of participation. Simple melodies tend to induce rocking and swaying in young viewers. The bouncier the tune, the more intense the physical reactions. With some songs the child almost seems compelled to "get up and dance." The more the child knows the words to a song, however, the greater the verbal as well as physical response. Thus, a song with a bouncy melody might at first induce dancing; then, as the child becomes more familiar with it, he is more likely to rock back and forth in his chair while singing along.

There is one essential condition that must accompany the use of music. A child's attention will be lost if the music is associated with static visual material. To be effective, music and sound effects must be integrated carefully with movement in the program's visual content. If the visual elements are static (e.g., a seated orchestra playing, a stationary folk-singer accompanying himself on his guitar), the music —no matter how appealing in itself—will not attract or hold the child's attention. A static visual presentation apparently stymies physical participation and violates a child's expectation that televised visual action will accompany what hears. Whatever the reasons for the failure to respond to music unaccompanied by visual action, the principle of synchronizing sight and sound to provide cross-modal reinforcement is once again apparent.

Another factor in eliciting children's attention is the use of repetition. It is impossible to produce television material that is always new and unfamiliar to all children, and our child-watching suggests that children would not like such material very much even if it could be produced. The reappearance of a familiar character, episode, or format often will recapture a child whose attention has drifted away. Repetition also provides opportunities to practice tasks as they become increasingly familiar, teaches the television formats and conventions that facilitate learning, and provides the bridge from familiar to new and unfamiliar concepts.

What pieces of material should be repeated and on what schedule? Segments can be repeated often or infrequently, with longer or shorter intervening intervals between repetitions, in their entirety or only in part, within a single program or across several programs, and exactly in their original form or with variations on that original form. We do not have detailed answers to these practical production decisions, but child-watching removes all doubt about the general importance of repetition.

Children seem to like certain pieces of televised material better after they have seen them several times. This seems especially true of short films or animation that build step-by-step to a humorous or incongruous outcome. This progression permits a child to anticipate each step in turn, while still holding the denouement in abeyance, saving the humorous outcome for the end but giving the child the safety of knowing that it indeed will occur after the child has followed the episode through its earlier steps.

Another factor determining increasing appeal with repetition is the child's initial reaction to a televised segment. If this first viewing contains some surprise for him, and also contains more elements than he can grasp in a single viewing, repetition permits the child to confront the grounds for his surprise and to sort out some of the complexities. In general, repetition thus offers opportunities to introduce the relatively complex concepts or situations which a child cannot easily understand fully from a single exposure. Far from being merely a vehicle for simple, rote, or memorizable material (although it certainly accomplishes that purpose very well), the repeated segment can act as a "mind stretcher," permitting the child to return repeatedly to a subject incompletely explored during its first presentation. Even exact repetition of a segment being repeated without change is probably experienced differently each time, giving the child the opportunity to explore all of its facets.

On *Sesame Street* the more common form of repetition has been to keep the content constant and to vary the formats in which that content appears. For example, teaching recognition of the letter "W" was the subject of three different animated films, four different segments videotaped for repetition, and a number of incidents using the live characters on *Sesame Street*. The letter "W" appears sometimes as a three-dimensional object, sometimes as a line drawing, sometimes as a cardboard cutout, etc., but always retains its distinctive features as a letter despite its different surrounding format. Almost every curriculum objective is presented in several different formats so that the child learns to generalize what he has learned across several different forms of appearance. Another form of variation in repeated segments, of course, is to keep the format constant while varying the content.

As with most other production and writing methods, the use of repetition carries its own list of limitations and *caveats*, and it must be used judiciously. Although repetition enhances some television approaches and adds to their appeal over time, other material suffers badly when repeated. For example, interest in slowly paced segments tends to decline with repetition. The length of the segment also seems a factor in how well it stands up with repetition; longer segments generally do not maintain attention as well with repetition as shorter ones. Lastly, when a segment presents many facets or perspectives that can be explored over repeated viewings, its appeal with repetition will be maintained; but when the child has exhausted these different facets, and no new elements are injected into the segment, its hold, upon repetition, is diminished sharply.

Directing Attention

We now have identified some of the elements of television production and writing methods that help to capture the child's attention or recapture it if it has drifted away. How do we take advantage of that attention to the television screen once we have captured it? Are there production and writing methods that will help the child to focus or direct his attention to the salient features of the material to be learned?

If such methods as music, sound effects, and repetition work to elicit the child's attention, other production and writing methods must be used to direct that attention, taking advantage of the narrow-focusing capability of television (to highlight relevant material and screen out or eliminate irrelevancies). At least three related methods provide some leverage here: (1) the use of surprise and incongruity, (2) the value of animation and pixilation techniques as means of directing a child's attention, and (3) the inclusion of the symbolic material to be learned within the televised dramatic action.

Children will direct their attention to what surprises them, to an image or event that violates their established expectations about the order of their world. They focus upon these deviations from their expectations because the deviations pose a puzzle. They are forced to confront them in order to reestablish a sense of order and regularity. The incongruity demands unraveling. Did the child actually see the surprising event correctly? If so, how could it have happened? Few people can let such violations of expectation rest without working hard to resolve them, and this motivation is a powerful one for children, apparently operating as early as the first year of life (Day and Berlyne, 1971; Kagan, 1970, 1971; Piaget, 1952).

Television provides several means of confronting children with such surprises and incongruities. Slow-motion and fast-action techniques show people and objects moving at unaccustomed speeds; one of the most appealing devices for children is the "pixilation" technique that produces the kind of speeded-up comic movements used so well by Buster Keaton and others in the days of silent movies. Also, stop-action technique is used, for example, to stop a horse's jump in mid-air, giving the child an opportunity to observe more closely the characteristics of the jumping horse, but also surprising the child through the novel experience of watching an animal in flight suddenly fixed in space. Running videotape backwards runs people and events backwards, providing other strange and unexpected visual experiences; for example, water flowing forward in a stream is suddenly stopped, and then magically flows backward into its source.

Other camera and editing techniques permit appearances and disappearances to occur far more suddenly than they do in the child's normal experience. This abruptness catches and directs attention. Close-up shots show unexpected characteristics of common objects; looking really closely at the skin of an orange or the surface of an automobile tire or a manhole cover reveals unanticipated properties of these objects. Long-shots, allowing views from unusually great distances, are another source of discrepancy. Who has not been stunned by the view of the earth from the astronaut's perch on the moon?

Since adults often spend considerable time in the effort to convince children of adult infallibility, one of the most remarkable and pleasing novelties for children is to observe adults making errors that children easily identify as such. One series of segments on *Sesame Street* was designed to exploit the interest for children of adults making obvious mistakes while trying to solve simple problems. "Buddy and Jim" are two adults who confront a series of such simple problems, but can never seem to get the obvious solution quite right. They attempt to place a picture on a wall by hammering the blunt end of the nail into the wall, fail to observe that the nail should be turned around, and then conclude that they must walk to the wall on the opposite side of the room in order to point the nailhead into the wall. In another segment, they conclude that making a peanut butter and jelly sandwich is an impossibly sloppy undertaking because both the peanut butter and the jelly always seem to end up on the outside of their sandwich. Here the source of incongruity is the spectacle of adults failing to solve problems which most viewing children already understand easily. And the element of surprise is augmented by the special appeal to the child in knowing that he, for once, knows more than the adults seem to know. These ingredients have a long history in children's programs; "Laurel and Hardy" and "The Three Stooges" traded on the same combination of incongruity and the child's occasional thrill of finding that he knows more than an adult.

We have experimented with other devices for surprising

the child. Using the television screen as a magical drawing-board creates the same kind of surprise as when an adult makes a mistake, adding to it the opportunity for the viewer to observe children correcting mistakes. For example, the viewing child sees the beginnings of a line drawing being formed on the set, representing the familiar form of an animal or an object. A group of unseen children is heard giving instructions in how to draw the object. In effect, the artist is the television set, since the lines appear as if of their own accord. As the line drawing is formed, however, certain lines are drawn incorrectly and the viewing child hears children's voices spontaneously commenting on the composition of the drawing and correcting mistakes as they appear. The television set making mistakes and the children correcting these mistakes provide an unanticipated experience that seems to hold special appeal for young children.

Another powerful production technique for creating incongruity is animation. It generates a wide variety of illogical surprises that fascinate young children. "In animation, anything can turn magically into anything else and children love it for the illogic that is a visual equivalent of their nursery rhymes and jingles and word games" (Kael, 1970, p. 229).

Certain animation techniques exert their magic by giving abstract symbols life and movement, permitting them to become part of the dramatic action. For example, in producing "clay animation," clay is molded in successive stages, each photographed on a single frame of motion picture film. When the film is projected, the clay appears to reform itself into a succession of shapes. In a typical piece of clay animation produced for *Sesame Street*, a small blob separates itself from a larger narrator blob and forms into the letter "E." Next, two "G's" are rapidly produced from the clay "E" and the three letters are aligned to spell "EGG." A clay egg forms behind the word and hatches to produce a baby eagle. The word "EGG" changes to "EAGLE," and the eagle eats the word.

But animation is only one way of directing attention. All forms of television production for children must find functional ways to bind educational content and visual events.

If the content remains superimposed or peripheral to the dramatic movement that children expect from television, that content surely will be ignored.

The forms of televised inaction that children almost always ignore are familiar. Most common is the "message monologue," where a single character appears on the screen, facing the camera from a more or less stationary position, telling the audience something. (Most in-school instructional television is forced to take this form due to insufficient funds; its failure to attract children's attention now is legendary.) Adding another stationary character to give the first stationary character someone to talk with does not help much. Such segments remain heavily loaded with verbal content that is not integrated into any form of visual action. Soap operas generally follow this format with, for example, two women seated on a living-room sofa, sipping coffee (which often is the extent of the action) while discussing their misadventures or the unseen misadventures of their acquaintances. Although these soap operas are not designed for children, and the tolerance of most adults for sheer, second-hand gossip far exceeds that of children, the static quality of their visual conventions is an excellent example of televised inaction that will not hold children's attention.

Action, then, is a key ingredient in children's television, and it assumes many forms and styles. One of its most familiar forms is perhaps the most criticized: zany, slapstick comedy that often also displays one person harming another. Our premises regarding the use of slapstick comedy for children are that the elements of zaniness and harm are not inseparable and that forthright, absurd comedy, even when the elements of harm are extracted from it, will retain its great appeal for children. Behind these premises is the speculation that slapstick's appeal lies mostly in its incongruity and surprise and not in its harmful outcomes. Thus, action on *Sesame Street* is, from time to time, just as nonsensically slapstick as the real world can be. Our general aim on children's television is for larger doses of wit, whimsy, and useful knowledge; but small doses of good, honest, forthright silliness can only make us more credible to our children who, after all, know as well as we do how absurd life sometimes can be.

Instructional content can be engaged directly in the visual events instead of being imposed upon them superfluously. In one episode, Kermit, the saturnine but gentlemanly puppet frog, involves the letter "W" in the action accompanying his lecture describing the letter's attributes. Indeed, in this instance, all of the action is initiated by the letter "W" itself, and Kermit becomes more and more perplexed by the letter's antics. In the first segment, the "W" deteriorates into its component parts as a consequence of the Cookie Monster's voracious appetite (W, to N, to V, etc.), with Kermit desperately trying to retain his composure and continue his lecture. In the second segment (illustrated by some episodes in Figure 1), the "W" comes to life as Kermit offers words beginning with "W," and the "W" itself acts them out. After such words as "walk" and "wander," the "W" engages Kermit in mock battle when Kermit continues with such words as "war," "weakening," and "woe is me!"

Sustaining Attention

To teach effectively, children's attention must not only be caught and focused, but also sustained. Often children's attention is caught momentarily, but they do not hold still long enough to persist in completing the task at hand. This "attention-span" notion is contained in the common complaint of teachers and parents that "I just can't get him (her) to pay attention!"

One obvious and appealing device in holding attention is humor. Since we traditionally have regarded humor as a slightly disreputable diversion from the hard, serious work of education, however, and since we often have accused teachers who indulge in it of coddling or currying favor with their students, we know virtually nothing about how to make humor instrumental to learning. Forms of education that rely upon captive students perhaps can continue to survive without such knowledge, but the televised teaching of children is so completely dependent upon the effective use of humor that some understanding of it is demanded.

a. Kermit the Frog delivering his lecture on the letter W. As Kermit says that the letter W is used in the words Walk and Wander, the W approaches him.

b. Kermit is surprised by the letter's behavior.

c. The letter begins to pummel Kermit.

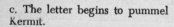

d. Kermit, about to succumb to the W's attack, sighs, "W is for weakening. Woe is me!"

SCENES FROM KERMIT THE FROG'S LECTURE ON THE LETTER W.

Can humor be analyzed? Humor probably is as much a matter of individual taste in children as it is in adults, and therefore it seems to defy neat generalization. Recall David Connell's admonition, when he was worrying about over-intellectualizing children's television, about the risks in analyzing the elements of a joke: nothing is learned and nothing remains to be laughed at. But since there is no more important ingredient in children's television than humor, it may be worthwhile to identify a few consistencies that do appear in what children find funny.

Several of these sources of humor contain the same surprising and farcical incongruities that I described earlier as being so useful in directing a child's attention. Slapstick comedy is a favorite with preschoolers and they find it more amusing than any other comedy form we have observed. They laugh when Ernie out-smarts Bert, when Bert retaliates, when the Cookie Monster foils one of Kermit's lectures, and when a chef falls down with his cakes and pies. The exaggerated physical action characteristic of slapstick seems related to its success with children. Although there are some forms of play with words that young children do find amusing, what seems funny to young children tends to be physical rather than verbal. Stand-up comedians attract little attention until they fall down, not necessarily because falling down is injurious but because it is unexpected.

Trickery always has been an essential element in slapstick comedy, where one person, through guile, takes advantage of another. But today a more advanced level of morality seems to characterize the slapstick comedy that amuses young children: the "underdog-turns-the-tables" form of justice. Here the person who is attempting to take advantage of another through trickery ends up at a disadvantage himself—being tricked through his own guile or cunning. For example, on *Sesame Street*, Ernie (innocent and guileless in this episode) encounters a shifty Salesman puppet dressed in trench coat and slouch hat, who tries to sell Ernie a collection of cut-out number 8's. The Salesman's manner is insidious and fraudulent; he flatters Ernie, agrees with everything Ernie says with a soothing "Riiiight," and engages in other forms of persuasion that clearly communicate his belief that Ernie is an easy mark. In earlier days of slapstick comedy, the episodes might have ended with the Salesman's successful sale. But today the episode results in Ernie gently frustrating the Salesman by having already acquired a large stock of cut-out numbers, although he has no 8's. Explaining that he has no money, Ernie offers to exchange his own number collection for the Salesman's 8's, depriving the Salesman of his opportunity to make a profit. The innocent Ernie has turned the tables and the would-be trickster instead becomes the victim. Justice is restored. Although *Sesame Street's* producers and writers had some early misgivings about how well young children would understand the intended salesman characterization and the justice represented in the "worm-turning" outcome, this and similar episodes, with repetition, were understood by young children, and were entertaining to them.

Another source of humor for children stems from the suspense of waiting for the incongruous to occur. Viewing children cannot predict the exact outcome, but they know that a particular format will follow a predictable sequence in its early stages and then proceed to an unexpected conclusion. For example, a series of short animated films is designed to teach counting backwards from ten. In these films, an identical situation—a countdown to a rocket blast-off—results in a variety of comic endings. The launch director counts off the seconds in a solemn voice as surrounding dignitaries wait expectantly. The numbers appear at the top of the screen as the countdown progresses. In every film but one, something catastrophic happens to embarrass the launch director: the rocket blasts off prematurely leaving the charred launch director sheepishly completing the countdown for his disgruntled audience; the rocket blasts off at the right moment but in the wrong direction and disappears into the ground; the launch director himself blasts off, his panic-stricken count of "Oooooone" fading in the distance, and so on. The naturally suspenseful situation of the rocket countdown is enhanced by the additional suspense of waiting for a particular form of disastrous pay-off, with the child's attention being drawn to the number sequence. The one exception to the consistently catastrophic launches is a successful launch which is greeted with cheers and waving of banners. This straight version itself becomes comic. The viewer who has come to expect incongruous disaster, in what precise form he cannot anticipate, now is surprised further by incongruous success.

Language can be a source of humor for children. Although play with words, divorced from action, must be used cautiously, most children do take pleasure in playing with language and certain emphases on verbal humor in *Sesame Street* are designed to promote this pleasure. Several catchphrases used repeatedly for comic effect have been widely recognized and repeated by viewing children as part of their spontaneous play away from the set: for example, "Cookie!" repeated in gutteral tones by the voracious monster puppet who plagues Ernie and Kermit the Frog; or the insidiously soothing "Riiiiight!" uttered by the mysterious salesman puppet. Children also enjoy certain large words or nonsense words that seem to roll around on the tongue: "bubble," "vigilante," "ukulele," "propeller," and "mumps" all seem to possess this magic.

Alliteration and rhyming in language also can be used to produce comic effects. One such use of alliterative word play is contained in "The Story of Wanda the Witch," an animated film designed to teach recognition of the letter "W" and its associated sound. Included in this film is a brief section at both beginning and end in which the witch uses her wand to write the letter "W" as an off-camera voice announces: "This weird story of Wanda the Witch is brought to you courtesy of the letter 'W.'" The story includes fifty repetitions of the sound of the initial "W" in one minute and sixteen seconds. The female narrator employs a harsh, penetrating vocal quality, appropriate to a story about a witch, amusing to children watching the film, and also effective in making salient the sound of the letter "W."

Again, a caution: although young children seem to enjoy word play, they do not respond well to puns and other plays-on-words. Puns inevitably depend upon the double meanings of words and phrases, and, perhaps because young children do not possess enough verbal sophistication or perhaps because puns generally are unrelated to television's visual action, they do not seem to interest or amuse young children.

In addition to sustaining the attention of young viewers, it should be emphasized that humor serves another function on *Sesame Street*: attracting parents and older siblings to share young children's viewing. Television's potential for providing shared experiences within families is great, but such sharing tends to be infrequent. To capture the interest of older family members, several forms of humor are used: verbal humor, spoofs on familiar television game shows and soap operas, etc. This principle of parent and sibling involvement, however, has its upper limits. Although every effort is made to induce family involvement instead of using *Sesame Street* as the traditional baby-sitter, nothing is included in the program solely to attract this older audience and nothing is made to depend entirely upon their participation with the young child.

The use of humor is one way to get parents and older siblings to watch with younger children. The appearance of well-known guest celebrities is another. Some celebrities, for example Batman and Robin, are enlisted because of their unassailable authority with four-year-olds. But others not so familiar to the pre-schoolers, like Burt Lancaster, Carol Burnett, and Odetta, are used for their appeal to the older members of the family. James Earl Jones was one of the first celebrities to offer to help by appearing on *Sesame Street*, and his performance yielded some unexpected returns.

We asked Mr. Jones, a stage and motion picture actor of imposing voice and appearance, to recite the alphabet in any manner he desired, so long as he paused long enough between letters to permit editing of the videotape. Mr. Jones' recitation of the alphabet takes a full minute and a half. He stares compellingly at the camera throughout. At the time the sequence was made his head was shaved for the role of Jack Johnson in the "Great White Hope" and it gleams in the close-up. His immense hollow voice booms the letter names. His lip movements are so exaggerated that they can easily be read without the sound. The performance should be seen by every actor who ever complained about his lines.

As Mr. Jones recites the letters, they appear beside his head. Each letter appears visually for a moment before it is named. Once named, the letter disappears, and another brief pause ensues before the next letter appears and is named. So powerful is Mr. Jones' presence that we were concerned that very young children might be frightened, but observation of viewing children established the contrary, and still further observation confirmed the presence of the "James Earl Jones Effect" (Gibbon and Palmer, 1970).

The effect appears in stages. The first time a child sees the Jones performance, he or she begins almost at once to respond to the implicit invitation to say the alphabet along with the performer. On somewhat later repetitions, the child begins to name the letter as soon as it appears, before Mr. Jones has named it; Mr. Jones' naming of the letter then confirms or corrects the child's identification of it. With still further repetition, the child begins to anticipate the printed symbol. As soon as the preceding letter disappears, the viewer names the next, saying the letter before Mr. Jones does. Even without the capability of two-way interaction between television and the viewer, the child progresses from following the instructional message to anticipating it. The pace of the presentation induces the child to shout out the next letter before it actually appears, its appearance then confirming or disconfirming the child's response.

The apparent value of anticipation in the James Earl Jones sequence led us to try to induce anticipation deliberately. When Pat Paulsen volunteered to perform, he was asked to recite the alphabet and the sequence of numbers with hesitations, as if he were unable to recall the correct sequence. The timing of the performance is roughly the same as Mr. Jones' performance: the letter appears, pause, letter is named, pause, letter disappears, pause, next letter appears, pause, etc., until Mr. Paulsen falters. At this point, the letter appearing next to his head flashes several times as if to remind him (or to induce him to think hard); Mr. Paulsen sneaks a quick look at the letter, names it in happy relief, and goes on. The pace allows children to anticipate, to respond overtly, and then to have their responses checked against the letter's or number's actual appearance. This anticipation effect, discovered by accident but apparently powerful in sustaining attention, now appears in a number of forms on *Sesame Street*.

Inducing anticipation is one means of inducing active participation. We assume that getting the child to respond verbally or physically promotes both entertainment and learning values, interrupts periods of physical passivity, and insures active rehearsal.

The ability to recite the alphabet is regarded by many as a relatively trivial skill. We had several reasons for including it on *Sesame Street*, however, and it illustrates our efforts to induce verbal and physical participation. We included alphabet recitation because (1) it can become a badge of competence for the very young child—an important displayable skill; (2) it seemed important to include in each *Sesame Street* program all of the letters of the alphabet, lest any viewer be misled to believe that the few letters stressed in each show were the complete list; (3) by presenting the letters visually, as their names are rehearsed, alphabet recitation constitutes a review of letters already learned and a preview of those yet to be taught; (4) presentation of the full alphabet may provide an opportunity to discriminate between visually or orally confusable letters; and (5) reciting the alphabet is a natural occasion for the type of overt participation that we sought in response to the program.

The traditional alphabet song is sung by adults on *Sesame Street* on several occasions, usually with children on the set joining in. On these occasions, the child at home is asked to sing along. The same traditional song has been used with less success in an animated film. This film shows a little girl who walks out on a stage apparently for an audition. An off-camera voice, presumably that of her mother, tells her when to sing and corrects her delivery during the song. The letters appear on the screen as the child sings. The film seemed amusing to the Workshop staff, and it initially tested well for appeal with children.

But when children were observed watching the program over a longer period of time, it was found that the film frustrated many of them. Children who had already learned the alphabet song and wanted to sing along found the interruptions confusing. The rhythm of the song was broken and the off-stage comments were distracting. Those who were still struggling to learn the song found the film difficult for the same reasons. Here is an instance where the intended humor apparently interferes with the intended instructional message.

Some educational conditions demand children's participation whether they willingly offer it or not. However, in response to televised invitations to react or participate, no matter how compelling the inducement may be, certain children will not display an active verbal or physical response. This is part of television's nonpunitiveness; the child may respond less energetically and enthusiastically than we hope, but each child is free to decline the invitation without fear of punishment or of attention of any kind. It should be recalled, however, that since television actors cannot respond in turn to the child's participation, congratulating the unseen audience for their supposed correct reactions may confuse the child who has not found the solution or who has confidently chosen an incorrect solution. It also may confuse the child who had declined to participate at all.

A final consideration basic to sustaining the child's attention over time is the use of a diversity of program elements. Children lose interest when the program dwells too long on one subject or remains too long at one pace or in one style. This "feeling of sameness" (Reeves, 1971) appears in several guises, loses the child's attention in each instance, and clearly indicates the need for diversity in characters, content, style, and pace.

For example, in the early planning of *Sesame Street*, we assumed that if the action on the street itself were tied to a common theme within each program (a pet show, a birthday party, a new character appearing on the street), the story line would link together the elements of each show, carrying the child along throughout the hour. This "story line" device for sustaining attention proved wrong, producing instead a feeling of sameness. Brief reports from the research staff (Reeves, 1971) documents this observation for two shows as follows:

Show 262: Pet Show. The children were very interested in this theme at the beginning. They were attentive, responsive, and loved Slimy the Worm. But, by the time first prize was awarded, the children were restless and inattentive.

Show 265: Ice Cream Machine. Most of the street action revolved around the installation of an ice cream machine on *Sesame Street*. By the time the ice cream man quit, hardly any children were still watching these segments. (Reeves, 1971, p. 2)

Also, a program tends to have the feeling of sameness if too many programming elements within it are similar in characters (no matter how attractive the performers may be), content, style, or pace.

Show 274. Folk-Singer. Nearly half of this program revolved around a folk-singer. This included his singing of six complete songs and snatches of several others. By the end of the program, only three of the six viewing groups were still intact and few of the children in these groups were watching anything.

Show 267. Animal Films. In this program, five animal films were programmed into the last half of the show: Mandrill Mother and Baby, Tree Kangaroo and Baby, Baby Reindeer, Animal Coverings, and Koala. In such a case, it is difficult to judge how attentive the children might have been to the individual films had they not occurred in the same program. (Reeves, 1971, p. 3)

The dangers of lack of diversity are readily apparent in these observations.

No production or writing technique ever works effectively if the characters shown (adults, children, puppets, animated figures, animals, etc.) are not appealing to children and do not portray a variety of distinctive and reliable personalities. The range of personalities among the several puppet characters (from James Henson's repertory company of "muppet" puppets) perhaps best illustrates the necessary diversity of characters in television for children. These puppets generally remain reliably in character across different episodes (a strong preference of young viewers) and can portray more exaggerated and therefore clearer roles and functions than human figures:

Oscar the Grouch: firmly and insistently contrary; from personal preference, he despises the standard virtues (friendliness, cleanliness, consideration for others, gregariousness, etc.) and thrives on what others reject (disorder, dirt, surliness in dealing with others, total privacy, etc.).

Big Bird: easily flustered and confused; prone to making obvious mistakes while remaining cheerfully undefeated and accepted (but not patronized) by others around him.

Kermit the Frog: half-pitchman, half-courtly-gentleman; tries hard to remain cool in the face of gathering chaos and usually succeeds with only minor, but visible cracks in his composure.

Ernie (most often, but not always, appearing in *Bert's* company): an appealing tease; often trapped by his own craftiness and cunning; retains a true sympathy and fondness for his would-be victims.

Bert: usually Ernie's straight-man, but more intelligent and less innocent than most straight-men; long-suffering and put-upon but retains a personal integrity and refinement that allows him to confront the intrigue and chaos gracefully; capable of delicate double-take and slow-burn acting.

Cookie Monster: voracious; sly in satisfying his incessant appetite yet aware of others and willing to understand their reasons for frustrating him; usually succeeds despite their efforts.

Grover: cordial and accommodating in a slightly gruff way; seeks opportunities to be helpful even when this places great physical and mental burdens upon him; often ends up in total exhaustion as he amiably extends himself to the utmost to cooperate.

Herbert Birdsfoot (often appearing in *Grover's* company): a careful and knowledgeable pedant: courteously accepts Grover's offers to assist in demonstrating Herbert's lectures by manipulating physical materials, visibly resulting in Grover's overworking and consequent exhaustion.

Roosevelt Franklin: an agile, quick-witted and quick-moving, street-language articulate Black child-puppet; knows a lot, likes to learn more and to show what he knows and can do; a learning-addict.

Roosevelt Franklin's Mother: nags and pushes Roosevelt a little (this does not seem to bother him much) but takes obvious pride in his knowledge and achievements: "Roosevelt Franklin—he sure does know his numbers!!"

Professor Hastings: verging on senility; gives comically confused lectures, interrupting each at unpredictable occasions for short naps; sporadically capable of remarkably clear insights that stand in marked contrasts to his general muddlement.

Sherlock Hemlock: a not-quite-competent detective who constantly searches for crimes to solve and prides himself on his detecting prowess; succeeds in deciphering certain clues but never quite arrives at a crime's final solution without assistance.

The Salesman: archetypical trickster who trades on the vanity and greed of others; often ends up as victim of his own avarice.

In addition to these distinctive puppets, an infinitely-expandable troupe of *Anything Muppets* come in all sizes, shapes, and appearances and can play any role from local grocer or postman, to members of a group of small boys and girls, to varied forms of monster, to a hip but somewhat seedy and disheveled musical group.

Beyond responding to puppets and animated figures, children generally prefer watching and listening to other children rather than adults. If the televised children are involved in some activity, especially when they are trying to solve a problem that the viewer can work through with them, attention is especially strong. Also, viewers particularly enjoy hearing other children's voices; several films that originally evoked only mild interest were much more appealing when children's voices were added to the sound track.

Televised children are most effective when they display distinctive and reliable personalities, but this is difficult to achieve. On *Sesame Street*, it seems especially important that the televised children be spontaneous and unrehearsed; nothing is more stilted and unnatural than child actors reciting lines from a prepared script. But when the televised children do respond freely and spontaneously, their behavior often is unpredictable and difficult to construct into a set of distinctive personalities. Distinctiveness of character often must be sacrificed for spontaneity and naturalness. If unpredictable behavior by children raises problems for teachers within the classroom and parents within the home, this same unpredictability presents continuous, unplanned crises for the on-screen *Sesame Street* cast. Since these cast members are not professional educators, the televised children's spontaneity of expression poses a constant threat of embarrassment. The adult cast's early reaction was to restrain children by restricting their opportunities to initiate or respond—much like the inexperienced university instructor who does not call upon students who threaten to interrupt his lectures with questions or comments. Slowly, some relaxation is being achieved as the cast learns to respond to the children's spontaneity with spontaneity of their own, even when this forces a radical departure from the planned televised lesson.

Watching adults or listening to them talk—especially when they are presenting "message monologues"—is much less appealing to children than watching other children. In the early planning of *Sesame Street*, we developed a continuing series of episodes called "The Man from Alphabet," featuring a bumbling adult detective hero and a super-reasoning child who unravels the clues and solves the crimes. Although these episodes seemed appealing to the educators and producers, they never held the attention of young children and the approach was dropped. Apparently, "The Man from Alphabet" simply talked too much.

Some attention to adults can be sustained if, instead of showing the adult speaker on the screen, the camera shows what he is speaking about, or if the adult shares the screen with children, directing his talk to them, or if the adult makes mistakes and provides opportunities to be corrected by children—in these instances the adult seems to use language that the child viewer can understand because he is talking to children. When an adult is on the screen by himself, however, children interpret this as part of adult television, not intended to be understood by them.

Presenting a diversity of distinctive characters inevitably means presenting the diversity of dialects natural to them. Although some misgivings were voiced during the early planning of *Sesame Street* about presenting any other language models than "correct" Standard English, we do present the full range of dialects, accents, and informal street language appropriate to the range of characters on *Sesame Street*. We have found no evidence that children are confused by this or learn "incorrect" language practices. The natural diversity of language simply reflects the natural diversity of characters. For example, Roosevelt Franklin, the Black child puppet, speaks a Black English dialect; Gordon—the adult Black male-identification figure—speaks both Standard English and Black English on different occasions or even changes his speech within a single segment, depending upon the situation and the other characters he is with.

Beyond these useful diversities in characters, content, and style, varied pace and mood are critical in sustaining attention. The appeal of any single segment is tied closely to the contrasts provided by the episodes preceding and following it. Both fast-paced and slow-paced material will hold children's attention (the common criticism that *Sesame Street* is continuously frenetic simply is inaccurate), but a slow, peaceful episode is more appealing when surrounded by fast-moving episodes than when it follows another slow, quiet piece. Interest in any particular episode is higher if it creates a pace and mood that looks, sounds, and feels different from the one that preceded it. The principle that visual action and contrasts appeal to young children need not mean that the action always must be rapid or frenetic to be effective; instead, the pace of the action should be varied.

Observations of dramatic improvements in intellectual skills around ages five to seven (White, 1965);—including the ability to sustain attention (c.g. Kagan and Kogan, 1970) —suggest that, for children below these ages, only television programs of short duration would be suitable. But, on the premise that only a program of sufficient total length would stand any chance of providing educational benefit, *Sesame Street* was designed to be one hour in length. The most common misgiving of educators was that this would be too long to hold young children's attention. This misgiving turns out to be wrong; when the segments within a program are varied in character, content, style, pace, and mood, young children's attention holds well over a one-hour period.

CONCLUSIONS

The list of things that television cannot do—and should not be expected to do—probably is far longer than the list of learning and teaching potentialities discussed in this paper. Television indeed may teach aggression to some children and induce physical passivity in others. It also may be severely limited as a teaching tool (one-way communication, inability to sequence material, failure to induce active responding, etc.); there is also the possibility that it may cause us to lose contact with each other and instead to seek and accept solitary, vicarious spectatorship as the normal course of human activity. While we should test television's upper boundaries in providing useful learning and teaching opportunities, we also should test its potential negative consequences and appreciate its inherent limitations.

This paper has discussed (1) some informal principles of learning and teaching, and (2) some production and writing methods that have been used experimentally in television for children. Since we have only vague, beginning glimpses both of these principles and of these production possibilities, our understanding of the relationships between them is tenuous and uncertain. Surely the principles of learning and teaching discussed here do not dictate directly the proposed production and writing strategies; all that these informal principles accomplish is to suggest conditions of learning and teaching that, at least, should not be violated in televised presentations for children.

Even this more cautious conclusion, however, is shaky. Developing television materials for children—and then observing children's responses to them—has been full of surprises and mysteries both for the producers and for the researchers using the visual medium to learn about how children learn. But for those of us who are experimenting in the effects of visual media upon children, a hidden impulse operates. Suppose we fail completely to discover anything more about how children learn; suppose television's capabilities and limitations remain a mystery despite our best efforts. Even so—once in a while, with a little luck—we connect, and hear a child laugh. That is worth most of life's satisfactions rolled into one.

REFERENCES

Arlen, M. J. *Living-room war*. New York: Viking, 1966.
Bandura, A. Social learning theory of identificatory processes. In D. A. Goslin and D. C. Glass (Eds.), *Handbook of socialization theory and research*. Chicago: Rand McNally, 1969.
Bandura, A., Grusec, J., & Menlove, F. Vicarious extinction of avoidance behavior. *Journal of Personality and Social Psychology*, 1967, 5, 16–23.
Bandura, A., & Menlove, F. Factors determining vicarious extinction of avoidance behavior through symbolic modeling. *Journal of Personality and Social Psychology*, 1968, 8, 99–108.
Berkowitz, L. *Aggression*. New York: McGraw-Hill, 1962.
Broadbent, D. E. *Perception and communication*. New York: Pergamon Press, 1958.

Brown, L. *Television: the business behind the box*. New York: Harcourt Brace Jovanovich, 1971.

Bryan, J. H., & London, P. Altruistic behavior by children. *Psychological Bulletin*, 1970, 73, 200–211.

Bryan, J. H. & Schwartz, T. Effects of film material upon children's behavior. *Psychological Bulletin*, 1971, 75, 50–59.

Bryan, J. H., & Walbek, N. Preaching and practicing generosity. Children's actions and reactions. *Child Development*, 1970, 41, 329–353.

Cole, M., Gay, J., Glick, J., & Sharp, D. W. *The cultural context of learning and thinking*. New York: Basic Books, 1971.

Collins, W. A. Learning of media content: A development study. *Child Development*, 1970, 41, 1113–1142.

Connell, D. D., & Palmer, E. P. Cooperation between broadcasters and researchers. Leicester, England: International Seminar on Broadcaster/Researcher Cooperation in Mass Communication Research, 1970.

Day, H. I., & Berlyne, D. Intrinsic maturation. In G. S. Lesser (Ed.), *Psychology and educational practice*. Glenview, Ill.: Scott, Foresman, 1971.

Deutschmann, P. J., Barrow, L. C. Jr., & McMillan, A. Efficiency of different models of communication. *AV Communication Review*, 1961, 9, 263–270.

Feshbach, S. The stimulating versus cathartic effects of a vicarious aggressive activity. *Journal of Abnormal Social Psychology*, 1961, 63, 381–385.

Gibbon, S. Y., & Palmer, E. L. *Pre-reading on Sesame Street*. New York: Children's Television Workshop, 1970.

Hartup, W. W., & Coates, B. Imitation of a peer as a function of reinforcement from the peer group and rewardingness of the model. *Child Development*, 1967, 38, 1003–1016.

Hovland, C. I., Lumsdaine, A. A., & Sheffield, F. D. *Experiments in mass communication*. Princeton, N.J.: Princeton University Press, 1949.

Kael, P. *Going steady*. New York: Little Brown, 1970.

Kagan, J. The determinants of attention in the infant. *American Scientist*, 1970, 58, 298–306.

Kagan, J. *Change and continuity in infancy*. New York: Wiley, 1971.

Kagan, J., & Kogan, N. Individuality and cognitive performance. In P. H. Mussen (Ed.), *Manual of Child Psychology*. New York: Wiley, 1970.

Lumsdaine, A. A. Instruments and media of instruction. In N. L. Gage (Ed.), *Handbook of research on teaching*. Chicago: Rand McNally, 1963.

Maccoby, E. E. Selective auditory attention in children. In L. P. Lipsett and C. C. Spiker (Eds.), *Advances in child development and behavior: Vol. III*. New York: Academic Press, 1967.

Maccoby, E. E. Early stimulation and cognitive development. In

J. P. Hill (Ed.), *Minnesota Symposia on Child Psychology.* Minneapolis: University of Minnesota Press, 1969.

Maccoby, E. E., & Konrad, K. W. The effect of preparatory set on selective listening: Development trends. *Monographs of the Society for Research in Child Development,* 1967, No. 112.

Moore, K. C. The mental development of a child. *Psychological Review Monograph Supplement,* 1896, *1,* No. 3.

Piaget, J. *The origins of intelligence in children.* New York: International Universities Press, 1952.

Pick, H. L., & Pick, A. D. Sensory and perceptual development. In P. H. Mussen (Ed.), *Manual of Child Psychology.* New York: Wiley, 1970.

Reeves, B. F. *The first year of* SESAME STREET: *The formative research.* New York: Children's Television Workshop, 1970.

Reeves, B. F. *The responses of children in six small viewing groups to* SESAME STREET *shows nos. 261–274.* New York: Children's Television Workshop, 1971.

Rosekrans, M. A. Imitation in children as a function of perceived similarities to a social model of vicarious reinforcement. *Journal of Personality and Social Psychology,* 1967, *7,* 307–315.

Rosenhan, D. L., & White, G. M. Observation and rehearsal as determinants of prosocial behavior. *Journal of Personality and Social Psychology,* 1967, *5,* 424–431.

Segall, M. H., Campbell, D. T., & Herskovits, M. J. *The Influence of culture on visual perception.* New York: Bobbs-Merrill, 1966.

Stevenson, H. W. Television and the behavior of preschool children. Minneapolis: Universitiy of Minnesota, 1971.

Surgeon General's Scientific Advisory Committee on Television and Social Behavior. *Television and growing-up: The impact of televised violence.* Washington, D.C.: U.S. Government Printing Office, 1972.

Travers, R. M. W. Transmission of information to human receivers. *AV Communication Review,* 1964, *12,* 373–385.

Travers, R. M. W. *Man's information system.* Scranton, Pa.: Chandlers, 1970.

White, B. L., Watts, J. C., *et al. Major influences on the development of the young child.* Englewood Cliffs, N.J.: Prentice-Hall, 1972.

White, S. H. Evidence for a hierarchical arrangement of learning processes. In L. P. Lipsett and C. C. Spiker (Eds.). *Advances in child development and behavior.* New York: Academic Press, 1965.

Woodworth, R. S. *Experimental psychology.* New York: Holt, 1938.

Yamamoto, K. Stimulus mode and sense modality: What's in it for education? *Teachers College Record,* 1969, *70,* 513–521.

11

The Breakdown of Schools: A Problem or a Symptom?

IVAN ILLICH

SCHOOLS ARE IN CRISIS and so are the people who attend them. The former is a crisis in a political institution; the latter is a crisis of political attitudes. The second crisis, the crisis of personal growth, can be dealt with only if understood as distinct from, though related to, the crisis of school.

Schools have lost their unquestioned claim to educational legitimacy. Most of their critics still demand a painful and radical reform of the school, but a quickly expanding minority will not stand for anything short of the prohibition of compulsory attendance and the disqualification of academic certificates. Controversy between partisans of renewal and partisans of disestablishment will soon come to a head.

The breakdown of schools, since it affects all members of the society, will become a fascinating and consuming preoccupation of the public forum. As attention focuses on the school, however, we can be easily distracted from a much deeper concern: the manner in which learning will be viewed in a deschooled society. Will people continue to treat learning as a commodity—a commodity which could be more efficiently produced and consumed by greater numbers of people if new institutional arrangements were established? Or shall we set up only those institutional arrangements which protect the autonomy of the learner—his private initiative to decide what he will learn and his inalienable right to learn what he likes rather than what is useful to somebody else? We must choose between more efficient education of people fit for an increasingly efficient society and a new society in which education ceases to be the task of some special agency.

All over the world schools are organized enterprises designed to reproduce the established order, whether this order is called revolutionary, conservative, or evolutionary. Everywhere the loss of pedagogical credibility and the resistance to schools provide a fundamental option: shall this crisis be dealt with as a problem which can and must be solved by substituting new devices for school and readjusting the existing power structure to fit these devices? Or shall this crisis force a society to face the structural contradictions inherent in the politics and economics of any society which reproduces itself through the industrial process?

The problem-solving approach to deschooling could serve as a means to tighten the alliance between the military, the industrial sector, and the "therapeutic" service industries. Deschooling, as a merely administrative program, could be the accommodation which would permit the present political structure to survive into the era of late 20th century technology.

On the other hand, the crisis of school could be understood as a breakdown of the most important, respected, non-controversial sector of society, the branch which employs 60 of the 140 million full-time institutionally active Americans as either pupils or teachers.

In the U.S. and Canada huge investments in schooling only serve to make institutional contradictions more evident. Experts warn us. Charles Silberman's report to the Carnegie Commission, published as *Crisis in the Classroom*, has become a bestseller. It appeals to a large public because of its well-documented indictment of the system—in the light of which his attempts to save the school by manicuring its most obvious faults palls to insignificance. The Wright Commission in Ontario had to report to its government sponsors that post-secondary education is inevitably and without remedy taxing the poor disproportionately for an education which will always be enjoyed mainly by the rich. Experience confirms these warnings: students and teachers drop out; free schools come and go. Political control of schools replaces bond issues on the platforms of school board candidates and —as recently happened in Berkeley—advocates of grassroots control are elected to the board. On March 8, 1971, Chief Justice Warren E. Burger delivered the unanimous opinion of the court in the case of Griggs *et al.* vs. Duke Power Co. Interpreting the intent of Congress in the equal opportunities section of the 1964 Civil Rights Act, the Burger Court ruled that any school degree or any test given prospective employees must "measure the man for the job" and not "the man in the abstract." The burden for proving that educational requirements are a "reasonable measure of job performance" rests with the employer. In this decision, the court ruled only on the use of tests and diplomas as means of racial discrimination, but the logic of the Chief Justice's argument applies to any use of educational pedigree as a prerequisite for employment. "The Great Training Robbery" so effectively exposed by Ivar Berg must now face challenge from a congeries of pupils, employers, and tax-payers.

In poor countries schools rationalize economic lag. The majority of citizens are excluded from the scarce modern means of production and consumption, but long to enter the economy by way of the school door. The legitimization of hierarchical distribution of privilege and power has shifted from lineage, inheritance, the favor of king or pope, and ruthlessness on the market or on the battlefield to a more subtle form of capitalism: the hierarchical but liberal institution of compulsory schooling which permits the well-schooled to impute to the lagging consumer of knowledge the guilt for holding a certificate of lower denomination. Yet this rationalization of inequality can never square with the facts, and populist regimes find it increasingly difficult to hide the conflict between rhetoric and reality.

Upon seizing power, the military junta in Peru immediately decided to suspend further expenditures on free public schooling. They reasoned that since a third of the public budget could not provide one full year of decent schooling for all, the available tax receipts could better be spent on a type of educational resources more nearly accessible to all citizens. The educational reform commission appointed by the junta could not fully carry out this decision because of pressures from the school teachers of the APRA, the Communists, and the Cardinal Archbishop of Lima. Now there will be two competing systems of public education in a country which cannot afford one. The resulting contradictions will confirm the original judgment of the junta.

For ten years Castro's Cuba has devoted great energies to rapid-growth popular education, relying on available man-power without the usual respect for professional credentials. The initial spectacular successes of this campaign, especially in diminishing illiteracy, have been cited as evidence for the claim that the slow growth rate of other Latin American school systems is due to corruption, militarism, and a capitalist market economy. Yet now the hidden curriculum of hierarchical schooling is catching up to Fidel and his attempt to school-produce the New Man. Even when students spend half the year in the cane fields and fully subscribe to "fidelismo," the school trains every year a crop of knowledge consumers ready to move on to new levels of consumption. Also, Dr. Castro faces evidence that the school system will never turn out enough certified technical manpower. Those licensed graduates who do get the new jobs destroy, by their conservatism, the results obtained by non-certified cadres who muddled into their positions through on-the-job training. Teachers just cannot be blamed for the failures of a revolutionary government which insists on the institutional capitalization of manpower through a hidden curriculum guaranteed to produce a universal bourgeoisie.

This crisis is epochal. We are witnessing the end of the age of schooling. School has lost the power, which reigned supreme during the first half of this century, to blind its participants to the divergence between the egalitarian myth which its rhetoric serves and the rationalization of a stratified society which its certificates produce. The current collapse of schools is a sign of disaffection with the industrial mode of production. The dropout manifests consumer resistance which rises faster in the service industry than in the market for manufactured goods. The loss of legitimacy of the schooling process as a means of determining competence, as a measure of social value, and as an agent of equality threatens all political systems which rely on schools as a means of reproducing themselves.

School is the initiation ritual to a society which is oriented towards the progressive consumption of increasingly less tangible and more expensive services; a society which relies on world-wide standards; large-scale and long-term planning; constant obsolescence through the in-built methods of never-ending improvements; the constant translation of new needs into specific demands for the consumption of new satisfactions. This society is proving itself unworkable.

Since the crisis in schooling is symptomatic of a deeper crisis of modern industrial society, it is important that the critics of schooling avoid superficial solutions. Inadequate analysis of the nature of schooling only postpones the facing of deeper issues. Worse still, superficial reforms can ease present tensions only to promote a smooth transition from antiquated industrial forms to a post-industrial society which would lack even the saving graces of the present system.

Most school-criticism is pedagogical, political, or technological. The criticism of the educator is leveled at what is taught and how it is taught. The curriculum is outdated, so we have courses on African culture, on North American imperialism, on Women's liberation, on food and nutrition. Passive learning is old-fashioned, so we have increased student participation both in the classroom and in the planning of curriculum. School buildings are ugly, so we have new learning environments. There is concern for the development of human sensitivity, so group therapy methods are imported into the classroom.

Another important set of critics is involved with the politics of urban school administration. They feel that the poor could run their schools better than a centralized bureaucracy which is oblivious to the problems of the dispossessed. Black parents are enlisted to replace white teachers in the motivation of their children to make time and find the will to learn.

Still other critics emphasize that schools make inefficient use of modern technology. They would either electrify the classroom or replace schools with computerized learning centers. If they follow McLuhan, they would replace black-boards and textbooks with multimedia happenings; if they follow Skinner, they would compete with the classical teacher and sell economy packages of measurable behavioral modifications to cost-conscious schoolboards.

The pedagogical, the political, and the technological critics of the school system do not call the institution itself into question. Nor do they recognize the most important effects of schooling.

I believe that all these critics miss the point because they fail to attend to what I have elsewhere called the ritual aspects of schooling—what I here propose to call the hidden curriculum, the structure underlying what has been called the certification effect. Others have used this phrase to refer to the environmental curriculum of the ghetto street or the suburban lawn which the teacher's curriculum either rein-forces or vainly attempts to replace. I am using the term hidden curriculum to refer to the structure of schooling as opposed to what happens in school in the same way that linguists distinguish between the structure of a language and the use which the speaker makes of it.

THE HIDDEN CURRICULUM

The traditional hidden curriculum of school demands that people of a certain age assemble in groups of about thirty under the authority of a professional teacher for from 500 to a thousand times a year. It does not matter if the teacher is authoritarian so long as it is the teacher's authority that counts; it does not matter if all meetings occur in the same place so long as they are somehow understood as attendance. The hidden curriculum of school requires—whether by law or by fact—that a citizen accumulate a minimum quantum of school years in order to obtain his civil rights.

The hidden curriculum of school has been legislated in all the united nations from Afghanistan to Zambia. It is common to the United States and the Soviet Union, to rich nations and poor, to electoral and dictatorial regimes.

Whatever ideologies and techniques are explicitly transmitted in their school systems, all these nations assume that political and economic development depend on further investment in schooling.

The hidden curriculum teaches all children that economically valuable knowledge is the result of professional teaching and that social entitlements depend on the rank achieved in a bureaucratic process. The hidden curriculum transforms the explicit curriculum into a commodity and makes its acquisition the most secure form of wealth. Knowledge certificates—unlike property rights, corporate stock, or family inheritance—are free from challenge. They withstand sudden changes of fortune. They convert into guaranteed privilege. That high accumulation of knowledge should convert to high personal consumption might be challenged in North Vietnam or Cuba, but school is universally accepted as the avenue to greater power, to increased legitimacy as a producer, and to further learning resources.

For all its vices school cannot be simply and rashly eliminated: in the present situation it performs certain important negative functions. The hidden curriculum, unconsciously accepted by the liberal pedagogues, frustrates their conscious liberal aims because it is inherently inconsistent with them. On the other hand, it also prevents the takeover of education by the programmed instruction of behavioral technologists. While the hidden curriculum makes social role depend on the process of acquiring knowledge, thus legitimizing stratification, it also ties the learning process to full-time attendance, thus illegitimizing the educational entrepreneur. If the school continues to lose its educational and political legitimacy, while knowledge is still conceived as a commodity, we will certainly face the emergency of a therapeutic Big Brother.

The translation of the need for learning into the demand for schooling and the conversion of the quality of growing up into the price tag of a professional treatment change the meaning of "knowledge" from a term which designates intimacy, intercourse, and life experience into one which designates professionally packaged products, marketable entitlements, and abstract values. Schools have fostered this translation; still, they might not be its most effective agents. The new media people might be able to distribute knowledge packages more rationally, more efficiently, and more intimately; many of them would like nothing better than to eliminate school administrators out of touch with the latest technology.

Personal knowledge is unpredictable and surprising with respect both to occurrence and outcome, whereas official knowledge must be anticipated and directed to measurable goals. Personal knowledge is always incomplete because there are always further questions to be asked. Official knowledge is always unfinished because there are always newer packages to consume. The progress of personal knowledge is governed by intrinsic rules of inquiry. The acquisition of official knowledge is measured by compliance with extrinsic rules of attendance. Personal knowledge is confident even while incomplete because it obeys its own restlessness. Official knowledge rests uneasy because its current value depends on institutional acceptance. Official knowledge only can solve puzzles within the present framework; personal knowledge only can lead to investigation which aims at change.

Schools are by no means the only institutions which pretend to translate knowledge, understanding, and wisdom into behavioral traits, the measurement of which is the key to prestige and power. Nor are schools the first institution used to convert knowledge to power. The Chinese mandarin system, for example, was for centuries a stable and effective educational system in the service of a class whose privilege depended on the acquisition of official knowledge. About 2200 B.C. the emperor of China is said to have examined his officials every third year. After three examinations he either promoted them or dismissed them forever from the service. A thousand years later, in 1115, the first Chan emperor established formal general tests for office: music, archery, horsemanship, writing, and arithmetic. One in every hundred who presented himself for competition with his peers—and not for competition against some abstract standard—was promoted through the three degrees of "budding geniuses," "promoted scholars," and those who were "Ready for Office." The selection ratio of the exams to three successive levels was so small that the tests them-selves would not have had to be very valid in order to be useful. Promotion to a scholarly rank did not provide entitle-ment to any of the coveted jobs: it provided a ticket for a public lottery at which offices were distributed by lot among the mandarins. No schools, much less universities, developed in China until she had to begin waging war with European powers. Voltaire and many of his contemporaries praised the Chinese system of promotion through learning acquired. The first civil service examinations in Europe and the U.S. used the Chinese system, directly or indirectly, as a model. Civil Service testing was introduced by the revolution in 1791 in France, only to be abolished by Napoleon. The English Civil Service system began as a selection for service in India by men familiar with the Chinese system. Congress-man Thomas Jenckes, one of the fathers of the U.S. Civil Service, sold his program to Congress in 1868 by praising the Chinese system.

For a while, public schools parlayed the consumption of knowledge into the exercise of privilege and power in a society where this function coincided with the legitimate aspirations of those members of the lower middle classes for whom schools provided access to the classical professions. Now that the discriminatory effects of the use of schooling for social screening has become more apparent, a new man-darin system becomes an appealing alternative to many people. Christopher Jencks, misread by uncritical followers, could easily turn "tuition vouchers" into identification tags of the new mandarins. It becomes equally tempting to use modern techniques for seducing individuals to the self-motivated acquisition of packaged learning. This can be done without the protection of schools in a society already trained to conceive of valuable learning as a commodity, rather than as an act of total participation by an individual in his cul-ture.

AN EXPANSION OF THE CONCEPT OF ALIENATION

Since the 19th century we have become accustomed to the claim that man in a capitalist economy is alienated from his labor; that he cannot enjoy it, and that he is exploited of its fruits by those who own the tools of production. Most countries which appeal to Marxist ideology have had only limited success in changing this exploitation, and then usually by shifting its benefits from the owners to the New Class and from the living generation to the members of the future nation state.

Socialist failures can be explained away by ascribing them to bad readings of Marx and Engels or to inadequacies of the original theory. Then again, blame can be transferred to war, blockade, or invasion. Or it can be interpreted in terms of inherited sociological conditions, such as a particular type of rural-urban balance. Whatever the argument, however, Marxist orthodoxies and revisionist heresies and value-free rebuttals now put up smokescreens against independent analysis.

The concept of alienation cannot help us understand the present crisis unless it is applied not only to the purposeful and productive use of human endeavor, but also to the use made of men as the recipients of professional treatments. Language reflects this alienation when it translates these verbs into substantives which make it possible to say that "I have" leisure, learning, transportation, rather than that "I do" enjoy, learn, move, or communicate. An expanded understanding of alienation would enable us to see that in a service-centered economy man is estranged from what he can "do" as well as from what he can "make"; that he has delivered his mind and heart over to therapeutic treatment even more completely than he has sold away the fruits of his labor.

Schools have alienated man from his learning. He does not enjoy going to school: if he is poor, he does not get the reputed benefits; if he does all that is asked of him, he finds his security constantly threatened by more recent graduates; if he is sensitive, he feels deep conflicts between what is and what is supposed to be. He does not trust his own judgment and even if he resents the judgment of the educator, he is condemned to accept it and to believe himself that he cannot change reality.

The mutation of the concept of revolution cannot occur, however, without a rejection of the hidden curriculum of schooling and the correlative attitude toward knowledge, for it is this curriculum and this attitude which turn out disciplined consumers of bureaucratic instructions ready to consume other kinds of services and treatments which they are told are good for them. The converging crisis of ritual schooling and of acquisitive knowledge raises the deeper issue of the tolerability of life in an alienated society. If we formulate principles for alternative institutional arrangements and an alternative emphasis in the conception of learning, we will also be suggesting principles for a radically alternative political and economic organization.

Just as the structure of one's native language can be grasped only after he has begun to feel at ease in another tongue, so the fact that the hidden curriculum of schooling has moved out of the blindspot of social analysis indicates that alternative forms of social initiation are beginning to emerge and are permitting some of us to see things from a new perspective. Today it is relatively easy to get wide agreement on the fact that gratuitous, compulsory schooling is contrary to the political self-interest of an enlightened majority. School has become pedagogically indefensible as an instrument of universal education. It no longer fits the needs of the seductive salesmen of programmed learning. Proponents of recorded, filmed, and computerized instruction used to court the schoolmen as business prospects; now they are itching to do the job on their own.

As more and more of the sectors of society become dissatisfied with school and conscious of its hidden curriculum, increasingly large concessions are made to translate their demands into needs which can be served by the system— and which thus can disarm their dissent. I here describe some of these attempts under the general label of *cooptation*.

As the hidden curriculum moves out of the darkness and

into the twilight of our awareness, phrases such as the "deschooling of society" and the "disestablishment of schools" become instant slogans. I do not think these phrases were used before 1970. Now in some circles they have become the badge and criterion of the new orthodoxy. Recently I talked by amplified telephone to students in a seminar on deschooling at the Ohio State University College of Education. Everett Reimer's book on deschooling had become a popular college text, even before it was published commercially. Unless the radical critics of school are not only ready to embrace the deschooling slogan but also prepared to reject the current view that learning and growing up can be adequately explained as processes of programming, and the current vision of social justice based on it (more obligatory consumption for everybody), we may face the charge of having provoked the last of the missed revolutions.

The current crisis has made it easy to attack schools. Schools, after all, are authoritarian and rigid; they do produce both conformity and conflict; they do discriminate against the poor and disengage the privileged. These are not new facts but it used to be a mark of some boldness to point them out. Now it takes a good deal of courage to defend schools. It has become fashionable to poke fun at Alma Mater—to take a potshot at the former "Sacred Cow."

Once the vulnerability of schools has been exposed, it also becomes easy to suggest remedies for the most outrageous abuses. The authoritarian rule of the classroom is not intrinsic to the notion of an extended confinement of children in schools. Free schools are practical alternatives; they can often be run more cheaply than ordinary schools. Since accountability already belongs to educational rhetoric, community control and performance contracting have become attractive and respectable political goals. Everyone wants education to be relevant to real life and so critics talk freely about pushing back the classroom walls to the borders of our culture. Not only are alternatives more widely advocated; they are often at least partially implemented: experimental schools are financed by school boards; the hiring of certified teachers is decentralized; high school credit is given for apprenticeship, and college credit for travel; computer games are given a trial run.

Most of the changes have some good effects. The experimental schools have fewer truants; parents have a greater feeling of participation in the decentralized districts; children who have been introduced to real jobs do turn out to be more competent. Yet all these alternatives operate within predictable limits, since they leave the hidden structure of the schools intact. Free schools which lead to further free schools in an unbroken chain of attendance produce the mirage of freedom. Attendance as the result of seduction inculcates the need for specialized treatment more persuasively than reluctant attendance enforced by truant officers. Free school graduates are easily rendered impotent for life in a society which bears little resemblance to the protected gardens in which they have been cultivated. Community control of the lower levels of a system turns local school board members into pimps for the professional hookers who control the upper levels. Learning by doing is not worth much if doing has to be defined as socially valuable learning by professional educators or by law. The global village will be a global schoolhouse if teachers hold all the plugs. It will be distinguishable in name only from a global madhouse run by social therapists or a global prison run by corporation wardens.

In a general way I have pointed out the dangers of a rash, uncritical disestablishment of school. More concretely, these dangers are exemplified by various kinds of *cooptation* which change the hidden curriculum without changing the basic concept of learning and of knowledge and their relationship to the freedom of the individual in society.

The rash and uncritical disestablishment of school could lead to a free-for-all in the production and consumption of more vulgar learning acquired for immediate utility or eventual prestige. The discrediting of school-produced complex curricular packages would be an empty victory if there were no simultaneous disavowal of the very idea that knowledge is more valuable because it comes in certified packages and is acquired from some mythological knowledge-stock controlled by professional guardians. I believe that only actual participation constitutes socially valuable learning—a participation by the learner in every stage of the learning process, including not only a free choice of what is to be learned and how it is to be learned, but also a free determination by each learner of his own reason for living and learning and the part that his knowledge is to play in his life.

Social control in an apparently deschooled society could be more subtle and more numbing than in the present society where many people at least experience a feeling of release on the last day of school. More intimate forms of manipulation are already common as the amount learned through the media exceeds the amount learned through personal contact in and out of school. Learning from programmed information always hides reality behind a screen.

Let me illustrate the paralyzing effects of programmed information by a perhaps shocking example. The tolerance of the American people to United States atrocities in Vietnam is much higher than the tolerance of the German people to German atrocities on the front, in occupied territories, and in extermination camps during the Second World War. It was a political crime for Germans to discuss the atrocities committed by Germans. The presentation of U.S. atrocities on network television is considered an educational service. Certainly the population of the United States is much better informed about the crimes committed by its troops in a colonial war than were the Germans about the crimes committed by its SS within the territory of the Reich. To get information on atrocities in Germany meant that you had to take a great risk; in the U.S. the same information is channeled into your living room. This does not mean, however, that the Germans were any less aware that their government was engaged in cruel and massive crime than are the contemporary Americans. In fact, it can be argued that the Germans were *more* aware, precisely because they were not psychically overwhelmed with packaged information about killing and torture, because they were not drugged into accepting that everything is possible, because they were not vaccinated against reality by having it fed to them as decomposed "bits" on a screen.

The consumer of pre-cooked knowledge learns to react to knowledge he has acquired rather than to the reality from which a team of experts has abstracted it. If access to reality is always controlled by a therapist and if the learner accepts this control as natural, his entire worldview becomes hygienic and neutral: he becomes politically impotent. He becomes impotent to know in the sense of the Hebrew word *jdh*, which means intercourse* penetrating the nakedness of being and reality; because reality for which he can accept responsibility is hidden for him under the scales of assorted information he has accumulated.

The uncritical disestablishment of school could also lead to new performance criteria for preferential employment and promotion, and most importantly for privileged access to tools. Our present scale of general ability, competence, and trustworthiness for role assignment is calibrated by tolerance to high doses of schooling. It is established by teachers and accepted by many as rational and benevolent. New devices could even be developed, and new rationales found both more insidious than school grading, and equally effective at justifying social stratification and the accumulation of privilege and power.

Participation in military, bureaucratic, or political activities or status in a party could provide a pedigree just as transferable to other institutions as the pedigree of grandparents in an aristocratic society, standing within the Church in medieval society, or age at graduation in a ₊chooled society. General tests of attitudes, intelligence, or mechanical ability could be standardized according to other criteria than those of the schoolmaster. They could reflect the ideal levels of professional treatment espoused by psychiatrist, ideologist, or bureaucrat. Academic criteria are already suspect. The Center for Urban Studies of Columbia University has shown that there is less correlation between specialized education and job performance in specialized fields than there is between specialized education and the resulting income, prestige, and administrative power. Non-academic criteria are already proposed. From the urban

---

* Ed. Note: Unfortunately, semantics is applicable. The term *intercourse* is used in the sense of communication.

ghetto in the United States to the villages of China, revolutionary groups try to prove that ideology and militancy are types of learning which convert more suitably into political and economic power than scholastic curricula. Unless we guarantee that job-relevance is the only acceptable criterion for employment, promotion, or access to tools, thus ruling out not only schools but all other ritual screening, then deschooling means driving out the devil with Beelzebub.

The search for a radical alternative to the school system itself will be of little avail unless it finds expression in precise political demands: the demand for the disestablishment of school in the broadest sense and the correlative guarantee of freedom for education. This means legal protections, a political program, and principles for the construction of institutional arrangements which are the inverse of school. Schools cannot be disestablished without the total prohibition of legislated attendance, the proscription of any discrimination on the basis of prior attendance, and the transfer of control over tax funds from benevolent institutions to the individual person. Even these actions, however, do not guarantee freedom of education unless they are accompanied by the positive recognition of each person's independence in the face of school and of any other devices designed to compel specific behavioral change or to measure man in the abstract rather than to measure man for a concrete job.

Touchstone for Revolution.

Deschooling makes strange bedfellows. The ambiguity inherent in the breakdown of schooling is manifested by the unholy alliance of groups which can identify their vested interests with the disestablishment of school: students, teachers, employers, opportunistic politicians, taxpayers, Supreme Court justices. But this alliance becomes unholy and this bedfellowship more than strange if it is based only on the recognition that schools are inefficient tools for the production and consumption of education, and some other form of mutual exploitation would be more satisfactory.

The insurmountable problems of inefficiency, consumer resistance, and political scandal which the school system can no longer hide could be solved by more rational, attractive, and specific learning packages, the diversification of educational procedures, and a cloud-like dispersal of production centers. A new educational lobby could even now be organized on behalf of more effective training for jobs and social roles, more job-related measurements, and more benevolently cooperative acculturation. The hidden curriculum of schooling could be transmuted into the unseen mask of a therapeutic culture.

We can disestablish schools or we can deschool culture. We can resolve provisionally some of the administrative problems of the knowledge industry or we can spell out the goals of political revolution in terms of educational postulates. The acid test of our response to the present crisis is our pinpointing of the responsibility for teaching and learning.

Schools have made teachers into administrators of programs of manpower capitalization through directed planned behavioral changes. In a schooled society the administrations of professional teachers become a first necessity which hooks pupils into unending consumption and dependence. Schools have made learning a specialized activity and deschooling will only be a displacement of responsibility to other kinds of administration, so long as teaching and learning remain sacred activities separate and estranged from fulfilling life. If schools were disestablished for the purpose of more efficient delivery of knowledge to more people, the alienation of men through client relationships with the new knowledge industry would only become global. Deschooling must be the secularization of teaching and learning. It must involve a return of control over what is learned and how it is learned to persons, and not a transfer of control to another, more amorphous set of institutions and their perhaps less obvious representatives. The learner must be guaranteed his freedom without guaranteeing to society what learning he will acquire and hold as his own. Each man must be guaranteed privacy in learning, with the hope that he will assume the obligation of helping others as well as himself to grow into uniqueness. Whoever takes the risk of teaching others must assume responsibility for the results, as must the student who exposes his capacity to learn to the influence of a teacher; neither should shift guilt to sheltering institutions or laws. A schooled society must reassert the joy of conscious living over the capitalization of manpower.

The touchstone of mutation in education is the honest recognition that most people learn most of the time when they do what they enjoy doing. Most people are capable of personal, intimate intercourse with others unless they are stupefied by inhuman work or snowed under by treatment with programs. Once this is admitted, we will understand that to increase learning opportunities means to facilitate communication between the learner and his world, between the learner and his fellows, between the learner and those who can point him towards traditions and methods tested by their experience. Once we take hold of the simple insight that personal knowledge is always predictable but never unconnected, we will undertake the real task of setting up institutional arrangements which guarantee the freedom necessary for independent inquiry. We will multiply the roads, bridges, and windows to learning opportunities and make sure that they are opened at the learner's bidding.

THREE RADICAL DEMANDS

Any dialogue about knowledge is really a dialogue about the individual in society. An analysis of the present crisis of school leads us, then, to talk about the social structure necessary to facilitate learning, to encourage independence and interrelationship, and to overcome alienation. This kind of discourse is outside the usual range of educational concern. It leads, in fact, to the enunciation of specific political goals. These goals can be most sharply defined by distinguishing three general types of intercourse in which a person must engage if he would grow up.

Get at the facts, get access to the tools, and bear the responsibility for the limits within which either can be used. If a person is to grow up, he needs in the first place access to things, places, processes, events, and records. To guarantee such access is primarily a matter of unlocking the privileged storerooms to which they are presently consigned.

The poor child and the rich child are different partly because what is secret for one is patent to the other. By turning knowledge into a commodity, we have learned to deal with it as with private property. The principle of private property is now used as the major rational for declaring certain facts off-limits to people without the proper pedigree. The first goal of a political program aimed at rendering the world educational is the abolition of the right to reserve access necessary for the purpose of teaching or learning. The right of private preserve is now claimed by individuals, but it is most effectively exercised and protected by corporations, bureaucracies, and nation states. In fact, the abolition of this right is not consistent with the continuation of either the political or the professional structure of any modern nation. The end of property protection would mean the abolition of most professional secrets and the consequent removal of the rationale for professional exploitation. This means more than merely improving the distribution of teaching materials or providing financial entitlements for the purchase of educational objects. The abolition of secrets clearly transcends conventional proposals for educational reform, yet it is precisely from an educational point of view that the necessity of stating this broad—and perhaps unattainable—political goal is most clearly seen.

The learner also needs access to persons who can teach him the tricks of their trades or the rudiments of their skills. For the interested learner it does not take much time to learn how to perform most skills or to play most roles. The best teacher of a skill is usually someone who is engaged in its useful exercise. We tend to forget these things in a society where professional teachers monopolize initiation into all fields and disqualify unauthorized teaching in the community. An important political goal, then, is to provide incentives for the sharing of acquired skills.

The demand that skills be shared implies, of course, a much more radical vision of a desirable future. Access to skills is not only restricted by the monopoly of schools and unions over licensing, there is also the fact that the exercise of skills is tied to the use of scarce tools. Scientific knowledge is overwhelmingly incorporated into tools which are highly specialized and which must be used within complex structures set up for the efficient production of goods and services for which demand becomes general while supply remains scarce. Only a privileged few get the results of sophisticated medical research, and only a privileged few get to be doctors. A relatively small minority will travel on supersonic airplanes, and only a few pilots will learn how to fly them.

The simplest way to state the alternatives to this trend toward specialization of needs and their satisfaction is in educational terms. It is a question of the desirable use of scientific knowledge. In order to facilitate more equal access to the benefits of science and to decrease alienation and unemployment, we must favor the incorporation of scientific knowledge into tools or components within the reach of a great majority of people. These tools would allow most people to develop their skills. Any peasant girl could learn how to diagnose and treat almost all the infections which occur in rural Mexico if she were introduced to the use of techniques which are now available but which were un-dreamt of by the doctor of a couple of generations ago. In poor countries most people still build their own houses, often using mud or the covering of oil barrels. Now we want to give them low-cost, pre-packaged housing—thus moderniz-ing them into regarding housing as a commodity rather than an activity. We would better provide them with cement mixers. Certainly the tools used in learning—and in most scientific research—have become so cheap that they could be made available to anyone: books, audio and video tapes, and the simple scientific instruments in whose use is learned those basic skills which form the basis for the supposedly advanced skill required of the very few who might have to operate an electron-microscope.

Insight into the conditions necessary for wider acquisition and use of skills permits us to define a fundamental charac-teristic of post-industrial socialism. It is of no use—indeed it is fraudulent—to promote public ownership of the tools of production in an industrial, bureaucratic society. Fac-tories, highways, heavy-duty trucks, etc., can be symbolically "owned" by all the people as the Gross National Product and the Gross National Education are pursued in their names. But the specialized means of producing scarce goods and services cannot be used by the majority of people. Only tools which are cheap and simple enough to be accessible and usable by all people, tools which permit temporary association of those who want to use them for a specific occasion, tools which allow specific goals to emerge during their use— only such tools foster the recuperation of work and leisure now alienated through an industrial mode of production.

The development and wide dispersal of simple and durable tools would discredit the special privileges now given to technocrats. The growth of science would not be jeopardized, but the progress of complex scientific technology at the service of technocratic privilege would become scandalous. This style of progress is now justified in the name of developing a necessary infrastructure. A new style of research would reveal this infrastructure as the foundation of privilege.

To recognize from an educational point of view the priority of guaranteeing access to tools and components whose simplicity and durability permit their use in a wide variety of creative enterprises is to indicate simultaneously the solution to the problem of unemployment. In an industrial society unemployment is experienced as the sad inactivity of a man for whom there is nothing to make, while he has unlearned or never learned what to do. Since there is little really useful work, the problem is usually solved by creating more jobs in service industries like the military, public administration, education, or social work. Educational considerations oblige us to recommend the substitution of the present mode of industrial production which depends on a growing market for increasingly complex and obsolescent goods, by a mode of post-industrial production which depends on the demand for tools or components which are labor-intensive, repair-intensive, and whose complexity is strictly limited.

Science will be kept artificially arcane as long as its results are incorporated into technology at the service of professionals. If it were used to render possible a style of life in which each man could enjoy housing himself, healing himself, educating, moving, and entertaining himself, then scientists would try much harder to re-translate the discoveries made in a secret language into the normal language of everyday life.

The level of education in any society can be gauged by the degree of effective access each of the members has to the facts and tools which, within this society, affect his life. We have seen that such access requires a radical denial of the right to secrecy of facts and complexity of tools on which contemporary technocracies found their privilege which they in turn render immune by interpreting their use as a service to the majority. A satisfactory level of education in a technological society imposes important constraints on the use to which scientific knowledge is put. In fact, a technological society which provides conditions for men to recoup personally (and not institutionally) the sense of potency to learn and to produce, which gives meaning to life, depends on restrictions which must be imposed on the technocrat who now controls both services and manufacture. Only an enlightened and powerful majority can impose such constraints.

If access to facts and use of tools constitute the two most obvious freedoms needed to provide educational opportunity, the ability to convoke peers to a meeting constitutes the one through which the learning by an individual is translated into political process, and political process in turn becomes conscious personal growth. Data and skills which an individual might have acquired shape into exploratory, creative, open-ended, and personal meaning only when they are used in dialectic encounter. And this requires the guaranteed freedom for every individual to state, each day, the class of issue which he wants to discuss, the class of creative use of a skill in which he seeks a match—to make this bid known—and, within reason, to find the circumstances to meet with peers who join his class. The right of free speech, free press, and free assembly traditionally meant this freedom. Modern electronics, photo-offset, and computer techniques in principle have provided the hardware which can provide this freedom with a range undreamt of in the century of enlightenment. Unfortunately the scientific know-how has been used mainly to increase the power and decrease the number of funnels through which the bureaucrats of education, politics, and information channel their quick-frozen TV dinners. But the same technology could be used to make peer-matching, meeting, and printing as available as is now the private conversation over the telephone.

On the other hand, it should be clear that only through the definition of what constitutes a desirable society, arrived at in the meeting of those who are both dispossessed and also disabused of the dream that constantly increasing quanta of consumption can provide them with the joy they seek out of life, can the inversion of institutional arrangement here drafted be put into effect—and also with it a technological society which values occupation, intensive work, and leisure over alienation through irrelevant and inadequate goods and services.

IV

New Approaches to
Socialization Research

The concluding chapter of this collection presents two papers in which eminent scholars of socialization and education reflect upon the possibilities of new approaches to these fields of study. Professor Urie Bronfenbrenner, from the Department of Human Development at Cornell University, has long established his reputation as an outstanding scholar of socialization processes. His paper, "A Theoretical Perspective for Research on Human Development," first published in this volume, describes the limitations of his own special field—scientific psychology—in the study of human development, and formulates an alternative model in the interactionist perspective, which he has earlier (if with less vigour) defended in his assessments of Parsonian functionalist theory of socialization. The merit of this article is that it does not stop with the formulation of some postulates but also spells out the concrete possibilities of his model in empirical research. "Sociology and the Study of Education" is the report of a Planning Conference for the National Institute of Education, written by seven experts from various fields and universities, including Professor Burton R. Clark from Yale and Professor David Riesman from Harvard. The paper is published here because it gives an excellent description of the present problems and future tasks of educational research. Socialization and education, however, can hardly be conceptually separated: while in former times education was the only available term, the introduction of the concept of socialization during the late Thirties was a symptom of a shift in interest from deliberate pedagogical action to the more unintentional elements affecting human development. Today the term education is more and more reserved for the procedures of the educational institutions, i.e., the school system. Yet the report on the present state of the sociology of education takes notice of the fact that family and school are related to each other in their combined effect on children. The effect of both these institutions as socialization agents must be the object of a renewed research effort, which should not shy away from new questions in order to find new answers if the social and psychological fate of our children should be less destined to alienation than ours.

12

A Theoretical Perspective
for Research on
Human Development[1]

URIE BRONFENBRENNER

THIS IS A PRESUMPTUOUS PAPER. In relatively brief compass, it purports to demonstrate that the scientific model typically employed for research on human development is critically impoverished—both theoretically and empirically; it then proceeds to present a new theoretical model alleged to be more adequate to the task.

I approach this rash endeavor from the peculiarly narrow perspective of my own discipline—scientific psychology. I use the term "narrow" advisedly. As we know, psychology borrowed its research model from the more prestigeful physical and biological sciences. Precisely because that model was designed to isolate physical and biological phenomena in their pure form, it is psychologically sterile.

I contend that the much-prized model of the experimental psychologist, as it is usually applied, is impoverished in at least four major respects:

First, it is ordinarily limited to a two-person system involving, or at least confining attention to one experimenter and one child—the latter typically—and significantly—referred to as a "subject."

The term "subject" reflects the second major restriction. The process taking place between experimenter and child is ordinarily conceived of as unidirectional; that is, one is concerned with the effect of the experimenter's behavior on the child, and not the reverse.

Third, this second participant in the system, the experimenter, is usually a stranger, nine times out of ten a graduate student, whose prior relationship to the child is nonexistent, or if existent, trivial in character.

Fourth, and most important of all, the two persons system exists, or is treated as if it existed, in isolation from any other social context that could impinge on or encompass it.

These four features so common in our experiments are hardly characteristic of the situations in which children actually develop. Thus in the family, the day care center, preschool, play group, or school classroom:

1. There are usually more than two people.
2. The child invariably influences those who influence him.
3. The other participants are not strangers but persons who have enduring and differing relationships with the child.
4. Finally, the behavior of all these persons is profoundly affected by other social systems in which these same persons participate in significant roles and relationships, both vis-a-vis the child and each other.

If all this be true, then much of our research is off the mark. We are using a theoretical model which is *ecologically invalid*. By ruling out of consideration the very phenomena that we most need to study, the model commits us to a science that is puny and trivial in comparison with the true nature of the processes which it purports to study. And we continue to employ this model in the mistaken belief that it constitutes our only hope for scientific legitimacy.

But, as we all know, times are changing, and, at least in child development, illegitimacy is on the rise. As a result, there is some hope of a new theoretical perspective.

In attempting to lay out the basic dimensions of that perspective, I make no claim to originality. Rather I have sought to consolidate and make explicit developments that are reflected, often only by implication, in scattered writings and researches, often on seemingly unrelated problems. In the interests of brevity, I shall identify the research evidence on which I have drawn only by reference rather than detailed description.[2]

To turn to the model itself. What properties must it have if it is to meet the major requirements already outlined?

1. *Reciprocality.* First and foremost, the model must be conceived as a two-way system, in which the behavior of each participant both affects and is affected by the behavior of the others. Thus, in a laboratory experiment, one would have to be concerned not only with changes in the child's response as a function of the behavior of an experimenter but also with the reverse; that is, the effects on the experimenter of the behavior of the child. The same consideration would apply to studies of other socialization systems such as parent and child, teacher and child, the child in the group, etc.

The importance of reciprocality as a defining property of any adequate model for the socialization process has been recognized in theoretical discussions (e.g., Bronfenbrenner, 1968; Gewirtz, 1969a, 1969b; Rheingold, 1969a), but in research practice the principle has been more honored in the breech than in the observance. For example, only a very few studies have analyzed mother-infant interaction as a reciprocal system (e.g., S. M. Bell, 1971; Gewirtz & Gewirtz, 1965; Moss, 1967), and none, to this writer's knowledge has examined interaction between infant and experimenter as a two-way process.

The property of reciprocality implies two important corollary principles which have received some attention in empirical work.

a. *The child as stimulus.* The child is to be viewed not merely as a reactive agent but as an instigator of behavior in others. To use the language of Kurt Lewin, the child has "demand characteristics" which tend to evoke certain patterns of response in others. Thus a young baby's "cuteness," and even more clearly its cry, invite, indeed almost compel a reaction from persons in its immediate environment. An adequate research model must take into account the almost inevitable impact of such demand characteristics on others, including the experimenter.

The role of the child as a stimulus and instigator or response has been stressed by a number of developmental psychologists, especially R. Q. Bell (1968, 1971). There are also a few direct studies of the phenomenon as manifested in the relation between mother and infant (S. M. Bell,

1971; Gewirtz & Gewirtz, 1969; Moss, 1967; Moss & Robson, 1968), but only the last is based on systematic analysis of the actual sequence of mother-infant interaction in a substantial sample (54 pairs). Nevertheless, all four studies show striking evidence for the predominance of infant-initiated over mother-initiated behavior in the first year of life. This writer has not been able to find any studies of this phenomenon for later ages.

As illustrated by Moss's research (1967), focusing attention on the child as a stimulus also brings to light the role of genetic and constitutional factors in giving both impetus and direction to the socialization process. Thus Moss argues persuasively from his data that the greater "soothability" of female versus male infants in the first weeks of life sets in motion a more rapidly converging pattern of mutual reinforcement and attachment which contributes to the emergence of sex differences in early language development and social relationships.

b. *The child as socializing agent.* The potency of the child as a stimulus takes on added significance in any situation involving protracted interaction between the child and another person. For, over a period of time, not only does the adult produce lasting changes in the behavior of the child, but *vice versa.* In other words, not only does the mother, or other consistent caregiver, train the child, but *the child also trains the mother*, a phenomenon of considerable importance for human development not only in terms of science but also of social policy on day care, children's institutions, etc.

The role of the child as a socializing agent has been emphasized by a number of writers (R. Q. Bell, 1968, 1971; Rheingold, 1969a), and Richard Bell (1968) has reinterpreted the findings of a large number of researches on socialization as possibly reflecting the influence of the child on the adult. But a search for direct studies of the phenomenon has proved unsuccessful. Despite considerable emphasis on the theoretical importance of this effect and some inferential evidence in support of its existence, as yet there appears to be no systematic investigation specifically focusing on and documenting the way in which a child, through such processes as reinforcement and modeling, produces enduring changes in the behavior of an adult, such as a parent, teacher, or—wonder of wonders—an experimenter.

In the absence of studies of this kind, it appears desirable to suggest some research designs which would make possible the analysis of socialization as a reciprocal process. Here are two examples of research currently under way.

1) *The effects of actual and attributed sex on adult-infant interaction.* James Garbarino[3] has proposed an experiment for testing directly some of the hypotheses on the genesis of sex differences in child rearing derived by Moss from his observational study (1967). The experiment employs the technique of cross-labeling developed by Condry and Garbarino, in which infants of each sex are identified by false names, with half of the girls being given boy's names and *vice versa*. Using a group of volunteer student caretakers, Garbarino proposes to examine the development of sex differences in the treatment of children as a joint function of actual and attributed sex. He hypothesizes that, even when the infants are cross-labeled, patterns of behavior associated with their actual sex will evoke differential response from the caretaker in terms of such variables as response to crying, talking to the infant, and, in particular, the frequency of responses contingent upon the infant's behavior.

2) *The impact of the child's initiative on mother-child interaction.* Bonny Parke[3] has designed an experiment to gauge the effect on the child's initiative in shaping the course of mother-child interaction. Working with a sample of preschool children she asks the mother to present the child with a story picture-book under two different sets of instructions. In one, the mother is asked to look at the story with the child "the way you usually do." In the other, the mother is told that the primary interest is in what about the book attracts the interest of the child; therefore the mother is to let the child take the initiative. The dependent variables relate differences in pattern of mother-child interaction instigated by the two sets of instructions, with

particular reference to the relative frequency of reciprocal reinforcement, imitation, and alternation from one participant to the other.

Both of these examples illustrate an important feature that distinguishes the present research designs from those traditionally employed in socialization studies. In the latter, the independent variable is typically the behavior of an adult and the dependent variable the behavior of the child. In the present examples, both adult and child behaviors are analyzed as dependent variables. The independent variable in each case is some systematic variation in the ecological situation—in the first example, actual *vs.* attributed sex of the child; in the second, an instruction influencing the extent to which the child is permitted some initiative in the interactive process.

A second distinctive feature of the research designs here proposed is that the dependent variables cannot be confined to the behaviors of the adult and child as separate individuals, but must describe properties of their interaction in a two-person reciprocal system. Thus it would not be sufficient to compute measures based on the frequency with which the mother engages in an action vis-a-vis the child or *vice versa*. One needs in addition indices which reflect the interdependency between behaviors of the two participants; for example, *the probability that an act of A is directly followed by an act of B, and vice versa,* or the number of *alternations* in action between A and B per unit of time. In computing such measures it would be important to take special note of *reciprocations in kind* (e.g., smile followed by smile) or *within the same modality* (e.g., vocalization followed by vocalization) as distinguished from non-imitative sequences (e.g., vocalization followed by eye contact). Finally, and most importantly, attention must be given to *convergence* phenomena, such as increased rates of alternation or homologous response over time, which would reflect the development and strengthening of a reciprocal system.

2. *Role Specification.* A second requirement of an ecologically valid model is that the roles of other participants besides the child be specified and systematically examined as independent variables. Two types of roles are usefully

distinguished. First, there are the persons who play specific and enduring roles in the child's life, such as mother, father, older brother, teacher, friend, etc. G. H. Mead (1934) coined the term *"significant other"* to designate this special kind of special relationship, and we shall follow his usage. A second type, presumably derived from the first, involves more *generalized roles*, such as male adult, female adult, older child, younger child, etc.

Significant others. It is a sobering fact, that whether from the point of view of science or social policy, in terms of direct observation and systematic study, we know more about the impact on the child of an unidentified stranger, who happens to serve as an experimenter, than of the child's own parents, family members, and other close associates. Although direct observational and experimental studies of mother-infant interaction during the first two years of life have shown a gratifying increase over the past decade (e.g., Foss, 1961, 1963, 1965, 1969; Kagan, 1971; Lewis, 1969), analogous investigations for children three years of age and older are still comparatively rare. There are a few observations of mother-child interaction in preschoolers (Baldwin, 1947; Caldwell *et al.*, 1970; Hilton, 1967; Lasko, 1954; Mussen & Parker, 1965; Rothbart, 1971), most of them focusing on the issue of differences in the socialization of first *vs.* later born children. But beginning with the school age child, virtually all the research on mother-child relationships still relies on far from adequate verbal reports.[4]

As for father-child interaction, direct observational or experimental investigations are extremely rare. Recently, two studies have appeared reporting the behavior of fathers toward infants in the first year of life (Ban & Lewis, 1971; Rebelsky & Hanks, 1971). The findings indicate that, although American fathers spend only 10 to 20 minutes a day attending to a child under one year of age, they nevertheless have an impact on the infant's response, particularly with respect to more distal interactions such as eye contact and vocalization. With the exception of these two researches, this writer has been unable to find any direct studies of father-child interaction until adolescence (Strodtbeck, 1958;

Rosen & D'Andrade, 1959), and both of these investigations are limited to boys.

Even more conspicuous than the absence of the father in research on child rearing is the absence of any other representative from the child's world besides his parents. For example, the effect on the child of interaction with his siblings, both older and younger, is virtually unexamined except in occasional clinical case studies. Even more striking is the complete exclusion of adult relatives. A search of the abstracts failed to reveal a single study of the role of such figures as grandmothers, grandfathers, uncles, or aunts, at least in Western countries. Perhaps investigators are prepared to assume that, in our modern mobile society with its shrunken nuclear family, such persons can no longer play a meaningful role in the lives of children. If so, then at least we should expect some attention to the principal agent who has taken their place as parent substitute—the ubiquitous member of every American family containing young children—the *babysitter*. But again the research annals are silent on the subject. To be sure, there is a growing literature on the reaction of the young child to a stranger (e.g., Morgan & Ricciuti, 1969; Rheingold, 1969b; Schaffer, 1966; Wahler, 1967) but, to date, attention has been limited to the immobilizing, anxiety producing impact of the initial encounter with no follow-up on the subsequent course of interaction of repeated contact over longer periods of time.

In summary, if we are to judge by the research literature, only if and when the child enters nursery, preschool, or school can other people besides parents significantly influence his life, and even these persons are limited to teachers and peers operating within an educational setting. The extended family, the informal peer group, older and younger children, other adults, the street, the neighborhood—all of these have remained outside the pale of direct investigation as agents affecting or *affected by* the developing child.

Generalized roles. This possibility that the young child may be differentially and significantly responsive to persons not only as particular individuals but as possessors of more generalized characteristics such as sex, age, or social background, has also been largely overlooked. Part of the reason derives from a scientific tradition which defines the experimenter as a neutral nonentity excluded from substantive consideration in the experimental design. Significantly referred to only as E, bereft of age, sex, or social identity, he is treated as if he were an interchangeable part of the research apparatus, like a light bulb. In point of fact, of course, the experimenter is not just anybody, but always someone of a particular age, sex, and social background. And in the few studies that have taken such factors into account, the evidence indicates that they can be of considerable importance. For example, differences in child's response associated with the sex of the stimulus person have been reported in the first year of life (Kagan & Lewis, 1965) and, in Soviet research, even within the first three months (Godovika, 1969). Differences in test performance as a function of race of examiner have been documented for both Negro and White children from the first grade onward (Abramson, 1969; Katz, Henchy, & Allen, 1968; Kennedy & Vega, 1965; Sattler, 1966; Turner, 1971). It appears likely that similar differences would be found in responsiveness to reinforcement, modeling, and other social influence techniques not only in terms of the race of the experimenter but also his ethnic and social class background as reflected in speech pattern, gestures, attire, etc. The further demonstration of such experimenter effects would have obvious and important implications for the interpretation of the ethnic and social class differences in performance so commonly found in the research literature.

Several studies reporting experimenter affects indicate the development, by preschool age, of a complex pattern of interaction between the sex of the examiner and the sex of the child (Bandura et al., 1961; Cieutat, 1965; Fryrear & Thelen, 1969; Gewirtz, 1954; Gewirtz & Baer, 1958; May, 1966; Stevenson, 1961; Stevenson & Allen, 1964; Stevenson & Knights, 1964). In general, performance appears to be enhanced when the child is presented with a model of the same sex and is reinforced by a person of the opposite sex, who also reinforces the model. The reader will note that this fairly intricate set of specifications defines a rather familiar and indeed universal structure in human societies—

the nuclear family. The pattern also calls attention to an additional essential requirement for an ecologically valid model for the socialization process. The model must be expandable from a two-person to a three-person system and beyond. This expansion, in turn, introduces new structural properties which add complexity and richness to the socialization process and its products.

3. *Two-Person vs N-Person Systems.* Expanding the socialization system to include more than two people increases opportunity for both role differentiation and reciprocal response. To take the classical example of a three-person system—the nuclear family, we have within it the possibility of differential allocation of parental roles between father and mother, and, now, instead of only one dyadic relationship, a total of three—mother with child, father with child, and mother and father. In each of these, patterns of reciprocal socialization take place which may duplicate, complement, or even contradict each other, with profound consequences not only for the behavior and development of the child but also of the two adults in their roles as parents, and of the nuclear family as a total system.

The special structural and functional characteristics of the nuclear family as a *triad* have been discussed from a broad theoretical perspective (Parsons & Bales, 1955) but empirical work has been largely confined to examining the role of such factors in the genesis of psychiatric disorders (Ackerman & Babrens, 1956; Alkire, 1969; Farber & Jenne, 1963; Goldstein *et al.*, 1968; Henry, 1956; Kohn & Clausen, 1956; Lidz *et al.*, 1958). Except for indirect evidence from the now extensive research of the effects of father absence (summarized in Biller, 1970 and Herzog & Sudia, 1970), there appears to be only one study focusing explicitly on the effects of varying patterns of parental role differentiation on development in normal children (Bronfenbrenner, 1961a, 1961b, 1961c). The results indicated that adolescents showing the highest degree of leadership and dependability tended to come from families in which parental roles were differentiated, with some division between father and mother in the spheres of discipline and affection. Since the results of this investigation were based on correlations between questionnaire responses and sociometric data, the findings are yet to be confirmed by an observational study. They receive some indirect support, however, from the interpretation of their experimental results offered by Rosen and D'Andrade (1959).

The father-mother-child triad is clearly not the only ecologically important example of a three-person socialization system. Another is provided by the mother in simultaneous interaction with a first and second child. Unfortunately, none of the existing studies of differences in socialization of first vs. later borns (Baldwin, 1947; Lasko, 1954; Hilton, 1967; Rothbart, 1971) has actually employed a three-person model. The observations focus on the behaviors of mother with each child separately, so that the interplay among all three parties, especially between the two children, is overlooked. Also, these investigations have concerned themselves with only one parent—the mother. Inclusion of the father of course produces a four-person system, with a geometric increase in the number of possible reciprocal relationships. Nor, from an ecological point of view, are the important participants limited to parents and children. Conceivably they might also include a grandparent, babysitter, teacher, etc. In terms of research strategy, however, it would probably be wise to assess the role of such ancillary participants first in triadic situations involving parent, child, and third party.

It should be recognized that the three-or more-person system provides opportunity not only for role differentiation but other configurational features that are foreclosed in only a two-person interaction. For example, with a third person present, there is the possibility of vicarious reinforcement or imitation in which the child, or adult, does not himself participate but is susceptible to what Bandura (1962, 1965, 1969) has called observational learning. Finally, a three-or n-person model permits the occurrence and analysis of a phenomenon of the greatest importance for socialization processes that has thus far received little systematic study: *the influence of a third party on the pattern of reciprocal interaction between the other two.*

4. *Second-Order Effects.* Ordinarily, research on sociali-

zation is confined to what might be called *first-order effects* —the direct impact of one person on the behavior of another. But the pattern of interaction between two people, such as mother and child, can also be profoundly affected by third parties. Thus both mother and child may act differently toward each other in the presence of the father, younger child, or stranger. This is what is meant by a *second-order effect*.

The author has been able to find only one example of the systematic study of such second-order effects in the research literature. Though the context is a rather specialized one, the results are dramatic. I refer to the ingenious series of experiments by Rheingold (1969b) documenting the effect of the mother's presence on the young child's reaction to a stranger. Although when left alone with an unfamiliar person, ten month old infants exhibited considerable emotional distress, the appearance of the mother not only appeared to allay the fear of the stranger but instigated vocalization and exploratory behavior. It is as if the presence of the mother served as a catalyst enabling other kinds of interaction to occur.

Within the family system itself, the potency and magnitude of second-order effects are reflected in the now voluminous literature on the impact of father absence (see above) and birth order differences (summarized in Clausen, 1965), but direct evidence for the phenomenon is almost completely lacking. What is needed are observational and experimental studies of the changes that occur in patterns of interaction as a function of the presence or participation of the third party. Such a formulation points to the need, for example, of studying the effects of father absence not solely in broken families, but, more importantly, in families that are intact, and in terms of the father's influence not only on the child but on the mother and the mother-child dyad. Conversely, we can now envision a new aspect to the study of maternal behavior: the impact of the mother on the father-child relationship. For example, are there any consistent differences in the behavior of father with child as a function of the presence or absence of the mother? Or, to consider a less obvious second-order effect, does consistent reliance on a babysitter have any systematic influence on the mother-child relationship, or the capacity of the child to relate to other adults?

It is important to recognize that the source for a second order effect is not limited to another human being. For example, the recent research and discussion on the role of early stimulation in infancy has led to the development of new types of baby equipment. Thus a brochure recently received in the mail describes a "cognition crib" equipped with a tape recorder that can be activated by the sound of the infant's voice. In addition, frames built into the sides of the crib permit insertion of "programmed play modules for sensory and physical practice." The modules come in sets of six, which the parent is "encouraged to change" every three months so as to keep pace with the child's development. Since "faces are what an infant sees first," "six soft plastic faces . . . adhere to the window," including a distorted face of the type so often included in recent studies of perceptual development in infants. Other modules include mobiles (among them a "changing faces mobile"), a crib aquarium, and "ego building mirrors," Quite apart from the effectiveness of such devices for accelerating the infant's cognitive development, one may ask what influence they have on adult-infant interaction. Are they likely to increase the frequency, say, of picking up the infant, reciprocal eye contact, vocalization, or lead to its reduction?

At an older age level, an analogous issue of second-order effects arises with respect to television. Much of recent research and public concern about television in the lives of children focuses on the influence of TV violence. But perhaps an even more important phenomenon, both scientifically and socially, is the effect of television in reducing social interaction. As the author has written elsewhere (Report of Forum 15, 1970): "The primary danger of television lies not so much in the behavior it produces as the behavior it prevents—the talks, the games, the family festivities and arguments through which much of the child's learning takes place and his character is formed." It is this impact of television on the socialization processes within the family that needs to be investigated.

The role of television in changing patterns of interaction within the family points to the most potent form of second-order effect, one in which the external agent is not a single individual, but another ecological system that impinges on or encompasses the system in which the direct socialization is taking place.

5. *Experimental Human Ecology.* Perhaps the best documented example of a second-order effect at the level of ecological settings rather than individuals is the influence of social class on socialization practices and outcomes (for a recent summary see Hess, 1970). Subsequently, Tulkin, Kagan and others (Kagan, 1970; Lewis & Wilson, in press; Tulkin, 1970; Tulkin & Kagan, 1970) have identified reliable class differences in mother-infant interaction within the first year of life. Ecological differences of even larger order are of course found in cross-cultural studies (for a recent summary see Levine, 1970). But the difficulty with most investigations of this kind is that they shed little light on the processes through which cultural or class values come to affect child rearing practices, or *vice versa.* Clearly the connection is mediated through particular social structures and institutions in the society, such as schools, neighborhoods, places of work, and the like. An instructive example is provided by a recent observational study of mother-child interaction in Japan (Caudill & Weinstein, 1969). Utilizing Miller and Swanson's (1958) distinction between entrepreneurial and bureaucratic job settings, Caudill and Weinstein found that wives of independent business men were more likely to talk to, rock, and stimulate their babies than wives of a matched group of salaried personnel. The latter mothers were content to look, and remain passive.

Second-order effects at an older age level are demonstrated in Bronfenbrenner's study (1970b) of matched groups of Soviet children attending day schools and boarding schools. Consistent with the hypothesis of the study, children reared primarily in a single socialization setting (the peer collective in the boarding school) differed from those exposed to two somewhat divergent contexts (peer collective at school, family at home). Children brought up in boarding schools subscribed more strongly to culturally approved values and showed greater conformity to social pressures in their immediate environment.

In the foregoing examples, variation in ecological settings is observed as it occurs in society. But the full import of ecological systems for the development of both science and social policy is to be sought not in experiments of nature but in experiments of man—that is, through *the deliberate design, systematic manipulation and scientific analysis of new ecological settings that can affect primary socialization processes*. We refer to this approach as *experimental human ecology*.

There are few examples of this kind of experimentation in the research literature, but the few that do exist testify to its power and its promise. The most familiar is Skeels' (1966) remarkable follow-up study of two groups of mentally retarded, institutionalized children who constituted the experimental and control groups in an experiment he had initiated thirty years earlier (Skeels, Updegraff, Wellmann, & Williams, 1938; Skeels & Dye, 1939). When the children were three years of age, thirteen of them were placed in the care of female inmates of a state institution for the mentally retarded with each child being assigned to a different ward. The control group was allowed to remain in the original—— also institutional—environment, a children's orphanage. During the formal experimental period, which averaged a year and a half, the experimental group showed a gain in IQ of 28 points, whereas the control group dropped 26 points. Upon completion of the experiment, it became possible to place the institutionally-mothered children in legal adoption. Thirty years later, all thirteen children in the experimental group were found to be self supporting, all but two had completed high school, with four having one or more years of college. In the control group, all were either dead or still institutionalized. Skeels concludes his report with some dollar figures on the amount of taxpayers' money expended to sustain the institutionalized group, in contrast to the productive income brought in by those who had been raised initially by mentally deficient women in a state institution.

In seeking to explain the early gains showed by the children placed on the wards, Skeels calls attention to facts like the following. In each instance, one of the inmates in effect adopted the infant and became its mother; in addition, the entire ward was caught up in activities in behalf of "our baby." New clothes and playthings appeared, and the children were lavished with attention. Also, the several wards began to compete with each other in terms of whose baby was developing most rapidly.

All of these developments derive, however, from a deliberately-contrived ecological change—the restructuring of a social system in such a way as to maximize adult-child interaction.

A number of authorities have expressed serious skepticism about Skeels' dramatic results. Several of the crucial methodological issues raised by McNemar (1940) in his critique of Skeels' early work have in fact been refuted by the follow-up study and its clear demonstration that the early dramatic differences were not ephemeral either in their magnitude or durability. More recently, Jensen (1969) has called Skeels' work into question not on grounds of fact but of interpretation. Substantial gains in IQ, such as those reported by Skeels, he asserts, can be expected only in severely deprived children, whereas "typical culturally disadvantaged children are not reared in anything like the degree of sensory and motor deprivation that characterize, say, the children of the Skeels study."

In response to this criticism one need only point to a growing body of well-designed researches documenting significant and substantial gains in IQ and related measures for samples clearly representative of disadvantaged families (Gray & Klaus, 1970; Hodges et al., 1967; Karnes et al., 1970; Palmer, 1972; Schaefer, 1969a; Schaefer & Aaronson, 1972; Weikart, 1969). Of particular significance, in terms of second-order ecological effects, is the study by Karnes, which involved no work directly with the children themselves but only with their mothers. Fifteen mothers, all but one of them Negro, from economically depressed neighborhoods, attended weekly two-hour meetings over a 15 month period. The project provided transportation and costs of baby-sitters for the mothers' initially 12-24 month old infants. During the meetings,

. . . mothers in disadvantaged families were provided a sequential educational program to use at home in stimulating the cognitive and verbal development of their children and were instructed in principles of teaching which emphasized positive reinforcement. In addition to these child-centered activities, a portion of each meeting was devoted to mother-centered goals related to fostering a sense of dignity and worth as the mother demonstrated self-help capabilities within the family setting and the community at large. (P. 926)

Two types of control groups were employed—one consisting of children of similar family background,[5] the other of siblings of the experimental children, who had been tested previously at similar ages prior to the mother's enrollment in the training program. At the end of the 15 month period, when the children averaged three years of age the experimental group showed a 16 point gain in IQ over their matched controls and a 28 point gain over their own siblings, cared for in the same home by the same mother prior to her exposure to the program.

The rather powerful implications of this experiment are well summarized by the authors.

The 16-point Binet IQ difference between the infants whose mothers worked with them at home and the control infants nearly equals the 17-point Binet IQ difference between the experimental and control subjects in the Schaefer study, where the educational intervention was carried out by college graduates who served as tutors, visiting the child at home for 1 hour a day, 5 days a week, over a 21-month period. . . . Since at-home intervention by mothers can be budgeted at a fraction of the cost of tutorial intervention, the direction for further research in preventive programs of very early intervention seems clear. Further, programs which train the mother to serve as the agent for intervention hold potential for developing her self-help capabilities and sense of personal worth, pivotal factors in effecting broader changes within the disadvantaged family. Not only may the mother represent the ideal agent for fostering an improved school prognosis for the young disadvantaged child, but through group interaction she may extend this sense of responsibility for infant, self, and family to the wider community in which they live.[6] (P. 934)

Results paralleling those of Karnes are reported in a recent study by Levenstein (1970). Working once a week with a group of mothers of 2-3 year-olds from low income families, Levenstein demonstrated the use of books and toys as a means to stimulating mother-child interaction. Over a seven month period, the children showed a mean IQ gain of 17 points.

In the light of Karnes' and Levenstein's findings, it is noteworthy that of the more conventional intervention programs, in which the child is worked with directly, those showing lasting effects have involved a strong component of parent involvement (Gray & Klaus, 1970;[7] Weikart, 1969). Despite substantial gains at the end of the program, follow-up studies in other group intervention projects report gradual attenuation of differences between the experimental and control groups, with no significant effects after two or three years (Hodges *et al.*, 1967; Palmer, 1972; Schaefer, personal communication). And even before the dramatic effects of his tutorial intervention program had "washed out" at the end of two years, Schaefer (1969b) had concluded from a review of the literature: "Evidence that mean IQ scores increase during intensive stimulation and decrease after such stimulation is terminated (is) cited as supporting family centered programs." Additional results consistent with this conclusion come from the growing body of research on the effects of parent participation on the child's capacity to profit from intervention programs (Gilmer, 1969; Grotberg, 1969; Hoffman, Jordan & McCormick, 1971; Strickland, 1967; Weikart & Lambie, 1968; Willmon, 1969).

Such findings provide *post hoc* support for a general principle that guided the design and development of the Head Start program. Early in its deliberations, the Planning Committee of Project Head Start, of which this writer was privileged to be a member, stressed in its statements and memoranda to Government officials that the immediate objective of the program should be to effect positive changes *not* in the child himself (e.g., gain in IQ) but in his enduring environment in home, neighborhood, and community. The former, we emphasized, were easily achieved, but likely to be short-lived; only the latter could give promise for continuing psychological development.

As the foregoing statements imply, ecological intervention as a strategy both for the scientific analysis and enhancement of human development can not be limited to the establishment of preschool or parent education programs. The principle applies to the full range of ecological systems that directly or indirectly impinge on the world of the child and those immediately concerned with his welfare. For example, this author has argued elsewhere (Bronfenbrenner, 1972) that the key to an understanding of socialization in contemporary American society, and the Western world generally, lies in the phenomenon of segregation by age, and the alienation which such segregation produces. This segregation, in turn, is the unintended consequence of developments in many different aspects of contemporary life. A host of factors conspire to isolate children from the rest of society. The fragmentation of the extended family, the separation of residential and business areas, the disappearance of neighborhoods, super markets, zoning ordinances, occupational mobility, commuting, child labor laws, the abolishment of the apprentice system, consolidated schools, television, the decay of public transportation, separate patterns of social life for different age groups, the working mother, the delegation of child care to specialists—all these manifestations of progress operate to decrease opportunity and incentive for meaningful contact between children and persons older, or younger, than themselves.

Ecological changes are crucial not only for the solution of urgent social problems. They are also critical for the further development of adequate theory and research on the process of human development. It is the central thesis of this paper that most of the environmental variance in human capacities, motivations, and behavior derives not from first-order socialization effects within family, classroom, or peer group, but from the second order impact of other institutions in the society, such as the world of work, public transportation, or the structure of neighborhoods. Moreover, instead of attempting to study these in the scientifically confounded and, nowadays, often socially disintegrated form in which nature, or—more accurately—society gives them to us, we should endeavor to create new ecological arrangements designed simultaneously both to solve pressing social problems and to test important theoretical propositions.

I close with a few examples of possible research designs for such an experimental human ecology.[8]

1. A study currently under way is based on an adaptation of a Soviet pattern in which business organizations "adopt" groups of school children and establish relationships of mutual visiting, help, and interest in each other's work (Bronfenbrenner, 1970a). Such a program has been introduced in a New England community. The parents of the children are not directly involved, but changes are being assessed in the attitudes of parents toward their children and children toward their parents.

2. A related design involves giving older children some responsibility for the young in the primary grades. They are to escort the younger children to and from school, teach them games, help them with schoolwork, etc. Dependent variables include changes in the older children's school performance, career plans, reading interests, views on child rearing, and behavior at home.

3. An educational program is set up for couples expecting their first child. Both husband and wife must volunteer to be included but only one spouse is selected (on a random basis). After completion of the program and arrival of the child, observations are made of mother-infant interaction. Higher frequency of reciprocal response is predicted for mothers whose husbands attended the program than for the mothers who attended themselves.

4. A large business firm employing working mothers is persuaded to introduce, in selected departments, an option of part-time employment. Mothers volunteer for this option with the understanding that both the experimental and control group would be selected from among the volunteers. To compensate for the Hawthorne effect, the control group receives some other fringe benefit, such as longer vacation periods. The dependent variables in the study relate to changes in patterns of interaction within the family and their effects on child behavior and development.

5. Two comparable low-cost housing projects are selected which differ in that one of them has shops and services within easy walking distance, the other involves a trip by car or bus. The dependent variable is the amount of time

parents and other adults spend in interaction with school age children and the consequent effects on the children's behavior and performance both in and out of school.

Hopefully such investigations would have a beneficial effect simultaneously in two domains. They would contribute to making human beings more human—both in research, and in reality.

NOTES

1. The author expresses appreciation to his students, who have contributed significantly to the development of the ideas presented in this paper.
2. A more extended discussion of some of these studies appears in Bronfenbrenner (1972).
3. Graduate student. Department of Human Development and Family Studies, New York State College of Human Ecology, Cornell University, Ithaca, New York.
4. A notable exception is Rosen and D'Andrade's (1959) ingenious experimental study (see below).
5. The children were matched on family size, working status of mother, mother's birthplace, mother's education, presence of father or father surrogate, and welfare status.
6. The authors note in this connection that at a local meeting called to discuss the possibility of establishing a parent-child center in the community, twelve of the fifteen mothers attended "and were in fact the only persons indigenous in the neighborhood in attendance."
7. Gray and Klaus also found positive changes in the younger siblings of the target child, additional evidence of the power of second-order effects.
8. The practical, programmatic, and public policy aspects of these proposals are discussed in Bronfenbrenner (1972).

REFERENCES

Abramson, T. The influence of examiner race on first-grade and kindergarten subjects' Peabody Picture Vocabulary Test scores. *Journal of Educational Measurement*, 1969, 6, 241–246.

Ackerman, N. W. and Behrens, M. L. A study of family diagnosis. *American Journal of Orthopsychiatry*, 1956, 26, 66–78.

Alkire, A. A. Social power and communication within families of disturbed and non-disturbed preadolescents. *Journal of Personality and Social Psychology*, 1969, 13, 335–349.

Baldwin, A. L. Changes in parent behavior during pregnancy. *Child Development*, 1947, 18, 29–39.

Ban, P. L. and Lewis, M. Mothers and fathers, girls and boys: Attachment behavior in the one-year-old. Paper presented at the Meetings of the Eastern Psychological Association. New York: April 1971.

Bandura, A. Social learning through imitation. In M. R. Jones (Ed.), *Nebraska Symposium on Motivation 1962*. Lincoln: University of Nebraska Press, 1962. Pp. 211–269.

Bandura, A. Vicarious processes: A case of no trial learning. In L. Berkowitz (Ed.), *Advances in Experimental Social Psychology*, Vol. II. New York: Academic Press, 1965. Pp. 1–55.

Bandura, A. A social learning-theory of identificatory processes. In D. A. Goslin (Ed.), *Handbook of Socialization Theory and Research*. Chicago: Rand McNally, 1969. Pp. 213–262.

Bandura, A., Ross, P., and Ross, S. Transmission of aggression through imitation of aggressive models. *Journal of Abnormal and Social Psychology*, 1961, 62, 570–582.

Bell, R. Q. A reinterpretation of the direction of effects in studies of socialization. *Psychological Review*, 1968, 75, 81–95.

Bell, R. Q. Stimulus control of parent or caretaker behavior by offspring. *Developmental Psychology*, 1971, 4, 63–72.

Bell, S. M. The effectiveness of various maternal responses as terminators of crying: Some developmental changes and theoretical implications. Paper presented at the Meeting of the Society for Research in Child Development. Minneapolis, 1971.

Biller, H. B. Father-absence and the personality development of the male child. *Developmental Psychology*, 1970, 2, 181–201.

Bronfenbrenner, U. Some familial antecedents of responsibility and leadership in adolescents. In L. Petrullo and B. L. Bass (Eds.), *Leadership and Interpersonal Behavior*. New York: Holt, Rinehart, and Winston, 1961. Pp. 239–271. (a)

Bronfenbrenner, U. Toward a theoretical model for the analysis of parent-child relationships in a social context. In J. C. Glidewell (Ed.), *Parental Attitudes and Child Behavior*. Springfield, Illinois: Charles C. Thomas, 1961. Pp. 90–109. (b)

Bronfenbrenner, U. The changing American child—A speculative analysis. *Merrill-Palmer Quarterly*, 1961, 7, 73–84. (c)

Bronfenbrenner, U. Early deprivation: A cross-species analysis. In S. Levine and G. Newton (Eds.), *Early Experience and Behavior*. Springfield, Illinois: Charles C. Thomas, 1968. Pp. 627–764.

Bronfenbrenner, U. *Two Worlds of Childhood: U.S. and U.S.S.R.* New York: Russell Sage Foundation, 1970. (a)

Bronfenbrenner, U. Reaction to social pressure from adults versus peers among Soviet day school and boarding pupils in the perspective of an American sample. *Journal of Personality and Social Psychology*, 1970, 18, 179–189. (b)

Bronfenbrenner, U. Developmental research and public policy. In J. M. Romanyshyn (Ed.), *Social Science and Social Welfare*. New York: Council on Social Work Education, 1972.

Caldwell, B. M., Wright, C. M., Honig, A. S., Tannenbaum, J. Infant day care and attachment. *American Journal of Orthopsychiatry*, 1970, *3*, 397–412.

Caudill, W. and Weinstein, H. Maternal care and infant behavior in Japan and America. *Psychiatry*, 1969, *32*, 12–43.

Cietat, V. J. Examiner differences with Stanford-Binet IQ. *Perceptual and Motor Skills*, 1965, *20*, 317–318.

Clausen, J. A. *Family size and birth order as influences upon socialization and personality: Bibliography and abstracts.* New York: Social Science Research Council, 1965.

Farber, B. and Jenné, W. C. Family organization and parent-child communication: Parents and siblings of a retarded child. *Monographs of the Society for Research in Child Development*, 1963, *28*, #7.

Foss, B. M. *Determinants of Infant Behavior.* Volumes I–IV. London: Methuen, 1961, 1963, 1965, 1969.

Fryrear, L. L. and Thelen, M. H. The effect of sex of model and sex of observer on the imitation of affectionate behavior. *Developmental Psychology*, 1969, *1*, 298.

Gewirtz, H. B. & Gewirtz, J. L. Caretaking settings, background events, and behavior differences in four Israeli child-rearing environments: Some preliminary trends. In B. M. Foss (Ed.), *Determinants of Infant Behavior, IV.* London: Methuen, 1969. Pp. 229–295.

Gewirtz, J. L. Three determinants of attention seeking in young children. *Monographs of the Society for Research in Child Development.* 1954, *19*, #59.

Gewirtz, J. L. Mechanisms of social learning: Some roles of stimulation and behavior in early human development. In D. A. Goslin (Ed.), *Handbook of Socialization Theory and Research.* Chicago: Rand McNally, 1969. Pp. 57–212. (a)

Gewirtz, J. L. Levels of conceptual analysis in environment-infant interaction research. *Merrill-Palmer Quarterly of Behavior and Development*, 1969, *15*,

Gewirtz, J. L. and Baer, D. M. The effect of brief social deprivation on behaviors for a social reinforcer. *Journal of Abnormal and Social Psychology.* 1958, *56*, 49–56.

Gewirtz, J. L. and Gewirtz, H. B. Stimulus conditions, infant behaviors, and social learning in four Israeli child rearing environments: A preliminary report illustrating differences in environment and behavior between the only and 'the youngest' child. In B. M. Foss (Ed.), *Determinants of Infant Behavior, III.* London: Methuen, 1965. Pp. 161–184.

Gilmer, B. R. Intra-family diffusion of selected cognitive skills as a function of educational stimulation. Nashville, Tennessee: George Peabody College for Teachers, DARCEE Paper and Reports, 3:1, 1969.

Godovikova, D. B. Osobennosti reaktsii mladendsev na "fizicheskie" i "sotsial'nye" zvukovye razdrazhiteli. (Special features of infant reaction to "physical" and "social" auditory stimuli *Voprosi psikhologii*, 1969, *6*, 79–90.

Goldstein, M. J., Lewis, L. J., Rodnick, E. H., Alkire, A., & Gould, E. A method for studying social influence and coping patterns within families of disturbed adolescents. *Journal of Nervous and Mental Diseases*. 1968, *147*, 233–251.

Gray, S. W. and Klaus, R. A. The early training project: A 7th Year Report. *Child Development*, 1970, *41*, 909–924.

Grotberg, E. H. *Review of research—Project Head Start, 1965–1969.* Washington, D.C.: Research and Evaluation Office, Project Head Start, OEO Pamphlet 6108–13, 1969.

Henry, A. F. Family role structure and self-blame. *Social Forces,* 1956, *35*, 34–38.

Herzog, E. and Sudia, C. E. *Boys in fatherless families.* Washington, D.C.: Office of Child Development, 1970.

Hess, R. D. Social class and ethnic influences upon socialization. In P. H. Mussen (Ed.), *Carmichael's Manual of Child Psychology,* Vol. II. New York: John Wiley, 1970. Pp. 457–557.

Hilton, I. Differences in the behavior of mothers toward first- and later-born children. *Journal of Personality and Social Psychology,* 1967, *7*, 282–290.

Hodges, W. L., McCandless, B. R., Spiker, H. H. *The development and evaluation of a diagnostically based curriculum for preschool psychosocially deprived children. Final Report, University of Indiana Project #50350.* Washington, D.C.: U. S. Office of Education, 1967.

Hoffman, D. B., Jordan, J. S. and McCormick, F. *Parent participation in pre-school day care.* Atlanta, Georgia: Southeastern Educational Laboratory, 1971.

Jensen, A. R. How much can we boost IQ in scholastic achievement? *Harvard Educational Review.* Winter 1969, *39*, 1–123.

Kagan, J. *Change and continuity in infancy.* New York: Wiley, 1971.

Kagan, J. and Lewis, M. Studies of attention in the human infant. *Merrill-Palmer Quarterly,* 1965, *11*, 95–127.

Karnes, M. B., Treska, J. A., Hodgins, A. S., and Badger, E. D. Educational intervention at home by mothers of disadvantaged infants. *Child Development.* 1970, *41*, 925–935.

Katz, I., Henchy, T., and Allen, H. Effects of race of tester, approval-disapproval, and need on Negro children's learning. *Journal of Personality and Social Psychology,* 1968, *8*, 38–42.

Kennedy, W. A. and Vega, M. Negro children's performance on discrimination test as a function of examiner, race, and verbal incentive. *Journal of Personality and Social Psychology,* 1965, *2*, 839–843.

Kohn, M. L. and Clausen, J. A. Parental authority behavior and schizophrenia. *American Journal of Orthopsychiatry,* 1956, *26*, 297–313.

Lasko, J. K. Parent behavior toward first and second children. *Genetic Psychology Monographs*, 1954, *49*, 97–137.

Levenstein, P. Cognitive growth in preschoolers through verbal interaction with mothers. *American Journal of Orthopsychiatry*, 1970, *40*, 426–432.

LeVine, R. A. Cross-cultural study of child psychology. In P. H. Mussen (Ed.), *Carmichael's Manual of Child Psychology, Vol. II*. New York: John Wiley, 1970. Pp. 359–614.

Lewis, M. A developmental study of information processing within the first three years of life: Response decrement to a redundant signal. *Monographs of the Society for Research in Child Development*, 1969, *34*, #133.

Lewis, M. and Wilson, C. D. Infant development in lower class American families. *Human Development*, in press.

Lidz, T., Cornelison, A., Terry, D., and Fleck, S. Intrafamiliar environment of the schizophrenic patient: VI. The transmission of irrationality. *Archives of Neurology and Psychiatry*, 1958, *79*, 305–316.

May, J. G. A developmental study of imitation. *Dissertation Abstracts*, 1966, *26*, 6852–6853.

McNemar, Q. A critical examination of the University of Iowa Studies of Environmental Influences upon the IQ. *Psychological Bulletin*, 1940, *37*, 63–91.

Mead, G. H. *Mind, Self and Society*. Chicago: University of Chicago Press, 1934.

Miller, D. R. and Swanson, G. E. *The changing American parent*. New York: Wiley, 1958.

Morgan, G. A. and Ricciuti, H. N. Infants' responses to strangers during the first year. In B. M. Foss (Ed.), *Determinants of Infant Behavior, IV*. London: Methuen, 1969. Pp. 253–272.

Moss, H. A. Sex, age, and state as determinants of mother-infant interaction. *Merrill-Palmer Quarterly*, 1967, *13*, 19–36.

Moss, H. A. and Robson, K. S. The role of protest behavior in the development of the mother-infant attachment. Paper presented at the Meeting of the American Psychological Association. San Francisco: September, 1968.

Mussen, P. H. and Parker, A. L. Mother nurturants and girls' incidental imitative learning. *Journal of Personality and Social Psychology*. 1965, *2*, 94–97.

Palmer, F. H. Minimal intervention at age 2 and 3 and subsequent intellective changes. In R. K. Parker (Ed.), *The Preschool in Action*. Boston: Allyn & Bacon, 1972.

Parsons, T. and Bales, R. F. *Family socialization and interaction process*. Glencoe, Illinois: Free Press, 1955.

Rebelsky, F. and Hanks, C. Father's verbal interactions with infants in the first three months of life. *Child Development*, 1971, *42*, 63–68.

Report of Forum 15, White House Conference on Children, 1970.

Rheingold, H. L. The social and socializing infant. In D. A.

Goslin (Ed.), *Handbook of Socialization Theory and Research*. Chicago: Rand McNally, 1969. Pp. 779–790. (a)

Rheingold, H. L. The effect of a strange environment on the behavior of infants. In B. M. Foss (Ed.), *Determinants of Infant Behavior*, *IV*. London: Methuen, 1969. Pp. 137–166. (b)

Rosen, B. C. and D'Andrade, R. The psychosocial origins of achievement motivation. *Sociometry*, 1959, *22*, 185–218.

Rothbart, M. K. Birth order and mother-child interaction in an achievement situation. *Journal of Personality and Social Psychology*, 1971, *17*, 113–120.

Sattler, J. M. Statistical reanalysis of Canady's "The effect of 'rapport' on the IQ: A new approach to the problem of racial psychology. *Psychological Reports*, 1966, *19*, 1203–1206.

Schaefer, E. S. A home tutoring program. *Children*, 1969, *16*, 59–61. (a)

Schaefer, E. S. The need for early and continuing education. Paper presented at the 136th Annual Meeting of the American Association for the Advancement of Science. Washington, D.C., 1969. (b)

Schaefer, E. S. and Aaronson, N. Infant education research project: Implementation and implications of a home tutoring program. In R. K. Parker (Ed.), *The Preschool in Action*. Boston: Allyn & Bacon, 1972.

Schaffer, H. R. The onset of fear of strangers and the incongruity hypothesis, *Journal of Child Psychology and Psychiatry*, 1966, *7*, 95–106.

Skeels, H. M. Adult status of children with contrasting early life experience. *Monographs of the Society for Research in Child Development*, 1966, *31*, #105.

Skeels, H. M., Undergraff, R., Wellman, B. L. and Williams, H. N. A study of environmental stimulation: An orphanage preschool project. *University of Iowa Studies in Child Welfare*, 1938, *15*, #4.

Skeels, H. M. and Dye, H. B. The study of the effects of differential stimulation on mentally retarded children. *Proceedings and Addresses of the American Association of Mental Deficiency*. 1939, *44*, 114–136.

Stevenson, H. W. Social reinforcement with children as a function of CA, sex of E, and sex of S. *Journal of Abnormal and Social Psychology*, 1961, *63*, 147–154.

Stevenson, H. W. and Allen, S. Adult performance as a function of sex of experimenter and sex of subject. *Journal of Abnormal and Social Psychology*, 1964, *68*, 214–216.

Stevenson, H. W. and Knights, R. M. Social reinforcement with normal and retarded children as a function of pretraining, sex of E, and sex of S. *Journal of Experimental Child Psychology*, 1964, *1*, 248–255.

Strickland, J. H. The effect of a parent education program in the language developmnet of underprivileged kindergarten children. *Dissertation Abstracts*, 1967. Pp. 1633a–1634a.

Strodtbeck, F. L. Family interaction, values, and achievement. In D. C. McClelland, A. L. Baldwin, U. Bronfenbrenner, and F. L. Strodtbeck, *Talent and Society*. New York: Van Nostrand, 1958. Pp. 135–194.

Tulkin, S. R. Mother-infant interaction in the first year of life: An inquiry into the influences of social class. Unpublished doctoral dissertation. Harvard University, 1970.

Tulkin, S. R. and Kagan, J. Mother-child interaction: Social class differences in the first year of life. *Proceedings of the 78th APA Annual Convention*, 1970. Pp. 261–262.

Turner, C. Effects of race of tester and need for approval on children's learning. *Journal of Educational Psychology*, 1971, 62, 240–244.

Wahler, R. G. Infant social attachments: Reinforcement theory, interpretation, and investigation. *Child Development*, 1967, 38, 1079–1088.

Weikart, D. P. *Ypsilanti Carnegie Infant Education Project. Progress Report.* Ypsilanti, Michigan: Ypsilanti School Department of Research and Development, 1969.

Weikart, D. P. and Lambie, D. Preschool intervention through a home teaching project. Paper presented at the American Educational Research Association. Ypsilanti, Michigan: Ypsilanti Public Schools, 1968.

Willmon, B. Parent participation as a factor in the effectiveness of Head Start Programs. *Journal of Educational Research*, 1969, 62, 406–410.

13

Sociology and the Study of Education

BURTON R. CLARK, together with: *Orville G. Brim, Jr.,*
Bruce K. Eckland, Dan C. Lortie, James P. Pitts, David
Reisman, and Martin Trow

IN THE BRIGHT SUN of its best days, the sociological imagination reflects the light and shadow of man's relation to man.
Sociology assumes man in the group, organization and
society, given purpose as well as restrained by his social
bonds. It treats man as a creature of idea, norm, and belief,
set free as well as compelled by symbols shared by many
minds. The analyses of sociology naturally include man
guided by rational pattern and possessed by logical thought;
but the sociological quest particularly quickens at the edge
of rationality, where group tie and social compulsion, tradition and sentiment, enter heavily in social exchange. An
imaginative sociology earns its way in sensitivity to man's
full repertoire of interaction and response.

In our effort here to help develop the agenda of a productive national institute of education, several other features of modern sociology come to mind. One is empirical
range and stubborn concern with complexity. Much of the
best sociology is catholic in taking into account a variety
of factors. There is a willingness to deal with the connected
effects of historical, social, and psychological forces. In
attempting to see various aspects of reality in their joint
interaction, sociological analysis thereby sometimes achieves
a useful approximation to the way the world works. Other
disciplines have other research strategies at the center of
their efforts; e.g. that of attempting to isolate the effects of

* Report of a planning conference for the National Institute of Education,
July 30–31, 1971, at Washington, D.C.

specific variables that are seen as appropriate to the concerns of the field. The inclusive strategy in sociology, committed to the interacting complexity of the empirical world, seems clearly a useful one in a major national effort to develop research that leads to policy and development.

This catholic empirical coverage also entails a growing willingness to move across ordinary disciplinary boundaries. There is a sense of the simultaneous relevance of historical, social structural, normative, and psychological forces, in, for example, the massive problems discussed below of educational inequality, teacher discontent, and institutional competence. We sense that an increasing number of men in other fields are similarly oriented, especially as they confront the awesome problems of education. A willingness to range across disciplinary lines is a characteristic of useful social science for a national institute of education.

Lastly, the field of modern sociology assumed some years ago the posture of searching for the unintended and unanticipated consequences of purposive social action, a matter of the greatest importance for the role of social science in public policy. The posture presses the researcher to estimate consequences in numerous directions, for various persons and groups, practices and values, in the process of proceeding from research to the making of proposals for policy and reform. The tunnel vision necessary in the dark hours of examining a three-variable relationship becomes a terrible blindness in moving from research to development. Again, our concern here is surely shared with some colleagues in other disciplines. A social science appropriate for a national R and D institute should be sensitive to the range of issues and factors that are most important for various public policies.

The disciplinary characteristics that we are emphasizing are highly relevant to the study of the institutional web that constitutes "Education." The educational domain is rooted in history, entangled in the current structure of community and society, and yet must face and predict the future that the young will have as their own. The enterprise is possessed by values that conflict, norms that contradict, and commitments that divide, as well as the common understandings that unite and the acts of cooperation that bring mutual joy. Education is notably a center of sentiment, since it taps deep emotions in parents, offers "intangible" psychological and social rewards to those who work its halls, plays on nostalgia in the hearts of citizen and lawmaker, and bears heavily on each of us in turn in the sensitive years of developing personal identity and social belief. We should have expected what we fast have been learning: that this burdened social institution is opaque to the penetration of the quick glance and resistant to the ready assistance of the rational plan. The effort to grasp and solve the evolving problems of modern education clearly needs the sensitivities of many approaches. It will require openness and flexibility as well as the sustained application of the best of received method. It will need the patience, caring and determination that we find in the best practitioners of the arts of teaching and administration. The characteristics of sociology discussed here are ones that we believe can help.

To convey more specifically our perspectives, our judgments as to what is important, and our awareness of inevitable dilemmas among competing good things, we wish here to highlight six major aspects of the situation in modern education that appear eminently important in the light of current sociological interests and perspectives. We believe each topic bears on the three problem areas of inequality, quality, and resource effectiveness. Each warrants a major research effort in its own right or in some combination of foci within the larger areas.

EDUCATIONAL INEQUALITY AND SOCIAL STRATIFICATION

The problem of educational inequality is enormously complicated. We here note a number of aspects.

The Definition of Inequality

When examining either the causes or consequences of educational inequalities, disadvantages or the like, we need to distinguish between inequalities in the structure of opportunities and inequalities in the structure of rewards. The first form deals with how different educational roles are allocated to individuals, essentially whether they are ascribed or achieved. Here one is concerned that there not be discrimination by race, class, religion, or sex in the offering of available opportunities to the young, that schools and colleges fairly select, sort, and certify. The second form, inequalities in the reward structure, refers to quantitative and qualitative differences in the kinds of education students receive and in the institutions that serve them. Here one is concerned with how the educational system is stratified, e.g., the prestige system of colleges, and how educational resources are used, e.g., the proportion of people who will receive a college education. In any given age cohort, everyone obviously does not receive the same amount or quality of education.

Simply estimating the magnitude of educational inequality becomes confusing when these two forms are not made distinct. Root causes and social consequences are even more muddled. Equality of educational *opportunity* may be increasing in a given period, but may not be remarked, if observers are taking note largely of the retention of status differentials within the system. Such elementary disentanglement of various meanings of "inequality" is essential, especially in light of the fundamental contest between "populist" and "elite" definitions of education (discussed below) that lies deep in American culture.

The Family and Equal Opportunity

The nuclear family as we know it today is only one of numerous forms which have been adopted by human societies at different times and in different places for rearing children. The modern American family, of course, competes with a variety of socializing agents in influencing the growing child. Among these is the school. Some schools clearly "develop the child" and transmit the core values of the larger society from one generation to the next with little direct interference from the family, e.g., the private boarding school. But, as various studies have pointed out, academic achievement is apparently far more dependent, across the population, upon family background than upon whatever influences most schools exert. The advantages or disadvantages that parents confer upon their children are increasingly viewed as the prime factor inhibiting equality of educational opportunity. The view directs attention to the structure and milieu of the family. It leads toward solutions that involve alternative support structures and intervention, direct or indirect, between the child and his parents.

Wise men who care about their society should lose a lot of sleep over this matter, since basic values are in conflict and the dilemmas are enormous. The challenge ahead suggests that we must somehow prohibit the transference of social status from parent to child, thereby to allow each child to compete fairly and succeed on the basis of his own merits. Yet it is almost impossible to over-estimate the extraordinary lengths that many advantaged parents will go to in order to protect their children's advantages. And we immediately face the questions: if equality of educational opportunity indeed cannot be achieved except at the expense of the family, then shall we diminish the family? Is the price too high to pay? As we pursue a course toward equality of opportunity, are we prepared to help cause a major redefinition of parent-child relationships and the functions of the nuclear family? If so, are we prepared to provide for rearing our children by other means? Will the task be left to the schools, to which it already appears to be gradually falling? Do we tip the balance in favor of social disintegration when we help erode the institution most fundamental to the social orders of the past? We tinker not at the margins here but rather attempt to take into our hands one of the vital centers of the social structure. We can hardly do too much research on the family-schooling relationship, since we shall need great sophistication in diagnosis and great skill in developing new patterns and strengthening some of the old.

The Assumption of Failure of Educational Achievement

The current view that black and brown students fail to achieve at desirable levels in educational institutions because of family, cultural, and personality deficiencies seems often to contain the assumption that previous lower-class strata made more effective use of education. But if features of the labor market were more important than academic training for previous lower *stratum* mobility, then a more modest definition of education's possible contribution would be appropriate or more demonstration would be needed that academic training is definitely becoming more crucial. More light on the impact of the labor market in the mobility of entire lower social strata might not only shift emphasis to political economy, but also help set the stage for realistic expectations of what a national effort in educational research and development might do in increasing social equality.

The Vices and Virtues of Educational Selection

The educational system stops or deflects some students while encouraging others to go on to higher levels and obtain the more advanced certificates and degrees. Some observers feel that the system is too decisive at various levels in discriminating between the successful and the unsuccessful. The selection process, moreover, is difficult to defend when its supporters cannot clearly demonstrate that the criteria used to sort and select have direct relevance to latter occupational success and may even often mislabel on the probability of later educational success. The arguments against educational selection often appear compelling, and are applied increasingly to the higher levels of education.

Yet, we should not overlook the possibility that (a) our schools and colleges generally may be more meritocratic—use more universalistic standards for advancement—than the world of work, and (b) loosening the meritocratic or allocative function of education may create more inequality of opportunity than presently exists, leaving the most important educational decisions (e.g., who goes to college and where) to fall once again upon the family, social heredity, or politics. If indeed our economic system arbitrarily discriminates against racial, sex, and other "minorities" to the extent that some observers have indicated, one could argue for more rather than less universalistic standards in educational selection and a closer rather than a looser fit between educational attainment and occupational placement. At least we should proceed cautiously in condemning our schools and colleges for setting standards and for not expecting everyone to achieve them. Unlike the world of work where the norms of achievement frequently and perhaps necessarily are evaded, e.g., in job rights and seniority, schools may be the more important arena for "letting the best man win."

The Stigma of the Categorical Program

Stubborn educational problems follow from the social ranking of occupations and social groups and of levels and types of schooling that prepare for variously-ranked jobs and adult locations. The problem is now an old one in vocational education at the secondary level; the British have had much experience with the lack of a "parity of esteem" for their several major forms of secondary schooling; and community colleges feel the status crunch as the "lowest" tier in higher education. The problem becomes measurably sharper when special and highly visible programs are mounted which are directed solely at the bottom stratum of society. The stigma that soon flower become debilitating for institutions and persons alike. They are among the most basic of the "non-rational" adverse consequences of policies made in social welfare and education with other ends in view.

Serious investigation of stigma effects, in our efforts to reduce inequalities in educational opportunity, might well lead to a posture of avoiding efforts earmarked for a social stratum and of advocating programs which would strive for a common minimal level of achievement. Allowing for individual differences, the society might attempt to insure that each individual have requisite reading, mathematical, and learning skills which would permit him or her to compete for advanced education or jobs. This approach would be congenial with an emphasis in the early years of schooling on diagnosis and feedback to the student, rather than labeling and elimination. It might also be appropriate to reform of the general educational structure in which the comprehensive public school restricts itself to certain basic skills while alternative settings for education and socialization host various other functions.

Social Destratification in Education

Some social critics have argued for less social differentiation in the educational reward structure, i.e., more equality in the quality of our schools and in how much schooling people receive. This could simply mean a basic education for all, as in a "right to read" program; or, it could mean common higher education for everyone; or, it could mean making every institution equally distinguished or undistinguished. At least three critical issues are involved:

(1) how far and at what stages in the educational process does destratification make good sense? As a general rule, status differentials in formal education increase as students progress. At what point do such differentials become self-defeating, if they do?

(2) to what extent can we ignore the manpower needs of the nation? Our educational system is geared in many ways to its utilitarian value and the efficient use of human resources. Educational differentials are connected to differentials in the labor force. The connection requires closer examination.

(3) diversity and individuality are widely seen as desirable goals. But destratification, to be successful, may end up removing the sources of variation and creating sameness, rather than removing simply the invidious comparisons that arise from individual or group differences. Thus, one of the most serious problems in providing variety in education, as well as in most human experience, is that of attempting to maintain diversity while avoiding the stigmatizing effects of status ranks. To try to do both may be our impossible dream,

but at least it is a critical matter for research and policy to develop greater sensitivity on points of balance and the payoffs of various combinations of effort.

INSTITUTIONAL VARIETY AND RESILIENCE

As we turn our attention to the sources of diversity and free individuation, there is so much that we need to know about how educational institutions are formed, how they survive, and how they are recreated. We still know so little about how men and women and other resources are mobilized for new enterprises; about how purpose is made operational and a productive organizational identity achieved; about the gains and losses of the flexible posture as compared with those of the singular commitment; and, notably, about the dilemmas inherent in the organizational means of serious innovation—the charismatic beginning, the ideological fervor, the fear of routinization.

The extent of individual choice and the level of voluntariness among students, teachers and administrators at all levels of education depends on the extent of institutional differentiation and uniqueness. For real choice there must be real alternatives, and we are struck with the contrast between the amount of choice available in American higher education, based on its marked internal differentiation, and the little choice available in primary and secondary education because of a lack of differentiation. There is much concern nationally with a higher measure of voluntariness at all levels and much research and experimentation are needed on how to achieve and maintain a desired range of variation within and between individual schools and sets of schools.

Yet the dilemmas here are imposing and the problems immense. Varied schools raise the spectre of differential treatment and increased inequality. To be organizationally flexible and responsive to consumer choice brings the possibility that while some schools become seriously better some others will go from bad to worse. Clearly, choice ought not be near-infinite, and in fact will not be because of the constraints of organizational, economic, and political realities. In a society with strong impulses toward bureaucratic order and much influenced by traditions of equal treatment, we apparently do not stand in danger of becoming unhinged by too much variety. Rather, the leverage of experimentation and reform will probably need to be in the latter direction.

There will also be great advantage in studying the resilience of schools and colleges. Educational institutions often seem to have uncommon capacity to somehow get the work done and stagger on to another year. They have people who work desperately hard, the "Thank-God-for-Joe" people: teachers whose hours never end, registrars who see that the grades get in and the seniors graduated in spite of anarchic faculty. They have reserves not only in the form of under-utilized resources but in devoted people whose time and energy can be stretched to meet sudden overloads on the system, as when bed and board as well as classrooms must be found for another one hundred unanticipated freshmen. In this regard, we can ask: why haven't our inner city schools broken down even more than is already the case? They remain stitched together in part by bureaucracy and the pay check, but there seems so much not accounted for by formal structure and rational calculus. Clearly, distinguished schools and colleges are frequently loaded with a momentum of mystique. But even the places that operate at the bottom of the barrel, often defined as grubby and mean-spirited, seem to possess cadres of devoted workers. Deep belief in "education" or in the immorality of failing the young is probably a prime resource of these institutions. Yet, as belief is chipped away, hedonism spreads, and despair deepens, there are limits to the resilience of the devoted.

Such matters warrant high priority in research—sensitive probing of the depths of institutional reserve and the ways of building resiliency. We can define a central task of institutional leadership as that of enhancing resilience. We can encourage an R and D effort that will help administrators at local, state and national levels to better comprehend and fulfill this task.

GOVERNMENTAL STRUCTURE AND THE
EDUCATIONAL PROCESS

There is so much that depends on who has the power! And whoever has it, there are various pressures and limits on that power. We have spoken of voluntariness as linked to the differentiation of schools and the encouragement of organizational uniqueness. Immediately, we encounter the organizational-political question of what range of variation is possible within and between schools, under different forms of organization and coordination, at different stages of historical development, under different degrees of legitimacy, and in different value climates. How much variation can a single board of education allow among the schools under its jurisdiction? There is a tendency for parents and others in the community to define differences invidiously and to demand that all schools be leveled up or down, on the ground that we cannot allow a wide variation, some parts of which are going to have "bad" consequences for students. Questions of institutional differentiation thus become questions of the governing structure. Much variation probably means many governing boards. In any event, the nature and quality of the educational processes in the schools are directly linked to alternatives in governmental structure.

At the same time, we need to look into the possible long-range, unanticipated and unintended consequences of such major changes in governmental structure as are now being advocated in the use of a voucher system together with a more viable private sector and a more decentralized public sector. What if the long-range effect is to deepen and institutionalize even more the existing cultural and social differences within society? The matter needs the most searching kinds of analysis.

SCALE AND ITS EFFECTS

The scale of educational organization works its effects in a great variety of ways. Small scale tends to require a greater mixing of students of different characteristics, even ages, in the same classrooms, where large scale allows more specialization in teaching and more differentiation by student characteristics. The problems of communication and coordination change markedly and there is considerable difference in the closeness and stability of relationships. Large scale seems to promote standardization around massive specialized operations and finally a routinzation of paths and careers that reduces individuality and local variety. The many effects seem to sum to fundamentally different qualities in the educational experience and in the occupational life of teachers and administrators. Scale seems even to alter basic sentiments, as when teachers, students, parents, and administrators in the very large district all come to feel powerless. We suspect that the economies of scale of the economist taper off much later on the growth curve than the social and psychological gains of increasing size. Much sensitive inquiry from a number of disciplines is needed and soon, for we shall hardly learn too much too fast on this matter compared with the rate at which the large is replacing the small.

THE HISTORICAL AND IDEOLOGICAL BASES OF DISCONTENT

Behind much of our discussion thus far there has run the theme of the tension between the broad currents of populism in American society, which are apparently growing in strength, and the traditional concerns of the training of elite groups and the conditions for elite achievement. Populism is inherently the enemy of variations, as it defines all differences as potential inequalities, and all inequalities as inequities. Rooted in American history and current social thought, the tension between this view of equality and the elite views of selection and excellence may well be the central one in American society. It surely is moving up to the center of the stage in educational problems: how to maintain distinctive institutions and yet have control by a populace that opposes elitism and hierarchy; how to select and reward by merit in the face of popular opposition to the differences in status and other rewards that are entailed. Major discontents directly follow: traditionalists concerned with excellence, merit, and support of the esoteric view with great alarm the reforms that are based on the populist thrust; reformers fixed on the importance of removing all inequalities are sorely impatient with the stubborn capacity of some groups and institutions to maintain distinctions and differences.

Many of us wish to play to both sets of values and to use research and development to gain insight on alternative sets of combined effort that will realize some of one and some of the other. "Equality and achievement" may well be at the heart of the concerns of the NIE and of the relation of social science to public policy in education. Here we would like especially to encourage historical and comparative research that will help us stand for awhile outside the entire value system of our own contemporary society, the better to view the main drift in current affairs as well as to learn from the wisdom of other men in other times and places.

THE VULNERABILITIES OF TEACHING

Issues of inequality, quality, and effective use of resources in education are very much bound up in the nature of the teaching role and the characteristics of teaching as an occupation. Recruitment plays an important part, as does preparatory work in the teacher training segments of the university and the college. But we are most of all impressed with the vulnerabilities of the career and social position of American classroom teachers. Two aspects of their existence stand out: the teachers' growing lack of protection against public attack and their increasing proclivity to feel malaise and even despair.

The sources of the vulnerabilities of American teaching are rooted in the societal definition of public schooling, the structural arrangements built to provide it, the nature of teacher tasks, and the state of technical culture in the occupation. The ideology that underlies the American public school system assumes widespread and even universal educability. Many teachers internalize the expectation of universal accomplishment; when they cannot reach all the children, they feel acute discomfort. The ideology has spurred Americans on to more demanding efforts, but there are also some negative consequences for those who are being so spurred. The structures built to implement the ideal of universal school, in turn, are based on compulsion, to the point where the participants in teaching and studying are likely to experience their mutual relationship as coerced. Students have little choice, the teachers somewhat more but still relatively little compared with the formal rights of other professionals. In this coerced relationship, the teacher is expected to motivate and manage the students; the load of motivational difficulties falls on him or on her.

Then, thirdly, the tasks of the teacher are particularly peculiar in their intangibility. Goals are ambiguous and lacking in consensus. The teacher confronts difficult questions of emphasis and action. He finds it most difficult to ascertain whether he has been effective. Confronted with various indeterminacies, teachers develop strategies to reassure themselves. But their own stratagems are often thin, easily pierced by the external critic who assesses them against conceptions of universal benefit. As a result, discouragement is a repetitive motif in the talk of teachers. Finally, the trade knowledge of teachers remains in a weak condition. Teaching continues as a hit-or-miss affair in which some excel and others do not. The system lacks the capacity to diffuse whatever it is that in some instances produces high effectiveness.

Clearly we need research and development based on the natural setting of teaching. Abstract formulations must give way to close analysis of the actual demands faced by the classroom teacher and to strategies which take the group nature of classrooms into account. Some recent reform efforts deal with parts of the situation; e.g., voucher plans enhance voluntarism, performance contracting narrows objectives to clearly stated cognitive goals and makes provision for their measurement. More broadly, it is time for us to think about ways in which the assumed centrality of schools in formal socialization should be altered. We need to inquire into alternative arrangements for socialization and social allocation. If we inquire seriously into what modern schools cannot achieve, we may gain a better balance in our expectations for teachers. We might even so reshape the role of teaching that it would be less conducive to a life of despair and to the various passive and active reactions to frustration that seem irrational or non-rational to others.

There are many other matters that are of fundamental importance: the many subtleties involved in teacher-student relations in the reforming of classroom environments; the dilemmas of planning and coordination in relation to voluntary effort and local variety; the necessity of seeing personality and individual action in the context of specific social settings. We have said nothing, in addition, about the importance of basic demographic information, and of straight ethnographic reporting on what a huge aggregation of people are variously thinking and doing in schools and colleges. And then there are the open-ended topics of life-long education and alternative structures of socialization. But the six topics briefly set forth here are sufficient to suggest our perspectives and emphases and to set in themselves an imposing agenda.

As a final note, we should like to emphasize the importance of the observation of human events. Education may be heavier than air, in the view of many observers, but somewhere out in the field there are men and women who are making it fly. Let us go look and listen, in many places and with great patience. As we observe the inventiveness of the creative practitioners, we can forge the concepts and assemble the descriptions that will lead others to understand and to achieve. If the National Institute of Education is to help temper the educational winds, it will need watchers out on the many terrains of reality. It is there that we will find the best and the worst—and will sense most fully how here, in education, if at all possible, we may improve man's relation to man.

RECENT SOCIOLOGY

An annual collection of articles on new developments and recent issues in the field of sociology.

EDITOR: Dr. Hans Peter Dreitzel

III. ON DISTORTED COMMUNICATION

CLAUS MUELLER
Notes on the Repression of Communicative
Behavior

JÜRGEN HABERMAS
Toward a Theory of Communicative Competence

IV. LABELING OTHER PEOPLE

PETER MC HUGH
A Common-Sense Perception of Deviance

ARLENE K. DANIELS
The Social Construction of Military
Psychiatric Diagnoses

V. EPILOGUE: THE CRITICAL PARADIGM

TRENT SCHROYER
Toward a Critical Theory for Advanced
Industrial Society

Recent Sociology No. 3
The Social Organization of Health

I. HEALTH AS A SOCIAL PROBLEM

ALFRED H. KATZ
The Social Causes of Disease

HARRY R. BRICKMAN
Mental Health and Social Change: An Ecological
Perspective

II. OUR CHEMICAL ENVIRONMENT: POLLUTION AND DRUGS

LAMONT C. COLE
Playing Rusian Roulette with Biogeochemical Cycles

RICHARD H. BLUM
Normal Drug Use

III. OUR SOCIAL ENVIRONMENT: POVERTY AND STRESS

RODGER HURLEY
The Health Crisis of the Poor

Y. SCOTT MATSUMOTO
Social Stress and Coronary Heart Disease in Japan

CHARLES C. HUGHES and JOHN M. HUNTER
Disease and "Development" in Africa

IV. OUR MEDICAL ENVIRONMENT: NEGLIGENCE AND
COMMUNICATION BARRIERS

DAN CORDTZ
Change Begins in the Doctor's Office

RAYMOND DUFF and AUGUST B. HOLLINGSHEAD
The Organization of Hospital Care

V. HEALTH AS A POLITICAL PROBLEM

RICHARD LICHTMAN
The Political Economy of Medical Care

THOMAS J. SCHEFF
On Reason and Sanity: Some Political Implications
of Psychiatric Thought

Recent Sociology No. 4
Family, Marriage, and the Struggle of the Sexes